FGP ATELIER

PRO
GRES
SION

HATJE
CANTZ

FGP ATELIER is an intercontinental practice led by Mexican-born architect Francisco González Pulido, whose mission is to contribute to social and economic advancement through the alignment of the core principles of design, science, and technology. The work of the Atelier is guided by transparency, openness, and freedom. These values are reflected in an approach to process and collaboration, as well as in the buildings and spaces that result. Logic, intuition, multidisciplinary collaboration, scientific research, and work experience drive the design of active spaces as well as infrastructure and urban networks that respond to atmosphere, ecology, comfort, economy, culture, and technological context. In working towards the dissolution of archetypical interventions, the user's experience of these spaces and buildings is valued over typology in order to ground their ultimate value in human existence.

I WANT TO DEDICATE THIS BOOK TO GERGANA, FABRICIO, AND VENETA ESTEL.

AXONOMETRIC PERSPECTIVE

a view of the object in its abstract form

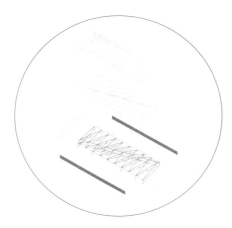

BUILDING SYSTEMS

dissecting the kit of parts

DIVINE DETAIL

the spirit of the project encapsulated in a singular moment

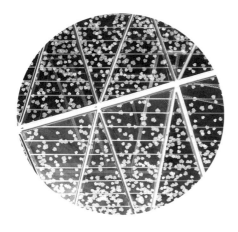

USER INTERFACE

representation of the human interaction

BY DEFINITION, PROGRESSION IS THE PROCESS OF MOVING GRADUALLY TO A MORE ADVANCED STATE. IN MUSIC, IT REFERS TO THE MOVEMENT FROM ONE NOTE OR CHORD TO ANOTHER. IN THAT SENSE, THIS BOOK IS ABOUT THE PROCESS AND CONDITIONS IN WHICH PROJECTS EMERGE, EVOLVE, AND ASCEND. THE FOCUS IS ON THE CONTEXT IN WHICH THE WORK IS CREATED. THIS IS NOT A BOOK CENTERED ON BUILDINGS. IT IS A PERSONAL JOURNAL ON THE RESULTS AT DIFFERENT STAGES OF EXPERIMENTATION WHEN DESIGN IS DRIVEN BY A SCIENTIFIC APPROACH. THE BOOK IS DIVIDED INTO THREE SECTIONS: VALUES, NETWORK, AND AMBITION, WHICH ARE UBIQUITOUS IN OUR PROCESS.

VALUE ASCENDS WHEN WE ACT ACCORDING TO OUR BELIEFS. OUR NETWORKS INEVITABLY CONTINUE TO FEED OUR FUTURES, IRRESPECTIVE OF THEIR NATURE. BUT IT IS OUR AMBITION THAT TRULY SETS US APART. I FIND THIS TO BE TRUE NOT ONLY IN ARCHITECTURE, BUT ALSO IN CONNECTION WITH ALL THE FIELDS THAT, SINCE CHILDHOOD, HAVE CONTINUED TO ABSORB MY INTEREST. FROM MUSIC, SCIENCE, DESIGN, ART, AND FASHION TO GUITARS, MOTORCYCLES, RUNNING, AND BUILDING. THEIR TRANSCENDENCE IS MORE IMPACTFUL WHEN ALL THREE ARE PRESENT AND INTERCONNECTED. THAT IS THE MOMENT WHEN PROGRESSION TAKES PLACE.

INDEX

	PREFACE BY MARK LAMSTER	10
	INTRO	18

I_VALUES

ONE	EDUCATIONAL PAVILION	28
	AESTHETICS OF THE SUSTAINABLE	52
TWO	LA HOJA	64
	PRACTICING HERE	84
THREE	TEC NANO	94
	ETHICS AND ARCHITECTURE	116

II_NETWORK

FOUR	DIABLOS STADIUM	130
	QIANTAN LOT 14	168
	TECHNICAL CONTEXTUALISM	200
FIVE	WISH	212
	GICC	230
	ALTERNATIVE FUTURES	252
SIX	HARMONY BRIDGE	262
	INFRASTRUCTURE AND (IN-)EQUALITY	278
SEVEN	SPACECRAFT	286
	CASA M5	300
	MONARCA	318
	HOUSING PLATFORM	330

III_AMBITION

EIGHT	TRANSPARENTE	344
	TWINNING	376
NINE	SMART SALON	386
	RADART	404
	PERVASIVE MEDIA	420
TEN	MODULAR	430
	GUADALAJARA T2	454
	AIFA	480
	DRY ARCHITECTURE	520

COLLABORATION	526
BIOGRAPHY	564
ACKNOWLEDGMENTS	566
COLOPHON	570

PREFACE

BUILDING FOR SPACESHIP EARTH:
ON THE ARCHITECTURE OF
FRANCISCO GONZÁLEZ PULIDO

Mark Lamster

I first met Francisco González Pulido at a Las Vegas casino, an unlikely place to find an ambitious young architect, or at least one interested in actually building, rather than the semiotics of The Strip. This was more than a decade ago, in the winter of 2010, and we were there for the unveiling of CityCenter, a mega-development of buildings by a roster of starchitects, name brands who could put some shine to the multi-billion-dollar complex.

Slight problem: the names grabbed your attention, but their buildings didn't. There was, however, an exception: a pair of golden towers that leaned away from each other, at what I would learn was a five-degree angle. Their hue came from fritted yellow glass set behind horizontal metal louvers, or fins, that wrapped the buildings. The effect was unusual, at once industrial but also bearing a sense of sophistication. They didn't preen, like some other buildings, but they commanded your attention: something was going on here, acts of genuine architecture rather than paint-by-numbers building for profit.

That direction seemed like something fresh, a descendent of the "high-tech" movement that had sprung out of England in the nineteen-seventies, but with an unexpected willfulness that pushed beyond a celebration of technical proficiency and into the realm of artistry.

The architect who gave the tour of this project was also unlike his peers. Over the previous day, a bevy of loafer-clad, clean-cut corporate deputies—the stars not being in attendance—toured us through the other buildings in the complex. And then there was the architect of those leaning yellow buildings, the aptly named Veer Towers, dressed sharply in a black leather jacket and looking not a little bit like Antonio Banderas. This was Francisco González Pulido, then a partner in the firm of Chicago architect Helmut Jahn.

González was unlike his peers in other ways. After a press tour of the Veer Towers, we bumped into each other and took a walk around the complex, pointing out the elements in the other projects that we found wanting, and discussing how they wound up that way. For an architect to be so frank with a critic was unexpected, but certainly enjoyable, especially as we seemed to agree on matters.

The next time I heard about González Pulido he was on his own and opening a ballpark in his native Mexico City. Baseball is a subject on which I consider myself fairly expert—I've written a book on the subject—but I had never seen a ballpark that looked like his stadium for the Diablos Rojos, named for team owner Alfredo Harp Helú. Over the last twenty-five years, the American ballpark has become a kind of architectural anachronism; even new parks are designed to appear old, with kitschy retro-styling that preys on a sense of nostalgia.

The Diablos park was something different: a work of daring technical precision that made its modernity its signature.

Which is not to say it was itself without a sense of history. The ballpark is in the Magdalena Mixhuca sports park, the complex that was the site of the 1968 Olympic Games. Among the facilities there is the domed Palacio de los Deportes, Felix Candela's magisterial essay in architectural engineering. As a boy, González Pulido was taken to games there by his father, but it was not the athletics but the structure, with its steel-cable supports and parabolic roof—that made a lasting impression. "That building to me was always a point of reference," he says.

Diablos is defined by its cantilevered roof system of parallel of white plastic sheeting held in place by an exposed system of steel trusses.

Getting such a complex system built was a challenge, economically, logistically, and bureaucratically. A factory was built on-site where fabrication of the trusses could be monitored and controlled. Even still, the weight of the canopies, which had been designed at no more than 300 tons, climbed to 600 tons each—the product of a compromised and immature building industry. To avoid such problems, as much as possible, the structure was treated as a kit of parts. "Whatever I could bring from a factory, I did," he says.

From above, the assemblage takes the shape of a squared-off arrow, the longer central panel acting as an awning that bridges the exterior and interior. Blending the two was a central concept. "Alonso De Garay and myself didn't want to build a container," says González Pulido. "We wanted a building that is really connected to the place. We wanted to make the building transparent, to make it a public space."

Opening the building up physically has engendered a reciprocal response from the community. Whereas the team previously had trouble filling its 5,000-seat ballpark, it now—at least pre-pandemic—is reaching the capacity of its new 22,000-seat home. That is significant, given the level of poverty in the surrounding community; instead of acting as a magnet for high-end development, the park engages with its neighbors, offering market space and amenities attractive to the local community.

This expansion of the ground of architecture, encompassing not just building but structural design and urban planning, is well timed, coming at a moment when professional boundaries seem to be inadequate to the demands of contemporary development. It is an intentional and necessary reframing, one that makes greater demands on the architect but allows for something more than the production of the kind of signature building that looks good in magazines (or on Instagram) but fails to meet broad public need.

As it is, the technical innovation that is a hallmark of González Pulido's architecture comes to him naturally.

His father, a mechanical engineer, had a business manufacturing parts for automobiles. Following a stroke, doctors thought he should leave Mexico City for cleaner air, and soon enough Francisco was splitting time between his mother in the capital and his father's ranch eight hours away in rural Tamaulipas. Isolation demanded ingenuity, which suited father and son. "He was a very inventive guy. 'We're going to turn this old truck into a four-wheel drive,' he'd say. I got pretty involved in building things. I think this is where my love for industrial buildings really formed, where I learned that simple forms can build interesting structures," says González Pulido.

He graduated high school in Ciudad Victoria and began his formal education in architecture at the Monterrey Institute of Technology. The focus there was on structural engineering, and that has suited him well. But the most formative experience of his time as an undergraduate was a year studying abroad at the University of Navarra in Pamplona. There was a discovery there, not just of Old-World architecture and urbanism, but of a sense of the social aspect of design, which had been largely absent from his technical training back in Mexico. He found a mentor in Joaquin Lorda, a professor of architectural history, and the two traveled Spain, with the elder Lorda pointing out elements with a stick he carried for such purposes. "He changed my perception," says González Pulido. "I was so interested in high tech, and then, hoo-boy, he was telling me you have to go up and hug these columns and feel the temperature."

After graduation, he returned to Tamaulipas, taking up a residential commission that had come to him through family connections. He treated it as a design-build project, living in a tent for two years. "The house will never change the history of architecture, but it changed my life," he says. That house brought more commissions, but building homes for the wealthy was not how he saw his future. He entered a competition, won it, but when the client found out it had awarded its multi-million-dollar project to an inexperienced twenty-seven-year-old working by himself, the job disappeared.

He returned to school, this time to the Harvard Graduate School of Design, where he was able to study not just architecture but business, planning, and development. When he graduated, a professor suggested he look into the work of Helmut Jahn, the Chicago architect known for projects of technical daring. Indeed, the office had recently begun a partnership with a structural engineer and an energy scientist, both based in Stuttgart. That appealed to González Pulido's technical background, and also his sense of social responsibility. "Research has always been an important part of my working method," he says. "How can I do something with less and less—not a as a philosophical posture, but as a response to the world we're living in."

The emphasis on structure and research appealed to González Pulido, as did Jahn's comprehensive philosophy of "design to the last bolt." He began at the firm as an intern and stayed for eighteen years. "He was a real force and an incredible mentor," he says of Jahn. "We always had a beautiful relationship." The Veer Towers was the first project he took entirely on his own. "He got pretty confident about what we could do together." If they shared a vision, their means of arriving at it were quite different. "He was a lot about trial and error," says González Pulido. "I form whatever I do in my head, and then I draw it. He's an absolute workaholic, his dedication, he stands for something."

González Pulido divides his time at Jahn into three six-year periods, during which he was working for, with, and then in partnership to Jahn. In that time, the office doubled in size, with González Pulido responsible for major projects in China and his native Mexico. Eventually, however, it became clear that, in order to pursue his own independent practice, he would have to separate from his mentor. His last day at the firm was in August of 2017. It was a bittersweet moment. "Why are we doing this?" Jahn asked. "There's no other way."

If there is any project that represents the direction González Pulido has taken now that he is on his own, it is for a building that he actually began while moonlighting at Jahn. And while he was drawn to the Jahn office in part by the opportunity to work at great scale, this project is practically toy-sized: just eleven meters square, a delicate little glass box. It is, in a way, a residential project, but the residents happen to be extremely delicate and highly sensitive: orchids.

This pavilion is located in the botanical gardens of the city of Oaxaca, itself situated in the Baroque-era monastery of Santo Domingo de Guzmán. The idea of inserting a modern structure in that architectural context was at first met with resistance. "They told me, 'you're building a UFO in beautiful Oaxaca,'" says González Pulido. They weren't far off. The pavilion does have an other-worldly sense about it, a crystalline spaceship that has landed from some verdant planet.

Although it appears simple—sheer glass planes framed by steel—it is anything but. Its secrets, however, are hidden. Its apparent fragility, for instance, is deceptive: the lightweight structure is built to withstand Oaxaca's seismic demands. "It's not about acrobatics or formal ambitions," says González Pulido. "It's very quiet in its aesthetics and its form, but it's very eccentric in the way it operates." Indeed, what is most remarkable about the building is that it maintains a steady temperature of seventy-two degrees with no air-conditioning system and clear windows without shades. The building is cooled using a geothermal system and an evaporative cooling system is used to provide water for the plants: pipes run deep into the ground, with solar-powered pumps pulling up cool water that can control the temperature and humidity.

The pavilion is effective at its primary function as a demonstration and research facility for orchids, but it has become something else, and equally important as well—a working model of sustainable building. "It's about what it takes to sustain life on this planet," says González. So perhaps UFO isn't such a poor metaphor for the building after all. Think of it as small craft docked on what Bucky Fuller called Spaceship Earth.

And so the journey that began in a tent in rural Tamaulipas continues now, at a grander scale. "I always felt that becoming an architect was about getting tools to realize my imagination," says González Pulido. That promises a future in which technological innovation is yoked to sustainability and social equity. It is an optimistic vision for modernism and for architecture, and it comes at a time when it is most needed.

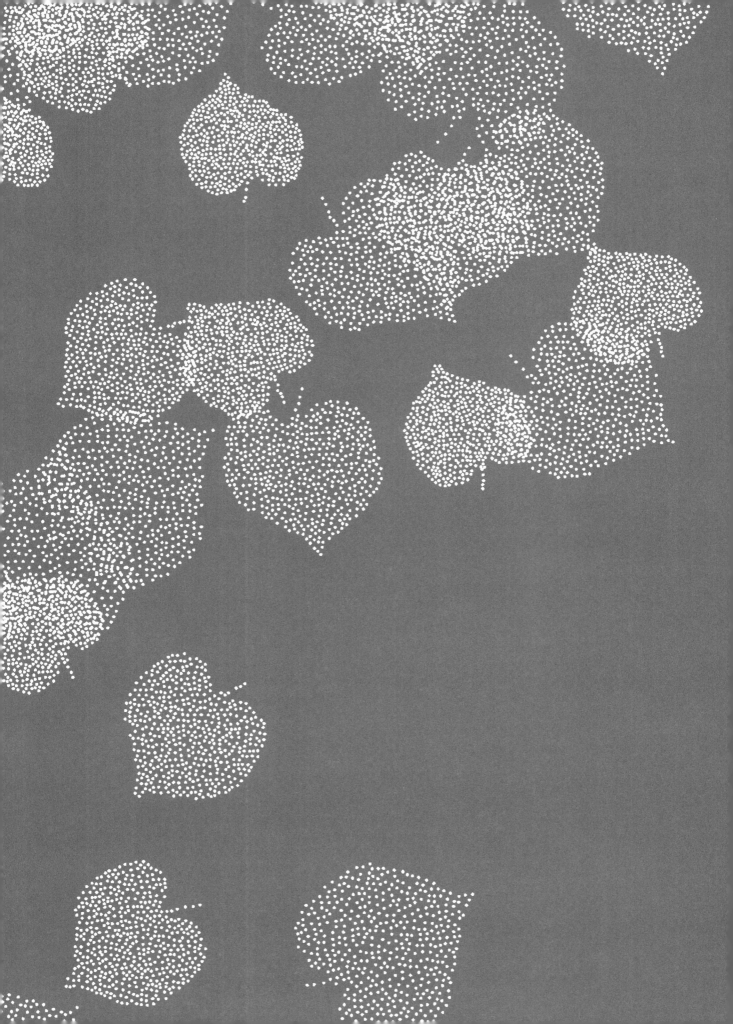

VALUES

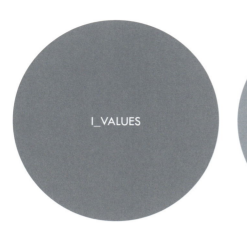

	ONE.	ONE.
I_VALUES	EDUCATIONAL PAVILION	AESTHETICS OF THE SUSTAINABLE
	TWO.	**TWO.**
	LA HOJA	PRACTICING HERE
	THREE.	**THREE.**
	TEC NANO	ETHICS AND ARCHITECTURE

INT

At a fundamental level, a building is simple. It is comprised of a foundation, walls, roof, and support structure. The walls in turn have openings to allow access, light, and ventilation. The building likely has some means of heating and cooling the space, a means of cooking meals, and a place to rest. The means of construction should be able to withstand wear over time, protect the interior from the intrusion of moisture and pests. In some cases, additional levels accessed by stairs might exist. In other cases, the building might grow sufficiently tall that an elevator is desirable.

As new elements are added and the scale increases, the building quickly becomes complex. Complexity begins to grow as buildings are designed for extreme heat and cold, seismic zones, hurricane winds, corrosive climates, and challenging soil conditions. New materials and construction techniques are introduced to meet these demands, further enhancing the complexity of the building. These buildings often take on programs whose specific requirements introduce new challenges. These might include acoustic, vibration, lighting, security, climate, ventilation, and circulation requirements. Each enhances the overall complexity of the building and the expertise required to make it successful.

In the context of increasingly complex buildings, it is important to understand how one makes the right decisions that will enhance the quality of the project and benefit the parties responsible for building the project as well as those who will inhabit it once complete. How does one determine the form? How does one balance the schedule for the completion of the project with the budget for the project? The answers to these questions are not found by simply consulting an expert or undertaking a calculation. They are found in guiding principles that have, in turn, been developed over decades of practice and experience in the field. The need for guiding principles is particularly important in the context of an architectural practice that designs buildings in diverse geographic locations as well as with a wide range of scales and typologies. The contents of this book share the principles that guide the work of FGP ATELIER and that have been honed over several decades of practice by Francisco González Pulido, FGP ATELIER Founder, Principal, and Design Director; Gergana González Pulido, Director, Interiors Practice; and the broader team. Through examining these principles, the themes, ideas, and goals that are common to the projects of FGP ATELIER emerge and provide a means of understanding how a diverse set of buildings relate—as well as what might come next.

This set of guiding principles is presented in a variety of ways. Each topic guided the selection of specific projects designed by FGP ATELIER. These projects in turn inspired the essays that conclude each chapter. Each takes one principle as its theme and unpacks how this principle, topic, or area of focus resonates beyond specific projects designed by the firm. They connect the themes within the essay to the broader practice of architecture as

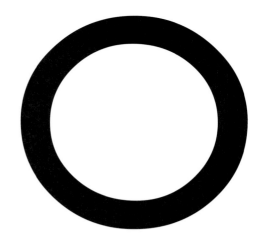

well as the state of our cities and world. These projects are presented through diagrams, plans, sketches, renderings, and photos of the completed project in order to illustrate the problems that were faced from start to completion and how the design solved those problems. While related to each essay, the projects ultimately go beyond the confines of the topics discussed as they become inhabited buildings subject to all the complexities of life. The projects and essays are framed by an introduction that clarifies the point of connection as well as commentary by Francisco González Pulido that offers insight into how the approach to the design developed and how particular problems were addressed and solved. This commentary is essential, since it illustrates González Pulido's vision, which has driven the team he has built and the mission and identity of FGP ATELIER.

The book is divided into three sections: "Values," "Network," and "Ambition." "Values" is comprised of three chapters that discuss sustainability, our practice, and ethics. This section explores the groundwork for our practice. Creating sustainable and resilient buildings, cities, and society is perhaps the most pressing problem facing the world. The question is not just a matter of climate, but of how we live together, support each other, create economies that benefit an expanding group of people, and create living environments that are healthy. The fragility of these systems can be seen in the devastating effects of the 2020 pandemic, which has caused a severe recession, and climate events that are becoming increasingly dramatic and devastating. For this reason, chapter 1 examines sustainability through the Orchid Educational Pavilion and "Aesthetics of the Sustainable."

Chapters 2 and 3 present our physical and philosophical perspective on our work and practice. Chapter 2 includes the essay "Practicing Here" and the new roof covering—La Hoja—for the central library of the Monterrey Campus of Monterrey Tec. This chapter offers insight into why the practice is based in Chicago, how the architectural history of the city inspires design, how the practice is influenced by its diverse communities and people, and how innovation is cultivated in projects such as La Hoja. Chapter 3 examines the ethics that guide our work through the nanotechnology building Tec Nano, designed for Monterrey Tec, and the essay "Ethics and Architecture." Ethics structures our philosophy, our aesthetics, and our actions. By asking ethical questions, the practice extends beyond design in order to enter into dialogue with the broader forces and concerns driving the world.

"Network" is comprised of four chapters that discuss how technical design is influenced by context, the alternative futures that planning can offer, the role that infrastructure plays in creating equitable cities, and challenges facing housing in the future. The projects included in this section are not conceived in isolation or independently of larger networks. They are defined by webs and relationships.

Chapter 4 is largely concerned with how history, style, and technology interact. This is examined in the essay "Technical Contextualism" and in the Alfredo Harp Helú Stadium in Mexico City and Qiantan Enterprise World Phase II in Shanghai. Chapter 5 explores the planning and broader context of a building as well as the capacity to push the limits of what a city can be. These issues are examined in the specific contexts of the 320-meter-high Guangzhou International Cultural Center and the hotel, office, and convention center Wish in Shanghai. Everything is brought together in the essay "Alternative Futures."

Chapter 6 looks at the infrastructure that serves the contexts explored in chapter 4 and the master plans discussed in chapter 5. The essay in this chapter, "Infrastructure and (In)Equality," and the project description of the two-kilometer-long Harmony Bridge in Guangzhou, PRC, consider the role that infrastructure plays in creating sustainable, human-centric, and equitable communities. The final chapter in the "Network" section considers how people live in the world discussed in chapters 4, 5, and 6. This chapter considers the challenges facing housing affordability, sustainability, and equity. The modular housing solution Spacecraft offers a way of using a compact unit that can be mass-produced and combined in various ways to accommodate different family sizes. The apartment building Monarca in Santander, Spain, looks at the way that a modular system such as Spacecraft can be deployed in a high-end apartment building. Finally, Casa M5 offers an example of a passive house constructed with limited time and money that achieves an ambitious design. These projects are accompanied by the essay "Housing Platform," which analyzes the housing crisis facing the world while also offering a few ideas for how it might be addressed.

While chapters 4 through 7 offer examples of current approaches to design problems, those included in the section "Ambition" suggest ways that the discipline of architecture can evolve in the future.

Chapter 8 proposes one direction by considering how a digital twin of a building can be created to aid owning, operating, maintaining, and using buildings. This possibility is explored through the essay "Twinning" and the renovation of the landmark central administration building, the Rectoría, at Monterrey Tec—a project that has come to be called Transparente.

If chapter 8 offers a largely invisible, inward-looking solution, chapter 9 proposes a complementary external, highly visible solution through the possibility of using media, screens, and mediation as a critical component of buildings and cities to help reconcile forces that come into conflict, but that may not ever have a chance to be resolved. These facets are explored in more detail in the essay "Pervasive Media" and the high-end hair salon Smart Salon, designed for the celebrity stylist Ted Gibson in partnership with Amazon. In looking at these possible directions for the field, our reflections go beyond the traditional scope of an architectural practice and consider the practical funding channels by which these solutions might be implemented. The final chapter brings together the areas of focus in chapters 1 through 9 by considering a construction method that has been used in past projects and might come to define future projects. The essay "Dry Architecture" expands on the notions of modular architecture and the kit of parts—important building blocks in many projects already realized by FGP ATELIER. How such an approach plays out in practice is a main theme of Felipe Ángeles International Airport at Santa Lucía, which will serve 84 million passengers when the final phase is completed. This chapter offers an opportunity to explore how the concerns raised throughout this book are addressed on a truly monumental scale. It suggests that deploying a module addressed to a human scale can be a highly effective means of confronting the immensity of the problems facing society today.

Ultimately, the goal of this book is to be provocative on multiple levels. It should inspire the reader through completed buildings often executed in challenging conditions. At the same time, it should be a catalyst for discourse and debate regarding what should be built and how a philosophy guides a practice, the design of future buildings, and the conservation of existing buildings. It is this conversation that will ultimately shape how our world appears and functions for decades and perhaps centuries to come.

CHAPTER ONE

I_VALUES

Creating sustainable, resilient, affordable, and equitable communities is the most pressing challenge facing our planet. Building, cities, infrastructure, planning decisions, and construction play a significant role in contributing to greenhouse gas emissions, the consumption of non-renewable fuel sources, creating large distances between commercial and residential sectors, and driving up the cost of living. At the same time, decisions can be made that reduce negative impact and provide a path towards genuine sustainability.

The Educational Pavilion is a "manifesto" that illustrates how to design sustainable architecture that can be a model for how to live more broadly. The Educational Pavilion is a small net zero building. The Pavilion is located within the former monastery of Santo Domingo de Guzmán—now the Botanical Gardens of Santo Domingo in Oaxaca, Mexico. Beyond the walls of the gardens, the region is one of the most biologically diverse ecologies in the world. The city of Oaxaca has a unique building tradition, labor force, and construction expertise that would ultimately play a significant role in the design. This process was driven by close collaboration with the engineers and local craftsmen who would be responsible for executing González Pulido's vision. The final result is a building that achieves exemplary waste, water, and energy performance through the use of solar panels and geothermal heating and cooling. The building also functions as an educational tool to teach visitors and students about the local ecology as part of an ensemble of cultural experiences within the garden.

CHAPTER ONE

Sustainability is not just a theme that runs throughout our work, but a fundamental force driving the form taken by the design, how the building is used, and how it functions. Our approach to sustainability goes beyond scoring systems or certifications by considering how the building can be uniquely tailored to its environment and intended use through the materials selected, configuration, orientation, and systems. This approach has been applied to a range of building types and scales. This is particularly challenging when working on large-scale, complex projects that require tremendous energy to operate, have very specific and often predetermined orientations, generate large amounts of waste, and are subject to very specific codes and construction requirements. Even in these projects, which range from airports to stadia, the goal has been to achieve net zero waste, water, and energy consumption.

The value placed on sustainability is discussed in greater detail in the essay "Aesthetics of the Sustainable." This essay discusses the relationship between energy performance and appearance as well as methods for achieving a sustainable building. It also looks at how sustainability cannot be confined to an engineering solution but must extend to how the building is constructed, the supply chain, the labor used, how the building is sited in the city, and how it is eventually used. The ultimate goal is to explore ways of looking beyond standard ways of documenting and classifying sustainability in order to concentrate more on high performance buildings, as well as how rethinking what needs to be built and what can be reused can support the broader sustainability of cities.

I_VALUES

CHAPTER ONE

I_VALUES

The importance of sustainability resonates throughout each of the chapters in this book. In chapter 2, which focuses on practice, it is traced in the renovation La Hoja that enhances the energy performance and usability of the central atrium of the library at Monterrey Tec. In chapter 3, sustainability is discussed as an ethical responsibility. Chapter 4 looks at the ways in which technical design standards can be tailored to local climate conditions while also integrating vernacular knowledge to reduce energy consumption. Chapter 5 considers how alternative planning strategies can support sustainability. In chapter 6, the role that infrastructure plays in creating sustainability cities is discussed. Central to this discussion is the way that infrastructure must serve communities more equally in order to extend opportunities and promote less energy intense habits, such as long commuting distances driven by the high cost of living in urban cores, which typically have the most jobs. Chapter 7 explores housing as a core unit of the city that can drive the reduction of energy consumption. Chapter 8 looks at how a digital twin can model energy performance to reduce consumption, while chapter 9 explores how media and mediation deployed in cities and buildings can help to reconcile forces such as unequal access to sustainable and resilient communities. All of these concerns come together in chapter 10, a discussion of how modular construction and manufacturing can help reduce waste and improve performance of buildings.

"IN MANY CASES, PROJECTS BUILT UNDER CHALLENGING CONSTRAINTS PRESENT A GREAT OPPORTUNITY TO DEVELOP A DIALOGUE BETWEEN LOCAL AND INTERNATIONAL CONSULTANTS WHILE ALSO INCORPORATING INSIGHT FROM AN INDIGENOUS WAY OF LIFE THAT CAN ENHANCE HOW THE BUILDING PERFORMS IN HARMONY WITH THE LOCAL ECOLOGY."

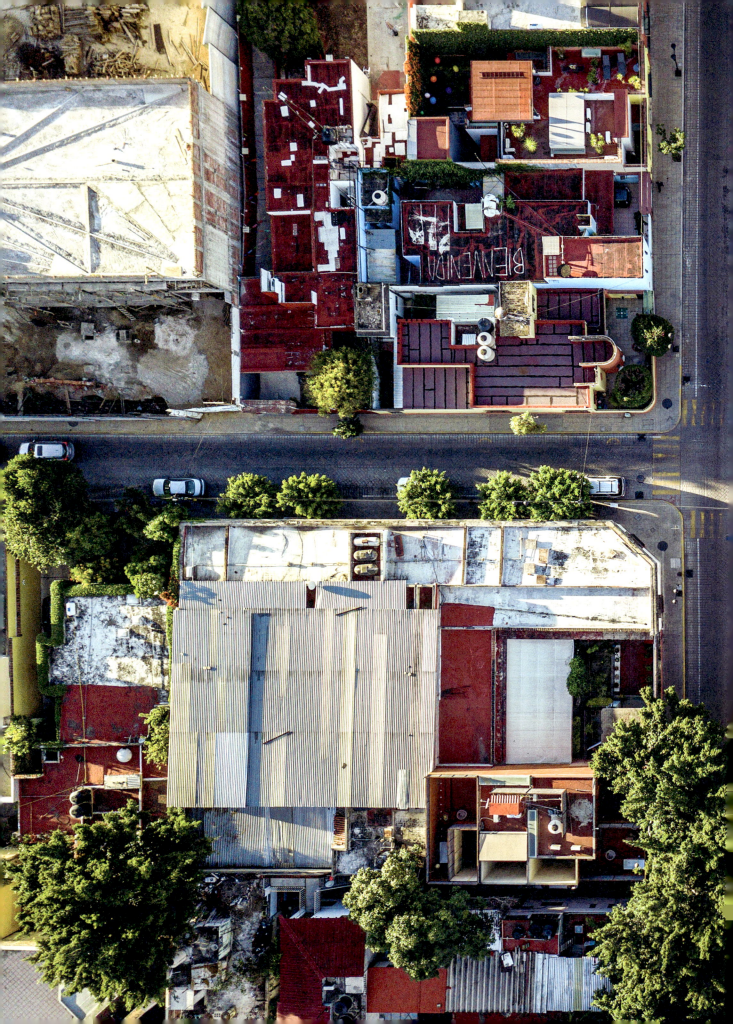

EDUCATIONAL PAVILION

INTRO

Mexican artists Francisco Toledo and Luis Zarate and the anthropologist and biologist Alejandro de Ávila began creating the cultural ensemble that would become the Botanical Gardens of Santo Domingo in the summer of 1994. It would be another four years before they would begin the first phase of planting and six more before they would begin contemplating a greenhouse that could support the growth of those species unable to survive in Oaxaca's extreme climate.

This diversity was essential to them. They wanted plants that would showcase the ecology of different regions in the state of Oaxaca. They would include those from both arid and humid climates, ranging from the low tropical zones to the temperate and mountain regions. The garden would represent the great diversity of climates, geological formations, and types of vegetation that characterize Oaxaca.

The purpose of this showcase would not merely be to collect a range of species, but also to show how this range of species functioned for the people who lived on the land over the course of several thousand years. In doing so, they hoped to show how the diversity of languages and cultures within the state corresponded to the diversity of plant life and how those plants were used to sustain and enrich human life. This would allow them to create an environment where people could understand how these elements were used for food, firewood, fibers, medicine, condiments, and dyes. Moreover, it would allow people to understand how they have served as a source of aesthetic inspiration, appearing in textile patterns, tiles, and architectural motifs over the course of several thousand years. In this sense, the reason they chose to call the garden "ethnobotanical" was because each element had a cultural meaning.

DESIGN

The project came about through a unique invitation from Toledo, Zarate, and de Avila to design an educational greenhouse. The design process began by carefully studying the context via its materiality, texture, pattern, color, and light. It quickly became clear that the Pavilion should reflect rather than compete with this context. It was important to create a lens through which this context could be seen and refined as well as a platform for learning more about this context and its ecology in the future. This involved a detailed conversation with experts to understand the precise growing conditions that would be required for the species grown in the Pavilion. This occurred through ongoing conversations with Alejandro de Ávila. Mathias Schuler and his company Transsolar were instrumental in understanding the thermal conditions in order to design the building systems that would be required to sustain the desired growing conditions.

GREENHOUSE
COMPLETED 2017
100 M2
OAXACA
MEXICO

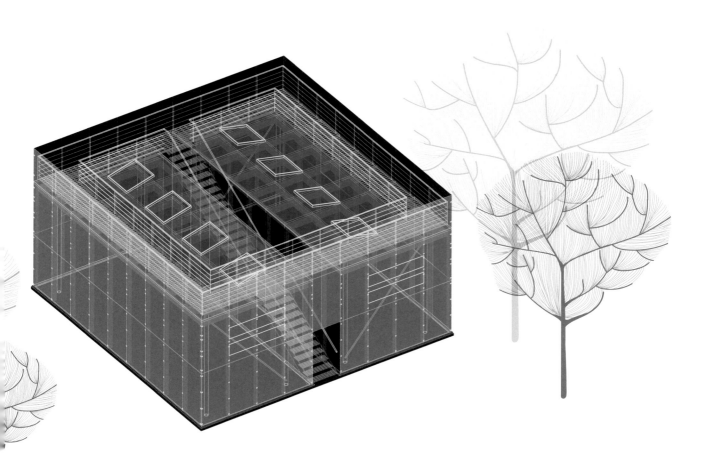

"IN THE PATH OF BUILDING THE IMMATERIAL ...
HOW THIN, LIGHT, TRANSPARENT, SELF-SUSTAINED CAN SOMETHING BE TO ACHIEVE THE 'INVISIBLE'... HOW FAR CAN WE PUSH THE LIMITS OF MATERIAL PROPERTIES ...
WHERE IS THE BOUNDARY?
THIS PAVILION IS A REFLECTION ON THE FRAGILITY OF LIFE AND THE DEDICATION REQUIRED TO SUSTAIN IT; IT IS THE PERFECT KIT OF PARTS, RIGHT DOWN TO THE NUMBER OF FASTENERS AND LINEAR METERS OF PIPING; IT IS THE BLUEPRINT OF WHAT A MUSEUM COULD OR SHOULD BE; IT IS EXPERIENCE AS A METHOD OF AWARENESS AND CONSCIOUSNESS OF THE RESOURCES INVESTED EVERY DAY IN BUILDING WITH LESS ..."

Following these preliminary conversations, González Pulido and Luis Zarate arrived at an initial concept: a two-chambered pavilion whose climates could each be controlled independently. These would be separated by a staircase that would allow the visitor to ascend to the roof. This would not only address the literal program, but also the metaphorical program of the building as one of learning, knowledge, and human connection to air and nature. The building would become more than a single program; it would become an object that would perform in its urban context.

Having determined the form and the structure, the systems and materials that would be employed were refined on the basis of Francisco González Pulido's concept of invisible systems. Werner Sobek further developed the structural system, while Schuler designed the geothermal. At the same time, local craftsmen and material suppliers who ultimately would build the Pavilion were added to the team. Many of these men were from trades in the city that were more accustomed to restoring historic structures. They brought an attention to detail that allowed them to build a highly sophisticated modern work of architecture with the craftsmanship that has defined the buildings of Oaxaca for centuries.

The result is a building that provides a unique experience within the Botanical Gardens through its materiality, transparency, and the way that it frames the garden and the city. It is a reflection of the fragility of life on earth. As an entirely self-sustaining ecosystem, it challenges visitors to consider how they might live in a more sustainable manner as well as to reflect on what is required to sustain life over the coming centuries.

The pavilion expresses greater freedom and sustainability in order to help the inhabitant live a more productive and creative life. It marks a shift from a strictly formal approach to dwelling relying on rigid

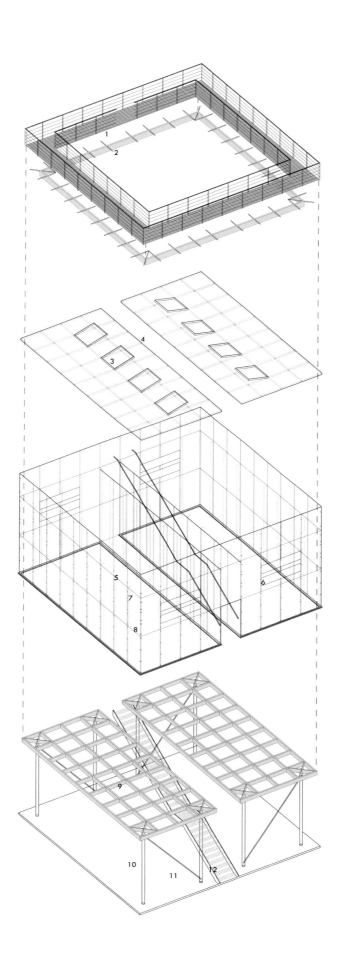

1. GLASS BALUSTRADE
  + STAINLESS STEEL RAILING
2. STEEL GRATING PLATFORM
3. GLAZED ROOF PANELS
4. OPERABLE ROOF FLAPS
5. SINGLE GLAZED ULTRA CLEAR GLASS
6. OPERABLE INTAKE FLAPS
7. COMPRESSION STAINLESS STEEL CLIPS
8. STEEL MULLIONS
9. TAPERED STEEL STRUCTURE
10. STEEL COLUMNS
11. BRACING TENSION CABLES
12. STEEL GRATING THREADS

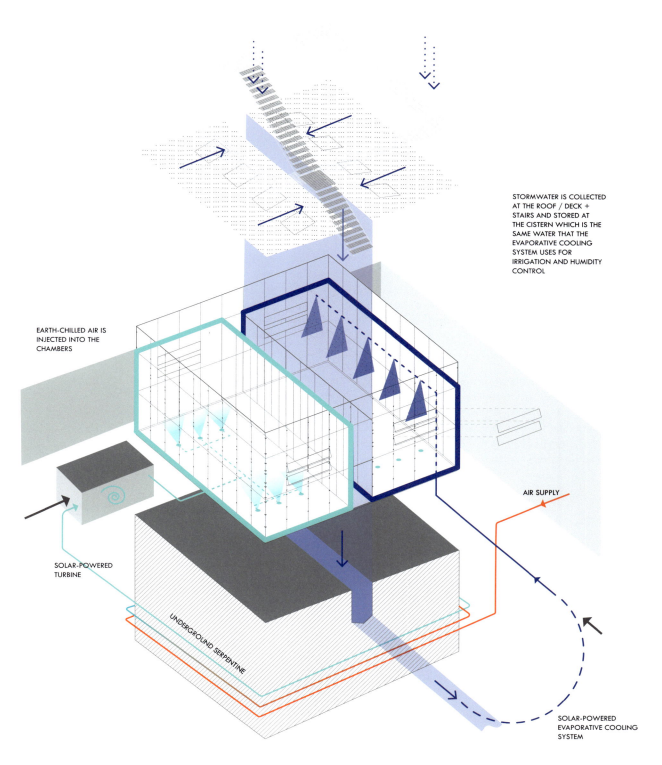

fixed geometries that can be deployed to any site around the world to an ecological approach that does not merely optimize energy performance or integrate the architectural object into a broader system, but rather manifests the ecology in an architectural language defining materiality, tectonics, and a hierarchy of systems, spaces, and programs.

The Pavilion is conceived as a contemporary cultural building that, in contrast to its historic context, is designed around the idea of minimum use of resources and minimum environmental impact. It is a self-sustaining "machine" for harvesting. The idea of total transparency was critical in the design. The flooring planks for the staircase and the viewing platform are an open grid to allow light and views from all directions into the chambers. The visual effect that results becomes the central aesthetic feature of the building. The detail with which these panels are constructed, and the overall detailing of the building, is vital in creating a sense of cohesion and achieving a vision that draws on the history of modern aesthetics while also pushing beyond through performance.

The Pavilion builds on the tradition of the High-Tech movement in architecture, characterized by buildings such as Lloyds headquarters in London, the Centre Pompidou in Paris, and the Eden Project in Cornwall that made visible the mechanical and structural systems on which buildings rely. By contrast, the primary feature of the Pavilion is what is not visible. The result enhances the minimal aesthetic defined by clean lines and transparency. It allows the building to take a step back, so that both the surroundings and its contents come into focus. In doing so, the overall feeling of lightness is enhanced.

A sense of lightness is also found in the ability to climb the stairs to the roof and stand above the trees with the wind blowing through one's hair. The platform creates an opportunity to contemplate the curated plant contents from an elevated perspective. Underneath the staircase, rainfall is collected and stored in the complex's main well to be used by the evaporative cooling system that supports the cooling and irrigation systems.

SUSTAINABILITY & RESILIENCE

The Pavilion never truly vanishes. It is a subtle intervention through glass surfaces and steel detailing that creates new juxtapositions with the surroundings that activate these surfaces in exciting and unexpected ways. The technology that went into the refinement of the glass with minimal reflection and the steel components that hold the Pavilion together is brought into a visual play with the natural surroundings. This contrast between nature and culture, plant life and the mineral product of human refinement creates a framework for understanding both. Hopefully, in the process, the visitor is given a chance to appreciate both with greater depth than when they arrived.

The design is based on five elements: the west chamber ("hot chamber"), the east chamber ("cool chamber"), the central staircase (which collects rainfall), the viewing platform, and the "invisible systems" (geothermal, evaporative cooling, and power). The east and west chambers are rectangular glass boxes oriented on the north-south axis to provoke natural cross ventilation. They are located on either side of the central staircase and designed to run on slightly contrasting thermal criteria. The air-conditioning is provided through a geothermal system that injects cold air into the chambers.

The Pavilion does not use any power from the city grid to run the fans for the air pipe system and the sprayers for evaporative cooling. The evaporative cooling system of overhead sprayers are mounted at the nodes of the roof structure to create humidity for conditioning and harvesting. The electricity that is required is generated via photovoltaic panels that are mounted on the roof of the main administration building. Due to the sensitivity of the plants, no artificial lighting is required for day and night conditions, further reducing energy demand. The buried air pipe system uses one fan to pull outdoor air through a single intake cavity located in the east wall of the site's northeast boundary, where the ambient temperature is the lowest throughout the year. The air is then circulated through the buried air pipe network, which is approximately 132 meters in length and wraps around the greenhouse 10 meters below grade.

The viewing platform within the perimeter of the pavilion is constructed with a tight steel grating that provides partial passive shading to the interior of the chambers. Flaps located in the north and south elevations as well as on the roof regulate the temperature and humidity. The buried air pipe system and evaporative cooling was critical for achieving this goal.

"THE RESULT IS A BUILDING THAT PROVIDES A UNIQUE EXPERIENCE WITHIN THE BOTANICAL GARDENS THROUGH ITS MATERIALITY, TRANSPARENCY, AND THE WAY IT FRAMES THE GARDEN AND THE CITY. IT IS A REFLECTION OF THE FRAGILITY OF LIFE ON EARTH."

OBSERVATION DECK DETAIL

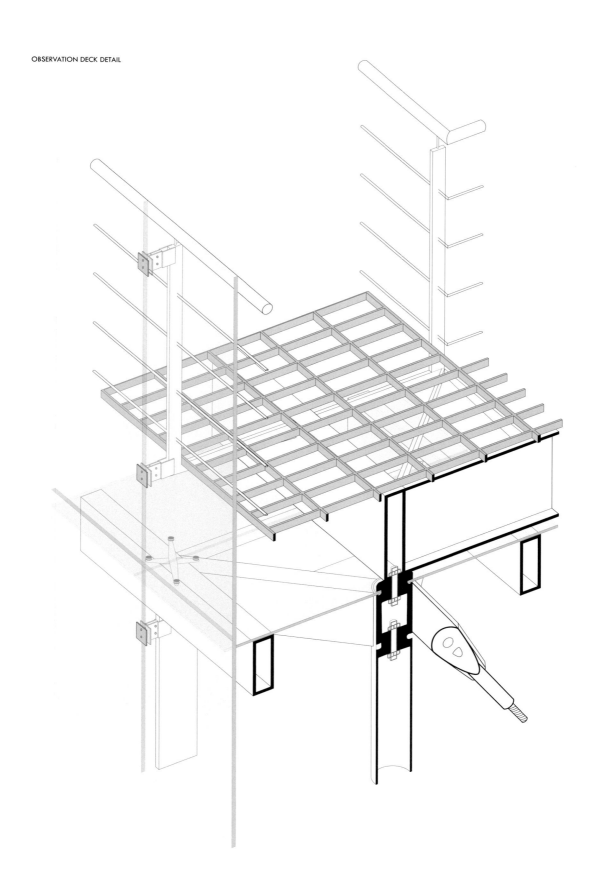

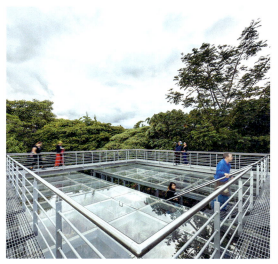

"THE CORE OF THE BUILDING WAS INVISIBLE SYSTEMS. THE GOAL WAS TO NOT SEE WHAT MAKES THIS BUILDING FUNCTION. EVERYTHING IS INTEGRATED INTO THE ARCHITECTURE AND THE OVERALL BUILDING EXPERIENCE."

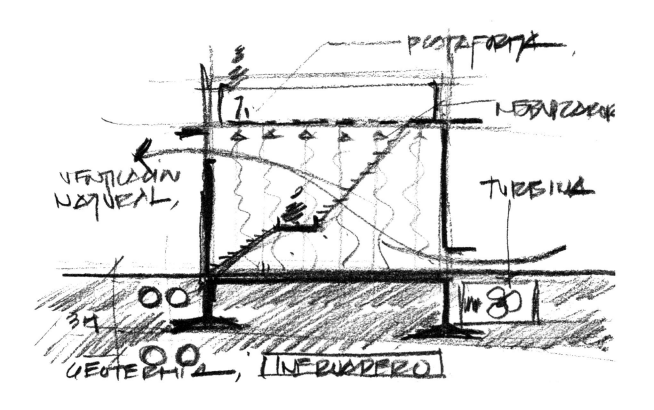

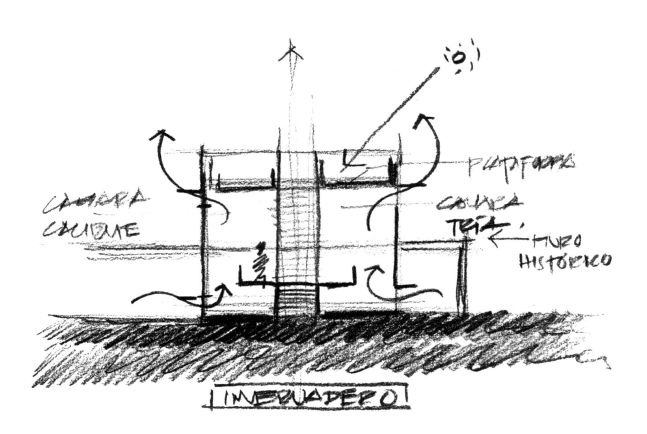

AESTHETICS OF THE SUSTAINABLE

1. "Aesthetics" and "Sustainability"

Aesthetics is typically defined as a set of principles associated with the appreciation of beauty, particularly in a work of art. Sustainability is typically defined as the avoidance of the depletion of natural resources in order to maintain ecological balance. The intersection of the two terms would then be a set of principles associated with beauty in avoidance of depletion of natural resources. This very broad field is narrowed if the focus is on how buildings can avoid the depletion of resources. In shifting the focus to buildings, a tradition of aesthetics in buildings becomes an important consideration. This tradition is concerned with determining the principles of beauty in a building largely through judgment. In this sense, discussing aesthetics and sustainability requires a system whereby a particular appearance of a building is tied to that building's sustainable performance and a framework for judging the specific nature of that connection and appearance.

An "aesthetics of the sustainable" is concerned with the intersection between nature and culture. In choosing to discuss both as connected terms, the idea that the sustainability of buildings is merely a technological question is rejected. Instead, sustainability is driven by behavior. Such behavior is framed by the natural environment. It is driven by the path of the sun, oceans and shores, rivers, fertility of the land, animals and insects, vegetation and agriculture, and the varied atmospheres around the world. This behavior defines the buildings that are built and how those buildings become embedded in natural systems. Engineers could take our cumulative knowledge and design a solution that would make the world sustainable but doing so would be meaningless, because it would fail to address the underlying systems that define the world at present.

This notion that sustainability is a social and behavioral problem, and that aesthetics are the set of principles that guide how this behavior is reflected in the built environment in a beautiful manner, is comparatively absent from the current discourse on sustainability in buildings. Over the last several decades, a style has developed associated with what has come to be known as sustainable design. The style can be seen in the wide range of "green homes" in cities around the world that boast passive systems, solar panels, and sustainably sourced materials. It can also be found in the designs of architects who work in harmony with the ecology of the site to develop buildings requiring minimal systems to sustain a conducive atmosphere. These buildings, when well designed, generally express an honesty of materiality, straightforwardness of structure, and organization around the habits of the resident.

AESTHETICS OF THE SUSTAINABLE

In large scale buildings, the sustainable is often manifested in advanced mechanical systems, double skins that prevent heat gain, green roofs and places for users to retreat outdoors, and a wide array of sustainable materials. They are certified by LEED, WELL, ISO, and other systems and standards that validate their status as sustainable. What, however, is the nature of their beauty? Do we connect what we consider beautiful in a sustainable building to the elements that make it sustainable? Or is this beauty tied to conventional criteria—proportion, composition, color, attention to detail, hierarchy, and transcendence—that have for centuries been used to evaluate art and architecture? And, in what way does an "aesthetics of the sustainable" help us to move beyond aesthetics as strictly visual and to an understanding of aesthetics as connected to the senses and the atmosphere?

One of the aspects that is missing from this approach is a balanced consideration of both the behavior and the building. Too often, sustainability is framed in strictly architectural, material, or construction terms. This is, in large part, a function of defining sustainability as something to be achieved in new buildings. What this approach misses, is a consideration of the broader systems that affect the building and the inhabitants. Chief among these systems are those networks of infrastructure that propel particular lifestyles that are not sustainable. These include roadways, flight paths, shipping channels, electric lines, and media networks. Media networks, in particular, play a significant role in propelling a culture of consumption that values the new over the tool or object that can be used over the course of generations.

These networks are propelled by capital structures that subject the vast majority of the world to a system concealing and alienating the individual both from their labor and from the natural environment. This is evident in the hundreds of TV and radio channels that support mass media. They distribute events twenty-four hours a day and have created a need for continuous drama and consumption. Since it is impossible to generate that volume naturally, media outlets have developed artificial ways to produce it. Architects too have become caught in this cycle of drama and celebrity. It is a clear human signal of a confused world showcasing an abbreviated form of personality defined by adding complexity into situations that require clear vision. One of the most devastating consequences has been the acceptance of design and production methodologies that segregate designers living in a reified sphere from builders grounded in materiality and the earth. The result is a social setting that proliferates throughout the world.

"OUR WORK AIMS TO GO BEYOND ANY ONE SYSTEM TO MEASURE SUSTAINABILITY. FOR US, IT IS NOT ABOUT GETTING POINTS OR MEETING THE LATEST STANDARD, BUT ABOUT SUSTAINABILITY AS A WAY OF LIFE THAT DRIVES OUR CRAFT."

AESTHETICS OF THE SUSTAINABLE

The point of calling attention to these systems is by no means to suggest that they should not exist or that a critical stance towards these networks should be taken in the design of a building. Instead, it is to suggest that the building be conscious through design decisions of how it is embedded in these networks, how these networks are defined by the natural environment, and how together they affect the environment. Moreover, it is to suggest that this intersection between nature and culture takes on a specific visual and sensory experience that defines how an occupant uses and appreciates the building. This appreciation is, at heart, a process of judgment and negotiation that defines an aesthetics of the sustainable.

2. Sustainability and the Modern Movement

The aesthetics of the sustainable described above has existed in how architects in the past have approached the design of buildings. Both ancient and modern architects and builders have used the natural environment to guide the design of buildings and to make them operate more effectively. This was particularly true for architects working prior to the advent of mechanical and electrical systems. They were required to use natural ventilation as well as water circulation and waste disposal to make the structures they designed function.

The rapid growth of cities during the eighteenth and nineteenth centuries left many overcrowded. Buildings were so tightly packed together that they could not take advantage of traditional means of integrating them within the natural environment. Instead, they were decorated with ornamentation and floral patterns standing in for a real relationship to nature. Modernist artists and architects understood this ornamentation to be artifice and sought to reframe the relationship between man and nature in the built environment. Frank Lloyd Wright grounded his reaction through the influence of natural characteristics of the midwestern prairie of the United States. It inspired both the low profile of his buildings, many of which were tied to the ground, as well as the patterns in the leaded-glass windows throughout his homes. These houses were also centered around the hearth as both a focal point for gathering and means of heating the home. Through the publication of the Wasmuth Portfolio in Germany in 1911, the work of Frank Lloyd Wright circulated in the studio of Peter Behrens, where Le Corbusier, Ludwig Mies van der Rohe, and Walter Gropius were all working as apprentices.

Each in their own way reframed the question of the relationship between nature and culture. Common to all was an alignment of culture with industrial

AESTHETICS OF THE SUSTAINABLE

technology and a fresh approach, or perhaps even a return, to the natural environment. These industrial objects were thought to possess an honesty through the way in which their form was derived from their function, which made them beautiful in a more authentic way than decorative art. These objects were, however, designed, and this design process often drew on classical systems of proportion and a deep understanding of how humans behave, see and hear, use space, and generally dwell. In this sense, modern aesthetics can be seen as a return to a more innate grounding of beauty distinct from the academic system that had arisen over the preceding centuries. The valuation of these technical devices was not strictly technological but tied to a deeper meaning that they conveyed and, ultimately, a morality driven by a quest for authenticity. However problematic this notion of modernist authenticity would prove to be, it did convey a quest to live openly and in harmony with one's surroundings, subject to one's own decisions and fate.

At the beginning of the twentieth century, great examples of the fusion between the idea of art and utilitarianism came about. Most were under the wing of abstract purism and based on Neoplatonic philosophy. This generation and many in those that followed were enamored with functional objects because there is a reason for their existence. It is the premise of their longevity. At the same time, this infatuation with the industrial would prove somewhat problematic when confronting how the building actually sits within the natural environment. Le Corbusier, perhaps more so than his German counterparts, was deeply interested in the relationship between building and nature. He ultimately placed man rather than the built form at the center of his design philosophy. The relationship between man and sun, water, and earth grounded all design decisions. While sometimes naïve in his estimation of how this would play out in the context of his five elements of architecture (pilotis, roof garden, free ground plan, free facade, horizontal windows), he did endeavor to introduce elements such as brise soleil, natural ventilation, planted roofs, and cities in gardens that would ground his architecture in a relationship to nature. Moreover, in his later work, he introduced a genuine phenomenological experience through light, sound, and color that satisfied functional needs with empirical forms and abstract elements that impact the senses and nurture the intellect.

Walter Gropius and the Bauhaus were pioneers of simplicity. Their fundamental idea relied on the principle of a simple form that would solve all the spatial and vital needs, which could be simultaneously respectable and genuine. They aimed to reconcile custom design and industrial production. All this was based on the application of essential design principles such as

"IT IS IRONIC THAT, IN A WORLD IN CONSTANT FLUX, THE MAJORITY OF BUILDINGS UTILIZE NON-ADAPTABLE CONSTRUCTION METHODS, AND MATERIALS AND SYSTEMS FAIL TO RESPOND TO THEIR ENVIRONMENTS LIKE LIVING ENTITIES."

AESTHETICS OF THE SUSTAINABLE

the extensive use of natural light and ventilation, simplicity of diagram and structural integrity. They sought to introduce new mechanical systems to genuinely make their buildings machines that could satisfy all the needs of the inhabitant, even if this was sometimes accomplished by working against the natural conditions in which the building existed.

Mies van der Rohe consolidated a new vision of architecture in which elimination strengthens content. This purity of approach, however, sometimes made it difficult for his buildings to function effectively in diverse climates. When commissioned to design a house on the outskirts of Chicago on the Fox River, Mies designed a structure—the Farnsworth House—with all-glass walls and one operable window located near the floor. There was no ability to provide cross-ventilation and no air-conditioning. Further, the porch had no screens and thus would likely have been a fantastic feeding ground for insects to breed, given its proximity to water. The house was unbearably hot in the summer and, owing to the single-pane windows, quite cold in the winter. Finally, while the house was elevated to prevent flooding when the Fox River overflowed its banks, rising river levels meant that the house was ultimately inundated with water.

The challenges faced by the Farnsworth House were echoed in buildings he designed around the world, which in turn inspired generations of buildings in the International Style. They often required intense air-conditioning to cool, lacked operable windows, and generally drew huge amounts of energy. In many ways, they reveal the slightly problematic use of machines as the inspiration for a building design, in part because they focus on culture to the detriment of nature. Many of the machines that inspired this modern aesthetics—from steamships, airplanes, and cars to factories and mass-produced consumer products—have proven to be significant contributors to climate change through their reliance on fossil fuels. Around the beginning of the twentieth century, we learned that simplicity and purism were premises for the creation of content and meaning. During the twentieth century, the same premises opened the door to complexity and contradiction in an attempt to achieve the same result. By the end of the twentieth century, the new challenge was (and still is) to generate more by using and wasting much less. Some call this principle the "lean economy," and it has become a model for a path forward in approaching sustainability in the built environment.

AESTHETICS OF THE SUSTAINABLE

This approach can be seen in the work of architects such as Buckminster Fuller who believed that the main purpose of architecture was to continuously achieve higher living standards at a lower cost of both resources and energy. Energy is taking a more active role in architecture as our energy consumption has become a critical parameter. More energy is used to operate buildings than to operate cars. To save is to maintain and to preserve translates into comfort. To generate equals sustainability. Operation costs are becoming as important as construction cost in the building industry. It is ironic that, in a world in constant flux, the majority of buildings utilize non-adaptable construction methods, and materials and systems fail to respond to their environments like a living entity. Paradoxically, the physical properties of buildings remain constant while internal and external agents impose permanent changes on them. The notion of what is possible to generate in the energy plan using mechanical means has kept us away from more adequate solutions. The beauty of what is sustainable should be defined by how humans live and the way in which buildings and systems take form to meet the criteria for living a productive life. The technologies that are employed should be in service of this life and should not become the focus of life.

3. Aesthetics of the Sustainable Today and Tomorrow

Today, the aesthetics of the sustainable is driven by recent data that describes a changing climate and the effects of this change on temperature, rainfall, sea level, natural disasters, and food production. It is also driven by an ecological approach to theory and practice in realms ranging from anthropology and cybernetics to architecture and urbanism. These trends have had the effect of creating a whole wave of buildings that address the notion of sustainability in one manner or another. On one hand, this could be the LEED and WELL certification programs; on the other, it could be the design of passive houses and the high-tech office building that makes use of double skins, operable windows, solar panels, and wind turbines, among other techniques.

Over the course of the last several decades, we had the opportunity to explore many different strategies to achieve sustainability. Whether visible or invisible, their presence is ultimately reflected in the appearance of the building. In the realm of planning, this has involved the design of buildings seeking maximum adaptation to the location, the possibility of changes in the use of a building, adaptability of the structure, and plan to recycle components when the building is no longer needed. In the realm of materials, the exploration has included the design of buildings that use materials derived

"THE BROADER IDEA IS THAT WHAT YOU COLLECT, YOU USE, AND WHAT YOU COLLECT COMES FROM THE ENVIRONMENT. YOU HARVEST THE SUN, WIND, AND RAIN, AND REUSE IT."

AESTHETICS OF THE SUSTAINABLE

from manufacturing processes that do not impact the environment via zero carbon and zero waste while conserving natural resources. In many cases, green roofs have been introduced. Using materials with low or zero volatile organic compounds has also been done. These designs also introduced highly insulated metal panels, high-performance, low-e coated glass, vacuum glass, transparent photovoltaic roofs with 15% light transmission, and ultralight systems that combine several functions in a single component such as envelope, insulation, and structure. Software has played an essential role in simulating how the building will interact with the natural environment and how specific materials will perform. As a building's digital twin, it has the capacity to simulate the operation of the building over the course of its life as well as how it interacts with the power grid, other buildings, and the natural environment.

Construction methods are an equally important component of a sustainable design and contribute significantly to the overall beauty of the building. A careful understanding of construction methods in a particular context is essential to achieving sustainable criteria. Differential construction methods are based on components made up of a variable number of elements that, individually, are comparatively simple in their design. Integral methods are based on a component made of a single material that then forms a unit. Integral methods of this kind have become a key characteristic of the concepts explored in the concluding essay of this book, "Dry Architecture."

Once a building is completed, it will be commissioned and open to its intended use. This use will require energy. It is therefore important to design the building in such a way that its mechanical systems are energy efficient, that daylight is maximized, and heat gain minimized, and that renewable energy sources such as wind-power generation and photovoltaic panels are used where possible. Other techniques, such as solar thermal absorption chillers, thermal inversions at night to draw air into space, earth duct pre-cooling, wind cones that support massive intake of cool air into the ground level, hot air exhaust, diffuse daylight, operable windows for cross ventilation, the highest level of negative pressure on roof to promote the highest draw, under-floor air distribution systems, solar vacuum tubes for cooling, high thermal mass, passive solar heat blocking, natural shading, natural light, solar absorption and heat reflection, geothermal systems, thermal shields, and collecting energy to heat water and supplement electrical needs have been explored to reduce the overall energy requirements. At the same time, it is important to consider how the building mitigates waste generation, how it might utilize waste through systems like a biodigester, how rainwater is collected and stored, and how rainwater relates to the watershed.

AESTHETICS OF THE SUSTAINABLE

These elements come together in the design of a building that may be considered beautiful based on satisfying the above criteria. It is in this context that an aesthetics of the sustainable should be couched. Ultimately, a sustainable approach to design and construction should reduce the cost of building rather than become a defining characteristic of a way of living that is only available to the wealthiest members of society. In this sense, an aesthetics of the sustainable should support affordable living for humanity as a whole. And, in this sense, it would be an aesthetics grounded in the universality of many as opposed to the few. At the same time, these structures must meet the centuries-old desire to create spaces in which our senses transcend the physical and attain to the metaphysical, almost unconsciously. They are places where form and space penetrate our psyche with the many forms of the psychological.

CHAPTER TWO

I_VALUES

All architecture firms are grounded in a studio practice. The studio is a place to draw, build models, research, experiment, critique work, present work to clients, and stay up to date on the state of the industry. Such a studio practice is located in one or distributed across several cities serving different markets. Each may take on its own identity while also existing as part of a cohesive global practice and brand identity. The specific nature of this identity is often tied to the culture of the firm and the extent to which it is seen as a desirable place to work. This is often driven by the type of work the firm does, the leadership culture, the pressure placed on team members, and the overall work-life balance.

The context of this space is just as important as the space itself. The physical space serves as a congregating point where members of the professional community of a specific city meet. The success of a firm is often contingent on access to a strong professional community and the capacity to grow as new projects arise. The context is also important because it defines the extent to which the studio is connected to the rest of a city via road networks and public transportation that make it possible to easily access desirable places to live. It is often important that the location balance access to housing that is affordable for all team members while also appealing to current and future clients. This is often connected to the history of the location, the significant buildings that might exist nearby, and parks and green space. These elements help to ground the practice in a historical tradition while also providing inspiration. The specific nature of this connection between the West Loop of Chicago and our practice is discussed in the essay "Practicing Here."

CHAPTER TWO

For our practice, the studio space allows for a number of pursuits that contribute to the overall success of the buildings. These include parametric modeling, 3D printing of models, the use of VR for presentations, ongoing material research and continuing education, the development of white papers based on research and dissemination via our website as a publishing platform, and the establishment of the Building Research Institute as an independent entity charged with developing new products, lines of research, and businesses that improve the future of the built environment. These tools have all been utilized in designing La Hoja, a new covering for the central library of Monterrey Tec in Monterrey, Mexico. This relatively small, experimental project is emblematic of our broader practice. It is highly contextual and tailored to the programmatic requirements. The specific manner in which these attributes were achieved is explored in what follows.

I_VALUES

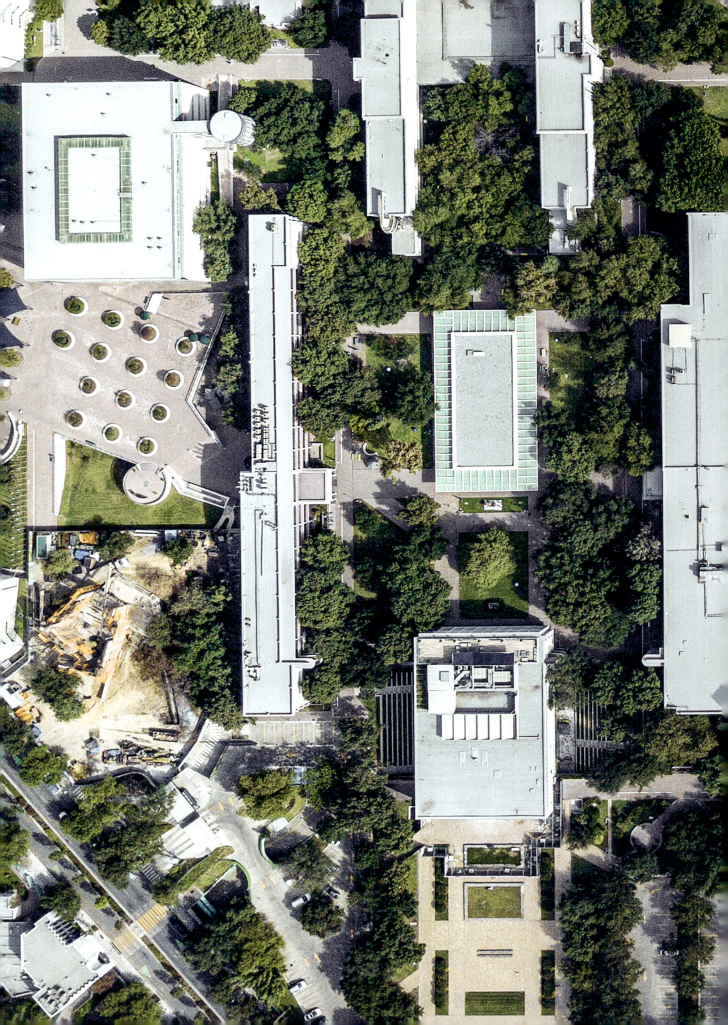

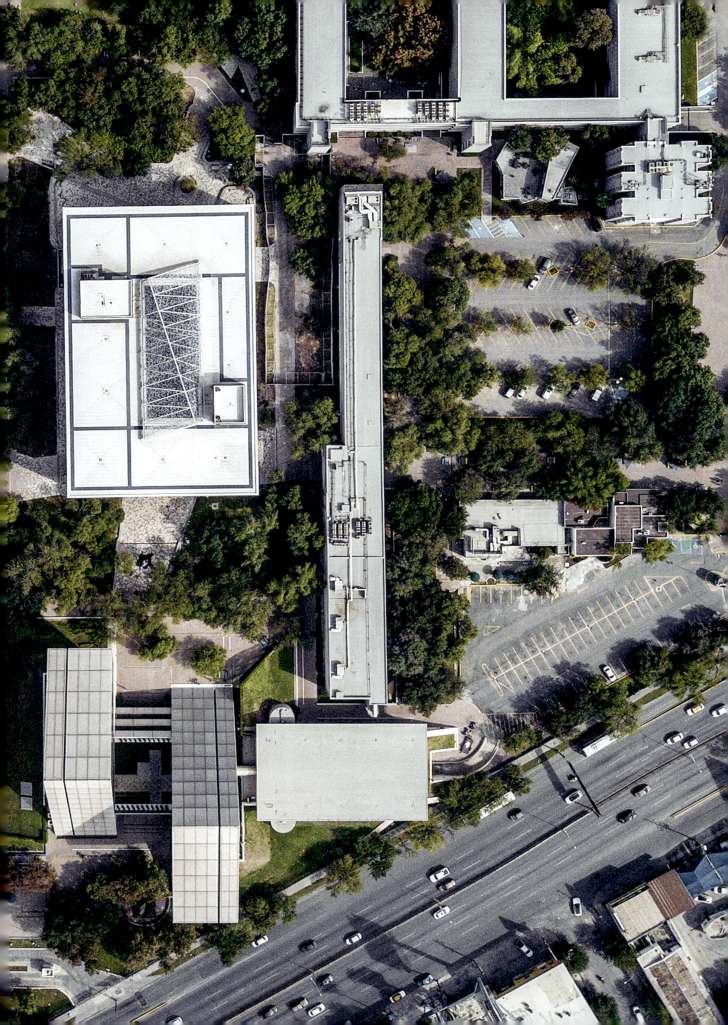

LA HOJA

INTRO

The commission involved creating a covering for the central space of the recently completed library at Monterrey Tec. The goal was to protect the space from rain, sun, and uncontrolled winds so that it could be used year-round. This was particularly important, because the space was underutilized and had become somewhat dysfunctional during storms, to the point that the lack of covering was creating a condition that was beginning to cause the deterioration of the building's courtyard.

The building in which the new roof is located was designed by Sasaki and Associates in a contemporary style defined by large stone and glass planes. The rigidity of the geometry is broken by a series of bridges crossing the space at varied angels as well as stairs connecting the different levels. It was important to pay homage to the geometry and style while also introducing a more whimsical element to the design. Doing so might help bring the space to life and create a dynamic environment that would attract people, so that it would become a central gathering space within the campus.

The trees on the lush campus inspired the creation of a veil simulating leaves falling on the surface via a pattern screened on ETFE. The falling leaves were further connected to the idea of evoking fall and the moment when the semester begins, when students are positive and excited by a new beginning. The ultralightweight structure will create new patterns as the sun moves across the surface and, in turn, provide a sense of time passing as one studies in the library.

The roof is defined by both the large figure of the leaf and also by the smaller leaves that make up this figure. The leaf itself comes from a tree that is native to the area—the white poplar, or *álamo blanco*. In some ways, the use of the leaf is intended to create an opportunity to reflect on our relationship to the natural environment and the impact that buildings have on the environment.

DESIGN

In designing the specific surface of the membrane, a wide range of potential patterns were explored. Parametric modeling tools were used to design the geometry of the roof. A physics engine was then used to simulate wind blowing leaves across this surface. Each leaf had a certain number of dots. The process required multiple simulations. This allowed the team to achieve a sense of randomness. In this sense, the pattern was designed directly via digital tools that were in turn linked to the digital printing technology that ultimately fabricated the membrane.

**ADDITION
COMPLETED 2019
600 M2
MONTERREY
MEXICO**

"AN INTERVENTION TO PROVIDE SHELTER AND CREATE A 'PLACE,' CONCEALED FROM EXTREME CLIMATE YET CONNECTED TO THE HISTORY AND THE NATURE OF ITS CONTEXT THROUGH PATTERNS OF WHITE POPLAR LEAVES THAT REMIND US OF WHAT PRECEDED US. OUR GOAL IS THE PRESERVATION OF THE MEMORY OF THIS PLACE; A STRUCTURAL INTERPLAY WEAVES THE ATRIUM, WHICH RESEMBLE TREE BRANCHES THAT ARE NO LONGER WITH US. LA HOJA IS A REFLECTION ON HOW OUR PATTERNS OF EXTERMINATION ARE UNDERESTIMATED AND EVENTUALLY FORGOTTEN."

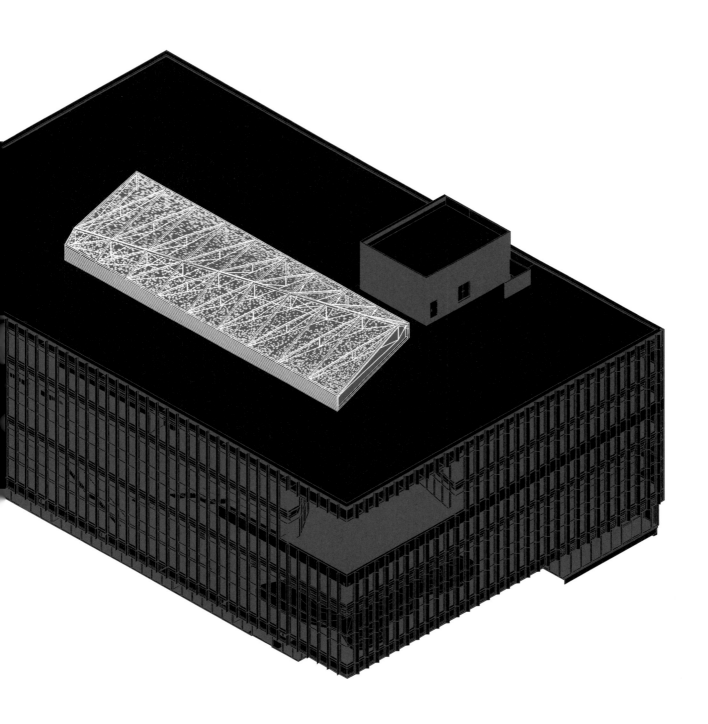

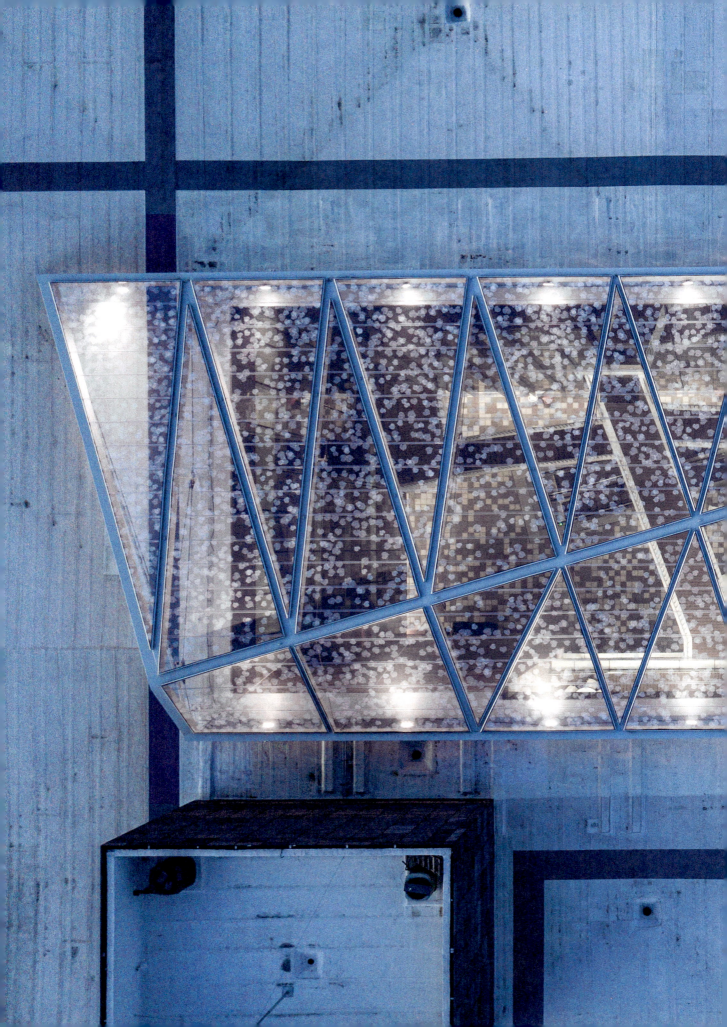

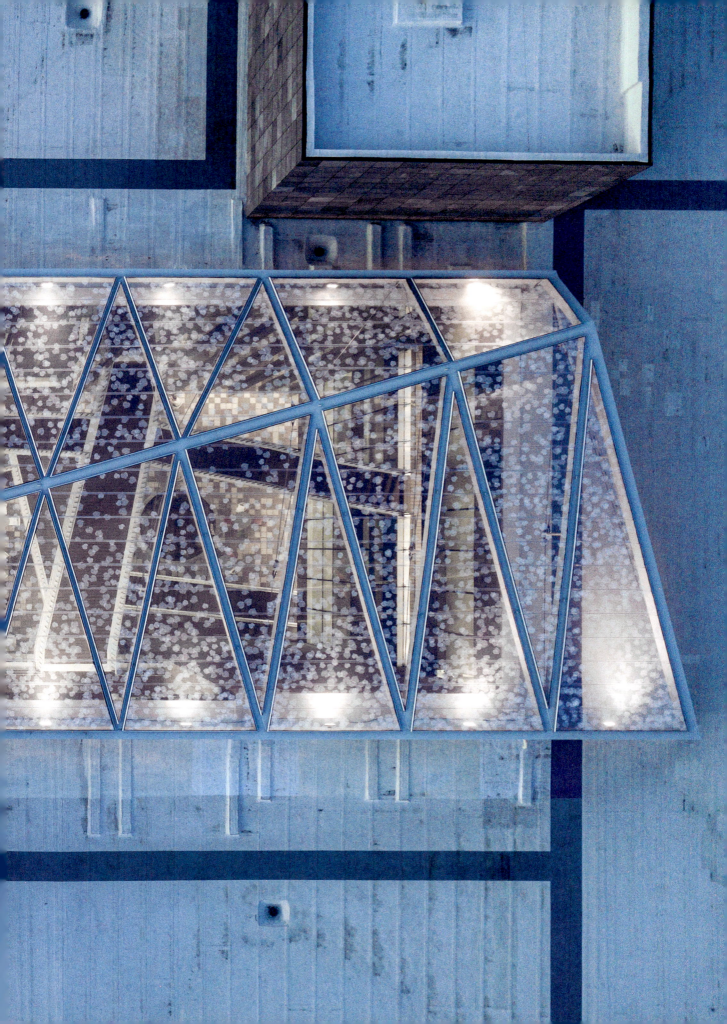

The surface of the roof is supported by a system of ten steel trusses set at an angle that would complement the angle of the bridges and stairs below. The triangular trusses would have a varying peak point that would follow a diagonal line from one corner of the atrium to the other. While a steel member would follow this diagonal peak, additional steel members would connect the two corners of the trapezoid in order to provide added stability. Below the surface of the roof, a network of tension cables completes the structural system. The structural system in turn supports the single-layer ETFE membrane that is held in tension along the perimeter.

The roof extends beyond the edge of the courtyard. In this sense, it is a cover rather than an enclosure. A wind study suggested that if an enclosure was created, the structure would have to be much more robust because the wind entering the courtyard from below would be trapped. This would have significant cost implications. By raising it slightly above the level of the roof, hot air can escape. Extending it beyond the edge also protects the courtyard from strong winds and rain.

The use of ETFE cladding material with a printed pattern reduces the potential for heat gain within the space. In addition, the use of natural ventilation along the perimeter of the roof systems allows for heat to escape while keeping water from entering the space. At the same time, the use of an ultralightweight structure reduces the overall embodied energy of materials and carbon cost of transporting those materials to the site. The result will be a space that does not significantly add to the energy load of the building.

The process of building the roof was challenging. The building is located in the center of campus with little room for staging the construction. In addition, students would continue to use the building throughout the construction process. The client was against putting a crane in the middle of the building. This meant that all materials had to be lifted from the side. In spite of these limitations, the project was finished both on time and on budget.

The intervention not only solved the initial problem but created a space that was not there before. This made it possible to introduce new programmatic functions into the atrium that enhanced the overall functionality of the library. In some sense, it has become the heart of the campus—a point where people meet and collaborate.

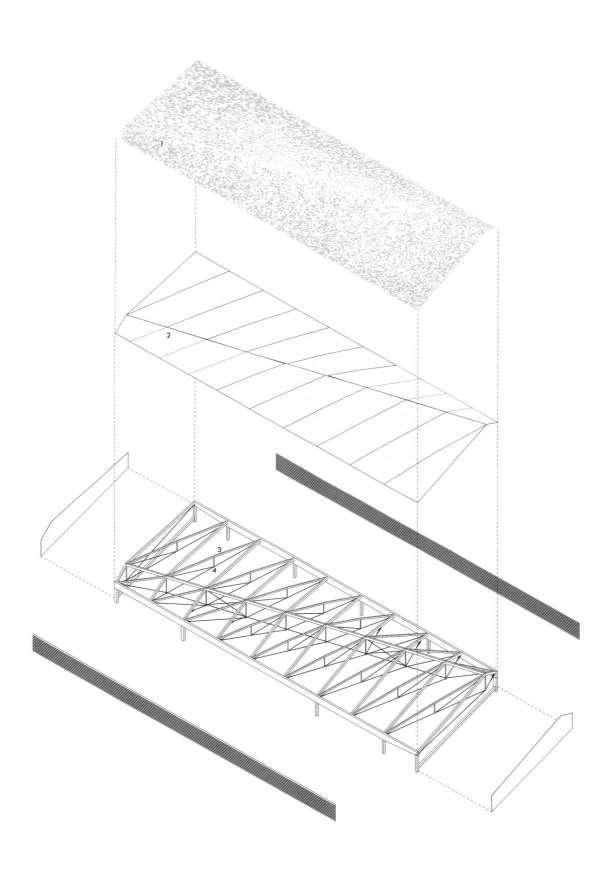

1. DIGITALLY PRINTED PATTERN
2. SINGLE LAYER ETFE ENCLOSURE
3. STEEL STRUCTURE
4. CABLE TRUSSES

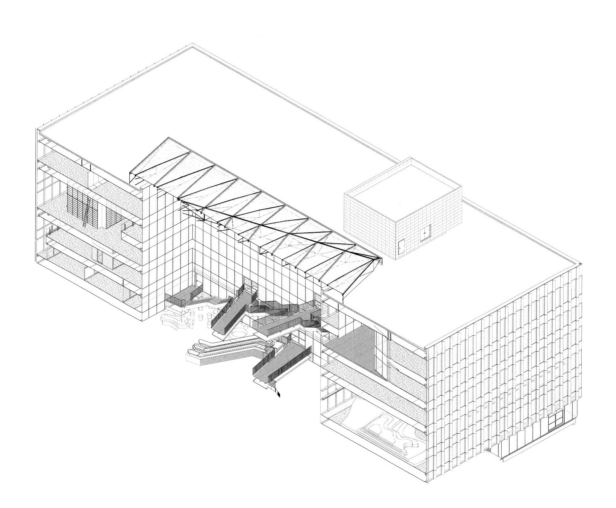

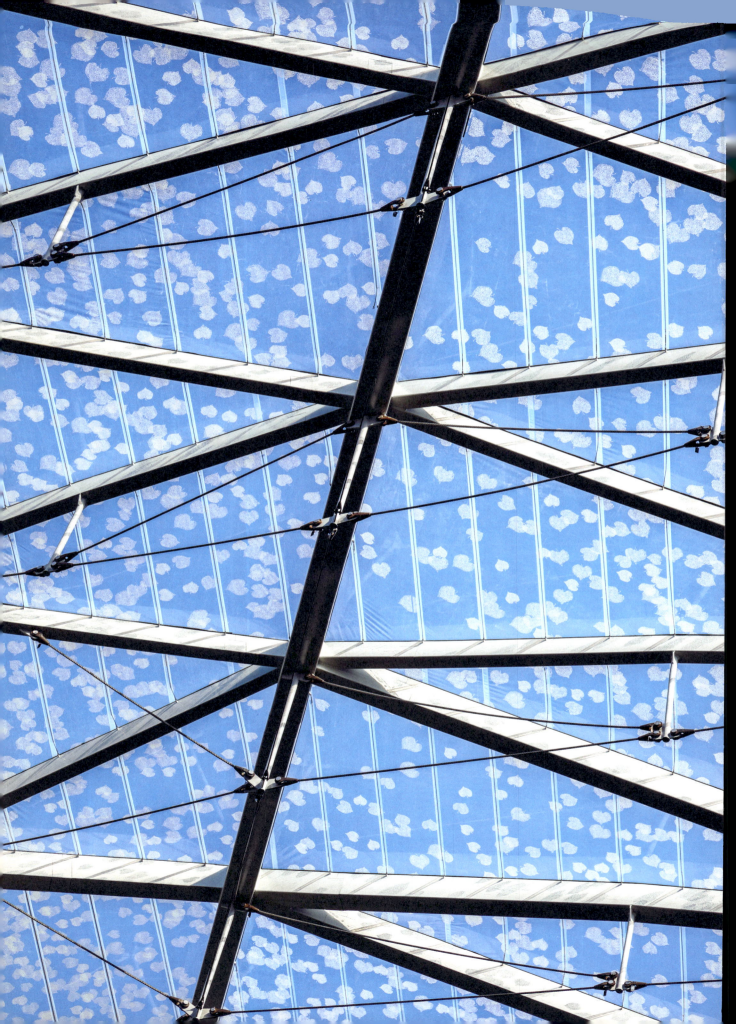

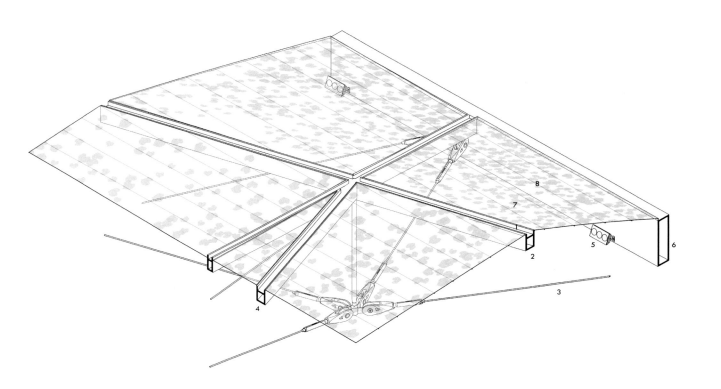

1. GUTTER
2. RIDGE STEEL STRUCTURE
3. CABLE TRUSS
4. SECONDARY STEEL STRUCTURE
5. INTEGRATED DYNAMIC LIGHTING
6. MAIN FRAME STEEL STRUCTURE
7. LEAF PATTERN DIGITALLY PRINTED ON ETFE
8. STAINLESS STEEL CABLES TO KEEP ETFE IN TENSION

GRASSHOPPER SCRIPT

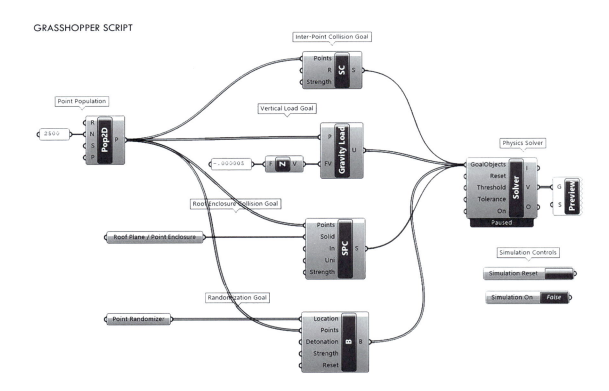

"A physics engine was then used to simulate wind blowing leaves across this surface. Each leaf had a certain number of dots. The process required multiple simulations. This allowed us to achieve a sense of randomness. In this sense, the pattern was designed directly via digital tools that were in turn linked to the digital printing technology that ultimately fabricated the membrane."

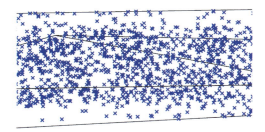

1_WIND BLAST

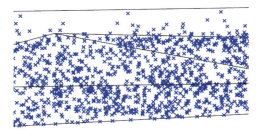

2

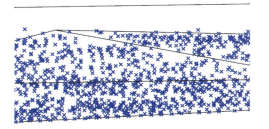

3

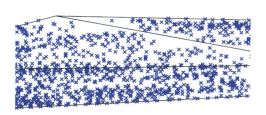

4_FINAL PLACEMENT

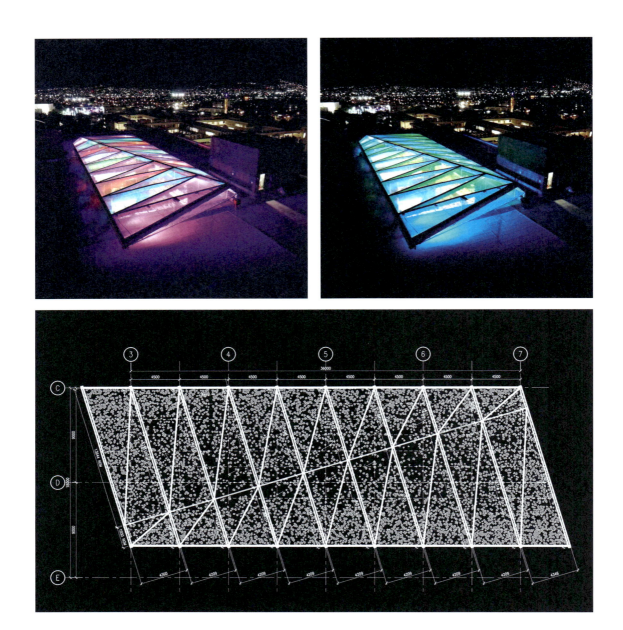

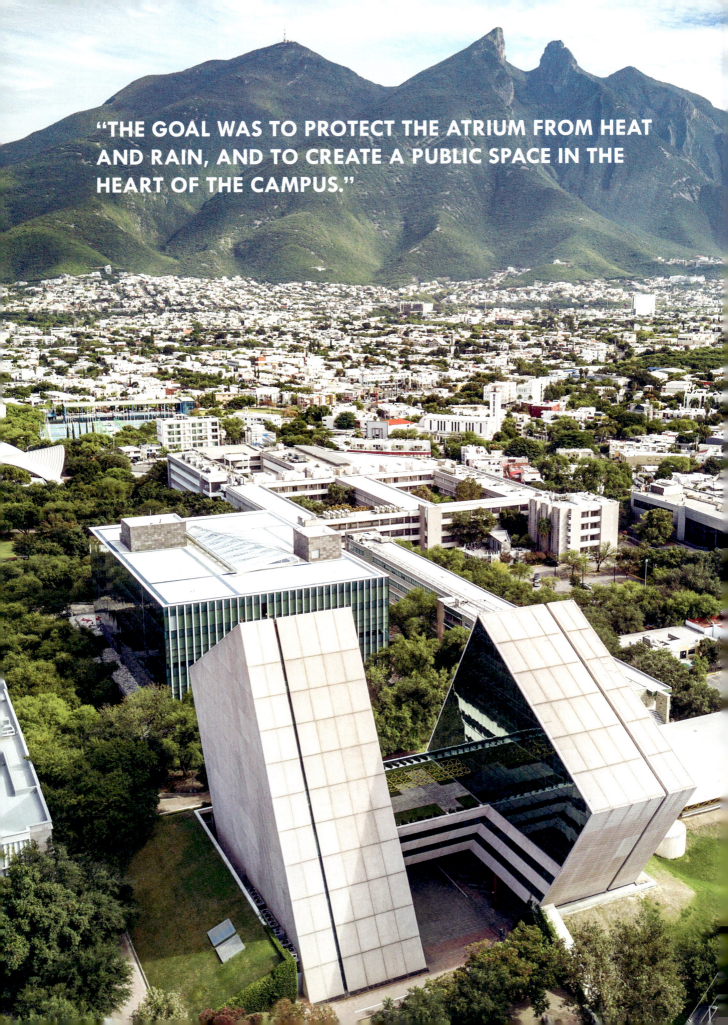

"THE GOAL WAS TO PROTECT THE ATRIUM FROM HEAT AND RAIN, AND TO CREATE A PUBLIC SPACE IN THE HEART OF THE CAMPUS."

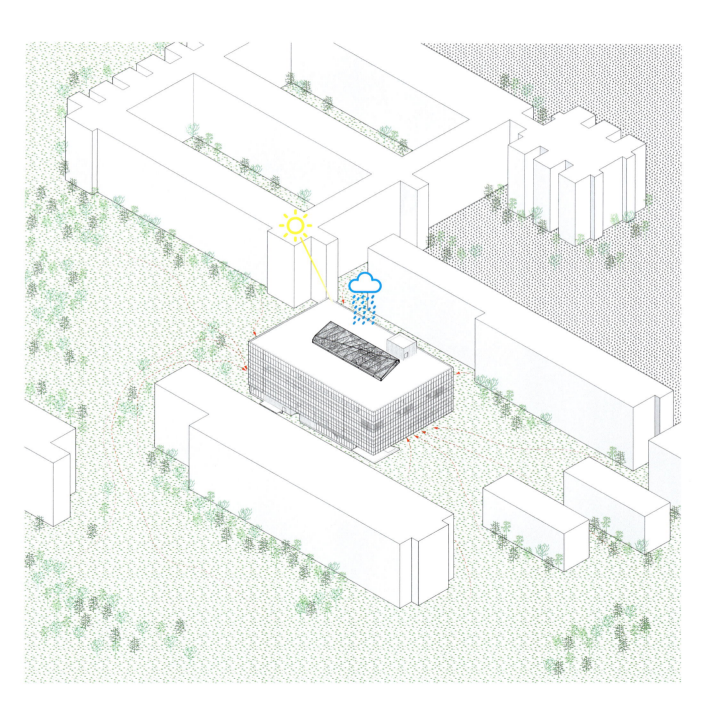

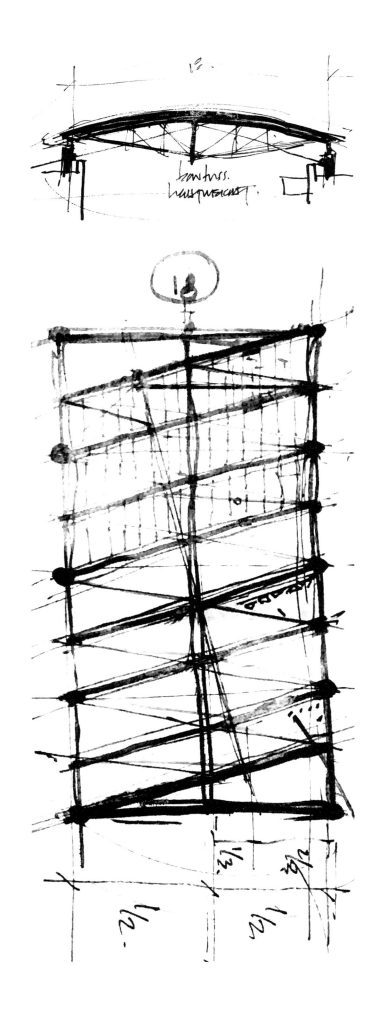

A) HOJAS DE ALAMO BLANCO, ESPECIE NATIVA, NL.
- SIMEZA
- ABSTRACCIÓN
- OVERLAP PATTERN.

'EL OTOÑO EN EL TEC REPRESENTA EL INICIO DE UNA NUEVA ETAPA EN NUESTRA VIDA PROFESIONAL, LAS HOJAS SE DEPOSITAN EN LA CUBIERTA SIMBOLIZANDO ESE MOMENTO'

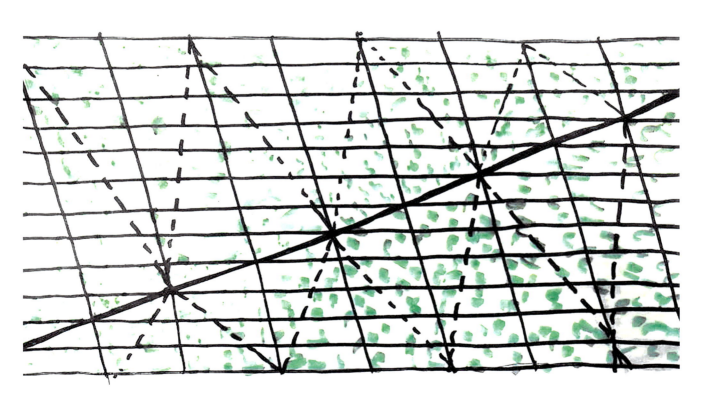

PRACTICING
HERE

The context in which a building is designed is as important as the context in which a building exists. Some choose to design in polished high-rises or historic office buildings from the early and mid-twentieth century. Our office is located in an early twentieth-century converted warehouse in the West Loop of Chicago. The industrial character of this area has always fascinated González Pulido. Before it began its rapid transformation, he would drive his motorcycle through the area to explore its rich character. This persistent fascination with the area ultimately led him to locate his new firm in the West Loop.

For those unfamiliar with the layout of Chicago, the city is defined by the shoreline of Lake Michigan. The lakefront itself is angled, running from southeast to northwest. This angle infuses the city with a need to move parallel to the lakefront along the diagonal. The result is a number of streets that cut across the otherwise regular grid in order to more efficiently traverse the large distances of the sprawling city. In addition to the lakefront, the city is defined by the Chicago River, which once drained into the lake before being reversed at the end of the nineteenth century in order to protect the city's water supply from contaminants being dumped into the river. The river runs essentially perpendicular to the lakefront before splitting, with a north branch following the angle of the lake before eventually rejoining the lake and a south branch running roughly forty-five degrees to the angle of the lake before eventually joining the Illinois River, which drains into the Mississippi River. Together, the river and the lake form the northern, eastern, and western boundaries of what has become known as the Loop. The Loop itself is formed by the elevated trains that loop the area before radiating in many directions to serve the different neighborhoods of Chicago. The area is home to the earliest skyscrapers in the world and many early, iconic examples of the International Style. It is home to professional service firms that include those working in finance, law, accounting, advertising, and architecture. It is also home to the city's jewelry district as well as a number of universities, government buildings, and private clubs. Over the last couple of decades, some historic office buildings have been converted into apartments, while other ground-up condo developments have also been constructed.

As the Loop became denser, the area to the west of the Loop—and west of both the river and the highway that parallels the river—became an attractive area in which to build. This began occurring in the late nineteen eighties and early nineties. While the Loop had been defined by the office typology, the areas to the north, south, east, and west were initially defined by generally luxurious residential buildings and later by factories and warehouses.

PRACTICING HERE

The heart of the area that would become the West Loop was Haymarket Square and a produce market around Randolph and Halsted. Randolph Street was home to a number of produce and grocery businesses located on either side of a very wide street whose dimensions were set by the proportions of the market building at Randolph and Halsted. North of Randolph, Lake Street has an elevated train line running above it. Fulton Street is one block north, and Carroll Street is one block further. Fulton was home to a number of butchers and meat-packers. Some of these were connected to the major packing houses located near the Union Stockyards on the South Side of the city. The existence of the industry itself was a direct result of Chicago's location in the country and the extent to which this location allowed it to serve as a transportation hub connecting the north, south, east, and west sections of the US. This same geographical advantage continues to drive Chicago's role as a global aviation hub. It also makes it an ideal place to locate an international architecture practice.

In addition to the produce and meatpacking industries, the area was also home to a number of luxurious mansions in the area south of Randolph. Ashland Avenue, in particular, was home to some of the largest in the area, including that of Mayor Carter Harrison—whose statue can be seen in Union Park just south of our office. After World War II, however, the area began to see significant decline and the area along Madison became known as skid row. Many of the mansions were demolished or converted into apartments. The area to the west of Ashland, however, remained somewhat stable until blight began spreading west during the nineteen-fifties and sixties. The decline of the neighborhood culminated in the devastating riots that followed the assassination of Rev. Dr. Martin Luther King, Jr. in 1968. The riots left many buildings burned and resulted in the departure of some of the last companies still located in the area, such as Sears, Roebuck and Co.,—taking many well-paying jobs with them in the process.

Following the decline, however, the area continued to be home to a range of thriving businesses as well as the monumental People's Stadium, which would later be demolished and replaced with the United Center, where the Chicago Bulls basketball team and the Blackhawks hockey team have won numerous championships. The area also remained home to some of the largest construction companies in the city, manufacturing, scrap metal and recycling, as well as the meatpacking and produce companies mentioned earlier. The area was a place where people looking for cheap rent for a new business or place to live could find space.

> "I WANTED THE ROOF TO FEEL ALMOST AS IF A MASSIVE LEAF HAD FALLEN ON IT. LIGHTWEIGHT CONSTRUCTION WAS THE WAY TO GO."

PRACTICING HERE

The major transformation of the area began in the late nineteen-eighties and early nineties as the Loop itself was being transformed by a wave of new office buildings fueled by the booming economy of the Reagan years. A few concrete steps were taken towards revitalizing the area and making it a more attractive and safer neighborhood. On one hand, medians were built along Randolph and Madison with planters. The medians along Randolph created local one-way lanes and a central two-way lane for through traffic. The desire was to clean up the congestion of trucks. However, the medians made it very difficult to back larger trucks into the suppliers along Randolph, thus precipitating their flight from the area. At the same time, a Planned Manufacturing District was created north of Lake Street that would ideally ensure the continued industrial use of the area.

These structural changes to the area coincided with broader societal trends that created conditions for various types of entrepreneurship. With new, innovative ideas came a need for space in which to produce new products and services—ideally in low-cost spaces with ample room to meet the specific demands of the endeavor. Restaurants began to arrive in the area and by the mid-nineteen-nineties, the hottest restaurants in the city were located on Randolph Street. At the same time, former industrial and commercial buildings that were generally masonry with timber columns and floors were converted to live-work lofts. These conversions were accompanied by a new wave of professional supply companies, such as those serving the film production and restaurant industries. They joined others that had remained to continue servicing the meatpacking houses along Fulton Street. As this occurred, preservationists began to consider the architectural merit of the buildings that had been constructed in the area over the last century. By 2015, the Randolph-Fulton Market District would be given landmark designation that would set specific preservation goals for the area. This would ensure that historic facades and architectural details would be preserved, even if the entire structure behind the facade was ultimately replaced.

The landmark district proved vital. Although there was much speculation that the area would see significant development, the 2008 housing crisis severely limited new construction in the area, and many projects that started construction were stalled. By 2011, however, people were beginning to explore new ways of developing real estate in the area. These efforts were led, in large part, by the real estate developer Sterling Bay and were made possible by relaxing the rules of the planned manufacturing district between Halsted and Ogden to allow higher density for commercial spaces and restaurants. These efforts coincided with a shift in how companies wanted to work. Instead

PRACTICING

HERE

of smaller floorplates that necessitated taking office space across multiple floors or sprawling suburban campuses, companies began to be increasingly interested in large open plans. They also wanted to locate offices in trendy urban areas with great restaurants and cultural destinations that would be alluring to the young professionals they hoped to attract in an increasingly competitive labor market.

The first major development to occur was the transformation of the Fulton Cold Storage Building into what would become known as 1K Fulton. The process involved thawing the ten-floor freezer—much of which was underutilized and filled with crystalline ice structures. After defrosting the building, the facade was removed, and the concrete frame left to air out for months before construction began. As this occurred, the developer Sterling Bay signed a deal with Google to become the anchor tenant. Having successfully completed 1K Fulton, they then purchased the entire block on which Harpo Studios was located, tore the building down, and erected a custom designed headquarters for McDonalds. With two of the world's largest corporations now anchor tenants in the neighborhood, many tech companies followed, as well as those companies that would serve McDonalds. This was followed by additional office space, several hotels, and a new wave of condos and apartments south of Randolph. At the same time, one of the largest land- and property-owners in the area, Sue Gin, passed away. Prior to her death, she had resisted turning her properties into luxury lofts and deeply respected the historical nature of the area. Her heirs, however, began the process of selling off her extensive holdings to developers who would upgrade them and attract commercial tenants. By 2017, development had pushed all the way from Halsted to Ogden—with many block-scale developments planned near Union Park. In 2019, it was announced that the Planned Manufacturing District would be modified all the way to Ashland in order to allow for higher density and for restaurants and bars.

The transformation of the area into a dense and pricey neighborhood whose real estate is as expensive as the Loop has led a number of the businesses and residents of the neighborhood to move elsewhere in the city. Many galleries have closed or moved farther west, due in no small part to the broader consolidation of the art market, the expansion of global art galleries, and increased focus on selling at art fairs. The few galleries that remain, for the most part, own the property they operate within. Those that have moved farther west into the roughly eight blocks between Ashland Avenue and Western Avenue have joined an area that bears a similar appearance to what the West Loop used to feel like. In the place of packing and produce, however, are brewers, coffee roasters, and distillers. They are joined by new light

PRACTICING HERE

manufacturing, custom motorbike shops, artists' studios, architects, florists, contractors, music and recording studios, artists' collectives, clothing makers, interior designers, and new technology companies.

Our studio is located right on the edge between the rapid development of the West Loop and the area to the west that is just beginning to experience redevelopment. We are here because we want to be surrounded by those who are making things while also remaining connected to the commercial activities of global brands. We also enjoy working in an area that is not finished. The various components are still in a process of being put together. It has a sense of being filled by potential. Walking around the neighborhood, one feels that it might still be possible to discover a new arrival or remark the departure of an older building. This allows us to both see the past and reflect on the quality of the future that is being built. It gives us an opportunity to fully interrogate urban form as it comes into existence and reflect on how it might be improved upon in the future.

Considering this success—and more fundamentally, what constitutes success—is essential as development continues to spread west. In the spring of 2021, construction will begin on a new CTA Green Line station located at Damen Ave. In addition, the owners of United Center have indicated interest in developing some of the many parking lots surrounding the stadium. Doing so would create a unique opportunity to bridge the significant gap between the development taking place in the West Loop and the residential neighborhood west of Damen. At the same time, it is important to consider the general poverty that dominates farther west in the neighborhoods of East and West Garfield Park. As development continues, will architecture that plays on the vernacular of the historic industrial buildings continue to dominate or will something new come into existence? Will the development be a model of sustainability? Will it integrate new urban technology? Will it be inclusive and affordable?

These questions, as well as what it means to live and work in a particular place, have taken on a new light in the context of the 2020 pandemic. Like many, we were required to work remotely for several months and found a new capacity to connect virtually and work efficiently. When we were able to return to our office, we rediscovered the incredible impact of the human connection in the design process. As we move into the future, we hope to embrace both the incredible power of working from anywhere and the capacity for innovation that comes from face-to-face collaboration.

CHAPTER　　　　THREE

It is too often the case that architecture and design professionals get caught up in the cycle of competing for jobs, offering preliminary concepts to attract clients, and then rushing to meet deadlines to deliver contractual obligations across various phases. In doing so, it is easy to lose sight of goals for a practice, a project, or the profession more broadly. This is an ethical question—both in terms of how architects behave across the phases of a project and as a question of what should be built in the world. In essence, it is a question of values.

As the grounding and groundwork that guides our ambition, ethics and ethical behavior is particularly important with complex projects that may push new limits, take risks, and desire specific rewards. They are also very important when different personal interests and desires get involved and when these desires affect the design and performance of the building. They are important when monetary or other compensation is at stake as well as when the reputation of the designer or client can be affected in either a positive or negative manner. This is particularly true with a very successful design for which all parties involved want to take credit.

One project, in particular, has presented both many opportunities and challenges. Tec Nano began as a request for qualifications issued to a small group of architects to design a bioengineering and nanotechnology lab building for Monterrey Tec. After being selected, the design for the building combined a number of different types of lab spaces with collaborative co-working spaces that will ultimately house corporate partners.

CHAPTER THREE

In designing for this program, the goal was to create a space supporting a highly interactive experience that would allow researchers to come into contact with the building, the outdoors, and each other. This collection of experiences would be facilitated by unique configurations on each floor and protected from the elements by a veil made of hexagonal shapes that alludes to the patterns one finds in nanotechnology. The result would be a dynamic interaction between indoors and outdoors that is rarely found in laboratory buildings.

While ethical questions are sometimes less prominent, they play an important role in all projects. In many cases, these questions arise even before a project is awarded, when the question of what is built and where it is built is brought to the foreground. This question was particularly relevant when considering whether to pursue work on the Felipe Ángeles International Airport At Santa Lucía. In other cases, questions of accessibility and inclusion arise. These questions were prominent in designing the Alfredo Harp Helú Stadium. While the development could have been inward-looking and exclusive, it was important to make it open to a wider demographic, both formally in terms of how it embraces the landscape and via discounted tickets for local community members. In other cases, the question of sharing credit for a concept or design arises. In all of these cases, it is important to remain committed to the broader vision for the building and what it can do for a community, rather than becoming distracted by concerns more connected to a practice or personal promotion.

I_VALUES

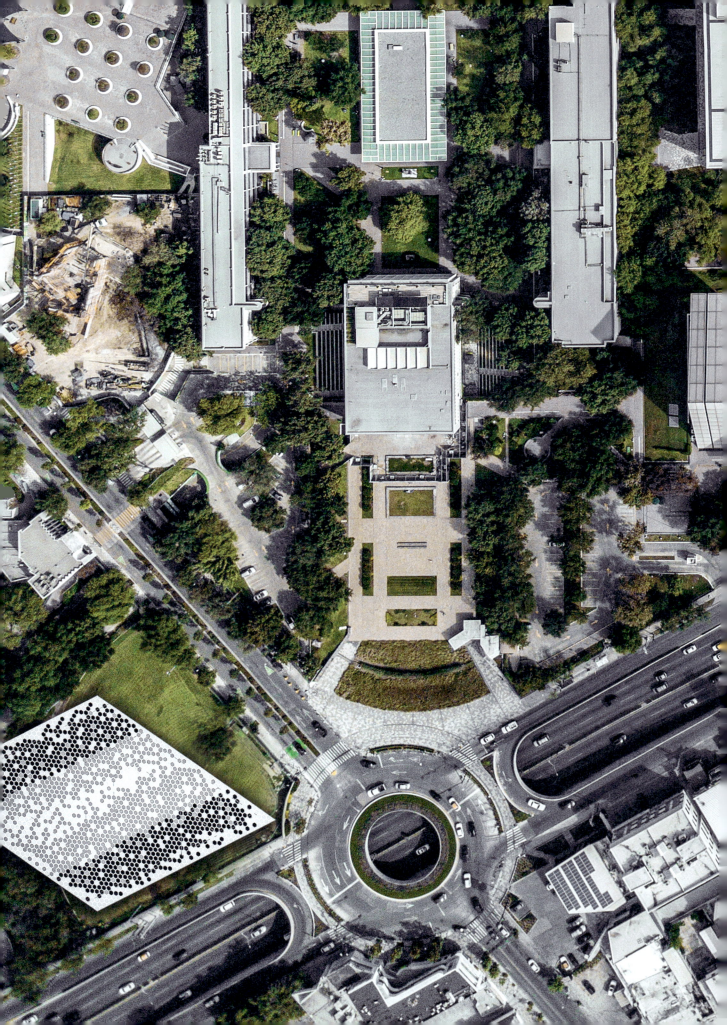

TEC
NANO

Biotechnology and nanotechnology are fast growing fields in universities. The Instituto Tecnológico y de Estudios Superiores de Monterrey (ITESM), also known as Monterrey Tec, has been developing a program that is focused on applied research, with direct collaboration with the manufacturing industry. Since its foundation, Monterrey Tec has maintained a close relationship with the local industry in many other fields. However, through bioengineering and nanotechnology, that role has expanded significantly to other parts of the world. Monterrey is leading a new technological revolution.

As a consequence of this trend, Monterrey Tec decided to commission a bioengineering and nanotechnology building that could house all the functions of research and development as well as incubators, accelerators, and collaboration spaces for scientists and corporations. The university issued a request for qualifications to a limited number of architects with experience in laboratory design.

The building site is located on the corner of Avenida Eugenio Garza Sada and Avenida Fernando García Roel on the campus of Monterrey Tec. This corner is effectively the entrance to the university and, as a result, is one of the most prominent sites on campus. The site is currently used as a softball field. The client hopes to maximize the value of this prominent site while also creating a building that serves as a gateway to the campus.

The site is defined in part by the angle of Avenida Eugenio Garza Sada, which runs at a roughly forty-five-degree angle from northwest to southeast. This angle is in contrast to the orthogonal north-south, east-west planning of the campus. Avenida Eugenio Garza Sada is a very fast-moving six-lane road. Four lanes of the road run under a traffic circle at the intersection of Avenida Eugenio Garza Sada and Avenida Fernando García Roel, while two lanes split off to connect to the level of the traffic circle. As such, a building on the site would have to address the orientation of the road as well as negotiate between multiple speeds of travel.

The campus itself is located in a dense urban setting surrounded by residential neighborhoods. The building typologies and construction techniques on the campus are quite diverse and range from concrete to glass and steel. The trend in campus architecture has been towards embracing contemporary design while also seeking to preserve the modernist legacy that defines some of the most noted buildings on campus.

NANOTECHNLOGY LAB
DESIGN DEVELOPMENT
30,000 M2
MONTERREY
MEXICO

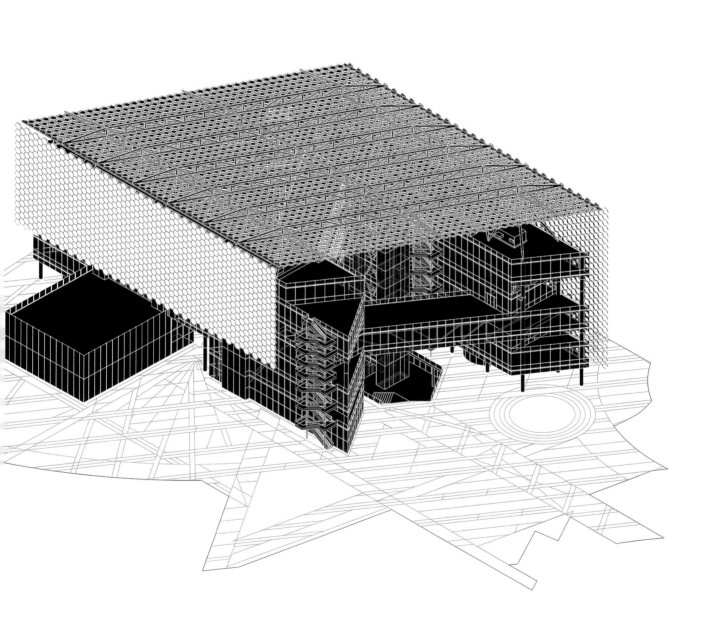

"A LIVING ORGANISM, AN ASSEMBLY OF FUNCTIONS THAT TRANSLATES INTO SPECIFIC SHAPES AND 'CONCRETE' SPATIAL EMOTIONS IN WHICH ACCURACY AND PRECISION ARE GUIDING DESIGN PRINCIPLES. TEC NANO REPRESENTS THE BUILDING AS THE ULTIMATE VISUAL REPRESENTATION OF A SYSTEM, A BUILDING AS A CAMPUS, A PLACE BOTH PHYSICAL AND METAPHYSICAL, PRAGMATIC AND MYSTIC, NUMERICAL AND POETIC, TECHNOLOGICAL AND PEDESTRIAN, HIGH-TECH AND LOW-TECH, URBAN AND INDUSTRIAL."

DESIGN

Tec Nano combines a number of different types of lab spaces with collaborative co-working spaces that will ultimately house corporate partners. In designing for this program, the goal was to create a space supporting a highly interactive experience that would allow researchers to come into contact with the building, the outdoors, and each other. This collection of experiences would be facilitated by unique configurations on each floor and protected from the elements by a veil made of hexagonal shapes that alludes to the patterns one finds in nanotechnology. The result is a dynamic interaction between indoors and outdoors that is rarely found in laboratory buildings.

In addition, the following goals were essential throughout the design process:
1) The building should look, smell, taste, feel, and sound like nanotechnology;
2) The building should be part of both the university and the community without compromising its main purpose;
3) The building should be linked to both the significant history of the campus and to the "new spirit" of Monterrey Tec through careful consideration of its urban context and Monterrey Tec's vision and goals;
4) Architecture, engineering, and science should work in a symbiotic relationship to create a building that brings the university to the forefront of sustainability and innovation through technology; and
5) The building should be flexible, adaptable, innovative, urban, socially engaging, and minimal in the use of resources.

The design process that ensued was quite complex and involved numerous iterations. This was in large part because the needs of the clients continued to evolve. The specific program and lab requirements changed multiple times. The overall budget and what was included within the budget continued to evolve. Throughout this process, however, the commitment of the client to the overall design vision for the building remained unchanged. Given the desire to retain this vision as the needs of the client and capacity to realize the project evolved, it was important for the design team and consultants to work diligently to help the client arrive at a position where they could build the design they had selected. This involved a high level of creativity in determining the correct structure, mechanical systems, layout, and size of the building. Through these efforts, it was possible to develop a bid set at the end of design development that could be accurately priced for construction. Having completed this exercise, it was determined that the building met the initial budgetary requirements.

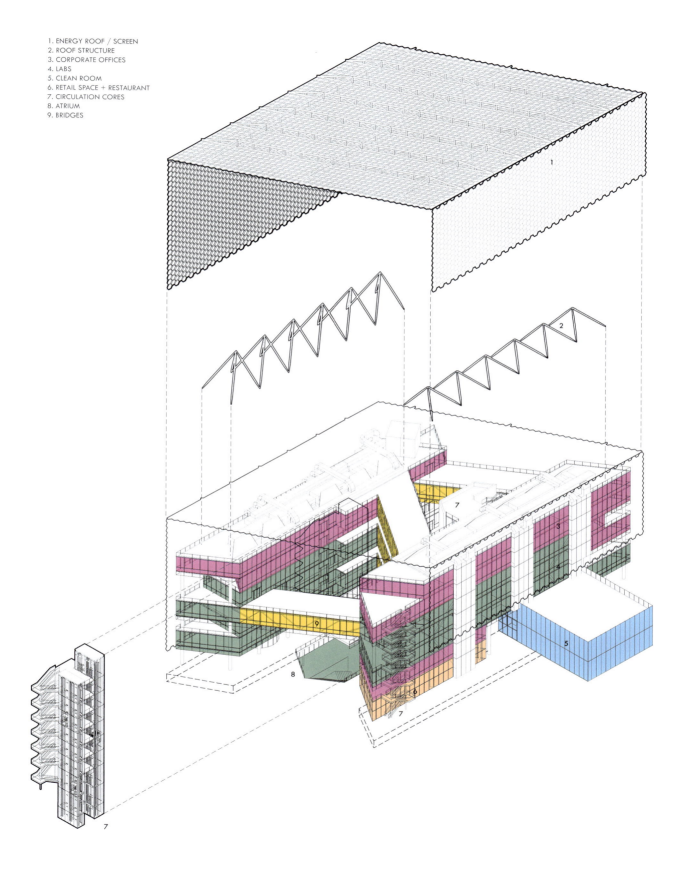

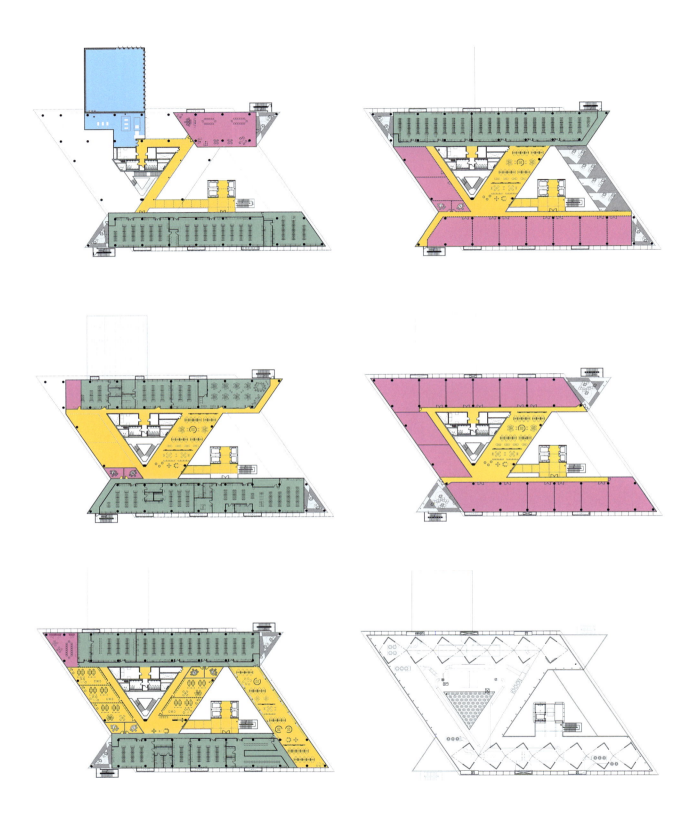

At this point it was unclear whether efforts to revise the building to meet budgetary requirements will be sufficient for the project to resume, the client has always remained committed to the core vision of the design. The basic building configuration is based on two north-south oriented slabs that are connected at each level by a series of diagonal bridges—originally eight but ultimately five in number. The slabs originally housed labs, but in the final design housed co-working spaces due to the vibration requirements of the labs. The initial vision was to house all parking, mechanical, retail, and the most vibration-sensitive labs, as well as the clean room, in four levels below grade. Ultimately, the clean room became an independent volume entirely isolated from the rest of the structure while the parking was moved off-site.

The bridges are connected to the west wing and articulated to the east wing to avoid the transmission of vibrations into the structure of the vibration-sensitive labs. The building structure of the wings is made of reinforced concrete, with composite on the bridges due to the large spans. The atrium is used as a natural exhaust shaft based on the stack-effect principle to transfer the spill-out air from the interior of the building to the outside by partially conditioning the open bridges and terraces in the atrium while reducing energy consumption.

The overall planning strategy seeks to harmonize the new building with the existing campus and the road network. This occurs through orienting the two primary lab volumes parallel to Avenida Eugenio Garza Sada and the central bridge parallel to the orthogonal grid of the campus. The additional diagonal bridges are set at a mirrored angle. The result is a new building that mirrors the orientation of the existing campus while also being connected to the road.

Beyond orientation, the landscape strategy seeks to create a large public plaza in front of the building with a paving pattern reflecting the orientation of the building. This paving pattern is intended to minimize the road that divides the new building from the existing campus through the use of the space by pedestrians while also making it possible for cars to travel over the surface when necessary. This strategy of connectivity is repeated in the openness of the central atrium to the campus and the overall image of the building as inviting guests to enter. It continues at the edges of the site as the landscaping seeks to extend the geometry of the building and knit this geometry together with the surrounding buildings.

SUSTAINABILITY

The energy, air handling, and water usage requirement of a bioengineering and nanotechnology lab present significant challenges in the context of sustainability. As a result, a range of strategies were introduced. The primary strategy was the use of an "energy screen" that would reduce the heat gain throughout the building and improve overall performance. It would also maintain daylighting in labs while reducing glare and the need for mechanical shading systems. In addition, the central atriums were conceived as natural ventilation chimneys that would help cool the building. Throughout the landscaping, porous paving strategies were used with the intention of capturing rainwater for graywater use in the building.

The most visible feature of the building is the roof/screen—the "energy screen." This shield is a lightweight aluminum and hybrid-membrane structure that acts as a rain and sunscreen and also as a source of energy. Equipped with three types of lightweight panels, it provides power for lighting, collects water, and protects and shades the atrium below to make the space usable year-round.

The bridges have four functions: as linkages between the two slab groups, buffer zones to maintain the labs under positive pressure, collaboration spaces, and terraces. The floor plates are column-free spaces that, in a 9.9-by-9.9-meter grid, provide utmost flexibility for different lab configurations, future uses, and growth. All the MEP feed lines as well as the four egress stairs are located in the same three-meter cavity formed by the facade and the "energy screen." The building's facade is an insulated window wall system that provides three different facade conditions based on the lab type. The panels can be clear, translucent, or opaque in order to respond to different thermal and daylight requirements.

POSTMORTEM

As the project progressed, it became clear that the program needed to change, the vision of the client had to be refined, and the technical demands of the building had to be understood in greater detail. In the process, it became clear that the original budget would not be sufficient to meet the client's goals. In this context, a range of other options were explored. This involved an analysis of how they could better understand how money was being spent and what was actually included in the ultimate budget—and, by extension, what was reasonable to include in the budget. In the end, the budget was revised, and a pricing exercise brought the design in line with the desired budget.

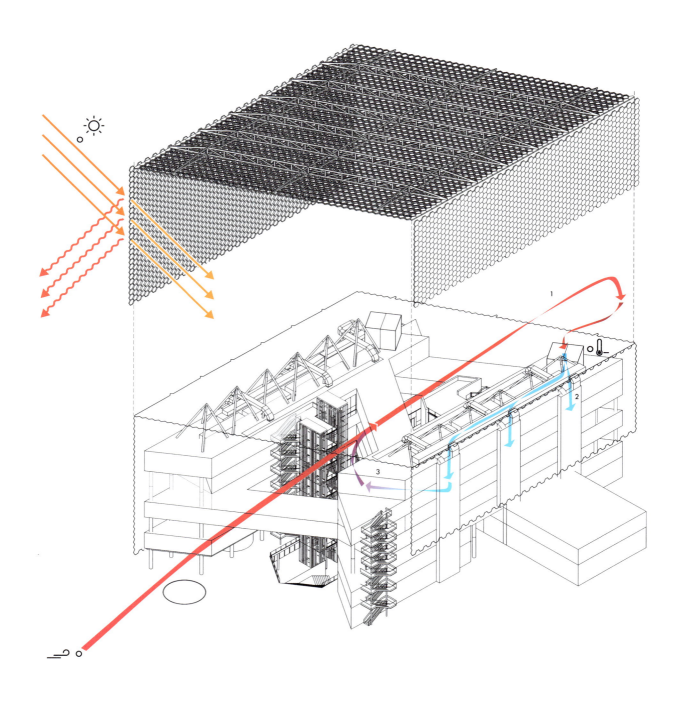

Unfortunately, this alignment was not enough for the client to move forward with the project past the pricing exercise and into design development. Such situations are particularly challenging for the architect when they have done everything in their power to help a project move forward successfully but are still faced with ignorance and doubt as to whether the building can actually be delivered as promised. At the same time, it became apparent that economics and business models associated with the building and with the density that would optimize the return on what amounted to the most prominent undeveloped site on campus were influencing the decision-making process. This was particularly difficult, as it was completely beyond the mandate of an architect.

Given these challenges, a considerable amount of time has been spent reflecting on how to improve the outcome. One of the primary strategies that could have been employed is a strategy that mirrors integrated project delivery. Integral to such an approach is the introduction of a phase 0 to clearly set all goals and establish a realistic budget. This would have allowed for greater stakeholder alignment, brought a contractor into the process from the beginning, and allowed for a uniform risk-reward structure that would encourage everyone involved with the project to work towards the project's success rather than concentrating on their own success. It would also have made it possible for the client to develop, test, and lock in their specific programmatic and business goals much earlier in the process.

In the end, no matter how complex the path a project may follow, the relationship with the client is very important. The hope remains that the ideas and images produced for this project will continue to live on in future work either for this or another client. Balancing the goals of the architect and the client remains a delicate act. Some of these challenges are discussed in the essay "Ethics and Architecture."

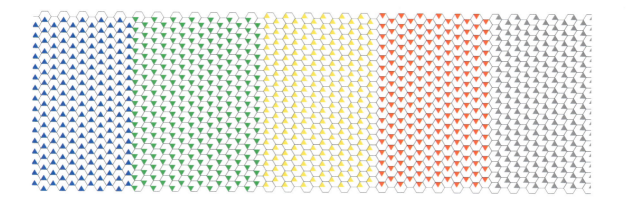

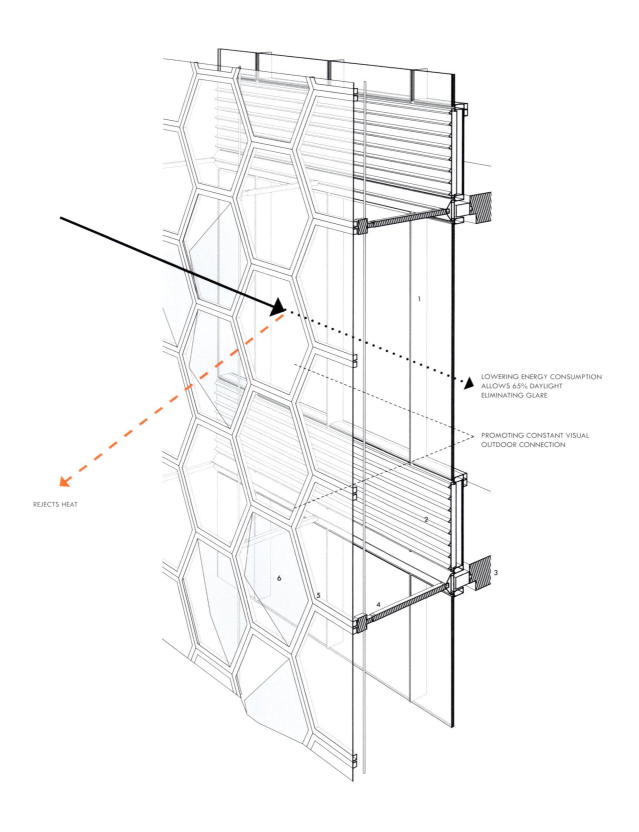

FACADE IN PTFE 65% PERFORATED

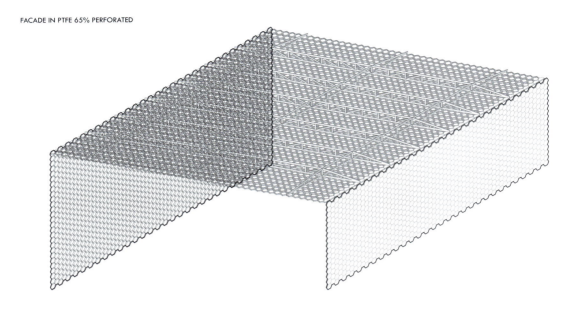

ROOF IN ETFE WITH 80% CERAMIC FRIT

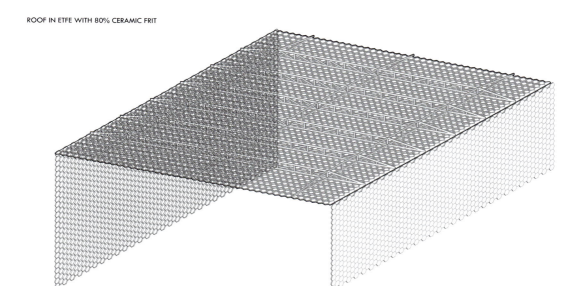

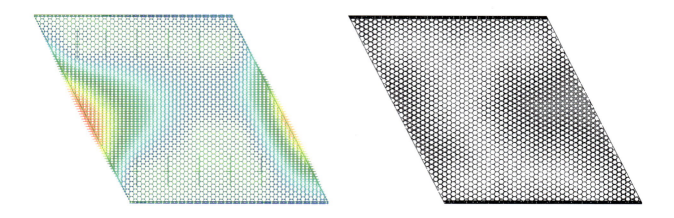

STRUCTURAL CONCEPT : THE HONEYCOMB STRUCTURE IS DENSER WHERE THE STRESSES ARE HIGHER

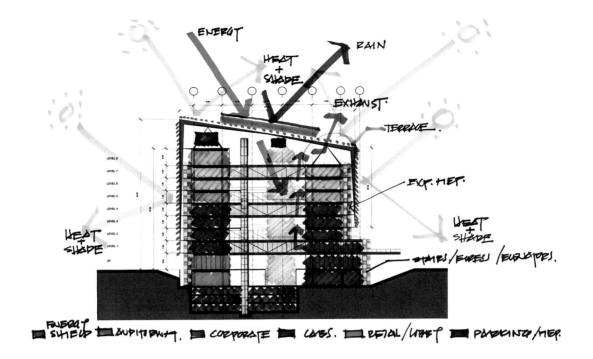
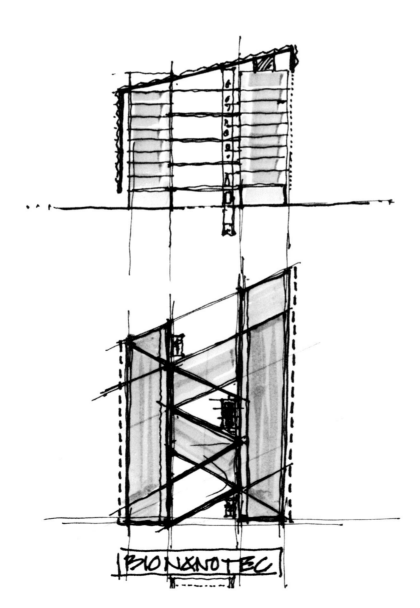

ETHICS AND ARCHITECTURE

1. Introduction

On the surface, one would think that designing and building are two very straightforward activities. A building is a collection of various material components bound together hierarchically in order to serve some purpose. They resist gravity and environmental conditions. Historically, they have done so very honestly through a clear relationship between material/form and the specific structural system and building enclosure. One can see how a column carries a load or how water is diverted away from the surface and foundation of the building via collection channels. It is the architect's responsibility to reflect the honesty inherent in a building. This honesty is tied to the building as a reflection of what it means for us to dwell and, at an even more fundamental level, to be here in this world with some purpose directed towards an end and guided by a value system, both individually and as a community. This purpose is reflected in the building's form, material, and style, which not only support the activities inherent to dwelling, but also communicate this support structure to others and to the next generation.

In an ideal situation, our habits are themselves honest, ethical, and oriented towards promoting the greater good. While this by no means implies that everyone needs to live in glass houses that display how honest we are through transparent facades, it does mean that the form of the dwelling and the things encountered are reflective of good intentions rather than covering over some more nefarious use. This is also not to say that buildings cannot be used for violence, merely that their form should reflect this use and that the purpose to which they are put should be guided by an ethical framework. In this sense, while wars may in some cases be necessary, it is important to ask whether a potential war is ethical and whether those called on to participate—even at the level of an architect—are not violating their own ethical framework and are fully aware of what they are contributing to.

2. What to Build and How?

The first question that should be asked is what should be built and how it should be built. In our view, a building should be an open, transparent, and lightweight structure that serves and inspires a broad community. Buildings should bring people together and foster inclusion. They should push the standards of sustainability through collaboration with the most forward-thinking engineers to become exceptionally high performing buildings. At the same time, it is important to consider whether a new building is required at all and whether the adaptive reuse of an existing building is possible. Doing so will

ETHICS AND ARCHITECTURE

not only preserve the heritage of a particular place, but also conserve the energy embedded in existing spaces.

A building should also create value. Our work seeks to deliver value across a number of categories, both qualitatively and quantitatively. With regards to quantitative value, a project should be delivered in a specific period of time, at a specific cost, with the capacity to generate a particular revenue, and the capacity to be durable over time. The building should perform to specific energy, waste, and water standards in order to ensure that it is sustainable. Quantitative value is also delivered through capacity to serve a particular number of people, ability to accommodate a certain type and quantity of flows of goods or services, and ability to integrate with external data.

Qualitative value is reflected in a space that makes a person feel good through light, material, texture, organization of program, height of ceilings, presence of special elements such as water, views that the building captures, feel of warmth or coolness, flow of air, and even smell. Qualitative value is also reflected in the extent to which a building takes on cultural significance as part of a history or narrative tradition. It imbues the building with a sense of meaning. This often occurs through a particular event that causes the building to be more than the sum of the parts that have made it. It becomes a place that attracts attention and interest over time—often contributing to the creation of quantitative value in the process.

Ultimately, it is this interaction between quantitative and qualitative value that lies at the base of creating value in our work. Each decision affects the other. Each element of a building and level of refinement that the building goes through is affected by their interaction. It is essential to insist upon balance throughout and at all scales in order to achieve a great building.

A building should also be honest. It should avoid illusion and eschew the dishonest use of materials and systems that disguise the building's underlying reality. This is a fundamental goal of every project undertaken. Such illusion is unfortunately seen all too often in projects whose primary goal is profit rather than good architecture. What constitutes "good architecture" is, of course, up for debate. In part, this question is even more tied to an ethical architecture than adherence to some specific aesthetic, stylistic, or cultural system. In our work, the idea of "good architecture" is derived from a wide range of buildings from different places and for different peoples. They inspire form, the organization of space, manipulation of material, and creation of community. In many ways, the diversity of buildings that drive our practice forms the basis of "technical contextualism."

"THE BUILDING WOULD BE QUITE SUCCESSFUL IN A POST-PANDEMIC WORLD. THE AMOUNT OF COVERED OUTDOOR SPACE WITH NATURAL VENTILATION WOULD BE ATTRACTIVE AS A SPACE WHERE COLLABORATION OCCURS ON MULTIPLE LEVELS."

ETHICS AND ARCHITECTURE

3. For Whom to Build

There are clients who may have considerable resources that can be invested in a project, but whose values do not align with our own. This is not a new phenomenon. Leaders have always needed to build cities and have always wanted to make monumental works to showcase their economic, military, and political power. Many of these past patrons presented serious ethical questions. Ancient monuments were, in some cases, constructed with slave labor. Roman society allowed slavery and violence to flourish. A considerable amount of the wealth created during the Renaissance was derived from plundering the New World. Colonial wealth was deeply connected to the slave trade and exploitation of indigenous populations. The pattern continued through the twentieth century with architects such as Giuseppe Terragni working in Italy during the Fascist period and even Le Corbusier getting wrapped up with a desire to build for the Vichy government.

What has changed in recent centuries, however, is the capacity of the architect to choose their own fate. In these cases, does one accept the commission and hope that, through design, one will be able to exert some influence and promote some form of change and progress? Is it possible to think that one can actually make the world better through architecture? Moreover, does one turn down the commission and watch as a competitor designs a building that sustains their practice? While in some cases, the line may be quite clear, in other cases the client may be lauded as one of the best companies to work for, creators of some of the best and most popular products, and yet still employ low-cost labor in Asia while also contributing significantly to the waste stream via the products that they produce. In asking these questions, it is important to rely on an underlying set of values and whether the project will significantly impact the community beyond the client such that it might serve a broader good.

With the understanding that a building can impact the environment as well as community, it becomes incumbent on the architect to probe how the profession and its products sit more broadly within society, politics, and the economy. Summary reflection reveals the role that a building and style can play in legitimizing a regime. The specific type of labor employed to construct the building could encourage low-wage or slave-like conditions. The nature of an urban configuration or infrastructure could divide a community and aid in segregation. Choosing to build public service buildings in one area versus another could contribute to long-term inequality. In this sense, the work of architecture has the capacity to touch all aspects of the world.

ETHICS AND ARCHITECTURE

Buildings have, of course, come to play a role that their designers could not have imagined, and people go to extreme ends to hide habits that they do not want others to discover. Secret rooms are built, doors are locked, and files are encrypted. At the same time, buildings are repurposed for new ends that may go against the original architectural intent; owners subdivide houses and apartments and pack them with people in unacceptable living conditions, charging high rents to those unable to find any other place to live and investing earnings from real estate in companies that produce weapons and degrade the environment, among other activities that might be deemed unethical and that go against the desires of the designer. At the same time, architects might be tempted to stray from an honest expression of program and material by so called "advanced" building systems that turn a building into an illusion. This occurs through facade systems that simulate a particular material, systems that appear solid when they are in fact hollow, dropped ceilings that disguise building systems, false floors that hide systems, and even through parametric surfaces and daring structural forms that make the building appear as an alien form without scale, proportion, or anything to which humans can relate beyond the spectacle of their virtuosic construction.

4. Creating a Better World

Our approach to value is guided by a desire to make the world a better and more sustainable place. Drawing on the tradition of aesthetics, determining "better" is a process of judgment—both individual and collective—that takes into account a number of categories: formal and material composition, alignment with a tradition, originality with respect to a tradition, conceptual merits, the sensation that is created as a feeling, emotion, and experience, what the work says and means, and the social and political implications. Each of these is delivered through the quantitative and qualitative routes mentioned earlier and are judged at the individual and communal level. Ultimately, the relationship between individual and communal judgment anchors a system that sets norms and standards that allow for a consensus to be reached about what is better and worse. In the process, a horizon or benchmark becomes the goal for the building.

A building must also strive to be something more than a building. It must participate in a process that helps us to realize our identity, why we are here, what our purpose is, and what our goals might be. The building must participate in the revelation of being and non-being. This occurs through the way in which one experiences and encounters elements that frame one's being, placing "being" in relief to allow one to learn and grow.

ETHICS AND ARCHITECTURE

This revelation is not universal but appears individually through encounter—often in an unexpected manner. Architecture can encourage or foreclose this appearance. This ultimately is a question of poetics that allow the sum to exceed the parts in isolation as an event—the grandest of which unifies people's experiences of what being is and draws people together to form a community.

5. Conclusion

In this context, architects must ask where they are going to draw the line with regards to what they are responsible for. While architects were once only responsible for creating drawing sets that would make it possible to erect safe buildings, they are now responsible for their environmental impact. While extending responsibility should not be a legal contract, architects should consider how far they want to go in advocating for a just, equitable, and ethical built environment and world. How far do designers want to go in making our habitat good for as many people as possible? What are the tools to do so—both from within the traditional realm of operations as well as others that might be appropriated from other professions?

To start, let us consider the relationship between architecture, speculative real estate development, the vastness of the construction industry, and the extreme amounts of capital that have been invested in these endeavors. The sources of capital that flow into these projects are complex, and it is often difficult to disentangle all the stakeholders of a joint venture, investment trust, or hedge fund. At the same time, the deployment of that capital can lead to unsustainable cities, apartments that are never inhabited, and generally to real estate whose only purpose is to create a place for capital to be parked. Meanwhile, the construction industry that builds these projects is often corrupt, while the materials used may not be sustainable or are extracted from the earth in less-than-humane conditions. In this sense, architecture is very much implicated in the web of consequences of late capitalism. As such, it is worth considering how the discipline can work within this system while also offering innovative approaches that allow existing stakeholders to benefit and that address some of the negative consequences of past practices.

ETHICS AND ARCHITECTURE

There will naturally remain considerable work to be done beyond these already expanded limits of architecture. Policies, programs, laws, and protections will need to be put into place to help combat inequality and create greater opportunity for men and women around the world. The precarious state in which many people find themselves will have to be addressed by taking a hard look at how the systems of late capitalism affect the majority of people around the world, the power structures that maintain them, and the people behind these institutions. In the process, the growing migrant crisis driven by violence, extremism, and climate change will have to be addressed. As this occurs, it is our responsibility as architects to remain informed. How do these policies, the world they change, and the people they affect impact habits and habitat? How can they guide the construction of an appropriate work of architecture for a new world? In some cases, laws that might be implemented and the world that might result should be anticipated. Having done so, the responsibility exists to render an image of a new world before it exists to inspire leaders and people to act so that it might one day become a reality.

Any utopia must be grounded in realities of the inhabited world and the practical levers and forces that can be manipulated to alter the world in the future. Doing so will help to better model the present in order to understand the variables affecting the future and how to bring about a desired end that will ultimately help reduce the risk inherent in any new building endeavor. This will reduce the waste of buildings that live only short lives and the violence inherent in their destruction. More importantly, perhaps, it will help us to reduce the violence that results from poorly planned cities that use infrastructure as a means of control, segregation, and the perpetuation of inequality. Ultimately, this will help to support broader sustainability of the built environment as the ethical horizon towards which the field of architecture must remain oriented.

"I FELT A TREMENDOUS RESPONSIBILITY TO THIS PROJECT—NOT JUST BECAUSE THIS WAS THE SCHOOL I ATTENDED, BUT BECAUSE I THOUGHT WE COULD DO SOMETHING INNOVATIVE WITH THE TYPOLOGY."

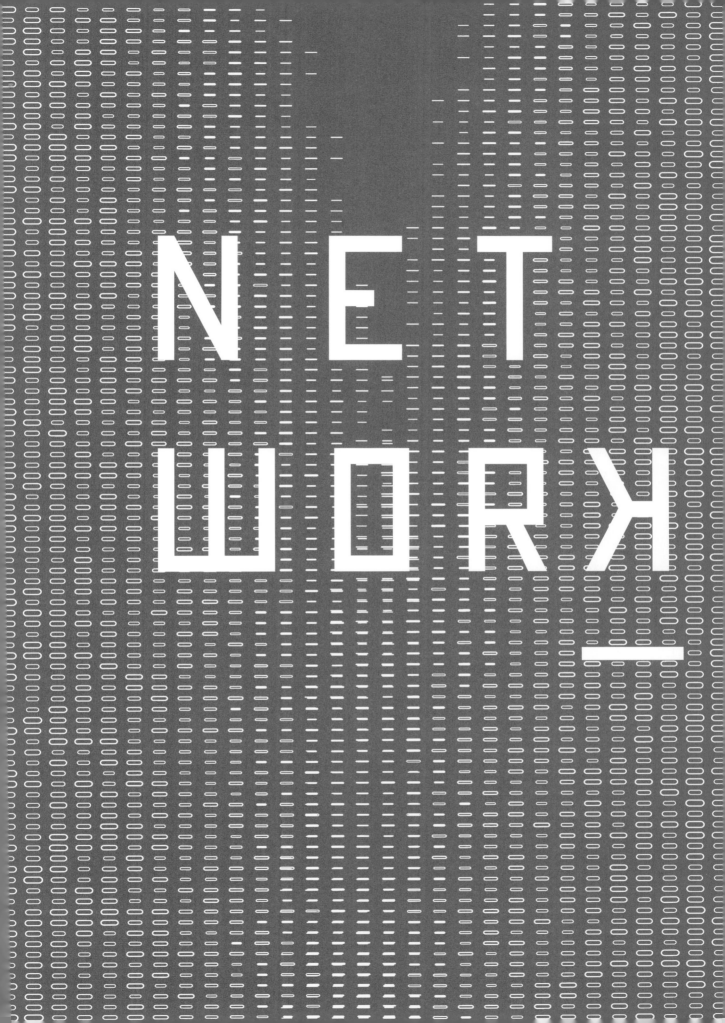

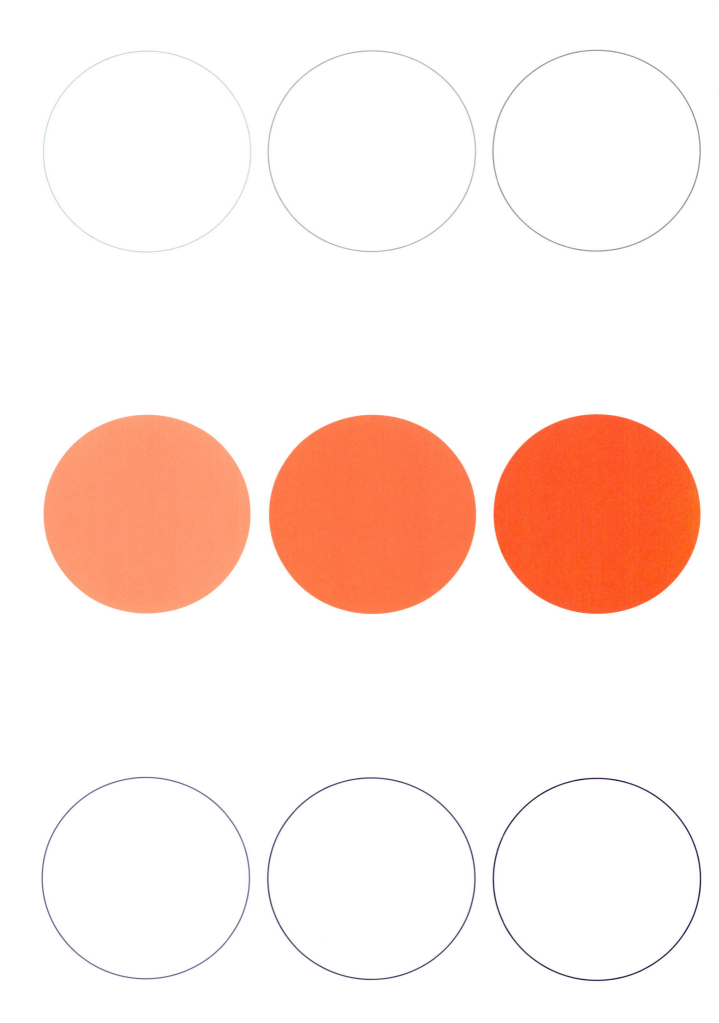

II_NETWORK

ONE.
DIABLOS STADIUM
QIANTAN LOT 14
TWO.
WISH
GICC
THREE.
HARMONY BRIDGE
FOUR.
SPACECRAFT
CASA M5
MONARCA

ONE.
TECHNICAL CONTEXTUALISM
TWO.
ALTERNATIVE FUTURES
THREE.
INFRASTRUCTURE AND (IN-)EQUALITY
FOUR.
HOUSING PLATFORM

CHAPTER FOUR

What does it mean to have a global practice? What knowledge and expertise does one bring to a specific project? What does the "global site" offer the designer? Our work in Mexico and China, in particular, provides an opportunity to explore these questions. When working in Mexico, it is important to be aware of the legacy of pre-Hispanic and colonial architecture. At the same time, we consider the legacy of modern architecture and Mexico's strong cultural relationship with Europe. This architectural context is complemented by the climate, seismic zone in some regions, and diversity of the ecosystem. Beyond the natural context, the political context of the last several generations, ranging from NAFTA to deregulation of various industries, adds another dimension to working in Mexico. Finally, the tradition of gathering and monumentality is an important driver of urban and architectural form. These all contributed to the design of the 20,000-seat Alfredo Harp Helú Stadium in Mexico City.

The architectural context of China is also defined by a historical imperial architecture accompanied by a strong artistic tradition and aesthetic philosophy. It too has a legacy of colonial architecture that was tailored to the specific climate in places like Hong Kong, Macau, Shanghai, and Singapore. These traditions are framed by the communist Cultural Revolution and the Great Leap Forward and a general depredation of anything associated with the imperial past and the cultural elites who sustained the aesthetics of society. It is also framed by a rapidly growing population and specific demographic characteristics of cities and towns across the country.

CHAPTER FOUR

The introduction of special economic zones allowing for experiments with capitalism further added to the diversity of the country while also playing a significant role in its explosive growth. It became apparent to many architects at a certain point that China was going to be a major market for new business. The rapidly growing population and expanding economy led to the construction of a wide range of housing, skyscrapers, and infrastructure. This process required extensive technical knowledge that was not necessarily readily available in China at the time. As a result, a number of international firms began flooding into the Chinese market.

It was in this context that international architects began researching places like the Pearl River Delta as the global economy was being transformed in the late nineteen-nineties and early two-thousands. Their research informed a great deal about how Western architects thought about context. A range of towers in Hong Kong, Shanghai, and Singapore began to set a new standard for what these cities would look like and how Western architects were expected to contribute to the future of urban infrastructure. At the same time, a new wave of infrastructure ranging from airports to bridges, stadiums, and opera houses as well as highly inventive residential and commercial projects began to arise that led to remarkable works of architecture by the world's designers. It was this context that guided the design of a number of projects throughout Asia and, in particular, the 80,000-square-meter Qiantan Enterprise World Phase II in Shanghai, whose anchor tenant would be the automaker Land Rover.

II_NETWORK

DIABLOS STADIUM

INTRO

When you look back at Alfredo Harp Helú Stadium—home to Mexico's Diablos Rojos baseball team—from the field, you can see through the center of the building below the owner's box to the trees. On each side, two bands of red cut across the field of vision to define the box level and upper balcony—a sharp contrast to the deep green of the field. Above, there is the canopy, the signature of the stadium, which provides shelter for thousands of fans by cantilevering over the seats and extending towards the entrance to shelter guests as they arrive. Below, seats colored with a gradient from red to dark gray with white interspersed descend from the entrance level to the field. To the right and left are a series of small pavilions roofed with lightweight textile fabric that lend a sense of intimacy to the vastness of the structure above.

This totality, however, is not something that you experience immediately upon arriving at the stadium. As you cross the bridge that connects the stadium to the surrounding community, you see the two three-pronged supports holding the tail of the central module forming the roof structure. Below, thousands of fans arrive and move towards the gigantic media screen above the opening that allows for a clear view towards the field. To the right and left you see the series of pavilions from which the support structure of the canopy rises. These pavilions appear grand yet light as a result of the striated openings of their surface. As one moves closer, it is clear that this is like no other stadium in the world and that, in addition to what will undoubtedly be an exciting game, an adventure exploring the building awaits.

The building is simply organized: a bowl with three levels of seating opening onto the playing field and six truncated pyramidal volumes housing services and circulation set a short distance from the seating. It is in this space, between the volumes and the seating, that all the drama beyond the game unfolds. These are spaces of encounter between guests, where they take a break from the game, buy concessions and souvenirs, and engage memorabilia from the history of the team and baseball in Mexico. Spaciousness is the fundamental quality of this place. It rises three stories and beyond to the roof soaring above. Circulation spaces form the perimeter—allowing people to look down from the upper floors to the entry level and across the space to others moving around the stadium.

This sense of permeability and openness is fundamentally different from most stadiums. Where the circulation space of many stadiums is a closed ring with little contact with either the field or the city beyond, this space provides clear orientation to both. The character of these spaces is enhanced by the support structure of the roof, which descends from the roof and plants itself firmly on the ground. The experience continues as one moves around the perimeter of the stadium, gaining glimpses of the action on the field in the process, before emerging beneath the tip of the wings of the roof above.

**STADIUM
IN COLLABORATION WITH
ALONSO DE GARAY AND
TALLER ADG
COMPLETED 2019
100,000 M2
MEXICO CITY
MEXICO**

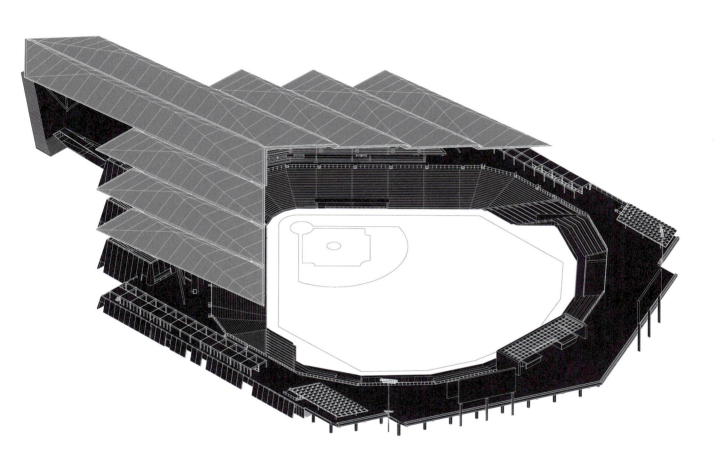

"THE URBAN REBELLION AGAINST THE 'CONTAINER,' THE KIT OF PARTS ON ITS GRANDEST SCALE, THE BUILDING AS AN INTRINSIC ELEMENT OF THE PUBLIC EXPERIENCE, THE DIABLOS STADIUM IS ROOTED IN THE GREEK AMPHITHEATER AS MUCH AS THE MESOAMERICAN BALL GAME, 'URBAN OPENINGS' THAT ARE BIGGER THAN 'WINDOWS,' INTROVERSION AND EXTROVERSION PLAYED OUT THROUGH INTIMACY AND TRANSPARENCY, THE ULTIMATE PARADOX OF LIGHTNESS."

Here, one is able to look back at the full expanse of the building and fully understand the scope of the design.

Having moved through the building, one is able to grasp its large scale clearly. Stadiums in general rank among the largest structures that one will encounter. This stadium, however, stands out because of its specific form. The roof does not merely provide cover, but is also a formal gesture and composition that thrusts towards the field and the city—drawing the eye of the visitor in the process. While many stadiums hold the guest in a contained experience that rarely allows one to look back out at the city, the Diablos stadium creates moments of connection that allow visitors to look back at the city from which they have come and attain a sense of scale in the process. The organization of the building as a series of separate volumes with space in-between breaks up the scale into units that can be conceptualized while providing room to see these different parts of the building. The result is a building with a sense of unity created by the roof that also contains elements that serve a diverse set of needs, provide scale and address the human body, and create a sense of intimacy amid the massiveness of the structure.

The story of the Diablos stadium begins with the team and the growing interest and prestige of the sport in Mexico. The origin of the sport in Mexico extends back to the eighteen-forties, when American military forces were stationed in Mexico during the Mexican American War. By 1925, the Liga Mexicana de Béisbol was founded. During the nineteen-thirties and forties, the Liga Mexicana served as an essential home to African American players from the United States, who were unable to play there until Jackie Robinson broke the color barrier in 1947. They were offered higher salaries and better conditions than in the Negro League in the United States.

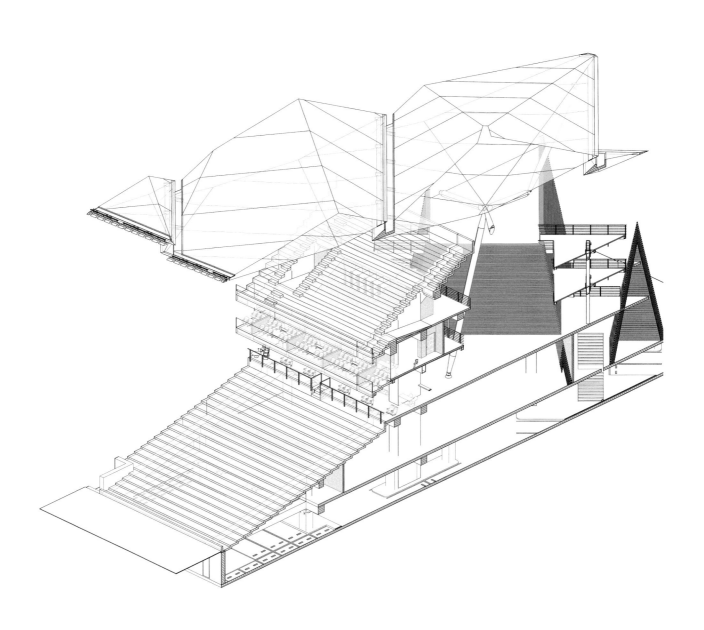

Don Alfredo Harp Helú grew up in this context and developed a love of baseball. He was raised as part of a highly intellectual business community and ultimately became a successful broker who built an investment bank that grew into the largest in Latin America. In the process, he continued to cultivate his love for baseball. This love culminated with the purchase of the Diablos Rojos baseball team in 1993. By the early two-thousand-tens, Don Alfredo began contemplating building a stadium that would be designed specifically for baseball. The new stadium that he envisioned for the Diablos Rojos baseball team would, in many ways, combine his interest in philanthropy and his love for baseball.

Twenty-one million people call Mexico City their home. As the sixth largest city in the world, it is faced with many of the challenges that global cities of this scale must reckon with. High-density zones require infrastructure to facilitate mobility, sanitation, and social services. The urban infrastructure must also be resilient to natural disasters. In the case of Mexico City, this means earthquakes and flooding. The city must also work as part of an international network of cities and as part of a broader economy, contributing and attracting goods, services, and talent.

For Mexico City, these challenges are particularly poignant. Unlike many of the cities of North America that were built at the site of little more than an existing trading post or broader temporary camp, Tenochtitlan, a vast and complex Aztec city, existed on the site of what would become Mexico City when Cortés arrived. The city was originally built by the Aztecs on an island of Lake Texcoco in 1325. However, little would remain, as Cortés razed much of the city during his conquest and then completed the job when he began rebuilding the city, leaving no trace of the Aztec city. He even went so far as to build Mexico City Metropolitan Cathedral over the ruins of the main Aztec temple.

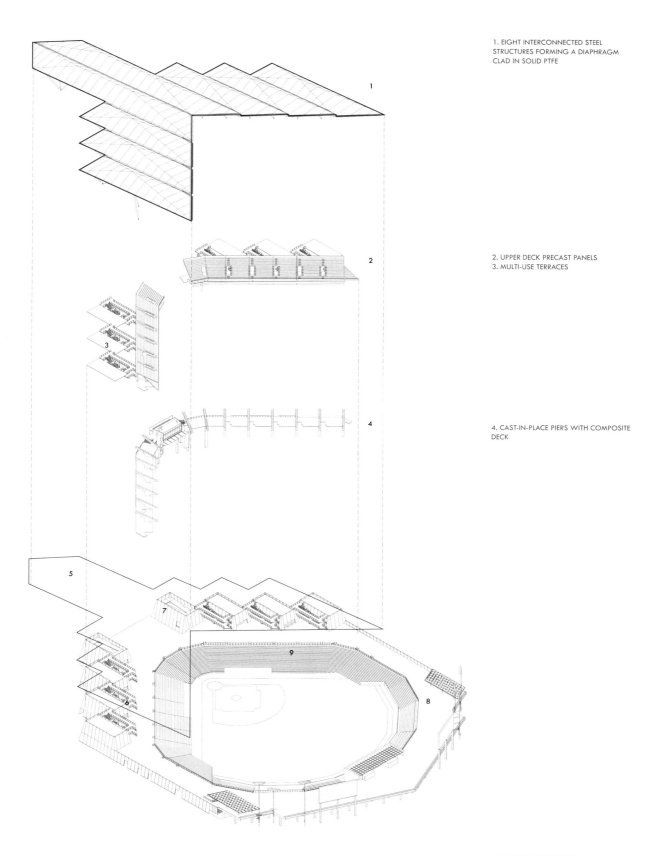

"ABOVE, THERE IS THE CANOPY, THE SIGNATURE OF THE STADIUM, WHICH PROVIDES SHELTER FOR THOUSANDS OF FANS BY CANTILEVERING OVER THE SEATS AND EXTENDING TOWARDS THE ENTRANCE TO SHELTER GUESTS AS THEY ARRIVE. BELOW, SEATS COLORED WITH A GRADIENT FROM RED TO DARK GREY DESCEND FROM THE ENTRANCE LEVEL TO THE FIELD."

The cathedral and the Zócalo onto which its doors opened would become the center of the colonial city, which would be laid out in a regular grid. The elite members of Spanish society would live in close proximity to the Zócalo, with the indigenous population forming irregularly planned villages on the periphery. The city would grow steadily from the center for the next hundred years until settlement reached the waters of the lake, subjecting many newly settled areas to flooding as a result. Draining the lake not only helped reduce the mosquito population, but also helped limit the spread of many diseases.

The site of the Diablos stadium is in one such area that was drained. Sited in the Barrio of Granjas Mexico, the area was historically utilized for farming. Because of its location, it was a strategic point for transit in the city. A significant waterway, the Iztacalco Canal, passed through the area along what is now Calzada de la Viga. Due to irrigation and quality of soil, the area became prime farmland.

The history of the area dates to 1309, when the island of Iztacalco in Lake Texcoco was settled by the Mexica, who later founded Tenochtitlan. When the lake was drained, the area was transformed into a maze of small communities, artificial islands, and solid farmland. The modern borough came into existence in 1929. The historic center of the borough corresponds to the original island and is centered around Plaza San Matías in the Barrio de Santa Cruz.

By the nineteen-eighties, however, little cultivation remained. In recent years, it has become a dense residential neighborhood in some areas and an industrial and commercial neighborhood in others. Generally speaking, the borough has some of the most neglected neighborhoods in Mexico City. At the same time, some of the former farmland was converted into a sports complex including the Palacio de los Deportes, designed by Felix Candela (1966–68), and the Foro

KING POST
CONNECTION

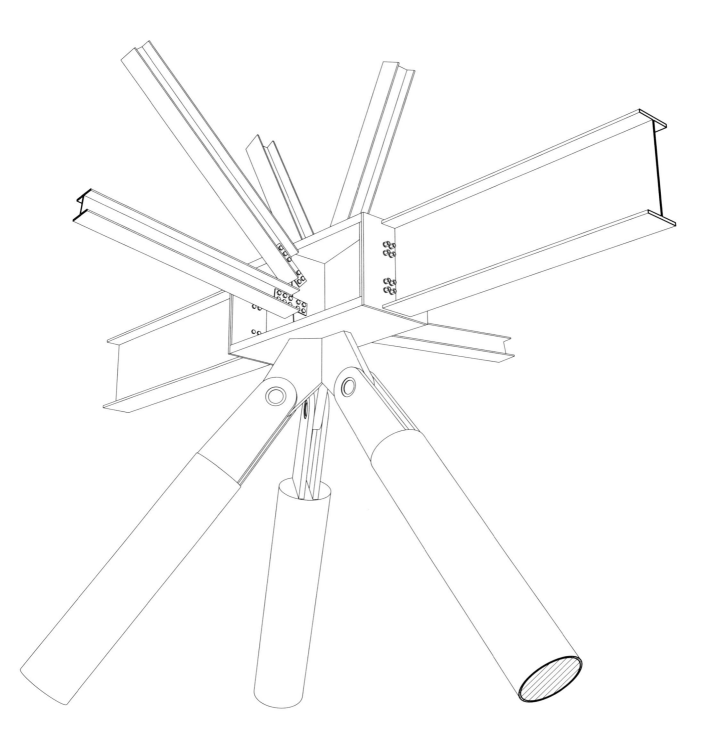

Sol Stadium (an earlier home of the Diablos Rojos baseball team), home to the 1968 Olympic Games. A Formula 1 racetrack would later be added. The site and the racetrack are constrained by significant transportation infrastructure that includes the Viaducto Rio de la Piedad to the north and the Canal Rio Churubusco to the south. The site can be accessed by car as well as via the No. 9 train line.

Beyond the immediate context of the stadium lies a city struggling to support a population that grew exponentially beginning in the nineteen-seventies. Growth was so rapid that it was difficult for urban infrastructure to keep up. Even before the boom, the existing urban fabric was not entirely equipped to handle the population. Although a metro system had opened in 1969 and wide boulevards such as Reforma were introduced during the Porfirian Era, shifts in political leadership, such as the Mexican Revolution and Independence a century earlier, resulted in discontinuity of urban planning efforts.

The result of this inability to fully plan the city and create an infrastructure framework supporting growth has meant a city that is divided between wealthier enclaves with lower density and excellent services and tightly packed neighborhoods—sometimes even shantytowns—that house the working class and urban poor. The new stadium would, in many ways, have to negotiate both of these worlds. While not literally straddling the line between rich and poor, the proximity to the working-class neighborhood and the wealthier contingent of baseball patrons creates a notable contrast that the design of the new building had an opportunity to address.

The design of the new stadium could have embraced its island-like setting within the interior of the racetrack and created an insular, inward-looking experience. This was not the path taken. Instead, the stadium seeks to integrate itself with the surrounding community. This occurs at the level of planning, programming, and aesthetics. At a formal level, this occurs through the way in which the roof extends towards the city and out over the field. The steps to the entrance plaza gradually descend to connect to the surrounding landscape. The truncated trapezoids are spaced such that visitors can see the program unfolding within.

At the programmatic level, the plaza of the stadium has been designated as a space for a marketplace on non-game days. Community members have the opportunity to sell locally produced wares and other objects. Batting cages are set up for the community to enjoy. Land has been designated for future urban farming.

On one hand, this decision reflects the agrarian history of the site. On the other hand, it is an opportunity to further engage the surrounding community by inviting them to cultivate their own plots of land. Doing so not only contributes meaningfully to the local culture and economy, but also brings life to the site on days when a game is not taking place. Finally, the intention was also to create a program of affordable tickets for members of the community who might otherwise not be able to attend a game.

The future vision of integrating a market would be a logical extension of the urban farming program. The market would bring life to the site throughout the year while also creating an outlet for local craftspeople and farmers to sell their products. It would create a vital and direct link between those visiting the stadium for baseball or other events and a community that is often cut off from such opportunities. The inclusion of such amenities would continue Don Alfredo's longstanding interest in cultivating young talent and supporting the broader popularity of the sport.

At the aesthetic level, the stadium references the history of urban form and ultimately becomes evocative of the Aztec city. The materiality of these truncated trapezoids further references the local context by using volcanic stone as part of the prefabricated concrete panels. Finally, the decision to clad the roof with a lightweight PTFE fabric membrane reflects a desire not only to provide the necessary shelter, but also a vision in which the use of light materials supports broader sustainability and the continued success of our cities.

These strategies work together to unite people. On game days, they come from a variety of sections of the city by car, with public transportation, and on foot. Once at the stadium, there are many ways for people to spend time. A considerable amount of time will naturally be spent cheering in the stands while watching the game. However, there are many sections of the stadium that are equally conducive to gathering. The family terraces offer a liminal space between the seating bowls and the concessions areas where people can casually congregate and devote their attention to the game or other concerns. The concessions area offers a temporary break, while the restaurants offer a longer break from the game in progress. Meanwhile, the terraces on the top of the truncated trapezoids offer a unique vantage point from which to view the surrounding city and landscape. This ability to see the city and mountains in the distance from these elevated planes was an essential goal of the design. The efforts to use architecture and the spaces that it creates to bring people together for ritual, gathering, entertainment, and sport are a fundamental and ancient aspect of civilization.

Each subsequent epoch has had the opportunity to redefine these spaces in order to tailor their form to the ways they might be used in the present incarnation of culture. During the modern epoch, limited reinvention of the stadium typology occurred. When stadiums were built, they often looked towards classical typology in order to evoke a return to past greatness. Instead, the great modernists focused on more fundamental questions of where we live and how we work. It was not until after World War II and the shift away from the concerns of modernity in philosophy, politics, and economics towards those concerns grouped under the rubrics of postmodernism and post-structuralism that true innovation and reinvention of the architecture of the stadium began to occur. Great structural engineers such as Pier Luigi Nervi, Frei Otto, and Felix Candela began rethinking how concrete and tensile structures could be deployed to reimagine the structure of stadiums and the extent to which large uninterrupted spans could be achieved. While not necessarily working within the same utopian ideological space as their modern predecessors, these and other architects and engineers extended the quest for material innovation, clarity of structural concept, and expression in form.

The Diablos stadium continues these pursuits while also exploring an approach that allows for a greater level of contextualism than the architectural vocabulary of either the universalist approach of modernism or the more fragmented approach of postmodernism might support. In the context of our practice, a truly universal approach to design is found in an understanding of how people experience space and form a connection to place. It is also expressed in how the design for the stadium is situated in relation to the surrounding community.

With the exception of the roof, which is the idea and design of Francisco González Pulido, the architectural design of the Diablos stadium is the result of a strategic fifty-fifty collaboration between the Mexican architects Francisco González Pulido — FGP ATELIER, Chicago, and Alonso de Garay — Taller ADG, Mexico City. González Pulido designed the roof and de Garay designed the landscape. They share credit for the design of the rest of the stadium. The design team wanted to create something that would be more than a stadium; rather, it would be an entire urban complex. The monumental, lightweight roof structure resembling the Diablos' trident would contrast dramatically with the predictable roof geometry that has historically defined baseball stadiums around the world. Indicative of the sky, the roof design would be sharp, translucent, luminous, and dynamic. Composed of lightweight steel wrapped in PTFE textile material, the roof would become an iconic symbol for the great city of Mexico.

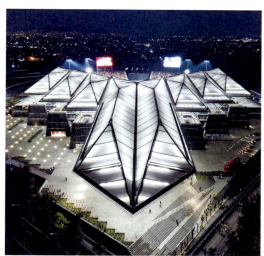

TECHNOLOGY & AESTHETICS

In contrast to the visual lightness of the roof, the base level is ceremonial and draws from many cultural cues. Designed using local materials from the Valley of Mexico and inspired by the pre-Hispanic era, the plaza-level design refers specifically to the court of the ancient Mesoamerican ballgame and emphasizes the connection between the earth and the heavens. The guiding concept was to establish the duality between pre-Hispanic Mexico, expressed in the base, and contemporary Mexico, expressed in the roof, which blends tradition, innovation, austerity, and technology into one space.

The relationship between the tools, techniques, and technologies used in design and construction are inextricably linked to the appearance that the finished building takes. Some would go so far as to suggest that the more the finished forms reflect these methods—as well as an overall mastery of them—the more "beautiful" the building will be to a broad group of people. It will connect to a deeply human capacity to master material, manipulate form, and create a solution to problems across a range of complex situations. The streamlined forms of the stadium are a direct expression of structural requirements, while the use of a PTFE textile cladding system responds to both the specific sheltering requirements of the program and the current state of material innovation. This attitude is carried throughout the building, as each element is reduced to its most essential characteristics so that one element can perform as many functions as possible. This is seen in the truncated trapezoid volumes that support the roof, house the support functions, and provide outdoor terraces as a break from the activities occurring on the field. It is also reflected in the goal of having the building operate with net zero energy, waste, and water through engineering elements such as the roof, which can collect water and provide room for solar panels.

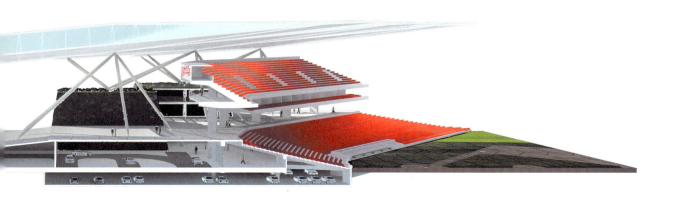

SUSTAINABILITY & RESILIENCE

At the same time, the lightness and transparency of the fabric structure allows light to filter through during the day and the stadium to glow at night. In both cases, the interaction of light with structure creates a heightened experience directly addressed to the inhabitant of the stadium. Such attention to experience is further reflected in how the truncated trapezoid forms are constructed from modular concrete panels incorporating volcanic rock, which renders a deep black surface that evokes the material used to construct ancient Mesoamerican temples. These forms reference the context of the stadium in Mexico City while also providing orientation to visitors as they navigate the expansive building.

Attending a single sporting event is sufficient to understand how potentially wasteful they can be. Fans fill myriad wastebaskets with disposable plates and cups, thousands of gallons of water are consumed by flushing toilets, and night games require extraordinary wattage to illuminate the field. This all occurs during the playing of a sport—one of the most sustainable activities imaginable—whose origins extend back thousands of years. In this context, it was important that the stadium reduce energy consumption, waste, and emissions as much as possible. The design strives for a net zero building using passive systems with minimal HVAC integration and active water reduction systems. The goal of sustainable design incorporating minimal ecological impact sets a strong precedent for a new standard of building in Mexico.

The strategy for achieving net zero energy began by determining a baseline for energy consumption: 1,250 MWh. This was made up of general lighting, space cooling, fans and ventilation, a wastewater treatment plan, space heating, pumps, receptacles, field and canopy lighting, heat rejection, and stand-alone base utilities. Overall consumption could be reduced through efficient lighting, lighting controls, air side economizer, demand control, VFD on fans, chiller efficiency, and energy recovery (museum and retail). This new number would be 62.3% of the baseline. In order to meet this demand, the team proposed generating solar energy on site and building a biodigester. With the biodigester working at full capacity, it could cover 23% of the baseline, and the solar panels could cover 35%—together nearly meeting the full demand of the stadium.

In order to achieve net zero waste, the team planned to divert 100% of recyclable waste from landfills and incinerators. The organic waste would be directed to a self-contained biodigester that would also collect ½ truckload of organic waste per day from off-site. The output would be electric energy for building use and organic fertilizer for landscaping. The biodigester could produce 64 KW by processing 2,000 tons of waste/year. The stadium

produces 50 tons of waste/year which will utilize approximately 2.5% of the biodigester's capacity. This would require an additional ½ of a small truckload of imported waste per day to provide the remaining 1,950 tons of waste. This would not only meet the net zero goal, but also divert a significant amount of waste from the neighboring area.

The goal was also to create a building where no potable water is used for irrigation, toilet flushing, and equipment water make up. One hundred percent of the non-potable water to be used originates from closed-loop water systems, appropriately purified without the use of harmful chemicals. One hundred percent of storm water and building water discharge would be managed on-site to feed the project's internal water demands. Municipal potable water would be used only to supply sinks, faucets, and showers when on-site potabilization is not be permitted. In order to achieve this goal, rainwater from the roof, plaza, field, and berm would be collected in a series of tanks. This water would then be treated with an advanced filtration system that would deposit the water in a tank for potable water that could also be used for fire protection. Meanwhile, water from the city sewer would be directed to an Ecolo wastewater treatment plant, a non-potable water tank, and then to the various fixtures throughout the stadium.

While not all of these goals were achieved, for reasons ranging from the politics and economics of garbage disposal in Mexico City to a decision to delay the installation of solar panels until a future date, many were implemented and the overall energy, waste, and water consumption of the building was reduced.

WATER MANAGEMENT DIAGRAM

1. MUNICIPAL WATER SUPPLY
2. ROOF RAINWATER COLLECTION
3. WATER TREATMENT PLANT
4. FIELD RAINWATER COLLECTION

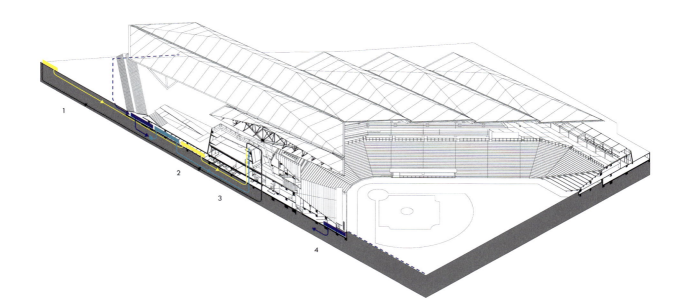

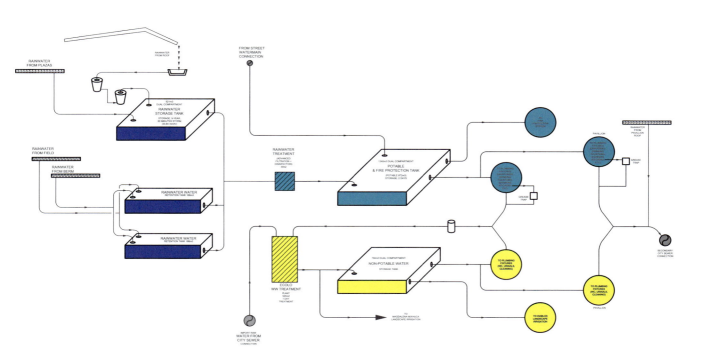

PRECAST CONCRETE CLAD TRAPEZOIDS

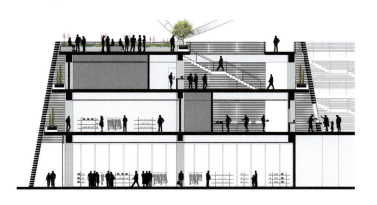
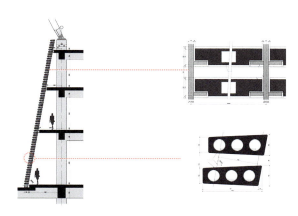

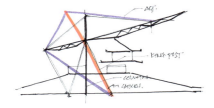 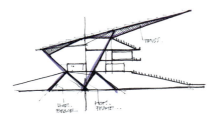 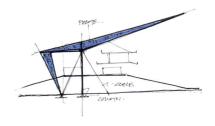

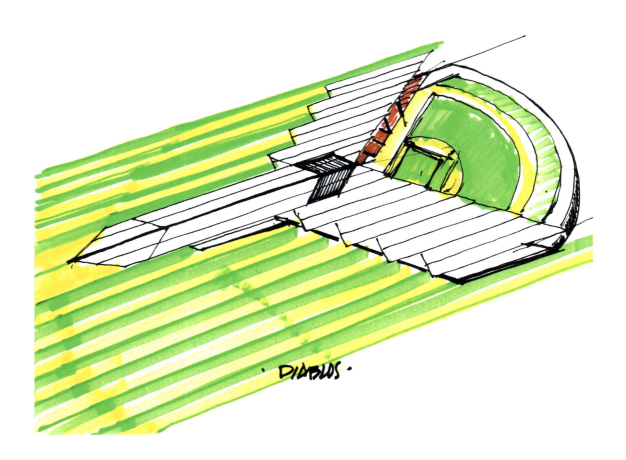

· DIABLOS ·

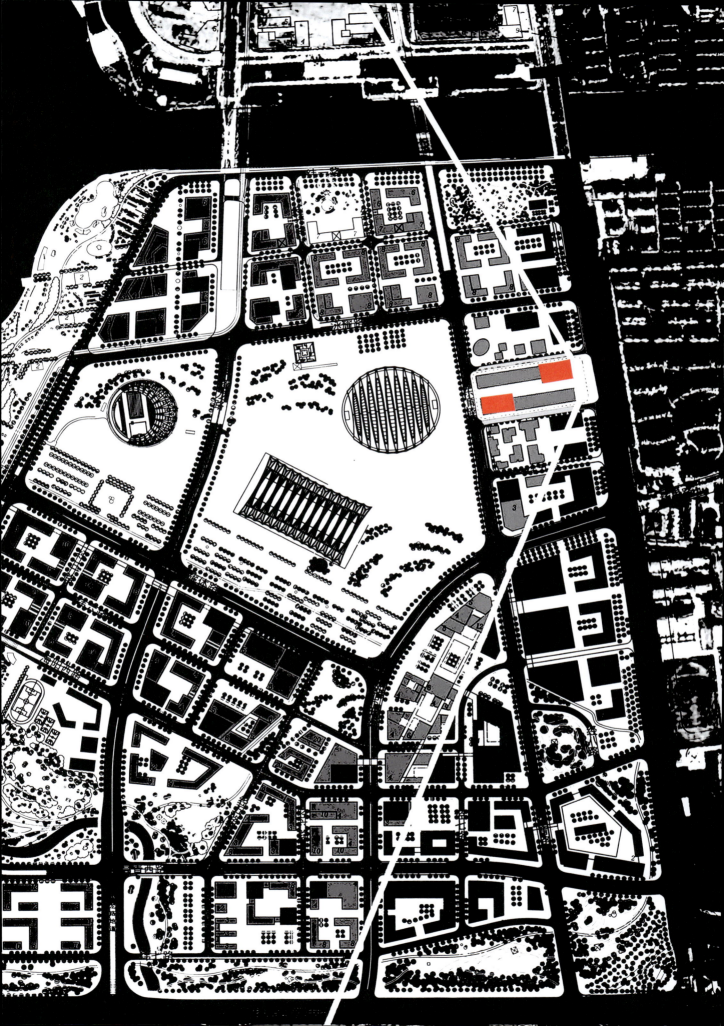

QIANTAN LOT 14

INTRO

The Qiantan Enterprise World Phase II in Shanghai is a two-tower structure and urban complex. Originally conceived as a speculative office complex, the project became home to the regional offices of the iconic British brand Land Rover soon after completion. The structures and urban plaza were meticulously thought out and designed to reflect the local culture, create a people-centric biophilic environment, and reflect the idea of a porous urban fabric.

Serving as a powerful metamorphic and symbolic tool, the buildings transform with the city's atmosphere through the application of a custom-fritted glass pattern which emulates Chinese bamboo when seen from afar. The patterned exterior surface not only pays tribute to the importance of bamboo in Chinese culture, but also contributes to the overall efficiency of the building by providing natural shade and privacy for occupants. The design honors Chinese culture and stands as a feat of imagination and technology. Designing the complex frit pattern was equivalent to putting together a giant puzzle. It would not have been possible without parametric tools and digital fabrication technology. The result is, in essence, a building with a lyrical, beautifully integrated skin that performs with light.

Like so many projects being built in China today, this project began while working on a master plan and tower proposal for the client on another site. The client had another site he was developing but was not entirely sure of the number of towers and the ultimate scale. He did know that it was going to be a spec office building whose ideal tenant would be an automaker. In recent years, the Pudong Area of Shanghai in which the project is situated had become the center of financial services in the city. As such, a growing set of adjacent businesses were continuing to flood the area and create ongoing demand for new office and retail space. While some developments were strictly dedicated to offices, the client was interested in creating a mixed-use building that could attract a unique anchor tenant as well as retail in order to become a place that would attract visitors from the broader area.

THE CLIENT

In setting out this goal, the client decided that the building would require parking for the retail and the offices above, ground floor and mezzanine retail, a public plaza onto which this retail could open, and a showroom that might be capable of attracting an automaker. The client wanted the showroom to be flexible so that it could meet evolving needs of the client and support ease of loading and unloading cars and other displays. The other retail spaces should be equally flexible and able to be divided or combined into a large space.

OFFICE-RETAIL
COMPLETED 2018
85,000 M2
HEIGHT 100M
SHANGHAI
CHINA

"IN MY MIND, I WAS SITTING IN THE MIDDLE OF WHAT FELT LIKE AN URBAN FOREST; WHILE REFLECTING ON THE MEANING OF THESE SURFACES, SLOWLY I UNCOVERED THE SUBTLE MESSAGES OF MOVEMENT IN A RIGOROUS CUBIST COMPOSITION, EVOCATIVE OF BAMBOO TREES AND REVEALED THROUGH LIGHT; AT THAT POINT THE BUILDINGS BECAME A 'BLACK CANVAS' FROM WHICH PATTERNS OF NATURE EMERGED, TOUCHED BY THE SUN, AND AS THE SUN MOVED, THE PATTERNS DISAPPEARED AND REAPPEARED: THE EFFECT WAS RHYTHMIC, A SILENT SOUND …"

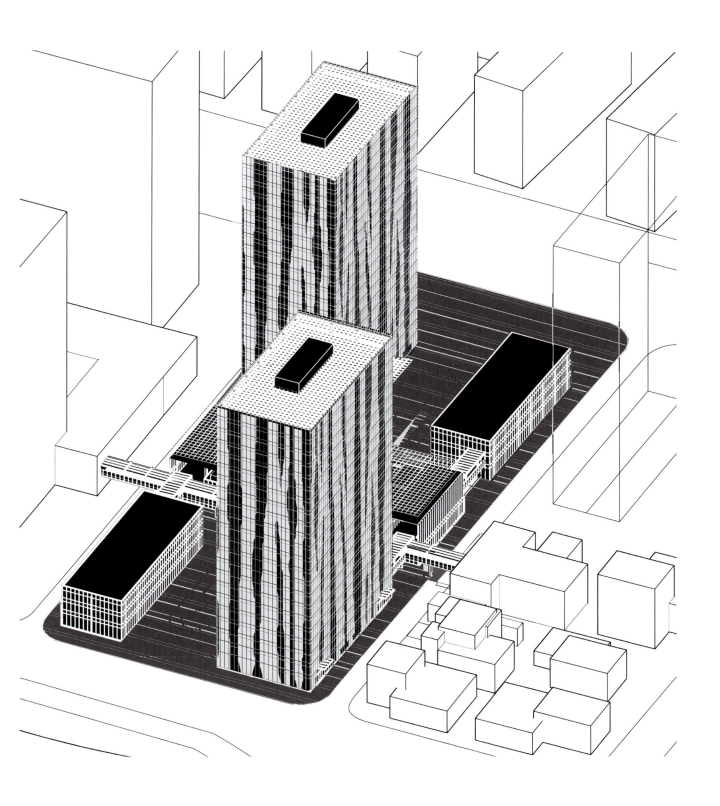

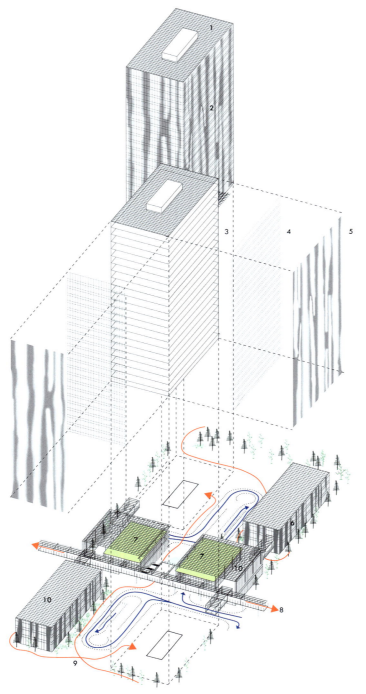

PEDESTRIAN

VEHICULAR

1. MECHANICAL ROOF DECK
2. OFFICE SPACE
3. COMPOSITE DECK
4. GLASS ENCLOSURE
5. BAMBOO PATTERNED CERAMIC FRIT ON GLASS
6. SHOWROOMS
7. GREEN TERRACES
8. BRIDGES
9. PARK WITH LINEAR PATTERN
10. RETAIL PAVILIONS

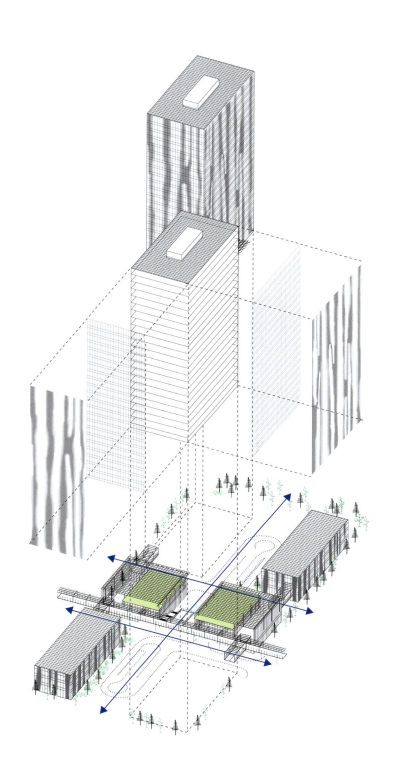

CONTEXT & URBANISM

The urban character of the building was particularly important. The client wanted the building to have its own unique sense of place and identity while also feeling connected to the surrounding area. In a city where buildings so often feel isolated by high-speed roads and the large scale of new blocks of buildings, the client wanted the project to convey a human scale. They wanted visitors to walk across the site, explore the block on foot, and find intriguing products in the process. This was essential, because the program would require two 100-meter-tall buildings totaling roughly 80,000 square meters.

These characteristics were particularly important because of the rapid rate at which the area was being developed and the significant competition to secure anchor tenants of new buildings. At the same time, the client was quite sensitive to the cost of the building, the procurement process, and how the building would be constructed. While they wanted a building of the highest quality that exhibited unique characteristics, they also wanted a design that would be economical and quick to build in order to satisfy the financing structure and economic model they had determined would make the building profitable and deliver a strong return on their investment. After delivering a building that came in on budget, the client was able to attract the very type of anchor tenant they had hoped the quality of the building would help them secure—Land Rover's Shanghai Regional Offices and Showroom.

Building a new structure in China's largest city—the world's second largest city with a population of 24.18 million, and a city possessing the world's busiest port—cannot be taken lightly. One has to consider how to make a positive contribution to the built environment of the city and hope that the new structure will overcome challenges and live up to notable past projects while also contributing to the urban fabric as a whole. This is particularly true in a city that has grown rapidly over the last several decades and whose growth has been largely fueled by real estate speculation seeking to maximize rentable space.

Shanghai was originally settled some 4,000 years ago. The ease of access to its port and location at the confluence of rivers has made it an attractive city ever since. After the British victory in the First Opium War in 1842, the city became a major trading port with the Occident. During the early twentieth century, it became the center of banking in China and a thriving, wealthy city. It was during the early nineteen-nineties that the economic reforms introduced by Deng Xiaoping resulted in intense redevelopment of the city and the return of finance and foreign investment.

The city's physical organization has evolved in conjunction with this history. Most recently, the incursion of European influence led to the construction of the Bund and French Concession as well as the introduction of European neoclassical styles that would come to mix with the historic temples and traditional townhouses. During this period, development was concentrated inland from the mouth of the Yangtze River, whose banks would often flood. The area that would become the Pudong District would require significant efforts to reclaim the land.

While the population continued to grow during the Maoist era, the extraordinary growth did not fully begin until the nineteen-eighties, when more residents flooded the city as country life became economically less viable. The economic liberalization of the nineteen-nineties and extraordinary wealth that was generated as a result made it possible to begin investing in a significant infrastructure system that would sustain and support growth over the coming decades. This would include a metro and light rail system with sixteen lines, a major expressway system, and new airports.

The infrastructure would make it possible to funnel millions of people through the city and deliver them to increasingly dense centers, where people would work in a new class of tall and super-tall buildings showcasing the city's new wealth and presence on the world stage. Pudong, more than anywhere else, is emblematic of this new wealth. Historically, the area along the east bank of the Huangpu River was largely farmland. Over a period of several centuries, the banks began to develop with wharfs and warehouses. The major inflection point for the area came in 1993, when the Chinese government established the Lujiazui Finance and Trade Zone—a Special Economic Zone that would allow the area to become the major financial services epicenter of the city.

In the coming years, the area would house the Shanghai Stock Exchange, major exposition centers, and some of the city's most iconic buildings, including the Oriental Pearl Tower, the Jin Mao Tower, the Shanghai World Financial Center, the Shanghai Tower, and the Shanghai International Financial Center, designed as a collaboration between Helmut Jahn and Francisco González Pulido. These modern skyscrapers directly face Puxi's historic Bund, a remnant of former foreign concessions in China. The rest of the new area includes the Port of Shanghai, the Shanghai Expo and Century Park, Zhangjiang Hi-Tech Park, Shanghai Pudong International Airport, and the Jiuduansha Wetland Nature Reserve.

Building in this context requires a unique sensitivity. On one hand, the city has a rich architectural history containing and combining Chinese and European styles. The scale of the city is remarkably diverse, ranging from the tallest buildings in the world to two- and three-story historic townhouses accessed via narrow alleys. The quality of new buildings ranges from the most sophisticated complex cladding and structural systems to buildings erected so rapidly that parts barely align. The aspiration of new buildings is often driven by a desire to appear modern and progressive. As such, the International Style and its derivatives has remained a guiding force for many of the buildings being constructed throughout the city. At the same time, as the country continues to evolve and progresses from a developing country to a developed country with less rapid annual growth, the specific nature of what clients want out of a project is changing.

In many ways, this change is a shift towards buildings that reflect the new China and the identity that has developed over the last two decades. This identity is one that embraces the duality of international citizenship and interfaces with the global capitalist economy while also embracing local cultural traditions that may

 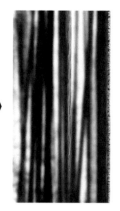 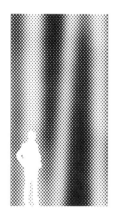 

 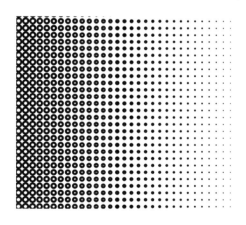

extend back centuries before the Cultural Revolution, as well as the continued dominance of the Communist Party and the central role that it plays in real estate development, banking, and guiding the structure of the economy.

The design consists of two classic modern structures with retail on the ground floor and mezzanine. Locating the two forms on either corner of the site while offsetting them created a dynamic urban plaza seamlessly connected to the surrounding area. It would be easy to build and could be delivered on-time and on-budget. It would, however, be the details—of the facade, the location of the lobbies and showroom, the character of the urban plaza, the design of the lobbies—that would give the building its true character and make it highly desirable. The specification of these features was done in such a way that it would not add significant cost or complexity to construction.

The intent of the design was to:
1) reflect Chinese culture,
2) create a porous environment,
3) inspire connectedness,
4) leverage technology, and
5) design a building that was recognizable in the skyline.

By incorporating a complex frit pattern on the glass-paneled facade of each tower through the use of parametric and digital fabrication tools, it was possible to create a pattern that depicts bamboo. The abstraction not only serves to distinguish a unique and dynamic building that changes with the light, but also to essentially reflect—both metaphorically and physically—two important aspects of Chinese culture. For perspective, China grows over 400 species of bamboo and the plant is frequently referenced in ancient Chinese literature. Bamboo is not only a symbol of traditional Chinese values but is also seen as a reflection of harmony between people and nature—which also harmonizes with the idea of a porous urban environment and biophilic design. The opacity rendered by the pattern also serves to cater to a still-developing need for privacy in the country while keeping everything open and welcoming. The bridges connecting the various structures serve a two-fold purpose—they reference the popularity of this design aspect in the country's culture while also contributing to an interconnected yet porous urban environment.

The idea behind creating such an environment is essentially people-centric with aspects of biophilic design. To combat the tendency to overdevelop, the inner area of the urban complex remained open. In this way, the landscaped, courtyard-like area enhances rather than degrades the surrounding

environment while also encouraging inhabitants and visitors to interact with nature and each other. Similarly, the addition of a rooftop garden on each tower promotes biodiversity while also contributing to health and wellbeing—yielding much more than just another aesthetically pleasing place.

The implementation of bridges that connect the various structures also play to the idea of interconnectedness and how the built environment can be used to enhance the connection between people. By leaving the large-scale buildings on opposite sides and on the outer lines, the inner area begins to take on the feeling of a small sanctum in the middle of an urban complex, yet also serves to provide a visual sense of arrival when transitioning between buildings. A contrast to the "walled city," the bridges imbue security and openness, are open twenty-four hours, and feature long expanses of uninterrupted glass rather than "fortress gates." By designing an open, modern space on the ground level, visual contrast between the scale of each building was created. While the towers are much taller than the surrounding buildings, they are perfectly situated so as to enhance rather than take away from the neighboring structures. The contrast in scale shines attention directly into the open showroom.

Rainer Schmidt Landschaftsarchitekten was critical in developing a strategy for creating an inviting and sustainable plaza. The result was a striated terrain operating at multiple levels, capable of breaking down the scale of the plaza in the vertical and horizontal dimension in order to address the experience to the scale of the human inhabitant. We worked in close collaboration to hone the vision for the series of green roofs and create intimate shaded zones, covered mezzanines, and expansive plazas.

The primary aesthetic feature of the building began with capturing an image of a bamboo forest. More specifically, a photograph was taken and used as inspiration. Naturally, this would not have been possible without the invention of the camera. The principles behind how a camera works have long been known and have guided the evolution of the aesthetics of architecture over the last several hundred years, if not far longer. Beginning with the Renaissance and the invention of perspective, the ability to translate between two and three dimensions with a high level of precision has played a fundamental role in design and construction. Stonemasons, in particular, were able to use theories of projection to understand how to translate complex curvatures onto the stones they cut, allowing them to produce intricate stairs and chamfered edges.

At this early date, the use of the camera obscura—essentially darkened a room with a small hole introduced in one surface—allowed the image of what was taking place outside to be projected onto a wall and traced if desired. Several centuries later, the use of photographic technology has aided architects in a variety of ways. On one hand, it has allowed them to better document and analyze a site on which a building will be constructed—both from above and on the ground. On the other, it has allowed them to go beyond perspective drawings of what a building might look like and to create what effectively are photographs of a building that does not exist. These renderings utilize principles similar to the ones that make photography possible, projecting light particles through a digital geometry to illuminate surfaces and then translating an axonometric space into a perspective aligned with the location of an imagined viewer. The result enables architects to explore more complex spaces, better understand how they will be experienced, and attain greater buy-in from the client and the broader set of people who might use the building. In recent years, this technology has been extended to include virtual and augmented reality, which allows the viewer to move through a perspectival space and use holographic or other means to introduce digital information into the real space one moves through.

In addition to using photography in the design process, new printing methods and materials have made it possible to cover vast surfaces with images. The ever-increasing resolution of photographs has made it possible to take an image of a piece of marble and create an expansive glass facade that appears to be made of stone. At the same time, large-scale projection technologies that can create highly legible images even during the day can be used to cover entire building facades. Inside, media screens have become increasingly ubiquitous and supplement both programs and architecture. The result is buildings whose atmosphere is increasingly defined by the capture and representation of images.

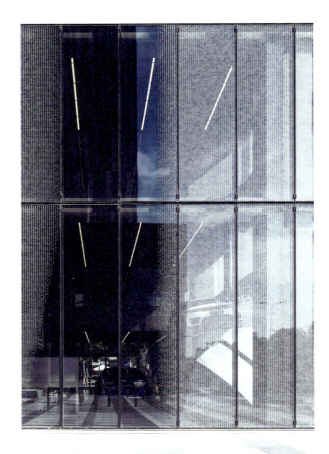

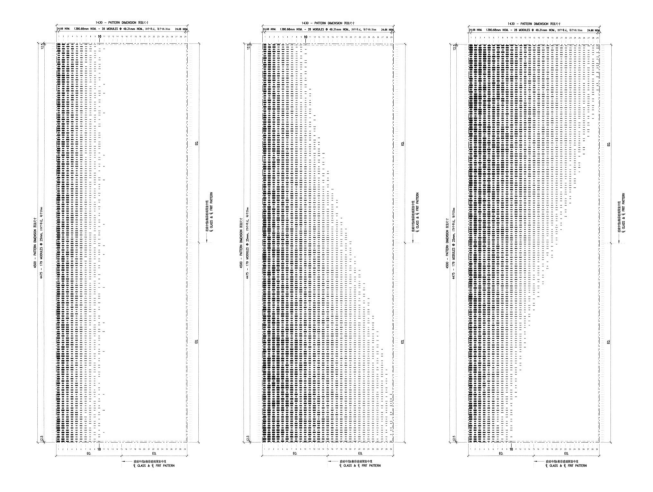

Qiantan Enterprise World Phase II takes a slightly different path. The buildings' unique facades were designed through the use of parametric and digital fabrication tools to create an abstract pattern that mimics bamboo. By printing countless dots on the surface of each glass panel in a predetermined yet complex frit pattern, the area is not only rendered opaque, but from afar, assumes the shape of bamboo. This pattern is achieved through the use of fifty-two unique fritted glass panels that have been combined in a range of manners to achieve the striated effect.

By utilizing parametric and digital fabrication tools to achieve the abstraction of the bamboo on each glass panel, the design concept for each tower was realized with 52 panels rather than the 500 it would have taken without the current technology. The use of technology also aided in creating vivid, distinctive imagery that truly renders the towers unique. By wielding every tool available, it was possible to build the cutting-edge towers at a much lower cost, with far fewer materials, and in a period of time that would not have been foreseeable in regard to this project even ten years ago.

Nor is the aesthetic experience of the building limited to how it is experienced from outside. Inside, office workers are given a remarkably transparent view through the floor-to-ceiling windows. The frit pattern, however, serves to provide orientation within a given space and helps to break up the potential monotony and large scale of the building's facade. The beauty of the building, in the end, is deeply connected to this process of abstraction. The viewer is able to identify with the underlying natural reference while also feeling pride in the technology used to transform the original image captured on a skin that performs both visually and in terms of how it supports reduced energy consumption through a rational process.

Just as the building draws upon this relationship between technology and aesthetics, it also draws upon the long legacy of modernism and the International Style that is prevalent throughout the city. The building exhibits a purity and an honesty that recall the icons of the International Style. The edges are highly refined and the geometry straightforward. This is nowhere more prevalent than in the lobby of the building, whose surfaces are defined by butt-jointed, back-painted glass that evokes the minimalism of the International Style. While the buildings of the International Style tended to express only minor stylistic variation, Qiantan Enterprise World Phase II has taken the International Style as a skeleton or framework for a skin uniquely tailored to the environment in which it lives, so that the building itself becomes its own species, suited to its habitat.

"THE BUILDING EXHIBITS A PURITY AND AN HONESTY THAT RECALL THE ICONS OF THE INTERNATIONAL STYLE. THE EDGES ARE HIGHLY REFINED AND THE GEOMETRY STRAIGHTFORWARD. THIS IS NOWHERE MORE PREVALENT THAN IN THE LOBBY OF THE BUILDING, WHOSE SURFACES ARE DEFINED BY BUTT-JOINTED, BACK-PAINTED GLASS THAT EVOKES THE MINIMALISM OF THE INTERNATIONAL STYLE."

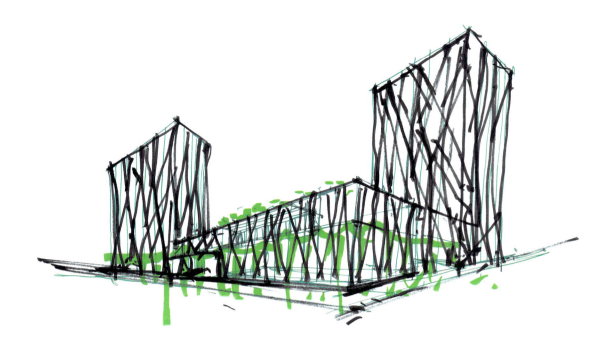
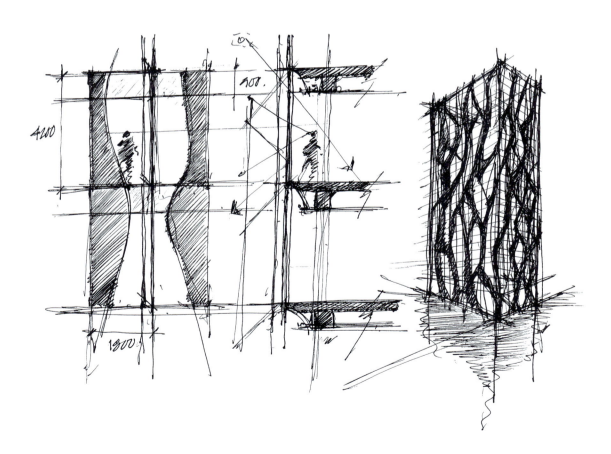

TECHNICAL CONTEXTUALISM

As technology has evolved, it has become increasingly possible to collaborate virtually and practice anywhere in the world. At the same time, considerable value should be placed in creating architecture that is contextual. Beyond striving to reflect the history, culture, economy, politics, and habits in the buildings, it is important to incorporate the local building tradition into the work. This can be done while also showcasing the high standards for design and construction developed over decades of practicing in some of the most rigorous building cultures. The standards that result have been discussed in the essays on the aesthetics of the sustainable, the manner of working at the intersection of architecture and engineering, and the ethics that guide an approach to design and the profession. The process of designing within a particular context is a process of adapting or adaptation in much the same way that one might think of an animal adapting to their environment through evolution. This process of adaptation leads to "technical contextualism"—a term that González Pulido coined five years ago to describe a central theme of his practice. The result is a building that addresses sun, wind, rain, habits, history, color, access, and desire through the form and organization that it takes.

The process of adapting universal values that guide our practice to a local context is, of course, a more complex process. First, it involves looking at the specific tradition of how buildings have been put together in the past. This is, fundamentally, to ask how space has been created. On one hand, it can be created through carving out space from a solid. It can be created by setting stakes to mark the limits of a future enclosure. It can also be created by adding solid material to other solid material to create a volume. Wood joints can be used to connect elements, straw can be combined with mud to create walls, and liquid concrete can be poured between temporary planes to eventually create a solid volume. Each strategy for creating space implies a specific set of expertise that must be accounted for. Moreover, each is the reflection of a particular climate, access to materials, and set of habits related to how people use space. By carefully considering the values that are reflected in these choices and how traditional building methods relate to global building trends and technology, it is possible to create rather unexpected formal, spatial, and organizational results that clearly reflect tradition while also attaining a precision and, in some cases, scale and connectivity with other building systems—often very advanced—that might not necessarily have been used historically. In doing so, new opportunities arise for the building to perform for those within the local context.

TECHNICAL CONTEXTUALISM

A critical component of a particular building culture is the extent to which that culture seeks to hide or reveal the systems or purpose of a given building. Some cultures have sought to create a high level of illusion, in which atmospheric effects appear as if by magic. Other cultures have, by contrast, endeavored to create buildings where every structural element, air duct, and piece of conduit powering the systems are visible. Structural forces can be clearly visible through the form that the building takes and how gravity is reconciled with the ground. In other cases, the building can take on a purity of form that hides the system that makes it stand. In still others, gravity defying formal gestures can occur that provoke a sense of wonder. In each case, the level of visibility and honesty of a building reflects the values of the culture that built it. While our own values are grounded in lightness, transparency, formal and programmatic legibility, and an honest use of materials, it is important to be cognizant of cultures with other values and seek ways of bringing our own perspective to a collaborative design process. In some cases, this might involve a juxtaposition. In other cases, a more layered approach might be desirable. In still others, an opportunity might arise for bringing values that critics feel are lacking in a given culture to a specific site and program via architecture.

The building tradition within a particular culture is always framed by a discourse that defines what is valued and the evolution of how a culture builds. This discourse can go beyond technical knowledge of the specificity of joinery or the way that concrete is mixed and define sought-after organizational, spatial, and qualitative attributes. This might include placing specific emphasis on certain aspects of a building, such as archways, peaks, axiality, asymmetry, or monumentality. Through focusing on these attributes, better and worse can be defined, better designers can be selected, and the quality of the built environment in service of the people enhanced. In understanding the diversity of these discourses, it is possible to learn how one's own background aligns or contrasts so that, when a design is produced, the process self-consciously celebrates diversity rather than treating it as an after-thought that disrupts the harmony of the overall design. This makes it possible for the building to address multiple constituencies in a cohesive manner and, hopefully, expand its audience and desirability over time.

Behind any discourse is a desire to build for a particular purpose. These purposes are often diverse and have evolved over time. They have ranged from the fundamental need for shelter to a desire to build a home for god on earth, a site for social or political gathering to a home for cultural events or objects. In defining these goals, there is often a specific group or person

"I WAS STRUCK BY THE WAY IN WHICH THE STEMS PROVIDED A UNIQUE VARIATION BETWEEN TRANSPARENCY AND OPACITY, CREATING A SENSE OF DEPTH AND SURPRISE IN THE PROCESS AS LIGHT WAS FILTERED THROUGH THE ATMOSPHERE."

TECHNICAL CONTEXTUALISM

who is responsible for setting the agenda and ultimately making the decisions about what is built. In the process, tensions often arise between competing groups who have different conceptions of what should be built. The design, construction, and even demolition process can, as a result, become the site where these tensions are played out. The building can, in turn, become a site where forces are reconciled. This notion is explored in greater detail in the essay "Pervasive Media." The result is a capacity for buildings to represent and reconcile specific material, cultural, and political forces. One of these forces can be the tension between local and global design traditions as well as local and global economies that might be brought into conflict through the procurement and construction process. Through understanding how a culture has dealt with such reconciliation materially through their architecture in the past, it is possible to utilize conventional tools to trace it in the present—thereby making that reconciliation legible and felt by those who live with the building rather than hidden beneath the surface or ignored entirely.

The success of these efforts and of the building culture as a whole are measured in great architectural achievements within a given culture. It is often the case that particular building cultures value specific typologies over and above other typologies. By valuing one building type over another, cities are given hierarchy, and structure is given to how people move through them. This reflects and informs habits, when people visit what types of places during a day, and how specific buildings fit within the arc of someone's life. Collectively, experiences of significant buildings give a group of people an identity that helps them to distinguish themselves from their neighbors. In doing so, they define their self-worth in terms that can be represented on the global stage. This process of identification with architecture and representation helps us to understand what it is about the built environment that a group values most and how to connect with this value system in future buildings. In many cases, the source of this identification is a technical achievement. Buildings such as the pyramids of Egypt, the Pantheon, Gothic cathedrals, the Eiffel Tower, and the John Hancock Building are examples. By bringing technical knowledge to these specific contexts, it is possible to connect with these traditions while also introducing additional insights that can lead to innovation and new landmarks that a people can call their own.

In considering these various aspects of the design, reception, and use of buildings, it is important to be aware of a building culture's relationship to the export of architectural systems from one culture to another. While the most recent example is the proliferation of the International Style in the form of steel and concrete frame curtain wall buildings, and more recently with

TECHNICAL CONTEXTUALISM

bespoke parametric buildings designed by celebrity architects, the tradition of architectural systems spreading around the world is quite ancient. It can be seen in the way post and lintel systems spread from Egypt throughout the Mediterranean, were expanded and codified by the Greeks, and transformed by the Romans into an entire urban planning system that could be used to build colonial cities throughout the Mediterranean. Similarly, the pagoda spread from China throughout Asia, and the Gothic style proliferated throughout Europe.

The spread of these systems and the way in which they confront preexisting traditions can lead to considerable conflict that must be reconciled in some manner or another. The confrontation can, in some cases, be rather benign and in other cases driven by power and control. This was the case with the way in which European powers sought to export their architectural styles throughout the world in what came to be referred to as colonial architecture. Such architecture is the opposite of "technical contextualism." Whereas "technical contextualism" resolves conflicting forces of globality and locality via the design process, colonial architecture does so through an awkward mash-up of local and global styles coupled with the infusion of local materials, patterns, traditions, and know-how to arrive at a finished product.

In each case, a given culture will have a memory of the confrontation that may be positive or negative. When designing in these contexts, it is important to take this memory into account, as well as the local aspiration for the future of the society and its building culture. While some groups may denounce the interference of a foreign tradition, others might embrace that tradition as emblematic of modernization and seek to excel within that tradition. In either case, it is important to take this process into account and explore how it is represented in design work as well as how this design work should be represented globally.

Beyond meaning, identity, and representation, integrating local and global building cultures—as well as the broader standardization of building cultures—has very significant consequences for economies, mineral extraction activities, transit routes, infrastructure, energy production and consumption, governments, and even political systems. It has led to specific supply chains, production capacities, innovation, and proprietary knowledge. The result has been new demand, lower costs, and wider variations in quality. The process has given rise to a need to develop and enforce global standards such as ISO, UL, LEED, and WELL that can be used to certify the quality of a building. This is particularly important in the context of public buildings that must

"SUCH AN APPROACH MIGHT ALLOW THE BUILDING TO APPEAR TO COME ALIVE IN AN URBAN CONTEXT WHERE MANY OF THE BUILDINGS APPEAR INERT AND INCAPABLE OF ADDRESSING THAT CONTEXT. THE BUILDING WOULD BECOME PART OF ITS ENVIRONMENT, BOTH BLENDING IN AND STANDING OUT."

TECHNICAL CONTEXTUALISM

withstand considerable wear, that seek to express ambitious form and program, and that must be safe for users. At the same time, global standards of quality are important in the context of a mandate for sustainability, so that they last as long as possible and do not waste the embodied energy of a building when it decays and must be demolished. As global sources of capital have sought to invest in a globalized architecture inspired by the International Style, such standardization has become even more desirable as real estate development becomes an increasingly integral part of how a country can diversify their economy, invest profit from other sectors, create genuine places for people to live, and represent their power and growth on the global stage. As this occurs, it is important to consider how local people have access to or are barred from this globalized space and what these lines of access mean for the society. In our work, we seek, when possible, to expand the presence of public space that is accessible to as many people as possible and that can help support the growth of diverse communities.

Incorporating these decisions into the design process leads to a series of capacities that can be reflected in the finished building. These include a reciprocal exchange of know-how, a bridge between local and global, a capacity to slow down global architecture and give it a greater sense of specificity, and the capacity to create more depth and meaning. The process also creates the opportunity to generate character through a specific experience tailored to the people who will be the prime first users, who in turn attract secondary users that together create the narrative of the architecture and its meaning. These capacities provide a clear, positive alternative to promoting a highly homogenous global architecture intended to serve as a vehicle for capital investment or formal or program-driven architecture intended to create a marketable image that can exist anywhere. Architecture of this type generally seeks to gain attention within the global political economy of images by outdoing previous images.

In attempting to embrace these ambitions in practice, it is important to keep in mind that no culture, building tradition, or context is alike. While common attributes exist, it is important to break down homogenous cultural identity into a specific situation of engaging a client and community through a design process. This makes it possible to understand how best to pursue the research that informs the process; structure contractual obligations and collaboration with local designers and consultants; incorporate advanced digital design tools and digital support services; relate to adjacent fields such as tradition, culture, and art; and reconcile our technical knowledge and values with the local context via a powerful building.

"IT IS IMPORTANT TO CONSTANTLY PROPOSE THE BEST SOLUTIONS TO CHALLENGING PROBLEMS THROUGH AN ITERATIVE PROCESS THAT ALWAYS SEEKS TO REFINE THE QUALITY OF THE DRAWING, DESIGN, AND CONSTRUCTION SO THAT THE BUILDING CAN TRULY BECOME ICONIC—NOT JUST AS AN IMAGE, BUT AS A TECHNICAL OBJECT THAT PERFORMS AT THE HIGHEST LEVEL FOR DECADES IF NOT CENTURIES TO COME."

CHAPTER FIVE

II_NETWORK

What is the relationship between a masterplan and a building? To a certain extent, the relationship is straightforward. The building relates to the city as a part to the whole. The building sits within a plot of land accessed or surrounded by a set of streets and connected to a broader network of streets, water supply, sewer system, energy grid, waste disposal service, telecommunications, internet, and delivery. When, however, none of these systems exists prior to the building—when the city in which the building will live is a future ambition—the relationship is less straightforward. It is not simply a matter of connecting the building to the existing networks; instead, it becomes a question of what that relationship should be, how that connection can be made most efficiently, and whether particular infrastructure networks should be designed in such a way that they serve the buildings of today and tomorrow in a better, more efficient manner.

The capacity to define the relationship between building and master plan allows greater flexibility by creating the opportunity to develop an ideal relationship rather than one defined by the predetermined context. It makes it possible to structure access, energy supply, views, and the relationship between built and unbuilt space in such a way that the building and master plan work in harmony. At the same time, parameters can be put in place that govern how future buildings will be developed. This strategy can be seen clearly in the district of Guangzhou, where the Guangzhou International Cultural Center (GICC) is located. In this case, the city developed a master plan for a new high-rise district where waterways, green zones, pedestrian walkways, mandated setbacks and densities, and rapid

CHAPTER FIVE

transit infrastructure governed how buildings were sited and designed. In responding to these planning requirements, the design sought to pay homage to the green and pedestrian zones through a grounded form that steps gradually to the central shaft of the tower. These stepped terraces are planted to pick up the greenery running in front of the building. The stepped form is further reflected in the design of the lobby, the open, transparent quality of which invites pedestrians to enter.

A very different relationship between building and master plan exists between Wish and its context. The master plan near Shanghai where Wish is sited is defined by a perfectly round artificial lake that forms the focal point of the development. Unlike the district where GICC is located, the master plan governing the placement of Wish is not tightly integrated with the city of Shanghai. Instead, it is defined by a loose network of roads, infrastructure, access points, and landscapes that make up the broader figure of the new master plan. In response to this context, the design of Wish picks up on the utopian nature of the master plant while also opting to create an island-like experience defined by a series of landscapes that frame the building. Both of the master plans in which Wish and GICC are sited were already determined before the buildings were designed.

In each case, there is a chance for an alternative future. It is not merely that there will be something where there was previously nothing, but that there will also be an opportunity for something innovative to arise. While this new relationship between building and context may seem formally novel, it offers a better solution to the problems presented by the client,

CHAPTER FIVE

program, site, and broader urban context than has been proposed in the past. Arriving at a better solution often involves looking beyond the surface of the urban context to uncover latent needs of the city and community that might not have been met by urban space in the past. The result offers the client a solution that is both integrated with its surroundings while also standing out as exemplary in order to attract broader interest. This in turn makes it possible for the new site to build on a deeper history as it becomes a place where people gather and live together for generations to come. Multidisciplinary collaborations are an essential aspect of a successful outcome. We believe in an "urban science" which embodies disciplines that go beyond the traditional structure of architecture and engineering to include psychology, sociology, culture, economics, and public health.

"THERE MUST BE SPATIAL RESONANCE FOR THE FORM TO BE RELEVANT. AND WHEN SPATIAL RESONANCE IS CREATED, IT ULTIMATELY TRIGGERS A LOT OF THINGS AROUND IT. THIS IS THE IDEA OF AN ENDLESS SPACE RADIATING IN ALL DIRECTIONS TO INSPIRE THE NEIGHBOR TO WANT TO BE PART OF THAT EXPERIENCE. IN THIS SENSE, THE GOAL SHOULD NOT BE TO BE THE BIGGEST OR TALLEST, BUT TO DELIVER THE BEST EXPERIENCE AND EXTRAPOLATE IT BEYOND ITS INITIAL LIMITS. THE HIGH LINE IN NEW YORK AND THE 606 TRAIL AND RIVER WALK IN CHICAGO ARE GREAT EXAMPLES."

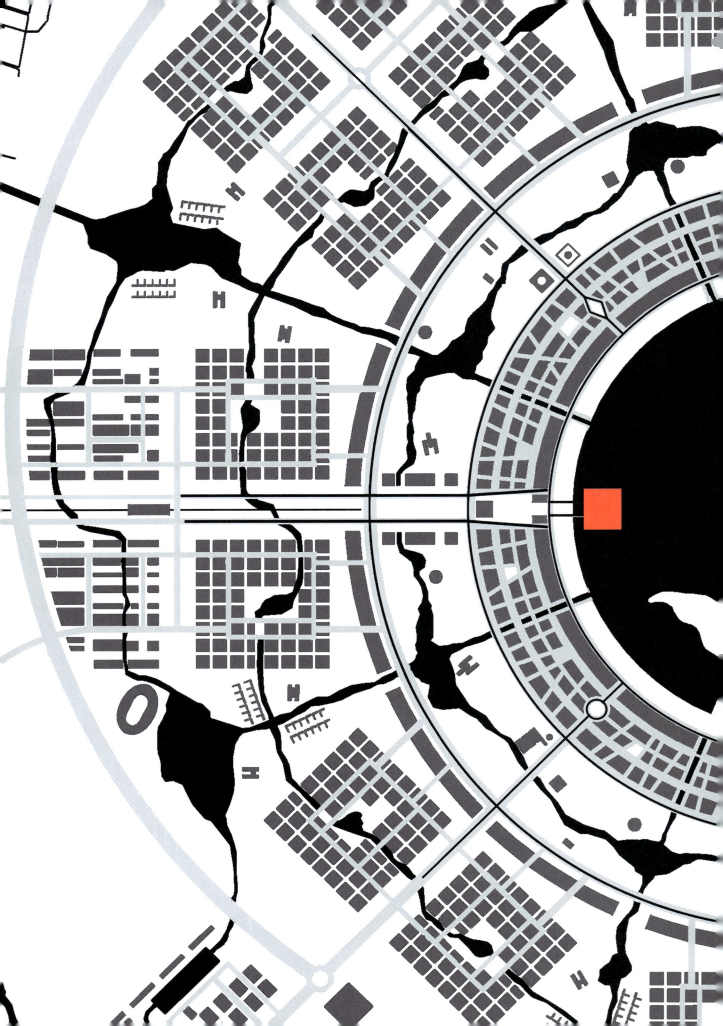

WISH

**HOTEL-RESORT COMPETITION 2014
160,000 M2
SHANGHAI
CHINA**

INTRO

The building known as Wish began several years ago as an invited competition. After several years of remaining on hold, our design was selected as one of two finalists. The project is located in Shanghai Lingang New Town—a new development that aims to attract international businesses and talent. The development will embody national development strategies and incubate developing industries. It will not only serve the functions of cultural facilities, entertainment, offices, and education, but also spaces for technological start-ups and financial entities. The site itself is strategically located in close proximity to airports, seaports, railroads, highways, and subways.

Wish is situated at the west of Dishuihu (Waterdrop Lake). It is meant to be an important architectural landmark in Shanghai Lingang New Town. The architectural form is a combination of perfect geometries that resonate with the shape of Dishuihu. The triangular void in the middle gives the building two additional faces. These new faces are extremely efficient in terms of fenestration, utilizing natural lighting by allowing southern light for residential areas and northern light for office space. In turn, the split wings join to form an apex in the center.

Wish was designed with the future in mind. It is a bold statement that responds to a bold context. Wish is the centerpiece of the lake; it will define the skyline of Shanghai Lingang New Town. The geometry comes from the interplay of three platonic shapes: the square, which is represented by the site, the circle, represented by both the lake and the shape of the building, and finally the triangle, the space between the two wings that opens like a gateway to the sunrise. During the day, Wish shines from east to west like a sun. At night, its image is reflected across the lake and is visible well beyond.

DESIGN

The initial idea was to have a simple disc propped up by a series of structural supports. This approach was then combined with the idea of a podium, which would be required to house the various conference, lobby, and other functions. The structure and facade were quite complex. With the facade, this was due in part to a desire to curve the glass, so that the surface would appear smooth rather than faceted. This would be achieved by limiting the size of the glass panels applying pressure to the edges of the parallelogram-shaped panels prior to construction. The size of the panels, however, had to be carefully calculated so that the correct curvature could be achieved while ensuring that the structural support system remained as light as possible. A great deal of effort went into working out the structure of the facade in collaboration with Werner Sobek.

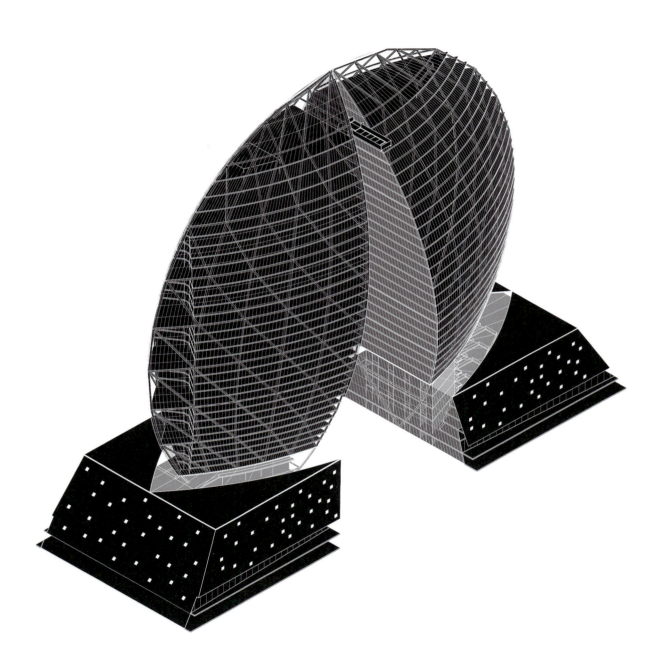

"IN SOME PROJECTS, THE SOLUTION CALLS FOR A UNIVERSAL SYMBOL. WISH IS THE CIRCLE, THE SQUARE, AND THE TRIANGLE; WISH STRIVES TO CONTAIN ALL THAT EXTENSIVE MEANING. WISH EMBRACES THAT TOTALITY: THROUGH ITS 160-METER-HIGH GATE, THE CITY AND THE LAKE ARE CONNECTED IN A SINGLE GESTURE. WISH IS A MIX OF UTOPIA AND CYCLIC MOVEMENT, ALL EXPRESSED IN EVOLVED PLATONIC FORMS SIGNALING TRANSFORMATION."

The final design merges two contrasting geometries and two different material regimes while further enhancing the structural stability of the disc. The trapezoidal podium serves as a landscape of sorts thanks to the greenery that climbs it sides. In many ways, this form was the source for the truncated pyramids that would be used in the Diablos Rojos baseball stadium in Mexico City.

The building's form responds to the natural division between the uses that it contains: the hotel wing faces south; the office wing, north. The overall geometry of the two concave wings is identical. As they reflect the richness of their respective programs, they become unique. As the office space strives for efficiency, so the hotel explores enchanting views through balconies, terraces, and sky gardens. Its concave geometry efficiently absorbs the southern light for living functions and northern light for business activities. The east and west faces are fully exposed. The striking geometry of the concave form, however, raised the question of how to approach the growing depth of the floor plate.

Given that the hotel required a relatively shallow floor plate, the possibility of an atrium and balconies was explored. The podium is not only the structural brace for the wings above, but also contains all the support functions, including exhibition, restaurants, amenities, meeting rooms, and auditoriums. Its architecture and materiality exist in contrast to the transparency of the wings. Punched architectural concrete clad in a green wall screen floats above the clear glass sliver that defines the entrance.

The landscape softly transitions from the organic and extroverted to the formal and introspective. The natural edge that touches the water is undefined, while the fields at the south and north ends of the island are a continuation of nature. A series of curvilinear paths and tall grass provide these fields with an untouched character.

As one gets closer to the east-west axis, the landscape gradually turns into a more formal arrangement of hedges, linear paths, "water steps," and a very formal yet humble grass field that leads to the lake through the wings. From the east and in the distance, the podium becomes part of the topography and the landscape, strengthening the presence of the wings as they emerge from it. An open-air viewing platform facing east provides a place to leave the building behind and reconnect with nature at almost 170 meters above the water level. At the top of the wings, a public space provides unparalleled views to the surroundings. The connecting point at the tip of the wings is not only structural, but also symbolic, as it represents the union of opposites.

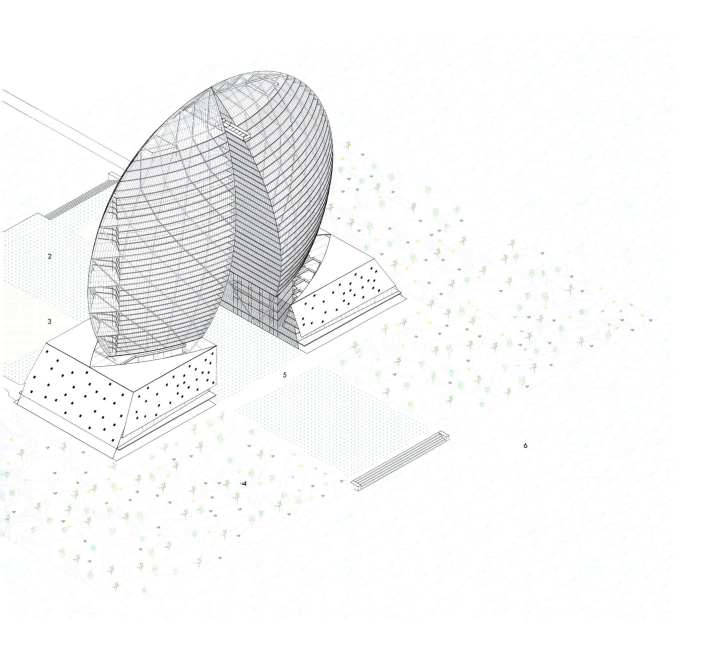

1. ENTRANCE BRIDGES
2. FORMAL GARDENS
3. REFLECTIVE POOL
4. WILD MEADOW MAZE
5. PROMENADE
6. LAKE

In the end, it is something of a hopeful building. The proposal has a certain calmness and is understated through a beautiful simplicity. At the same time, it is still dramatic. The bridge at the top where the two spherical forms meet extends out over the plaza below, uniting two places at the top of the building, creating what would be a natural location for a restaurant or observation deck. In many ways, the bridge completes the building, which is connected by the plaza, then disconnected through the primary volume, and then reconnected at the top.

Intuitively, the design makes the visitor want to be in the space as they enter the building. The gate not only makes a formal gesture to the lake, but also allows it to feel like an important place. From this open plaza, one either moves to the offices or to the hotel. This procession was designed in conjunction with the landscaping concept. The goal of this concept is to transition from the very formal front of the building to the more urban plaza and then on to the more natural, informal section before ultimately arriving at the lake. As a result, the building is rooted in the landscape.

Each wing has approximately 65,000 square meters of area. The carved-out space in the hotel portion responds to the lower floor-to-floor height required, and the setback space is needed to provide the rooms with an outdoor experience. The hotel rooms are smaller in the lower third of the wing, deeper at mid-section, with balconies and terraces, and both shallower and higher in the upper section.

Tom Willoughby—who was with WSP Global at the time—focused on developing the energy strategy and addressing the fact that the facade ran from east to west. This was not the right building for using a twin-shell facade. As a result, triple insulation with Argonne glass in one of the cavities was used to improve performance. Geothermal energy from the lake is used as a source of cooling for all functions, eliminating the need for cooling towers. The vast presence of sky gardens, balconies, and terraces provides a visual and physical connection to the outside, maximizing daylight and promoting a healthier environment through the use of natural ventilation. Automated shades will be incorporated to reduce heat gain and achieve a higher level of energy performance. The podium's massive green wall will also be used as thermal storage to passively support the cooling and heating systems and thereby reduce reliance on active sources of energy generation.

"THE GEOMETRY COMES FROM THE INTERPLAY OF THREE PLATONIC SHAPES: THE SQUARE, WHICH IS REPRESENTED BY THE SITE; THE CIRCLE, REPRESENTED BY BOTH THE LAKE AND THE BUILDING'S SHAPE; AND FINALLY THE TRIANGLE, THE GATE THAT OPENS TO THE SUNRISE."

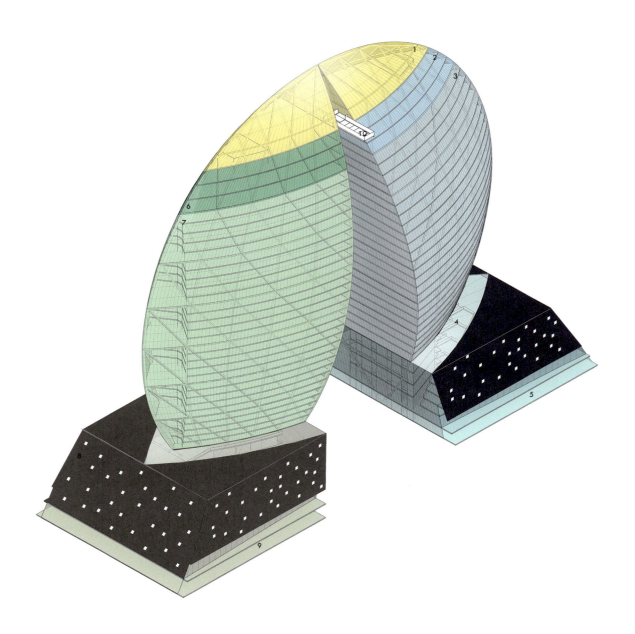

1. RESTAURANT
2. VIP SUITES
3. HOTEL
4. EXHIBITION SPACE
5. HOTEL AMENITIES
6. EXECUTIVE OFFICES
7. OFFICES
8. MEETING / CONFERENCE SPACE
9. RETAIL / OFFICE LOBBY
10. VIEWING PLATFORM

COMPOSITE STRUCTURE
WITH CONCRETE CORES

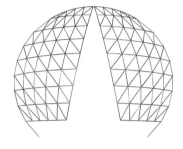
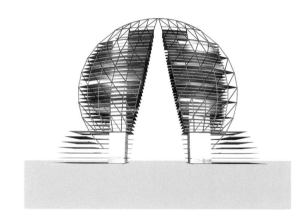

STEEL DIAGRID

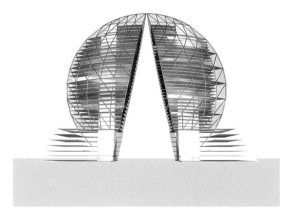

ENVELOPE

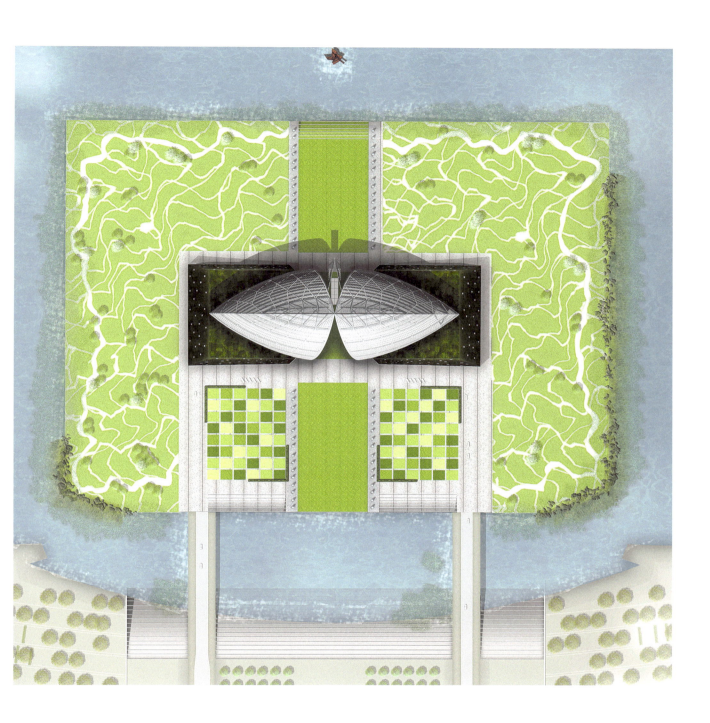

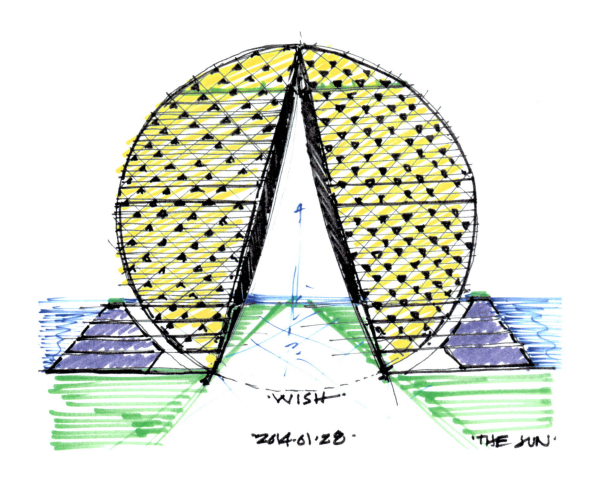
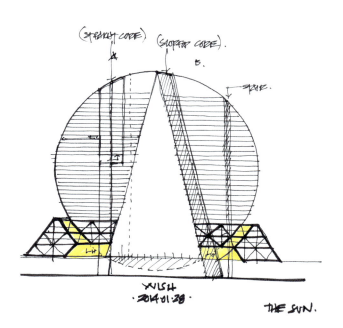
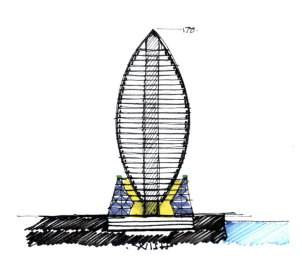

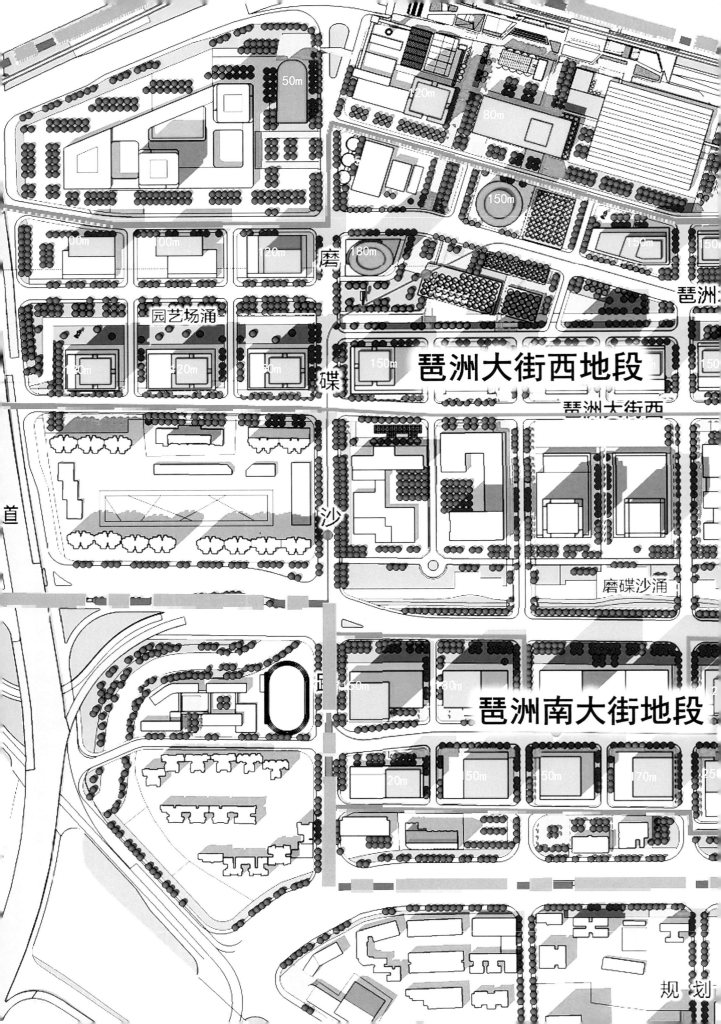

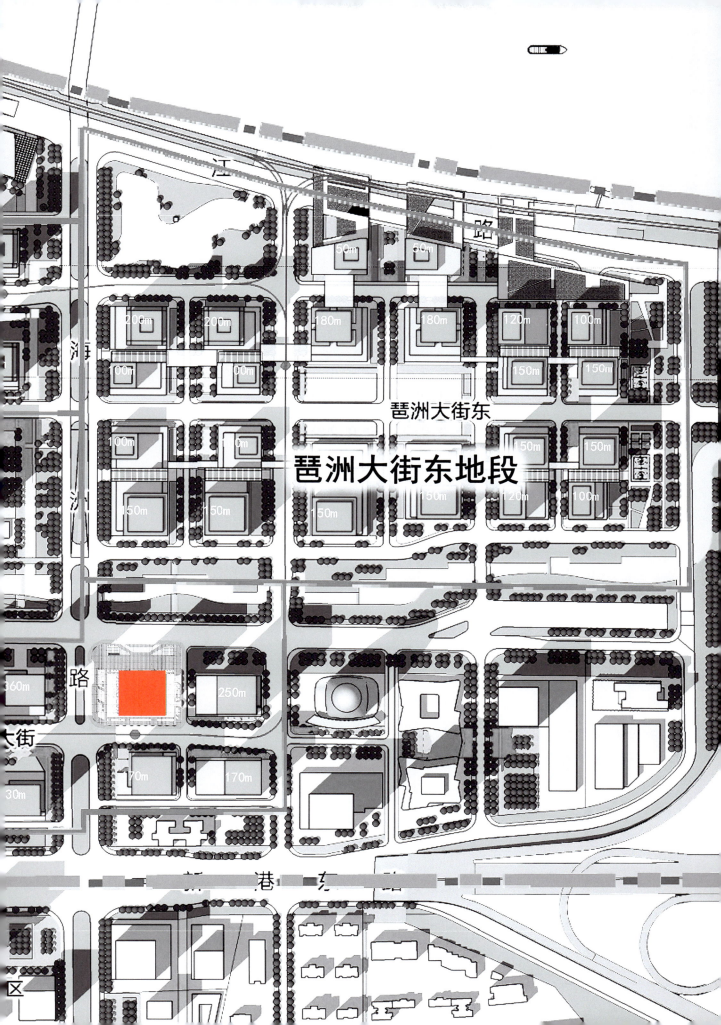

GICC

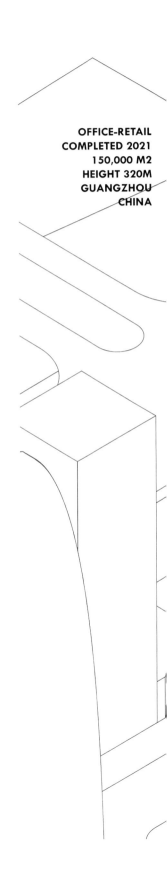

**OFFICE-RETAIL
COMPLETED 2021
150,000 M2
HEIGHT 320M
GUANGZHOU
CHINA**

INTRO

The Guangzhou International Cultural Center (GICC) was designed with a holistic vision in mind, in which architectural, engineering, environmental, functional, and technological principles respond to each other to create a timeless landmark. The building offers a place for human interaction in a tower "campus" comprised of a plaza, underground arcade connected to the subway station, forty-five-meter-high lobby, multi-level bookstore, sky lobby, and sky club. The goal is to achieve harmony and dilute the boundaries between public and private space. The design strives for urban openness, physical and spiritual connectivity, simplicity in functional organization, clarity in the use of materials and systems, efficient use of space and resources, and responsiveness to climate and orientation through a highly tailored building skin.

The site is located along a canal that branches off of the Zhujiang River. The tree-lined roadway Shuangta Road lies to the immediate north and connects the site to the small Modiesha Park (East Gate) to the west and the much larger park in front of the Guangzhou International Convention Center to the east. As such, Shuangta Road forms the primary axis of the zone and connects the site to the Convention Center. More broadly, the site sits within a district defined by the Zhujiang River to the north, the Huangpuchong waterway to the south, which bends to form the western boundary along Liede Avenue, and the S303 highway to the east. The building is situated in a context of similarly tall buildings in a rapidly developing section of the city. In order to enhance its connection to the city, a large public plaza is provided in front of the building's north facade. This urban gesture responds to the master plan guidelines. The lush green landscaping that runs along Shuangta Road is integrated into the site via a sunken garden surrounding the retail area.

DESIGN

GICC is the first development built by Southern Publishing and Media (SPM)—a prominent Chinese publisher. The program called for a bookstore to showcase their publications, speculative office space, a sky lobby for the publisher, office space for the headquarters, and a sky club. The bookstore is located over the first three levels in a podium that steps towards the shaft of the tower. The tower itself is anchored by a logical and efficient core. The facade is designed to address each of the cardinal directions to meet desired energy performance requirements. This occurs through horizontal fins on the east and west facades. By contrast, the north and south facades emphasize the verticality of the building while letting light and views flood the interior spaces. The building's footprint and massing were further defined by the city's planning limitations, which designated the setback from the street and the integration with the subway as well as the height of the building.

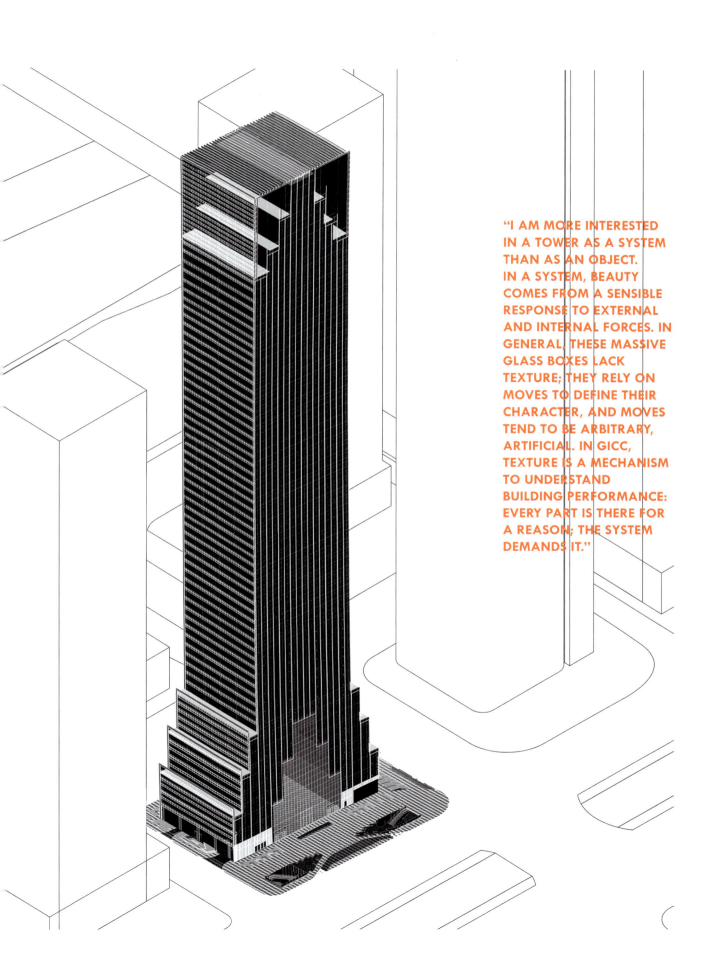

"I AM MORE INTERESTED IN A TOWER AS A SYSTEM THAN AS AN OBJECT. IN A SYSTEM, BEAUTY COMES FROM A SENSIBLE RESPONSE TO EXTERNAL AND INTERNAL FORCES. IN GENERAL, THESE MASSIVE GLASS BOXES LACK TEXTURE; THEY RELY ON MOVES TO DEFINE THEIR CHARACTER, AND MOVES TEND TO BE ARBITRARY, ARTIFICIAL. IN GICC, TEXTURE IS A MECHANISM TO UNDERSTAND BUILDING PERFORMANCE: EVERY PART IS THERE FOR A REASON; THE SYSTEM DEMANDS IT."

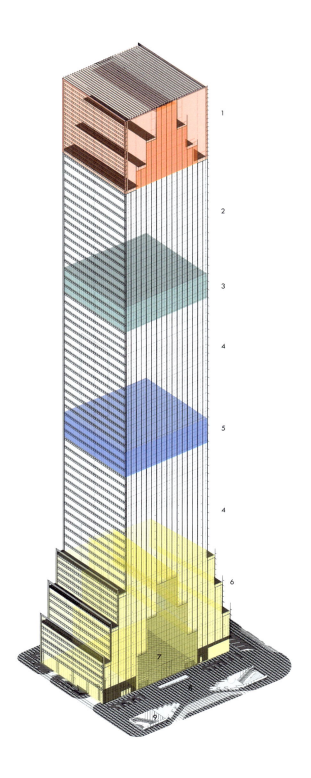

1. SKY TERRACE AND EVENT SPACE
2. HEADQUARTERS
3. MECHANICAL AND SKYLOBBY
4. OFFICE SPACE
5. MECHANICAL
6. PUBLIC PROGRAM
7. ATRIUM LOBBY
8. PLAZA
9. SUBWAY ENTRANCE

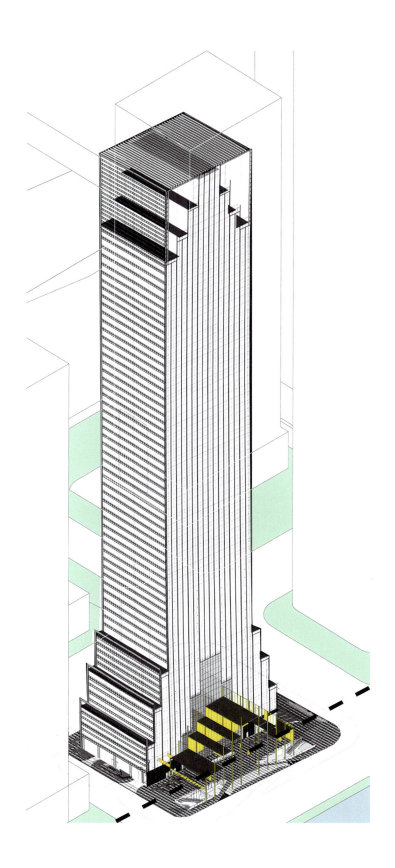

URBAN CORRIDOR + PROPOSED EXTENSION OF PUBLIC PROGRAM

The stepped design of the building is not only ideally suited to this cultural program, but also suggests the theme of ascent and the quest for knowledge. Its form is driven by the idea that sharing knowledge is essential to the formation of culture. Through culture, it is easier to overcome barriers and to grow and ascend as human beings. The articulation of the building as a peak also allows for a series of terraces with breathtaking views of the city. These terraces are sheltered by a series of screens that provide protection from the wind and rain. They also create a dynamic tension between the peak and the resolution of the building as an ideal rectangular form. Beyond creating functional green spaces, the stepped form of the building's peak creates a unique relationship between the lobby and the stepped terraces at the base of the building, giving the entire object a sense of cohesion across its large scale.

GICC is an expression of the client's cultural values. From the outside, its image is solid, classic, and inviting. It alludes to the idea of a company that is not a passing trend, but one that will stand the test of time—as will the solid mass of its building. The concept of the interior is a logical extension of the building's exterior. Just as the building reflects the idea of a company that is people-oriented, sober, and unique, the interior integrates the building's spaces and architecture, embracing their character and becoming a representation of these values in the everyday use of the space. The finishes, configuration, and materials used in the interior define the light and sound of the space, shaping the way each person in the building will perceive and interact with it.

In articulating this vision, the majority of the spaces reflect a consistency of materials and overall feel, with differentiation occurring in how these spaces are detailed. The exception to this rule is the grand lobby, which is given its own character and identity through the use of light-colored stone and a dynamically folded and illuminated large-panel system that covers the walls of the core and forms the primary backdrop of the north and south lobbies. The remaining spaces in the building makes use of darker materials and smaller panels. These spaces emphasize the continuation in the interior of the horizontal and vertical themes that define the exterior. Throughout the building, soft, mirrored aluminum finish is used on the columns; the elevators are defined by glass doors; aluminum strips are utilized on the floor of the lobby to form a visual connection between interior and exterior. In the public spaces, linear lights are used above a metal mesh ceiling that runs along a north-south grid, while in the basement and exterior spaces, linear lights are set in the ceiling plane.

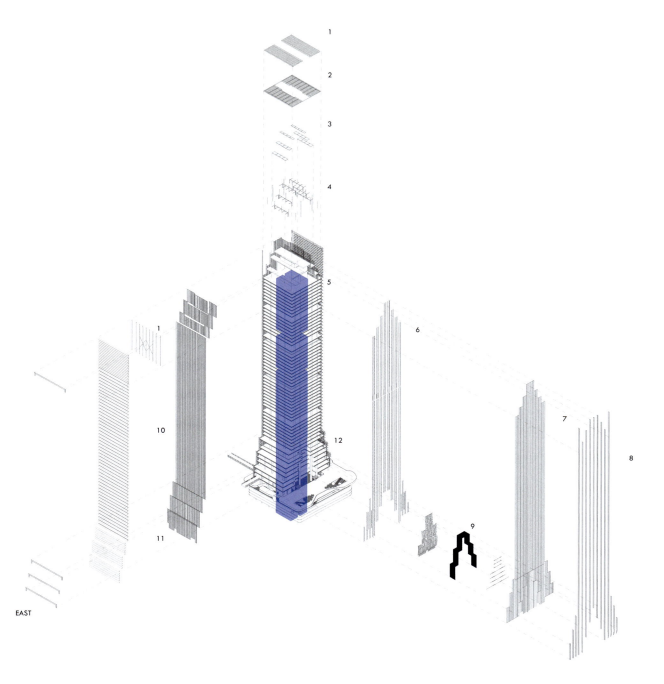

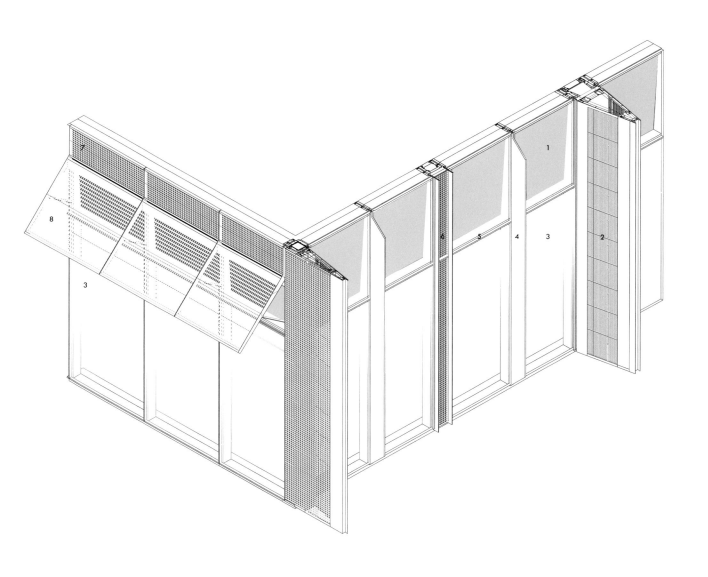

1. SPANDREL GLASS
2. PERFORATED STAINLESS STEEL MAIN PIER WITH INTEGRATED LIGHTING
3. VISION GLASS
4. SOLID STAINLESS STEEL EXTERIOR FIN
5. STRUCTURAL GLASS JOINT
6. U-CHANNEL EXTERIOR MULLION
7. PERFORATED STAINLESS STEEL SPANDREL PANEL
8. PERFORATED STAINLESS STEEL EXTERIOR SUNSHADE

In building the city, height has become the ultimate choice in developing density. Height has become an instrument for advancing technological progress and innovation. However, when it is disconnected from the dynamics of context and culture, height can become a superficial quality. More and more often, skylines are responsible for branding a city, but not necessarily for creating a place. GICC, by contrast, integrates architectural, engineering, environmental, functional, and technological principles to create a timeless landmark that serves not only the needs of the client but also the community at large.

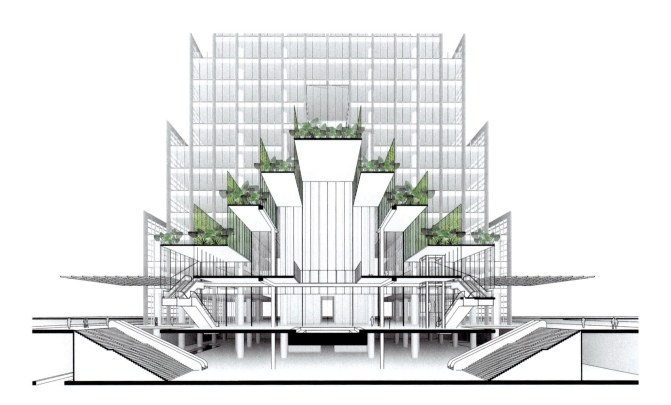

"THE STEPPED FORM OF THE BUILDING IS NOT ONLY IDEALLY SUITED TO THIS CULTURAL PROGRAM, BUT ALSO SUGGESTS THE THEME OF ASCENT AND THE QUEST FOR KNOWLEDGE. THE FORM AND SHAPE ARE DRIVEN BY THE IDEA THAT SHARING KNOWLEDGE IS ESSENTIAL TO THE FORMATION OF CULTURE, AND THAT CULTURE MAKES PEOPLE UNDERSTAND EACH OTHER BETTER—THAT, THROUGH CULTURE, IT IS EASIER TO OVERCOME BARRIERS AND GROW AND ASCEND AS HUMAN BEINGS."

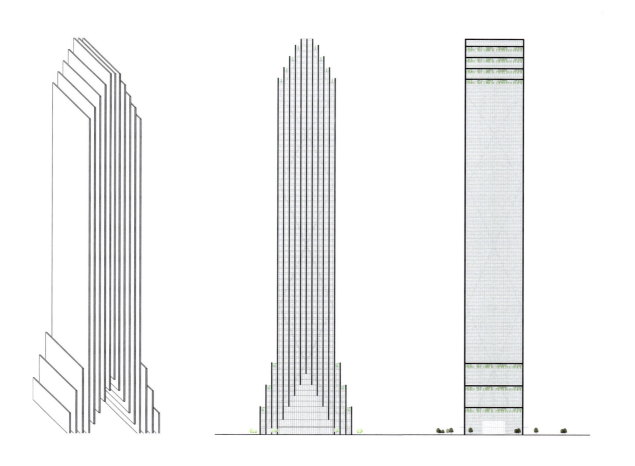

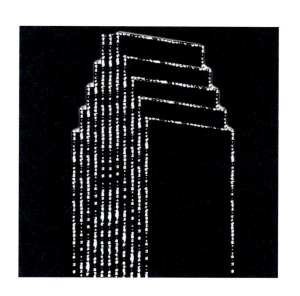
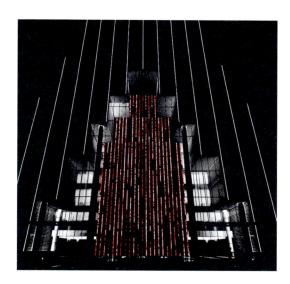
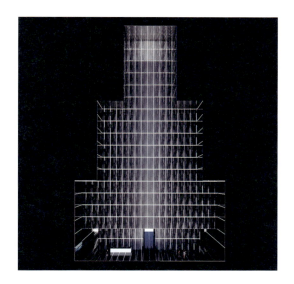
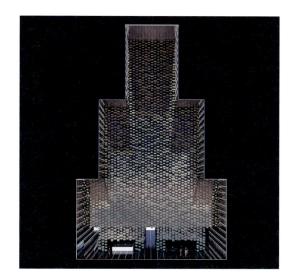

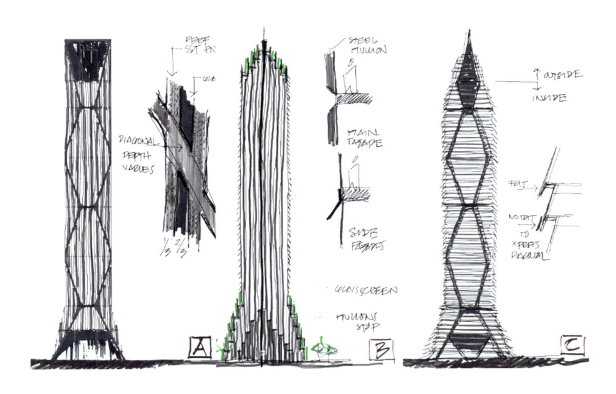
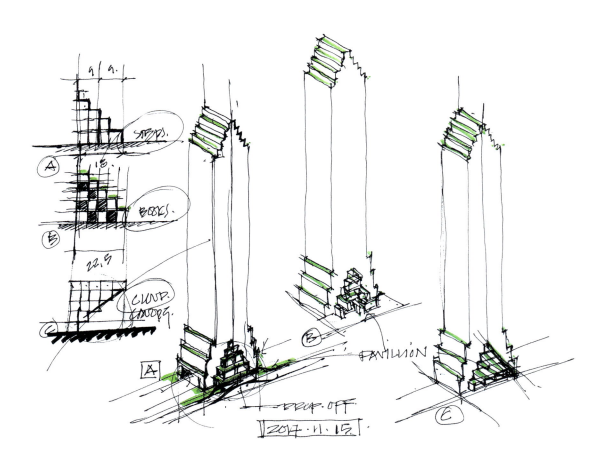

ALTERNATIVE FUTURES

The concept of "master planning" is somewhat problematic. The word "master" connotes a top-down strategy that has the capacity to anticipate a variety of future occurrences and demands in such a way that a successful framework of infrastructure, parcels, and amenities can be constructed to meet those demands. At the same time, the word "planning" is rather ambiguous and has referred to discourses ranging from interpreting statistics and setting policy to discussing urbanism and how one might design urban features. In this sense, planning can refer to setting a social agenda as well as the desire to build a new public plaza with a fountain or turn an unused train line into a park.

The concept of "master planning" has come to be associated with a century of grandly conceived plans for a wide range of cities. At the same time, these strategies have found echoes in efforts to build massive new cities in Asia and the Middle East as well as efforts to fill in sections of American cities that might have once been used for industry, infrastructure, or public housing, but that now lie adjacent to highly valuable property as a result of growth and revitalization and the shift of manufacturing overseas. While many of these frameworks have led to vibrant cities, the rigidity, monumentality, and homogeneity of others has led to cities and neighborhoods lacking life, diversity, and sustainability.

The core challenge of building cities lies in the fact that it is difficult to predict what will happen in the future. Technological developments can cause society, work, and urban form to take a variety of directions. Habits can lead to interest in living in an area with a particular density. Mobility patterns and abilities can lead people to cluster or disperse. The way that societies resolve conflicts can lead to a need to live in a certain manner. Furthermore, the stories that are told to motivate us and give meaning to our lives, while perhaps eternal, are always finding a contemporary expression that drives our collective desires. And, as new pressure is placed on the built environment by a changing climate, the way that people build and live will evolve in unpredictable manners.

At the same time, there is a strong temptation to create urban form that will shape how people live and, in the process, reduce indeterminacy. The hope is that the new framework will help to create habits that benefit society as a whole. This can be seen in Robert Moses's desire to deploy a network of roads across the New York Metropolitan region, his plans to create parks and beaches, and his efforts to develop thousands of affordable housing

ALTERNATIVE FUTURES

units. The negative effects of failing to listen to the people already living on the land he sought to develop—and those who would live in the units—also impacted the ultimate success of these plans.

In this context, there have been a number of attempts to refocus the way cities are built and designed, moving away from pieces of rigid infrastructure and towards more flexible strategies. These modes of urbanism seek to be more aligned with the variables that might affect a future. They aspire to get to the source by looking beneath the surface via analytic methods rather than solving an apparent problem with form. Some examples include digital master planning, ecological urbanism, socially engaged, community-based organizing and planning, and narrative urbanism. Each has sought to take a particular angle that will inform the tools used to design and implement a plan for the city of the future. They have sought to do so in such a way that the framework can evolve through interaction with a range of variables that reflect changing externalities.

Although there have been signs of conceptual progress in terms of rethinking how cities are planned, limited master planning has taken place in the United States outside the large-scale mega developments that private developers have been building in great numbers. Beyond these private developments, the primary concern is around zoning, economic development, reclamation of brownfield sites—and to some extent the planning of new neighborhoods and districts through the integration of some program, often related to art, culture, food, or entertainment—in conjunction with a private partner. The primary problem is a lack of integration, which leads to an inability to think across scales and explore the impact that decisions have on different groups. The result is an inability to create a unified model that can support enhanced productivity.

As a result of not having a central authority such as a municipality or planning commission interested in driving such an agenda, fragmented agencies and departments, which are often interested in competing ideas, and politicians drive the planning process. They often fail to see basic maintenance or a bold vision for the built environment as issues that can get them elected. This leads to enhanced power being placed in the hands of those private groups that are able to coordinate reinvestment in the built environment. At the same time, it leads to disinvestment in many neighborhoods that desperately need maintenance and new projects to address a range of problems, from housing shortages to a lack of affordable housing and insufficient community support and educational services.

ALTERNATIVE FUTURES

In this context, it is important to ask what an integrated approach would look like. At a fundamental level, such an approach would seek to combine some of the strategies mentioned earlier. Each of these approaches has a set of associated tools that can be utilized collectively to address different challenges facing the built environment and its inhabitants. These modes of urbanism can be integrated through FGP ATELIER's principles of 1) a systems-based strategy that aims for efficiency, transparency, openness, community, education, and lightness achieved via traditional means as well as the most advanced technology; and 2) an atmospheric approach that seeks to manifest those principles as a quality of space that is a lived experience. Such an experience is not an end in itself, but rather the zero point from which a broader narrative can unfold. This process is often facilitated by mediation. Historically, this mediation has occurred without coordination or integration and largely outside the purview of a designer, architect, or planner. In the essay "Pervasive Media," it is argued that designers should advocate for the control and planning of these mediating functions. It is also suggested that doing so would create a departure point for broader planning efforts. Introducing a story for the future of a community together with an engagement plan around that story could be an entry point that does not require the much broader investment needed for the implementation of a total plan, and it might even create or propel an economy that can support such a plan.

In order to integrate various past approaches through the use of mediation and narratives driving engagement with the city, an integral urbanism should be further codified. Beyond being an urbanism that uses mediation as a tool, it is an urbanism driven by the way people move through space, construct space, and are constructed by space. This approach is driven by interaction and addressed to experience. It values the tactile, touch, the haptic, contact with the ground, the walls, the earth, and the sky. It is driven by what it feels like to connect parts of the city. These are the paths and cues that orient us in space. They allow us to navigate and define habits of navigation and motion that are culturally specific. They help us to understand the elements that code a section of the city for a particular use. Together, they define the rhythm, the walkscape, and the way that they are constructed by and construct the lives of those who live there. This approach also helps us to see the class boundaries that are coded into the configuration of the city. It helps us to uncover the mythology of the city through places with specific value in particular parts of the city that are invested with narrative and poetry. Together these sites create a further level of orientation.

ALTERNATIVE FUTURES

As a whole, this type of approach stresses the value of encounter—with both the familiar and the unexpected. It helps us to understand the way that the city appears—both in terms of vistas that might exist and allow the city to show itself in its totality, and in terms of ways that it is represented. This makes it possible to understand the ways in which the city is fragmented and how it appears discretely. This determines how the city is hidden, how it fades into the night, what has vanished over time, what only locals know—the secrets, both good and bad. In essence, such an approach to urbanism seeks to provide a bridge between the body and the world that accounts for the logic that governs architecture and body. This occurs through an understanding of both spatial theory and how our mind operates, how value is derived, the process of understanding purpose and meaning, and the means of accounting for our origin and existence. In the process, particular attention is paid to those objects and media that can form a connection between these different realms.

On the surface, the 2020 pandemic might give pause to the idea of basing a planning practice on encounter, the tactile, or social engagement. However, as an approach that is derived from the needs of the body, it is in fact ideally suited to the moment. In this approach, the organization of space stems from the phenomenal perception of the body in space, rather than being dictated from above according to a more Cartesian approach. In the context of the pandemic, the specific needs of the body have changed, while the need for contact and connection have remained. In this sense, nothing has fundamentally changed. However, an opening has occurred that may create room to reevaluate the way planning is approached.

"I THINK THAT SOMETIMES WE ARCHITECTS PUT TOO MUCH EMPHASIS ON THE WAY THAT WE FORM THE PARTS AS OPPOSED TO HOW WE CONNECT THE PARTS. THAT EXPERIENCE, BETWEEN THE PARTS, IS GENERALLY MUCH MORE GRATIFYING THAN THE BUILDINGS THEMSELVES."

CHAPTER SIX

II_NETWORK

It is somewhat hard to fully distinguish whether infrastructure or buildings came first. In some ways, the migratory paths of early communities of humans could be seen as primitive roads facilitating a particular way of life. Roads, bridges, water supply systems, waste removal systems, energy production and distribution, and telecommunications and media networks, among others, evolved over several thousand years of recorded history. This evolution was driven by and supported growth. In many cases, the ability to harness various forms of energy made it possible to enhance agricultural output and sustain growing populations. As these networks became more complex, the infrastructure itself had to evolve and become increasingly technical. Historically, designing bridges, walls, and aqueducts might have been the responsibility of a multidisciplinary profession. As this infrastructure became more complex, however, this work became the purview of professional engineers. Architects, unfortunately, were increasingly relegated to the realm of aesthetics.

The relationship between architects and engineers changed dramatically during the twentieth century. Taking an approach that blends architecture and engineering has been an integral feature of our work presented in this volume. The opportunity to work specifically on a piece of infrastructure presented a unique opportunity to advance this relationship through an integral design approach. Harmony Bridge is intended to be a showpiece for the city of Guangzhou—a rapidly developing commercial and cultural hub in China. The brief called for a two-kilometer-long bridge across the Zhujiang River. The bridge would connect two crucial sections of the city as well as an island park.

CHAPTER SIX

The client wanted a solution that would be both functional and iconic. The result was a piece of infrastructure that explores the idea that a single piece of information, in this case sound waves, can inform everything from design to how the user moves, how the city functions, and even the city's overall capacity for growth, communication, interaction, economic strength, and unification.

In order to achieve this vision, Arup was brought on as a consultant and a multidisciplinary team was assembled. The design team explored a variety of methods of translating harmony into a visual form that could dictate the shape of the bridge were explored. The fins forming the skin were designed with three identical hinged segments that were derived from the form of waves. A deck covered with wide wooden planks was designed to stretch out into the viewing platforms and reach into the landscaped island. This approach would allow the bridge to generate an interactive harmonic sound as cars and people pass by: their respective vibrations transmit energy into the fins, which then vibrate and create sound. As this design progressed, consultants helped to optimize the structural system. Finally, a lighting artist designed a system addressed to the human scale to help travelers find harmony and focus on the music of the everyday that they otherwise might miss.

The oscillating nature of the waves balances the pedestrian and driver experience while crossing the Pearl River along the axis that ties the east and west ends of the city together. As the traveler listens, the promenade's deck offers a dynamic and sensuous procession by slightly rising and falling in relation to the roadway and by sliding in and out of its finned skin.

CHAPTER SIX

II_NETWORK

The pedestrian discovers unique vantage points from which to view the city. The viewing platforms allow the passerby to escape traffic, engage with the place beyond its physical limits, and find a moment of peace and solitude. The resulting design aspires to become a metaphor for harmony within the city of Guangzhou.

With projects such as the Harmony Bridge, it is important to consider the broader population that it will serve, its role in the urban infrastructure, and the way that it embodies our design principles and creates the possibility of an exceptional experience. In this sense, although the bridge may not actively reshape the way society develops, equitable wages, and access to affordable housing, it will hopefully serve as an inspiring experience for all, and, through the access to the green space that it provides, create equal opportunities for all to enjoy the natural environment of Guangzhou.

The notion of equality in infrastructure is something of a latent theme in the history of urbanism. Quite often, focus is placed on how infrastructure will support growth, enhance spending power, transform undervalued real estate into a neighborhood that will attract a new demographic, and create eye-catching showpieces as anchors of new developments. New projects rarely invite designers to create a piece of infrastructure that will address inequality. While there are numerous competitions for projects that generate innovative solutions to building for a range of demographics, few of these projects ever find funding. The ideas generated in the process often remain confined to the realm of academia.

CHAPTER SIX

This is particularly problematic because of the role infrastructure has played in creating divisions in cities, serving some neighborhoods better than others, creating profits during construction for exclusive groups, and generally contributing to the maintenance of existing power structures. In this context, it is important to continue looking for speculative opportunities to consider infrastructure. These projects are a chance to engage with a form of advocacy that will hopefully contribute to the positive transformation of the built environment.

II_NETWORK

HARMONY BRIDGE

BRIDGE COMPETITION 2016
2 KM
GUANGZHOU
CHINA

INTRO

Harmony Bridge is inspired by sound and harmony. The structural forms are organic and beautiful, modern and complex. The story behind the design of the bridge is a metaphor—one of harmony for Guangzhou. Harmony Bridge will be a tool for creating growth, communication, interaction, economic strength, and unity. It will do more than connect two points. It will unite people, allowing them to flow in harmony with both nature and city.

Guangzhou is a city of realized visions, a city where spirit endures through architectural icons. It is a city passionate about the beauty and mystery behind grand schemes, aiming endlessly towards the sky and across the landscape. The most ancient form of timber bridges are log bridges, which are created by felling a tree over a gap that needs to be crossed. Historical bridges also play an important role in the cultural life of the area where they have been built, providing meeting places for residents to exchange information, worship, and entertain. Harmony Bridge respects the history of ancient Chinese construction while providing an innovative icon for the city of Guangzhou.

The bridge will be one of the longest paths across the Pearl River and the linkage that will tie the city together across its west end. The design originates at the intersection of opposing forces: the technical and the natural, the formal and the informal, the horizontal and the vertical. The bridge is not only a connection between two points, but also reaches out to form multiple links to the landscape of the island and the river's shore. It is not only about traffic, but about people. It challenges the main direction of traffic by creating strong nodes and a network of pedestrian paths. It creates balance between contemplation and traffic. At the same time, the bridge will provide an interactive, harmonic sound created by passing cars and pedestrians as their respective vibrations transmit energy into the ribs. Finally, Harmony Bridge provides the possibility of finding a moment of peace and solitude in the middle of Guangzhou's dynamic urban artery. As one seeks to find harmony within oneself and with others, life becomes endless music.

DESIGN

Modularity and ease of construction guided the approach. Every rib of Harmony Bridge is different, but each is built using the same three segments. The total length of the bridge will be clad on both sides with vertical ribs spaced at variable intervals from 800 to 2,400 millimeters. The experience of the pedestrian walkway is both dynamic and sensuous: it gently rises and falls in relation to the roadway, softly shifting in and out of its ribbed skin. The ribs will be constructed as composite sections made by laminating two wooden blades on either side of a stainless-steel rib. The ribs and the promenade

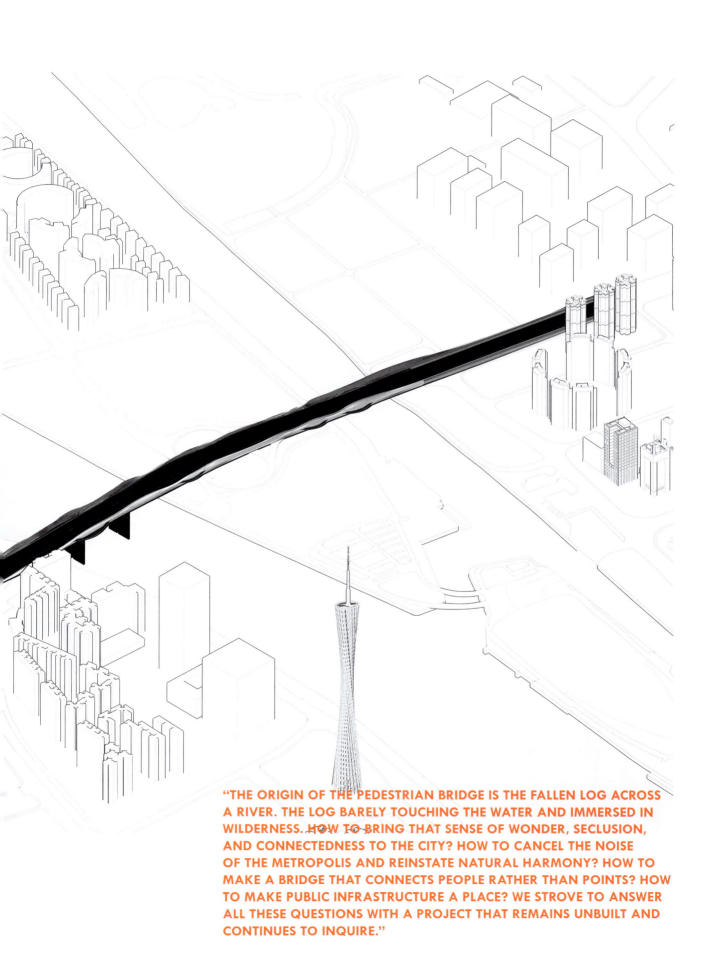

"THE ORIGIN OF THE PEDESTRIAN BRIDGE IS THE FALLEN LOG ACROSS A RIVER. THE LOG BARELY TOUCHING THE WATER AND IMMERSED IN WILDERNESS. HOW TO BRING THAT SENSE OF WONDER, SECLUSION, AND CONNECTEDNESS TO THE CITY? HOW TO CANCEL THE NOISE OF THE METROPOLIS AND REINSTATE NATURAL HARMONY? HOW TO MAKE A BRIDGE THAT CONNECTS PEOPLE RATHER THAN POINTS? HOW TO MAKE PUBLIC INFRASTRUCTURE A PLACE? WE STROVE TO ANSWER ALL THESE QUESTIONS WITH A PROJECT THAT REMAINS UNBUILT AND CONTINUES TO INQUIRE."

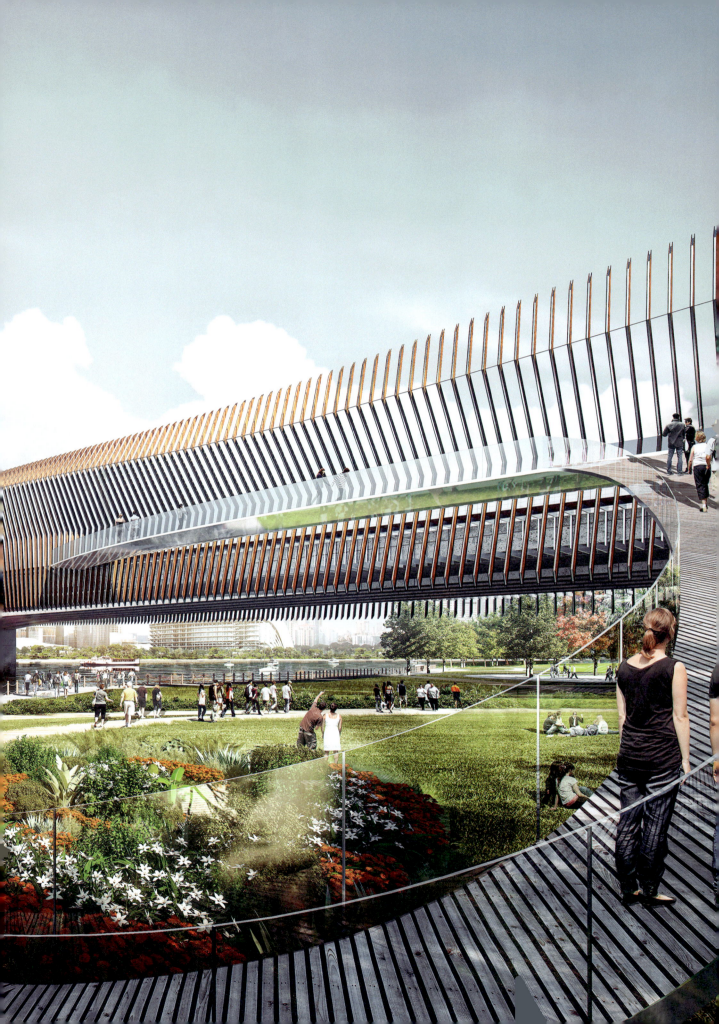

deck will be supported from the outer edge of the existing bridge's primary beams using hollow steel sections in cantilever. At times, the pedestrian walkway will be higher than the roadway, providing a sense of seclusion. Disconnecting pedestrian from vehicular traffic allows people to focus on the distant, echoing sounds that are orchestrated by the river and the city. The viewing platforms will allow the passers-by to escape traffic and engage with the space beyond its physical limits.

The landscape design is more than just a pattern of hardscape and softscape, it is an urban intervention that creates program in unexpected places. This approach is a powerful strategy for doing more than just connecting two points. It provides all the possibilities of interaction throughout the dynamic journey across. The landing points could be amphitheaters, playgrounds, retention basins, skateboard parks, extensions of extinct ecosystems, and much more. The design is based on that of the existing park, with its round garden and seating areas.

The theme of circles dominates the design of the park and the bridge. Circular elements with different uses such as a Zen Garden, a labyrinth, a yin-yang garden, a botanical garden, and play areas are added to complete and unify the landscape concept for the park. These elements include small plazas with fountains and seating areas for common activities or outdoor spaces for restaurants. The existing tennis fields are integrated in the new park and surrounded by hedges and other plantings. Fields for other sports activities such as football and climbing are also provided. In the eastern part of the park, trees have been planted to complete the wooded park landscape. Organically shaped paths connect the different spaces with the bridge and the river. On one side at the end of the bridge, there is a walkway for pedestrians to cross the road safely. Other small paths connect the bridge with the park. At the exit point, small gardens and plazas mark a connection to the park. On the banks of the river, circular terraces and landing stages are provided for boats.

The artistic lighting is recessed within the outer edge of the ribs to illuminate an urban icon on a colossal scale. The program lighting is recessed in the inner edge. It is soft and discreet and in tune with the human scale. The bridge connects the city at its very heart. It crosses the river, a sort of liquid monument at the origin of the city's existence. It is altogether a tool at the service of movement within the city as much as a support for circulation flows. It enables the dynamism of urban movement. Once night falls, all these elements shape a massive sculpture, and the bridge metamorphosizes into a grand signal on the scale of the city itself, inhabited by a soft, poetic pulsation. This pulsation derives from the urban energy of flows, soothing and settling the rhythm. As one crosses the river, walking on the bridge becomes an everyday event, a soft animation, an atmosphere of sensations that brings us closer to nature and nearby water.

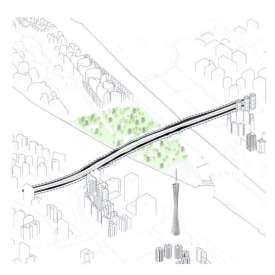
DYNAMIC SHAPE DERIVED FROM PENTATONIC SCALE

PEDESTRIAN AND VEHICULAR FLOW + ACCESS POINTS

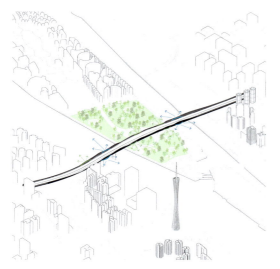
OBSERVATION DECKS

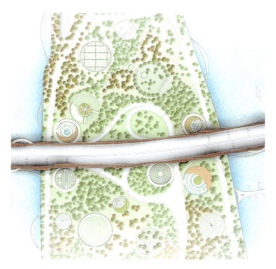
LANDSCAPE

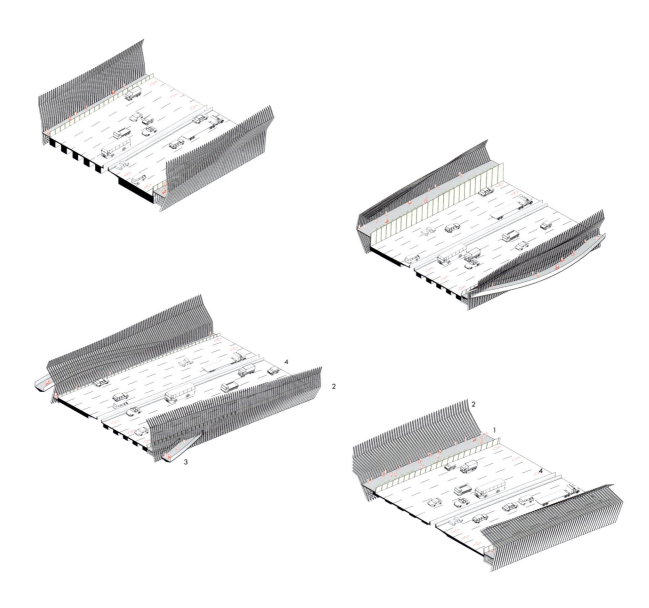

1. UNDULATING PEDESTRIAN PATH / ELEVATED PARK
2. WOODEN SKIN
3. SUSPENDED OBSERVATION DECK
4. VEHICULAR DECK

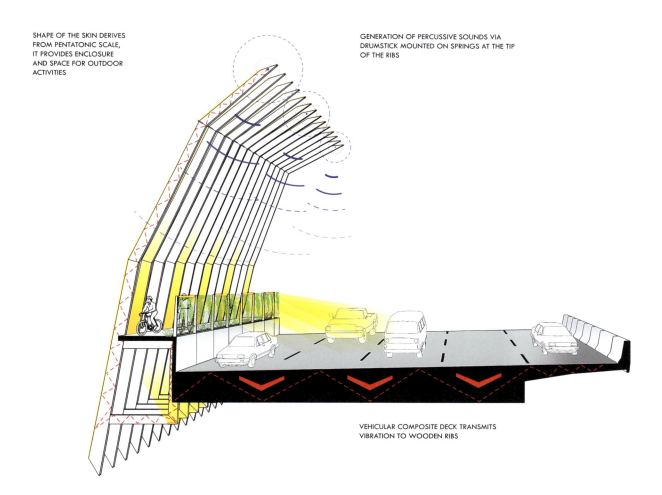

"IN COLLABORATION WITH THE LIGHTING ARTIST YANN KERSALE, THE PROPOSAL WAS TO SHOOT A VIDEO OF THE RIVER THAT WOULD THEN BE PROJECTED ONTO THE FINS. NORMALLY, A BRIDGE IS REFLECTED IN THE WATER, BUT IN THIS CASE THE WATER IS REFLECTED ON THE BRIDGE."

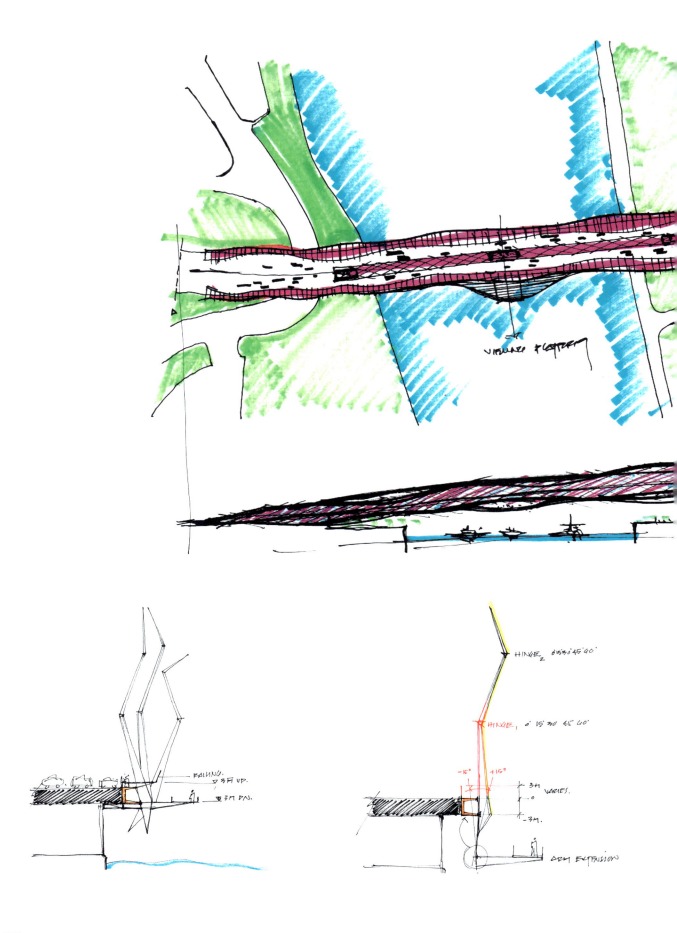

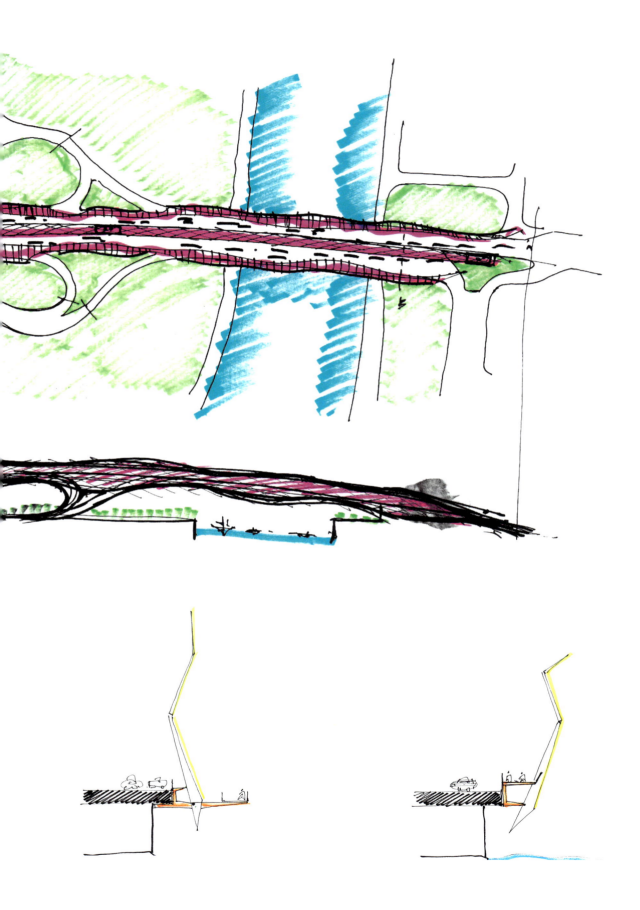

INFRASTRUCTURE AND (IN-)EQUALITY

Too often, the work of building and rebuilding our cities occurs in isolated parcels of varying scales driven by the ambitions of investment and profit. Direct spending by city governments mostly takes the form of infrastructure maintenance or tax incentives to developers to build projects. Rarely does a cohesive vision for a city or regional plan emerge.

This situation is unfolding in the context of a number of mega projects that have received national attention. These projects have drawn billions of dollars in investment and exist in light of a national affordable housing crisis that is making it difficult for many people to live near their jobs or in neighborhoods their families have called home for many decades. Many mega projects have been criticized for creating uninspired buildings anchored by amenities such as ultra-luxurious shopping malls, new cultural destinations, and exclusive green spaces. Even potentially transformative works of public art that might be seen as positive contributions to the cultural landscape have been met with skepticism as a result of their extreme cost and lack of a clearly positive impact in cities beset by extreme and increasing inequality.

Several projects in Chicago offer the broader city these opportunities and potential drawbacks. Many of these projects are situated along the Chicago River, are mega developments occupying a significant amount of land, support diverse typologies, are situated in former industrial areas, and would create an opportunity to bridge disconnected neighborhoods. These mega developments are taking place after a period in which few projects of this scale were attempted.

Common to many of these developments is the transformation of land and buildings once dedicated to industrial, meatpacking, and other food-related uses. While these industries once needed to be in close proximity to customers, logistics and customer bases have changed. It has also become increasingly difficult to get large trucks into those areas. Prices of this real estate are rising rapidly, which in turn makes it possible for owners to relocate. The redeveloped and new buildings have become quite attractive to many large companies, in part as a result of the large, open plans of historic loft buildings and the large blocks that have allowed developers to build large, uninterrupted spaces. These open plans and the capacity to house entire teams on one floor are conducive to trends in contemporary office design, both in Chicago and beyond.

The result of these trends is enhanced density that places greater stress on existing infrastructure, affecting infrastructure in close proximity as well as the system as a whole. It also increases the supply of different types of

INFRASTRUCTURE AND (IN-)EQUALITY

asset classes that could affect broader prices. At the same time, an enhanced sense of place with new amenities could make the area more attractive and lead to rising prices that could displace existing residents. This all occurs in the broader context of decaying infrastructure, ranging from overpasses to bridges, train lines, and urban lighting. The result could be a situation in which developers improve islands of infrastructure while receiving large tax breaks but fail to improve the system as a whole.

In this context, architects and urban planners need to think of ways to support development efforts while also combatting some of the negative effects. This is something explored in several of our recent projects. With the Qiantan Enterprise World Phase II in Shanghai, a campus was created with porous boundaries and a high level of connectivity with the surrounding area. The scale of the plaza is addressed to the body of the visitor, and public space are distributed across a series of levels connected by stairways to support a diversity of experiences. This strategy was also employed with the Diablos Rojos stadium, which is connected to the community through its form and through the way the stadium is programmed to include a market for the local community and discounted tickets for those living nearby.

In the context of larger infrastructure projects, FGP ATELIER has explored innovative ways of integrating infrastructure with broader programs to enhance the quality of life. This was the case with Harmony Bridge, which is integrated with a park and designed in such a way that it also functions as an artwork: the motion of the cars generates sound that can be experienced while crossing on foot or by car, and when illuminated at night, its image can be seen from a distance.

The developers behind these large-scale projects have adopted a similar strategy. They are integrating new transportation infrastructure and are also including cultural destinations. In many cases, they have taken steps to incorporate feedback from the existing community, which has led to the inclusion of more affordable housing and the reduction of height. At the same time, greater effort might be made to integrate these new developments with broader enhancement of the urban fabric. One way this might occur is by experimenting with new revenue models and digitally enabled capacities within the confines of a new development. These could become models implemented on a broader scale, potentially enhancing revenue for the city. One example is the revenue generated by bus stops throughout Chicago and other cities. Another might be the use of an upgrade to street lighting as a platform for new apps.

"HARMONY BRIDGE IS ABOUT CREATING AN EXCEPTIONAL AND PHENOMENAL EXPERIENCE THAT CALLS THE EXPECTED INTO QUESTION. IT IS ABOUT THAT MOMENT, A SPARK, WHEN ONE REALIZES WHAT IS HAPPENING—HOW THE BRIDGE IS PERFORMING—AND, IN THE PROCESS, UNDERSTANDS THE MAGIC OF THE BRIDGE."

INFRASTRUCTURE AND (IN-)EQUALITY

It is also important to consider the relationship between infrastructure and affordability, not just from the perspective of whether affordable housing is being built, but also whether places to live are being created in accessible areas connected to jobs. It is somewhat unfortunate that the political will and capital to invest in infrastructure that might serve communities which have faced disinvestment over the last half-century have not materialized. While this may be due in part to a lack of a cohesive plan for the city and financial policies that have prioritized other expenditures, it is also the result of the failure to imagine how a more multi-centered city could function. At the same time, investing in new infrastructure such as train lines, bus rapid transit, and public parks sometimes generates fear of rising property taxes and displacement. Combatting this potential fear would require a genuine set of policies and empowerment of local stakeholders. It might also require investing in lighter forms of infrastructure, such as free public Wi-Fi, which could provoke a gradual process of transformation.

These questions are even more essential given the 2020 pandemic. Infrastructure, perhaps more than ever, plays a crucial role in combatting illness and protecting people. It is essential to maintain strong supply chains supported by well-maintained transportation infrastructure. This infrastructure must be powered by clean energy that supports clean air, which in turn will reduce the risk of respiratory infections. At the same time, it is important that this infrastructure be increasingly resilient, both from a physical and an operational perspective, so that it can handle shocks to the system. This means that planning for these eventualities must secure monetary and human capital during non-stressful times so that they may be effectively deployed during disruptive events. These resources are often unequally deployed to different communities. Some neighborhoods have far greater access to transportation, food, and healthcare. To address these inequalities, it is essential for those who are being supported to take on greater social responsibility, both on an individual level and through electing officials who can effect such change on a broader level. One step towards this end might be to reevaluate tax-based financing and consider strategies of redistributing wealth to benefit a wider range of people within cities.

Beyond the specific nature of the infrastructure being built, it is important to consider the political, financial, and economic climate that might support such infrastructure. While promises have been made on a national and local level to make much-needed investment, little has happened. Moreover, it has been difficult for people to agree on what type of infrastructure should be created and who it should benefit. Should we build more levees to protect floodplains

INFRASTRUCTURE AND (IN-)EQUALITY

for increasingly common storms, or should we invest in infrastructure that allows us to live symbiotically with a changing climate? Should we support investment that improves the lives of the rural poor, or investment that makes the hearts of wealthy cities more attractive? Should we construct pipelines that transport energy, or build walls to help prevent illegal immigrants from entering the country?

The first step in answering these questions is to depoliticize them by removing them from a discourse littered with buzzwords and ideology. Instead, it is important to shift these questions to an arena led by planners, economists, sociologists, ecologists, and architects in order to have a rational conversation that will lead to a plan that can be deployed, tested, and revised. Of course, even with an arena and expertise for developing an infrastructure plan, it is essential to have a funding model to realize the vision. While the US government has been helpful in financing new roads, train lines, and energy infrastructure, and while there is increasing interest from private equity in financing infrastructure, there is not enough capital available to accomplish all that is required. One problem is that many banks refuse to invest in communities they consider risky. While once happy to lend to home buyers, these same banks hesitate when it comes to investing in the broader infrastructure and spaces in which business and life might grow. In this context, some have suggested the idea of a public bank that could be used to finance the construction of new infrastructure as well as support broader community development. Such a community bank could draw on the existing funds that cities invest with traditional commercial banks and set up their own specific criteria concerning risk, return on investment, and what types of enterprises they are willing to invest in to generate a return. This might allow for investments to remain local and enhance the quality of the community and, in the process, attract additional members.

The first step towards reinvesting in infrastructure and using this investment to enhance equality and even development across urban neighborhoods is bringing the fragmented planning agencies, foundations, think thanks, educational institutions, stakeholders, and design professional into greater alignment through a planning process that could generate a new plan for the city. The second step is to advocate for more equitable and long-term investment in a wider range of communities, as well as the people of those communities, empowering them to own their own homes and provide a far more stable and resilient home in which to live. In doing so, it is essential to continue to address the systemic failures of our society and advocate for the greater equality of all.

CHAPTER SEVEN

Our work is driven by creating different types of spaces in which people can engage in the activities that support a specifically human existence. This is not just a matter of providing food and water, but also of giving meaning to where and how one lives through narrative and poetry, making and maintaining that space through the use of tools, creating room for gathering, being with one another, and generally forming a habitat that is suited to our nature. Doing so goes beyond just creating four walls and a roof. These elements must reflect underlying values and support the broader dissemination of those values in order to support the existence of a wider and perhaps expanding group of people as part of a community.

This philosophy is reflected in the design of Casa M5. This project was executed with very limited financial resources and a quick construction time frame. In order to stay within the budget, a design-build strategy was adopted in which no formal drawings were produced. Instead, sketches were made and given directly to the contractor to build. The result is a home that conveys a sense of quality and luxury without costing a great deal. This approach guides a broader philosophy of housing and the question of housing for those with limited means in particular.

Casa M5 provided an opportunity to develop a low-tech, highly contextual solution leading to an ambitious home on a limited budget. While the economy of its construction can be applied to the broader question of how housing is designed, a more high-tech solution to the housing crisis facing cities around the world is explored in Spacecraft and Monarca.

CHAPTER SEVEN

Spacecraft began as a commission from Porcelanosa to showcase their products. Rather than simply design a kitchen or bathroom, the project proposed a modular housing unit outfitted with compact technology to support a highly efficient lifestyle within a minimal amount of space. This module became the basis of developing an entire building that could accommodate various configurations to address different family sizes. Monarca, on the other hand, provided an opportunity to explore a modular approach in the context of a high-end apartment development. The modular approach made for a very efficient building from the perspective of both constructability and energy efficiency.

These three projects suggest that a combination of a low-tech, design-build approach, a high-tech, modular approach, and the deployment of such a modular approach in higher-end settings, while fragmentary in themselves, might begin to address the broader housing crisis that society faces. On one hand, this is to say that simple, inexpensive structures built in a DIY manner may be appropriate for some contexts, while others might require a more manufactured, modular approach. The housing crisis, however, is not strictly a problem related to space we build to live in. It is tied more broadly to the structure of society and cities. It has also been affected significantly by new technologies and applications that have changed how we live, work, and move through the city. Through a deeper investigation of this transformative process and by employing a wide range of technologies and digital tools in addition to the conventional tools available to the architect and planner, it might be possible to create a platform and policy that guarantee the right to housing and promote broader generosity in society towards those with limited means.

CHAPTER SEVEN

II_NETWORK

Such a strategy would ideally empower people to take control of the space they inhabit rather than forcing them to deal with landlords and other power structures that stand between them and their right to live somewhere. It would, in essence, dis-intermediate the relationship between people and the place in which they dwell. This is a situation already afforded the wealthier members of society through home ownership. Homeowners are able to profit from this situation through appreciation and the option of renting out the space they own. A socially empowering strategy would remove the mediation of real estate in the process and create the opportunity to reframe this mediation through an alternative platform that, ideally, would be a publicly held asset. The question of what such a platform and its business model would look like is a concept explored in greater detail at the end of this chapter in "Housing Platform."

"WHAT FASCINATES ME ABOUT MASTER PLANNING IS THAT IT IS THE BEGINNING OF HOW TO USE THE EARTH'S RESOURCES SMARTLY. I THINK THAT, IN GENERAL, ARCHITECTURE TENDS TO NEGLECT THE VALUE OF WHERE IT IS SITED. THERE IS ALWAYS A HISTORY AND AN ECOSYSTEM THAT EXISTS PRIOR TO THE CURRENT INTERVENTION. THESE SYSTEMS HAVE RULES, STRUCTURE, AND FORM. BY ADOPTING A SMART STRATEGY, YOU CAN TAP INTO THEM AND USE THEM TO MAKE THE NEW MASTER PLAN FUNCTION BETTER THAN IF YOU JUST APPROACHED IT AS A BLANK SLATE."

SPACECRAFT

INTRO

Spacecraft began as a commission from Porcelanosa to feature their products in an innovative design. The design that resulted is for a highly efficient, compact living space that can be configured in different ways to accommodate various functions throughout the day. The design is a departure from the typical bathroom and kitchen spaces used to showcase Porcelanosa products; this space is one in which people can live. It utilizes natural materials such as quartz for the "wetbox," stone for the floor, and wooden screens for the walls. The two most interesting elements of the system are the "wetbox"—the centralization of all the technical equipment—and the screen that provide shade, views, lighting, storage, working surfaces, and a hanging system. As the screens unfold, they become work surfaces, a dining table, a kitchen counter, and a shelving area. The screens provide privacy on the wall that would include the fenestration. It is also pulled away from the solid walls to create a place for storing belongings. The bed unfolds from the quartz "wetbox," while the whole volume is mounted on a track to support the reconfiguration of the space.

In order to arrive at this solution, an analysis of the way people use a limited amount of space was carried out in order to determine the amount of space they need for a range of functions. This analysis built on the concept of "elastic space," developed by González Pulido while still a graduate student at Harvard. The goal of this elastic space is to contract and expand based on current needs. This elasticity would be achieved in part by moving the central volume housing the wet services to accommodate different programs in accordance with how the space is divided or unified. In the process, the space's materials and surfaces could adapt to its changing functions. This flexibility is enabled by a series of modular units that can be added or subtracted; they also accommodate shelving for different functions.

Having built a prototype, the module was used as a basic unit for a residential building. The 300-meter-high building has sixteen apartments per floor. The structure of the building is a spaceframe that accommodates each individual unit. There will be a series of different unit configurations across the floors. This will create a sense of randomness. The building's modular system can be repeated in a variety of manners within a broader building envelope. The spaces can be expanded or contracted to suit different demands while also connecting to other common or private spaces to enhance the functionality of the space or provide greater privacy. As this occurs, the relationship between the interior of the space and the walls at the perimeter of the building can be varied in order to create different degrees of transparency and privacy.

**MODULAR LIVING
CONCEPTUAL DESIGN 2015
37,600 M2
EUROPE**

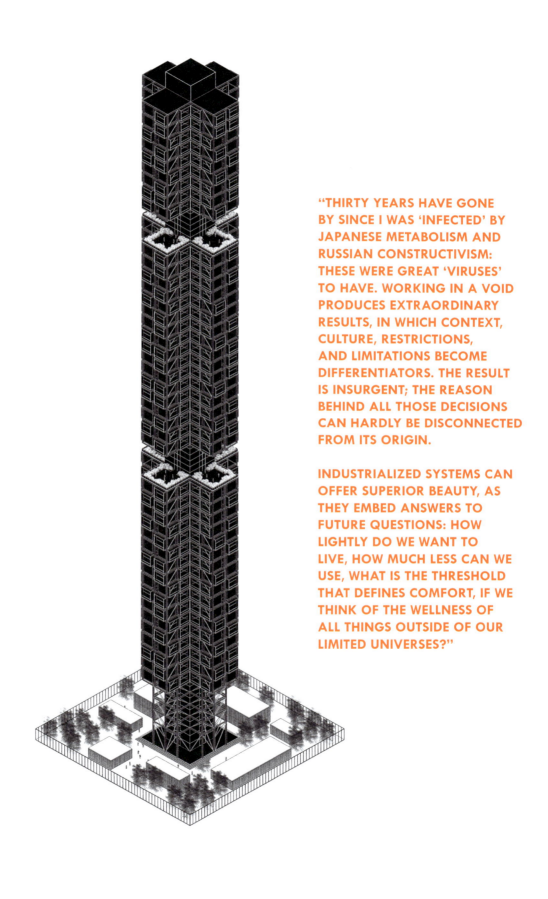

"THIRTY YEARS HAVE GONE BY SINCE I WAS 'INFECTED' BY JAPANESE METABOLISM AND RUSSIAN CONSTRUCTIVISM: THESE WERE GREAT 'VIRUSES' TO HAVE. WORKING IN A VOID PRODUCES EXTRAORDINARY RESULTS, IN WHICH CONTEXT, CULTURE, RESTRICTIONS, AND LIMITATIONS BECOME DIFFERENTIATORS. THE RESULT IS INSURGENT; THE REASON BEHIND ALL THOSE DECISIONS CAN HARDLY BE DISCONNECTED FROM ITS ORIGIN.

INDUSTRIALIZED SYSTEMS CAN OFFER SUPERIOR BEAUTY, AS THEY EMBED ANSWERS TO FUTURE QUESTIONS: HOW LIGHTLY DO WE WANT TO LIVE, HOW MUCH LESS CAN WE USE, WHAT IS THE THRESHOLD THAT DEFINES COMFORT, IF WE THINK OF THE WELLNESS OF ALL THINGS OUTSIDE OF OUR LIMITED UNIVERSES?"

Ultimately, the module units are sited within a tower structure that builds on the legacy of the Metabolists. The structure itself is, in this sense, quite conventional. The innovation lies in going beyond the Metabolists' tendency to attach the capsule units to the trunk by designing various common spaces that will appeal to a millennial resident while also allowing for more customization and flexibility of the unit itself. A high level of spatial and energy efficiency results from this modular system. At the same time, a great degree of creativity is given to the inhabitant through the way in which they are empowered to configure the walls, select finishes, and move the central volume over the course of the day. Such a system might be particularly impactful within dense urban situations where rents continue to rise rapidly. In implementing such a solution on a broader scale, it would be important to consider ways of ensuring that prices remain affordable rather than using the capacity to fit as many people into a building as possible as a tool for maximizing profit.

The modular units distributed throughout the tower are complimented by a series of ground floor amenities and elevated gardens that break up the modular units at two points along the vertical height of the tower. The ground-floor amenities include a fitness club, common lounge and entertaining space, a convenience store, and space for small retail. The amenities sit within a landscaped space defined by a series of mature trees. Collectively, the ground floor provides an animated horizontal experience in contrast to the verticality of the tower rising above.

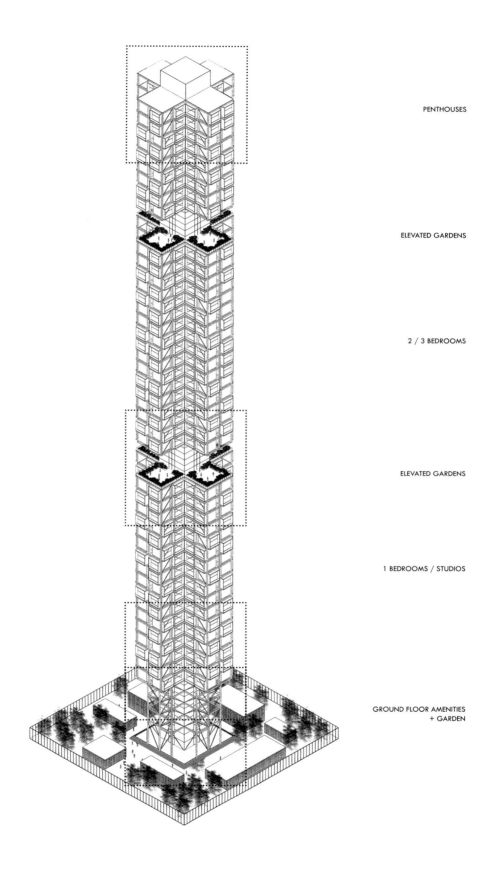

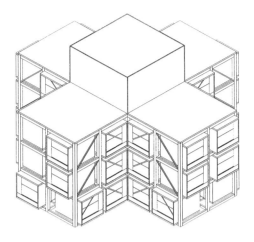

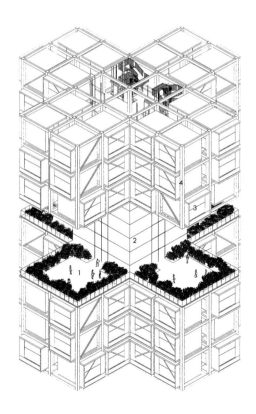

1. ELEVATED GARDEN
2. MECHANICAL AND VERTICAL CIRCULATION CORE
3. PREFAB LIVING UNIT
4. COMPOSITE SKELETON

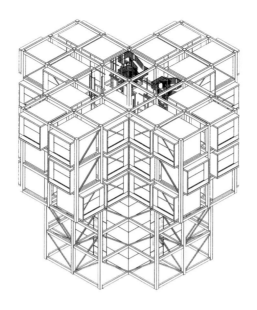

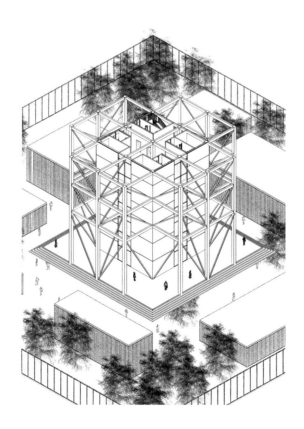

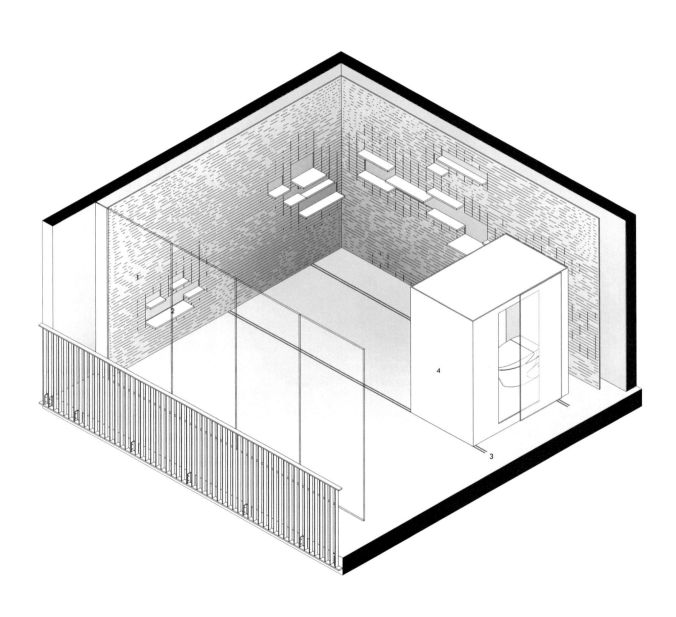

1. PERFORATED WOODEN WALL PANEL
2. OPERABLE SHELVES / SURFACES
3. WET BOX RAILS
4. QUARTZ WET BOX

16 UNIT PLAN DIAGRAM

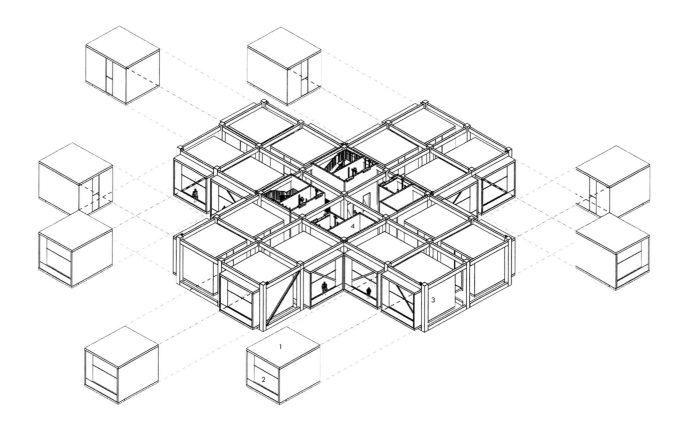

1. 5M X 5M MONOMATERIAL PREFAB UNIT
2. BALCONY WITH GLASS ENCLOSURE
3. COMPOSITE STRUCTURAL EXOSKELETON
4. MECHANICAL AND VERTICAL CIRCULATION CORE

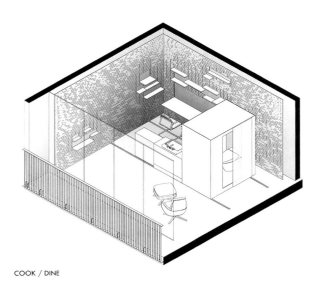

COOK / DINE

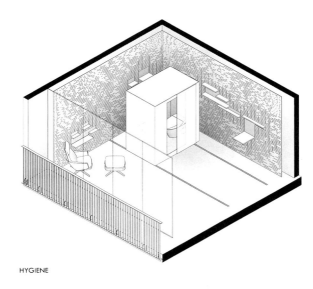

HYGIENE

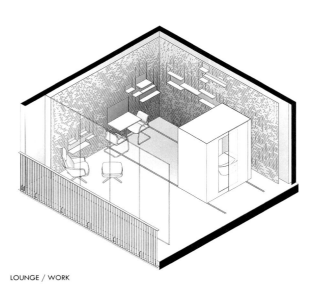

LOUNGE / WORK

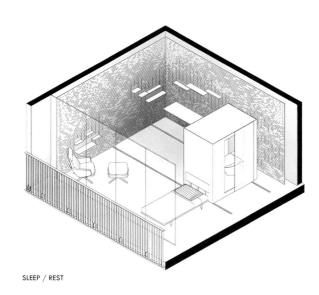

SLEEP / REST

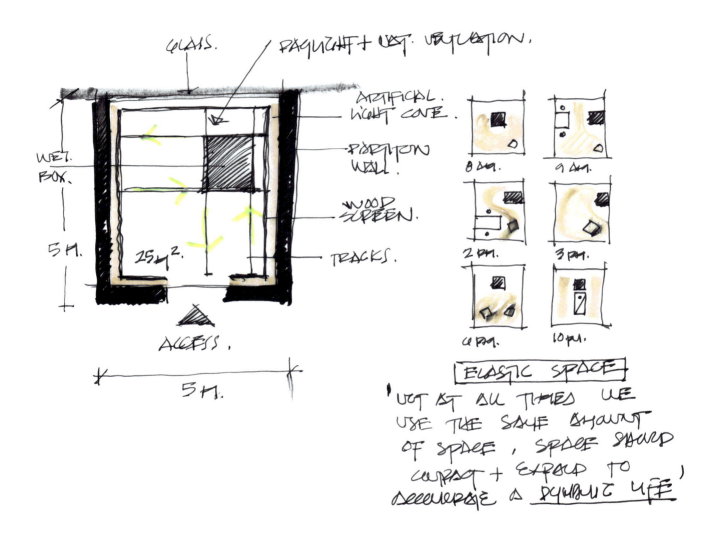

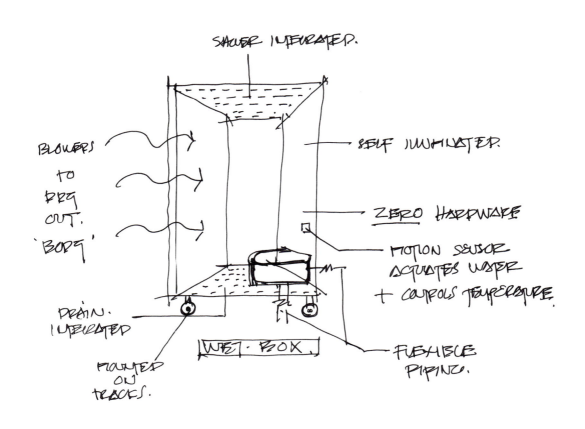

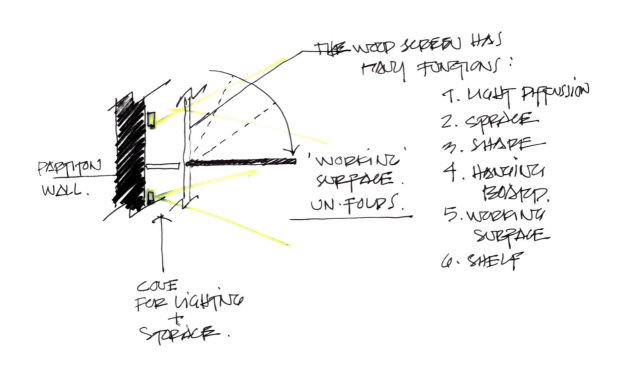

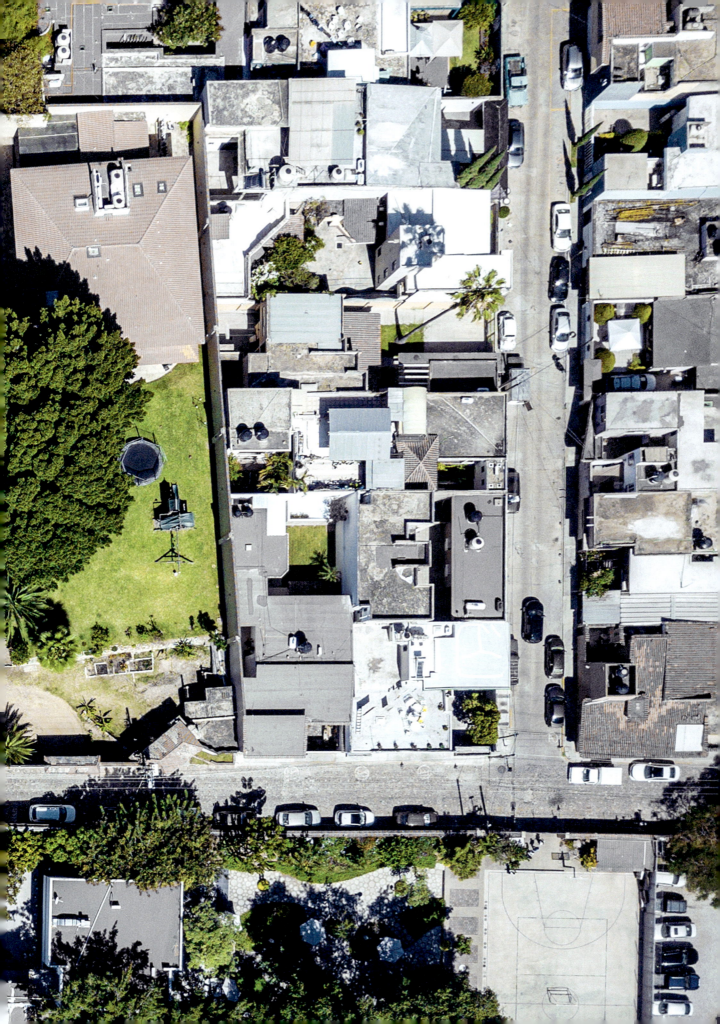

CASA M5

**RESIDENTIAL
COMPLETED 2013
500 M2
OAXACA
MEXICO**

INTRO

Located in Oaxaca, Mexico, Casa M5 is sited in the city center's main quadrant. The clients, Manuel and Maribel, wanted a new home with sufficient room for their three children, Manu, Miguel, and Marina—hence the name, M5. The clients had long owned a noted art gallery in Oaxaca and, through their involvement in the arts, had accumulated a large, diverse, and significant art collection. As a result, the new house also needed to be able to effectively display this collection.

The immediate neighborhood is largely residential. The surrounding properties include houses of varying scales. Some are quite large and are organized around a central courtyard and garden. The property immediately to the north is large and heavily wooded. Most of the properties sit behind a high wall that hides private activities from those on the street.

When the project began, the site was occupied by an existing summer house from the nineteen-thirties. There was no historic or architectural value to the house. As a result, the decision was made to tear the house down and begin anew. With this decision, however, came a desire to retain the historical typology of a house organized around a central garden and situated behind high walls that protect the privacy of the inhabitants and create continuity with the other houses on the block. After deciding to tear down the house, the decision was made to preserve many of the elements of the house and incorporate them into the new structure. This included solid wood doors, bathroom sinks, glass mirrors, brick, and even some furniture. In addition, the pool was preserved and restored. The house in turn was built around it.

The house was designed as the intersection of two ideas: a living gallery (spacious and with ample wall space) and a summer house (open and informal). The total area is approximately 560 square meters organized across two levels. The dramatic change in elevation from the north to the south boundaries of the property resulted in a project that was cantilevered, raised, and leveled in relation to existing site conditions. This created opportunities to introduce passive cooling strategies throughout the house, such as thermal mass and cross-ventilation cooling.

The project is divided into three indoor program spaces—the rear wing, the front wing, and the lower quarters—as well as three outdoor program spaces—the front, rear, and lower gardens. The rear wing is oriented east-west and houses all the private spaces—bedrooms, bathrooms, walk-in closets. It is raised 0.75 meters to allow the north wind to cool down the slab at night through radiation and to lower the temperatures of the bedrooms, thus

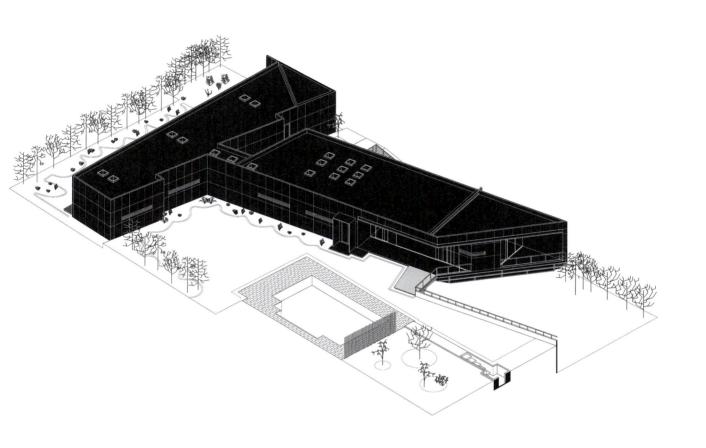

"I NEVER UNDERSTOOD WHY, WHEN THE WORLD OUTSIDE IS DYNAMIC, MOST BUILDINGS' RESPONSE IS STATIC. M5 IS A BUNKER AND A GALLERY, A HOME AND A GARDEN. ITS PREEXISTING BOUNDARIES—CLIMATIC, VISUAL, ACOUSTICAL, AND FUNCTIONAL—PREDETERMINED THE FORMAL RESPONSE OF ITS ENVELOPE AND DEFINED ITS MATERIALITY. M5 IS NOT ONLY A DIAGRAM IN PLAN; IT IS ALSO A SYSTEMS DIAGRAM. THE ELEMENTS OF DESIGN ARE CLEARLY THE ELEMENTS OF CONSTRUCTION; THE DIALOGUE IS MORE SCIENTIFIC AND LESS STYLISTIC."

eliminating the need for fans or air-conditioning. All the rooms in the rear wing were designed with large glass openings towards the back and front yards to allow cross-ventilation while capturing the predominant southeasterly winds.

The orientation of the wing also responds to the idea of creating a private zone for the family, the back garden. This goal is reflected in the thin strip windows facing the garden, which give the private area a bunker-like feel. This screening mechanism makes it possible for large gatherings to occur in the garden without allowing for views directly into the private portion of the house, yet still allowing for light and air circulation.

The front wing is oriented north-south and contains all the public spaces—gallery, living, dining, studio, kitchen, playroom. Half of the wing sits on the ground and the other half is in cantilever. The front wing is oriented towards the southeast, acting as a tube that brings the cool breeze from the southeast across all the spaces—which, in conjunction with the openings on the north side, creates a constant airflow throughout the house. The front and rear wings have a strong formal, visual, and operational relationship to the front garden. The family's intense social agenda comes to life in the confluence of these three spaces. The rear wing acts as a backdrop and spectator, while the front wing embraces the most public space of the house.

The entrance hall is designed as a gallery space with zenithal light around a central stair that connects the upper and lower ground floors. The lower quarters contain all large-format art storage, support rooms, general storage, mechanical and service functions as well a guest suite with independent access and its own private garden. This area is buried beneath the front wing, which is in direct contact with the ground and acts as a cooling chamber for the upper functions. The east wall of the primary living space of the house is defined by a corrugated metal surface that captures the shadows of the nearby trees as light passes through the leaves and branches. The lack of fenestration along this wall enables it to serve as the primary gallery wall, where the owners display their art collection.

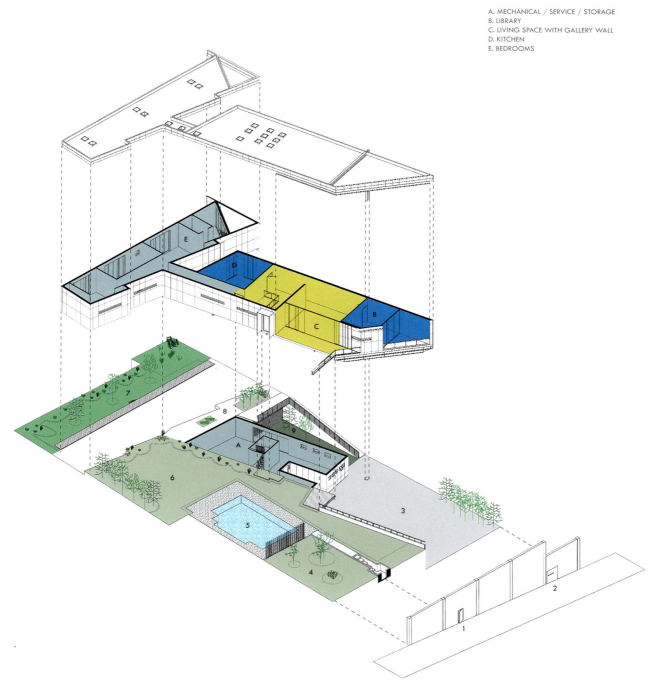

The house had to be built in six months with a very limited budget. Therefore, the use of steel was preferred for all the framing, while concrete panel infills and cast-in-place concrete were used for the foundation and service spaces. All the glazing systems are single panes suspended from the ceilings without the need for aluminum framing. The living and dining spaces are visually and physically connected to the main garden through an eight-meter, fully collapsible glass wall. When fully open, the effect is not only positive in terms of comfort, but also in terms of blurring the boundaries between private and public space. When the house is open, it evokes the feeling of a "beach house." The breeze, the noise, the smells, the music, and the visual richness and eclecticism of the art collection mingle in one continuous space.

Landscaping is predominantly based on cactuses and other indigenous species that require minimum or no maintenance. The existing trees (avocado and lime) have been preserved in their original locations. A small garden outside the kitchen provides chiles, tomatoes, lettuce, radishes, and some condiments. Exterior walking surfaces are covered by grass, gravel, and porous pavers. A large rainwater cistern was integrated in the lower quarters as the byproduct of adapting the program to the site conditions; it collects all the water that is consumed by the family and their guests for gardening, showers, toilets, and sinks throughout the year.

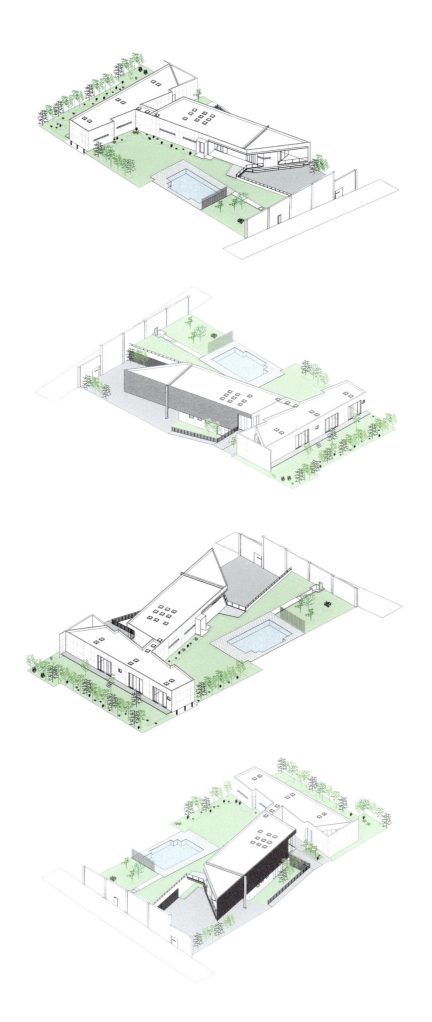

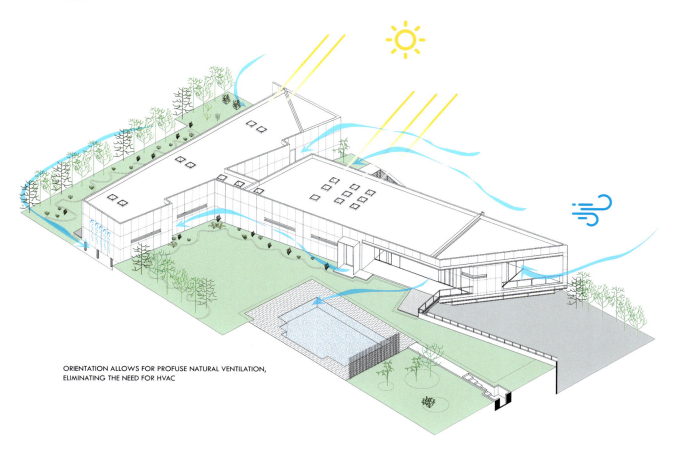

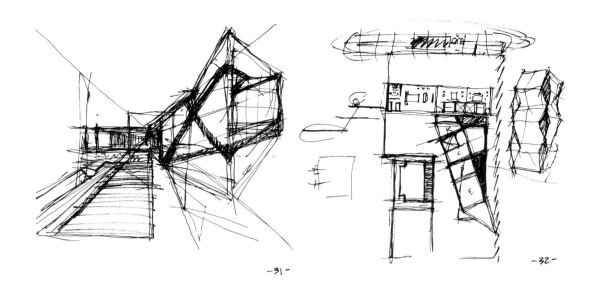

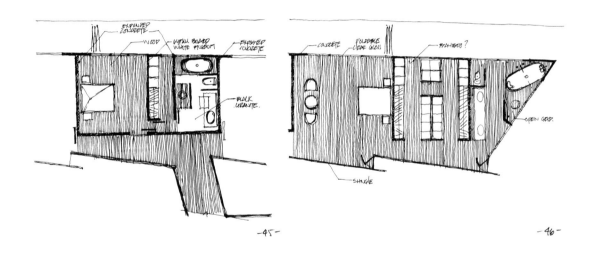

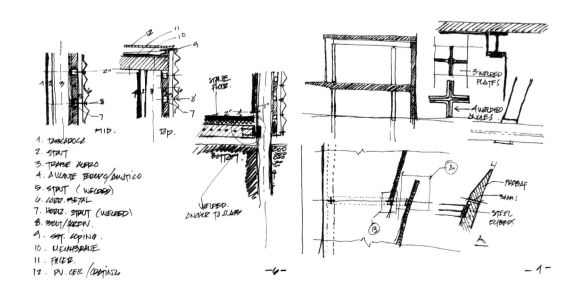

MONARCA

INTRO

Monarca is located on a magnificent site in the city of Santander. Located on the northern coast of Spain, Santander is the capital of the Cantabria region. The city is home to a significant port as well as the headquarters of Banco Santander. Much of the historic city was destroyed during the Great Fire of 1941. The city has a relatively low amount of sunlight year-round, even in comparison to other northern cities. This city is also home to the Palace of La Magdalena, which was built between 1909 and 1911 to house the royal family.

The commission called for two apartments per floor with the top two floors designated for the owner/developer, Paco García. García wanted a building that would be luxurious as well as express a certain level of honesty and straightforwardness in its design. It needed to respond to the architectural context of relatively new, postwar construction as well as the gradual slope of the site and the exceptional views of the city, the bay, and the sea. At the same time, it was important that all sides and orientations of the building be maximized to ensure optimal value for each apartment.

Generally speaking, the urban form of Santander follows the shape of the land mass that protrudes into the Bay of Biscay and forms the smaller Bahía de Santander, which gives shelter to the city's protected port. The long side of the blocks is oriented east-west with a general orientation towards the Bahía de Santander to the south. The city is at its most dense towards the south and gradually rises in elevation to the north, where its density gradually diminishes. The site is located in this interstitial zone between the dense historic city and the rural area to the north.

The building follows the form of the city and is primarily oriented towards the south. Although there is less sunlight than in other parts of Spain, it was still important to protect the interior from excessive heat gain. As a result, a double skin was designed that integrated wooden screens in order to give each of the apartments privacy while also allowing all of the screens to be hidden on cloudy days in order to maximize daylight. The south facade houses all of the public functions for the apartments, while the private functions are housed along the north facade. The southern facade also integrates a series of terraces that give it a sense of depth and texture. The shortest facades are on the east and west and house all of the services for the building.

DESIGN

The structure of the building is defined by a series of floor plates cantilevered over the lobby and common area at the base. The double skin essentially wraps over the north side of the building and hangs in front of the cantilevered floor plates. This makes it possible to open the ground level to

RESIDENTIAL PROPOSAL 2012
6,500 M2
SANTANDER
SPAIN

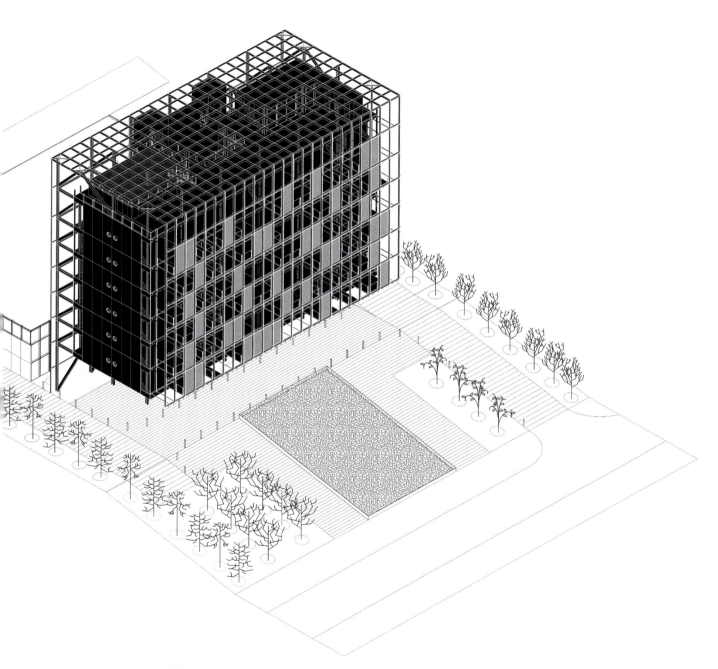

"ONE ORIENTATION FOR ALL FUNCTIONS: THE BUILDING IS A SERIES OF FLOATING GLASS PAVILIONS STACKED ONE ON TOP OF THE OTHER. THE MEDIATOR OF PUBLIC AND PRIVATE SPACE IS A MONUMENTAL GLASS SCREEN THAT ACTS AS A DOUBLE WALL, EXPANDING THE EXPERIENCE OF CITY LIVING BY DISSOLVING THE BOUNDARIES OF INTERIOR AND EXTERIOR SPACE. SECLUSION IS PROVIDED BY A SYSTEM OF LAYERS CONSTRUCTED WITH MOVABLE AND SWITCHABLE PARTS. FOR ME, HOUSING IS A NATURAL RESEARCH AND DEVELOPMENT PROCESS; THE INTIMACY OF INTERACTION PROVIDES INVALUABLE DATA TOWARDS ITS INDUSTRIALIZATION AND BEAUTY."

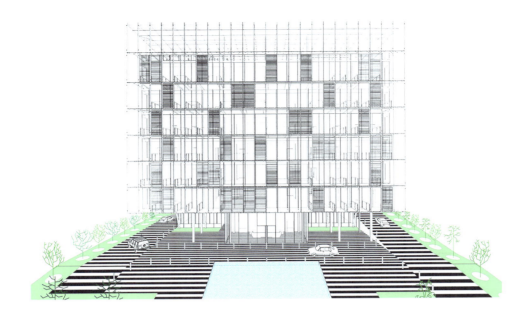

FACADE DAYTIME

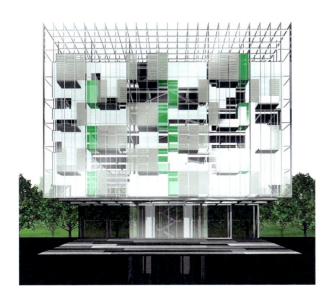

FACADE NIGHTTIME : INTEGRATED LED SYSTEM IN FACADE EMANATING AS A PLATFORM FOR COMMUNICATION

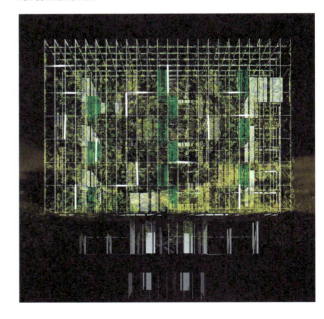

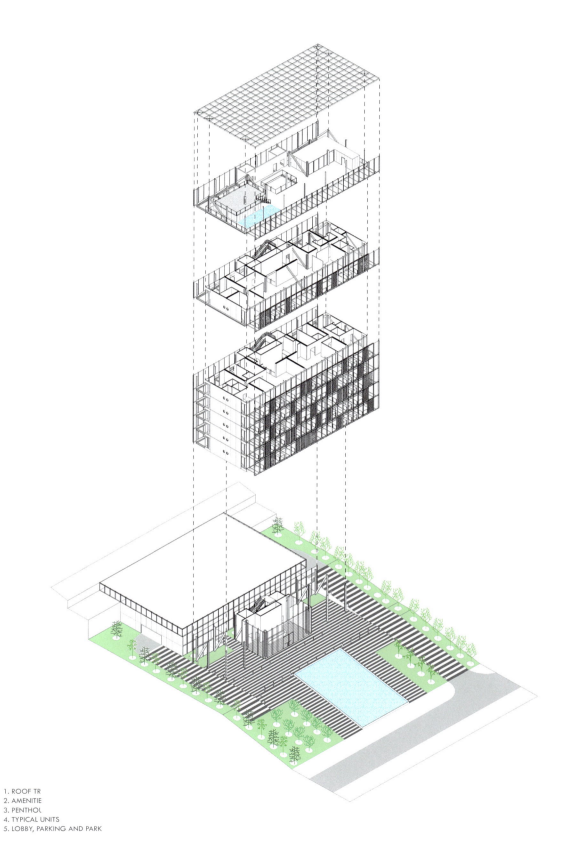

1. ROOF TR
2. AMENITIE
3. PENTHOU
4. TYPICAL UNITS
5. LOBBY, PARKING AND PARK

the landscape and create an inviting entry to the building. Parking spaces as well as a reflecting pool are located below this entrance. The outer southern screen is a dynamic artwork created in collaboration with a lighting artist. The intention is for the facade to blend with nature over the course of the day, so that the building is essentially camouflaged. At night it emits an entrancing glow of patterned vegetation.

The ultimate goal was to build the project with modular prefabrication techniques that allow for a rich layout based on a kit of parts. This would create a basic language that would unify the building while also supporting customization of the individual apartments in accordance with the owner's wishes.

Although Monarca is a high-end project, it expresses the same philosophy that pervades all of the projects discussed in this book. The design utilizes lightweight materials, efficient structure, a double skin to enhance energy efficiency, and modularity. In many ways, the project illustrates the idea that architecture of the same quality should exist for all types of housing. Furthermore, the design expresses a broader continuity with other typologies. It suggests that a similar approach to design can resonate across scales and budgets. Moreover, this approach fosters continuity in the spaces we inhabit rather than reserving expensive and extravagant design approaches for some typologies and less expensive for others. This concept is embedded in the DNA of FGP ATELIER and reflected in the buildings. It is examined in more depth in the final essay of this book, "Dry Architecture."

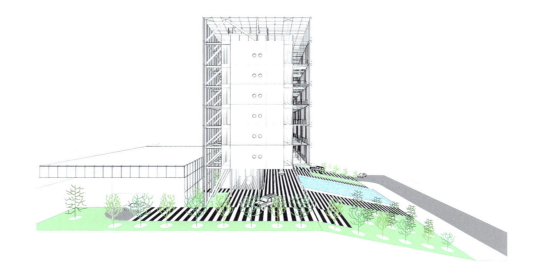

1. SINGLE-GLAZED EXTERIOR FACADE
2. INSULATED INTERIOR FACADE
3. RADIANT SLAB
4. NATURAL VENTILATION
5. BALCONY
6. WOODEN SCREEN

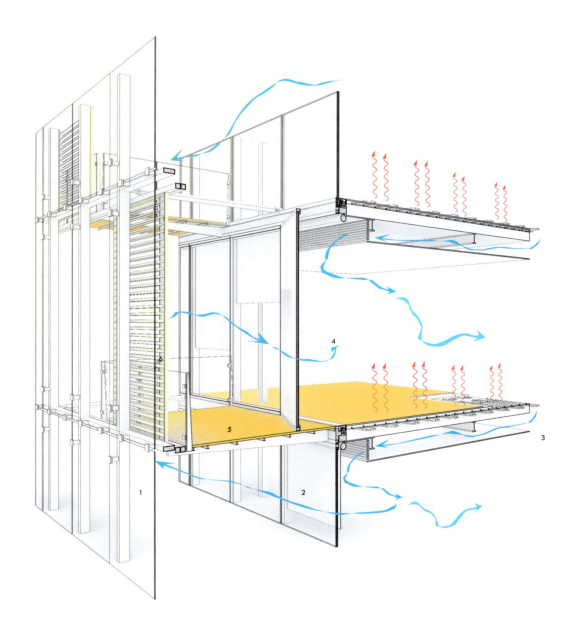

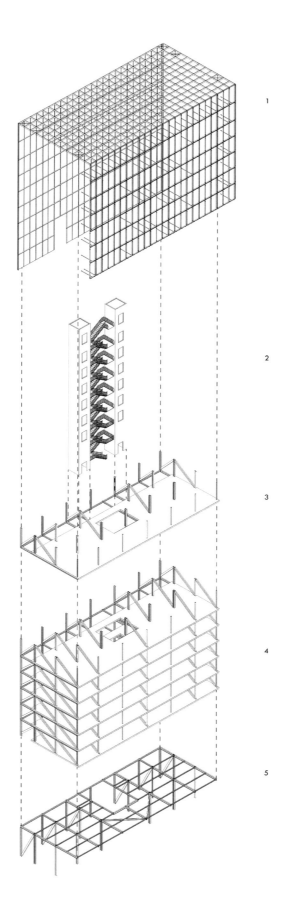

1. THERMAL ENCLOSURE
2. CONCRETE CORE
3. COMPOSITE SYSTEM
4. MODULAR SYSTEM
5. CANTILEVERED STRUCTURE

"THE BUILDING STRUCTURE IS DEFINED BY A SERIES OF FLOOR PLATES CANTILEVERED OVER THE LOBBY AND COMMON AREA AT THE BASE. THE DOUBLE SKIN ESSENTIALLY WRAPS OVER THE NORTH SIDE OF THE BUILDING AND HANGS IN FRONT OF THE CANTILEVERED FLOOR PLATES, GIVING THE USERS A PRIVATE OUTDOOR EXPERIENCE."

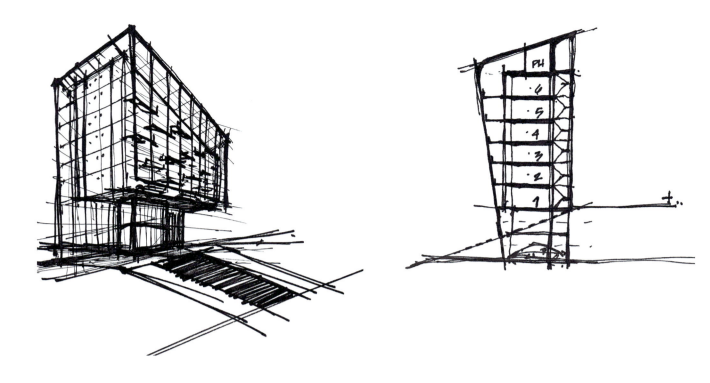
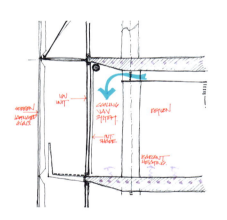
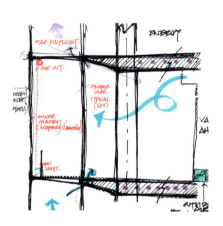
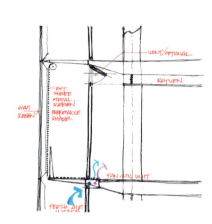
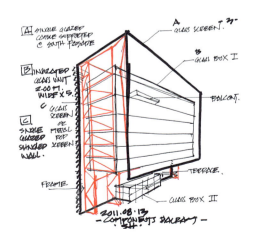
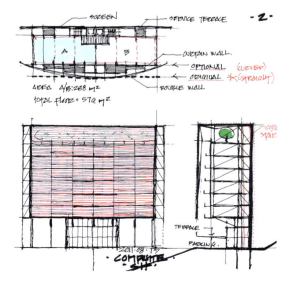

HOUSING PLATFORM: BEYOND AFFORDABLE AND MARKET-RATE HOUSING

The general inability to offer broad strategies for solving the growing crisis of affordable housing in America is related to a propensity to look at one aspect of the problem rather than exploring the interconnected web of past and present variables that go into defining the complexities of creating and offering housing at a cost that is aligned with income, jobs, location, and what people can afford to pay for a dwelling unit. This inability exists within the context of the history of how housing has been subsidized via government-backed mortgages, concentration of low-income families in high-rise buildings, and programs that offer tax incentives to developers. It also exists within the context of an approach to affordable housing that is largely concentrated on the very poor, rather than taking an approach adopted by countries such as France, which looks at the needs of the entire population—especially those of the working class, students, and the elderly.

At the same time, the entangled history of housing and racial discrimination, zoning laws guiding development and neighborhoods that develop a particular character and type of resident, systems of value that drive what should be attained from a housing unit, and the way in which community is built and our world transformed through work are often considered outside the immediate task of developing a design that can be built at low cost. It is important to fully analyze how the cost of other goods and services impacts what one can afford to pay for housing. The cost and benefits of transportation, digital, and social networks should also be considered, as should integrating new housing into employment channels. Most importantly, it is important to think beyond the division between affordable and market-rate housing to arrive at a situation in which all housing is affordable, and housing is seen as a right, not a privilege.

The 2020 pandemic has caused many to realize the expansiveness of housing insecurity while also raising concerns that the social safety net—if it exists at all—is quite fragile. The pandemic has further exposed the extent to which the high cost of housing disproportionately impacts those living on incomes considerably below the median. For many of these households, income has stagnated in the years following the Great Recession. Although the number of people employed is generally increasing, the wages of unskilled workers have not recovered, while those earning at the top of the economy have seen considerable growth. This has ultimately fueled the rapidly rising cost of housing in urban centers that once had large, stable low- and moderate-income communities. In this sense, the core problem of affordable housing is essentially low wages and insufficient access to training and jobs coupled with rising construction costs and rents.

HOUSING PLATFORM: BEYOND AFFORDABLE AND MARKET-RATE HOUSING

In this context, architects can play several roles, from contributing the design of new buildings that conform to the existing model of subsidized housing to exploring more novel solutions to reduce the cost of housing. One means of approaching the latter is through modular systems that can reduce the overall cost and duration of construction while improving quality. Modularity is a theme that runs throughout much of FGP ATELIER's work and is explored in greater detail in the essay "Dry Architecture." In addition, considering how space can be used more efficiently is critical to reducing the overall cost. Strategies for a more efficient use of space are explored in greater detail in the project "Spacecraft." At the same time, the legacy of housing discrimination, uneven development of cities, and the broader challenges of employment that we have touched on briefly remain deeply concerning. While we are currently working on "modeling scenarios" to address these concerns, it is also important to speculate on how our current approach to design might address them if given the opportunity in the future. What follows, then, is a thought experiment leading from a single modular unit to a network of such units distributed throughout a city or region and connected by a common platform that enhances their functionality.

One advantage of modular housing and prefabrication is its use of mass-produced and customized units based on the same general design while also maintaining a high standard of quality. When coupled with recent trends that embrace distributed rather than centralized affordable housing models, it become possible to explore how these units might be distributed, not just within a neighborhood, but throughout a city or even a region. Embracing this capacity would help decision-makers to look beyond preconceived distinctions between urban and suburban in order to examine the entire field of possible housing locations. It would help us to see beyond traditional boundaries that have divided neighborhoods throughout the city. Doing so would allow us to see the city as a field of characteristics, services, infrastructures, energies, flows, opportunities, employment centers, educational hubs, and broader active forms that could inform how new housing is sited and define the true cost of building and living in those homes. By looking at the city from an operational perspective, new housing can be tailored to the activities of the inhabitant, the amount of money those activities generate and cost, and their broader household economy. In this way, housing can be attuned to needs rather than to the equation of how much land, labor, and materials cost, what tax incentives are available, and how much minimum return on investment the developer requires.

"I BELIEVE IN THE UNIVERSAL RIGHT TO HIGH-QUALITY DESIGN. ACCESS TO GOOD DESIGN SHOULD NOT BE A QUESTION OF WHETHER YOU CAN AFFORD IT AND GOOD DESIGN SHOULD CERTAINLY NOT BE RESERVED FOR ELITE ARCHITECTURE."

HOUSING PLATFORM: BEYOND AFFORDABLE AND MARKET-RATE HOUSING

It would also help to understand how to balance location—such as inexpensive land on the extreme fringes of the city—with employment and cultural services that might be necessary to sustain life and that might be found within the more expensive core of the city. It would help to understand where the people who might benefit from affordable housing currently live—a condition that is just as important as any other site condition. In this sense, an integrated field analysis of broader cities and regions would help address the underlying problem of building "affordable" housing. It would help to understand the boundaries—sometimes physical and sometimes virtual—that limit where people can live and work. At the same time, it would help to understand the different types of communities that require housing. In doing so, would give rise to an opportunity to address the historic trend of breaking up existing communities in order to get people into affordable units that are often in distant or unfamiliar places without support services.

Opening the process of siting new housing to an expanded field that considers the region, its built environment, and its ecology will make it possible to look beyond the local conditions defining a plot of land acquired to build housing. Such an approach builds on the success of distributing new units throughout neighborhoods in conjunction with market-rate development. It also takes into consideration the capacity to integrate adaptive reuse and restoration. Moreover, a distributed, decentralized system comprised of an array of different people, situations, and cultures would create a network of housing and related services that support those who need affordable housing across boundaries. The potential embodied in these people could then be actively cataloged and cultivated as a personal development strategy that is integrated with a broader urban development strategy. This approach might allow for a housing strategy that germinates in a virtual sphere outside current racial discourses and explores ways of overcoming those divides that remain on the ground.

An affordable, distributed housing strategy would require a support program that helps new residents to connect with the broader social and economic system that ultimately is financing the housing. This could result in a new standard, creating pathways to agency for the residents. It would also require investing in housing at different levels of the economy and in different parts of the city. Within the context of those unable to afford market-rate housing near the jobs that they have been trained to fill or would like to fill, there are many subsets of the population in differentiated income brackets. Some people have invested hundreds of thousands of dollars in education and struggle to afford housing in high-cost urban centers near the jobs they have been trained to fill. On the other extreme, people with limited education

HOUSING PLATFORM: BEYOND AFFORDABLE AND MARKET-RATE HOUSING

teeter on the edge of poverty. For them, and everyone in between, it will be helpful to identify precisely the lines between different skills, incomes, and goals so that inhabitants can mature within one bracket while having the opportunity to progress to another bracket.

Housing and the supporting services it requires could be connected to each other through a digital platform and strategically located in relation to particular jobs, services, transportation, and other existing infrastructure. The number and scale of each support service as well as its specific adjacency would be based on location and population. The location would also be determined by how a new investment is placed in the context of existing "urban" conditions that is defined as the field of real, physical objects and active virtual forms that determine its appearance and functionality. This network of housing and support services would also be determined by how these generic spaces are customized and evolve. In deploying such an approach, it would be important to introduce people who can connect to other disciplines and coordinate the installation and initial inhabitation of "affordable" housing. This group—likely comprised of social workers, artists, and planners—would mediate between field analysis and the real spatial, cultural, social, and political conditions on the ground.

By introducing a platform that offers tools for making these decisions, greater interest in the place of dwelling can be established. This platform, moreover, can be virtual and incorporate a range of options that do not have to manifest immediately as a built product. Ultimately, this process might create opportunities during the planning process to better frame how new development is sited in a particular community. This process could create a space in which to negotiate different images associated with what inhabitants, developers, and other community members desire. It would be a space in which to explore what is possible within the context of a particular development.
In many ways, such a platform could integrate trends related to smart cities and the Internet of Things in order to connect to and control physical infrastructure. This would involve creating a single digital portal that would allow people to engage and monitor all aspects of the physical built world in which they live. They could pay their utilities and rent from one location with a single click. The platform could be used to track domestic finances and pay annual property taxes. People could arm and disarm their security system and monitor environmental air quality. They could even access a digital representation of their living space, inventory their belongings, purchase new belongings, and plan and execute physical improvements. It would also be a gateway for requesting services and emergency assistance if necessary.

HOUSING PLATFORM: BEYOND AFFORDABLE AND MARKET-RATE HOUSING

Ultimately, it is possible to imagine how this platform could be spread throughout the entire city and scaled to other cities. The fact that the platform would evolve from sites distributed across different sections of the city and different racial and economic groups is essential. This would allow such a platform to serve and benefit the widest possible range of residents from the beginning. The resulting platform would support community engagement through the feedback that the platform could provide. Ideally, such a platform would be guided by a set of principles to ensure equitable development. If revenue is generated via such a platform, it would be equally essential for such revenue to be allocated evenly across a geographic region.

Finally, it is worth considering how some of these reflections might intersect with those in the essay "Twinning." By integrating utilities with increasingly digitally enabled spaces that can be equipped with energy monitors, the platform could more effectively model energy use and create a better understanding of how to improve energy performance, reduce waste, and enhance the sustainability of the built environment. Although such a platform and a more equitable approach to affordable housing—one that sees the problem as going beyond the afflictions of the urban poor—remain a dream at the moment, our hope is that in the future, a broader community will arise and that, together, we can make progress in addressing one of the most pressing problems facing the world today.

"I WANTED THE WALL ADJACENT TO THE PROPERTY LINE TO BE AN OUTDOOR CANVAS THAT REFLECTS THE SHADOWS OF THE TREES. I SELECTED CORRUGATED METAL TO GIVE THE SHADOWS A GREATER SENSE OF DEPTH. ON THE INSIDE, IT IS THE LARGEST WALL FOR DISPLAYING ARTWORK. THIS WALL BEGINS IN THE LIBRARY—WHICH FORMS THE POINT OF THE CANTILEVER—AND EXTENDS THROUGH THE PUBLIC SPACES."

III_AMBITION

ONE.
TRANSPARENTE
TWO.
SMART SALON
RADART
THREE.
MODULAR
GUADALAJARA T2
AIFA

ONE.
TWINNING
TWO.
PERVASIVE MEDIA
THREE.
DRY ARCHITECTURE

CHAPTER EIGHT

The majority of projects designed today make use of digital design tools while also integrating digital and other media into the completed building. The renovation of the Rectoría at Monterrey Tec—Transparente—exemplifies both.

As the building had undergone a range of modifications over the years, fully understanding the existing condition presented a particular challenge. The available plans proved to be inaccurate in many ways. In this context, two options were available: traditional survey techniques that could correct those 2D plans or laser scanning technology to create a point cloud of the building that could then be translated into a BIM model. This model could then be integrated with the other digital design tools, ranging from CAD to virtual and augmented reality.

Not only were digital tools in the design process, the building itself also houses a range of media. On one hand, the building houses the largest collection of works by Cervantes in a rare book library. This library also includes the first letter that Christopher Columbus sent to Queen Isabella reporting on his discovery of the New World after returning to Spain (an edition printed in Rome in 1493) in addition to a number of other rare pieces of art and artifacts. The building itself is a platform for presenting programs, lectures, and movies to the student body and faculty. These activities are connected to the campus calendar and social media outlets of the university. At the same time, various options for online learning and e-courses are accessed there. Together, these features allow the building to perform digitally.

CHAPTER EIGHT

The possibility of creating a completely accurate, as-built model of the building via laser scanning technology led the design team to speculate on possibilities that went beyond the scope and deliverables of the project. This speculation involved considering the merits of creating a virtual digital twin of the real building, both during the design process and for use after construction was completed. Such a comprehensive model could serve as the basis for managing and operating the building. Through this digital model, the owner would be able to locate all the different building systems and connect this model to manufacturing specifications. If desired, they could even connect augmented reality platforms that might assist technicians as they addressed specific maintenance issues. Given the building's historical significance, such a model could serve as the basis for future renovations and additions.

Although these deliverables were beyond the scope of our work on the Rectoría, they reflect a new capacity for technology to greatly enhance the efficiency and sustainability of the built environment. Some of the broader implications and applications of such technology are explored in the essay "Twinning" and by the initiative One City by the Building Research Institute—the experimental branch of FGP ATELIER.

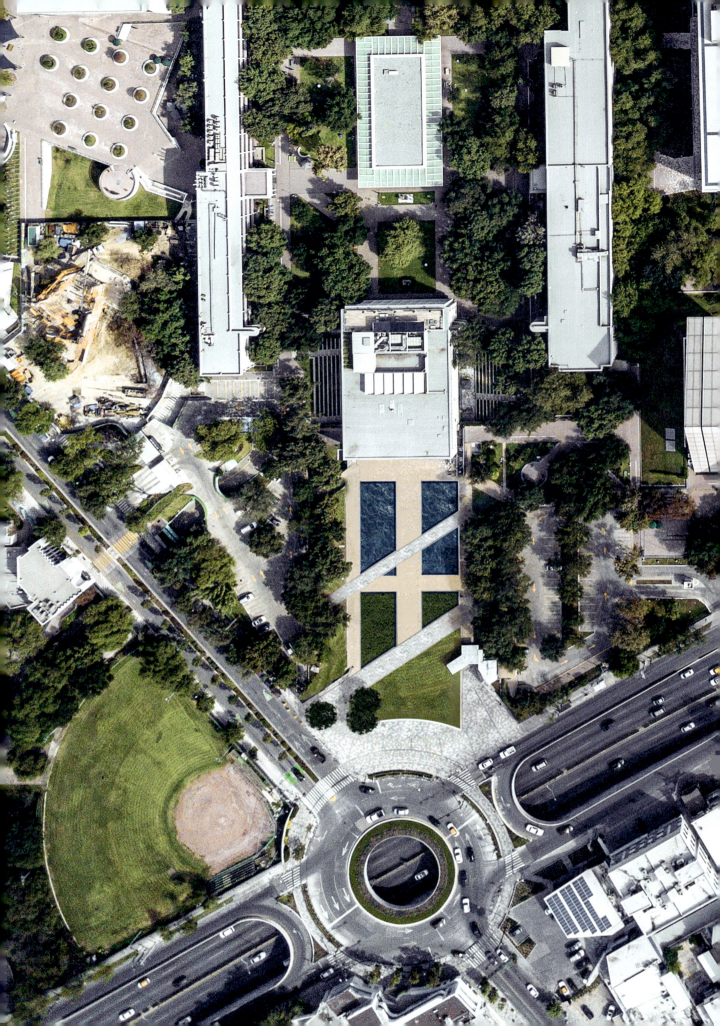

TRANSPARENTE

INTRO

The Rectoría at Monterrey Tec's primary campus in Monterrey, Mexico, serves as the central administration building for the entire system of campuses around Mexico. The building is the most iconic on the campus and one of the most important in the history of modern architecture in Mexico. Since its construction, its use has changed many times.

The building is defined by a mural by González Camarena that represents the battle between innovation and lack of purpose. Science is represented in the upper register, while the snakes and dark warriors occupying the lower register represent dark forces that will be conquered by innovation and technology. This mural anchors a primary volume of the building, which sits on a secondary volume defined by a recess in the primary facade and further distinguished by the use of glass, tile, and thin, linear-cut rough stone, as opposed to the larger, honed stone of the upper volume. A deep sense of modernism pervades. Banded windows set within a shallow box define the north and south facades. This strong linearity provides an elegant contrast to the monumentality of the primary facade. The recession of the lower volume creates a loggia defined by a series of circular concrete columns. The effect calls to mind the iconic works of modern European architecture set on pilotis. Loggias continue on the north and south side as additional volumes are carved out below the first floor.

The building is planned on a six-meter grid comprised of five by seven bays, with the primary axis running along the longer axis of the building. Organizationally, however, the building is defined in section by a series of double-height spaces, including the primary entrance lobby and the main lecture hall in the center of the building. Although these double-height spaces exist throughout, they are not particularly effective in creating connectivity between the levels. In fact, many of the spaces in the building feel disconnected from the others, leaving the visitor somewhat disoriented within the broader whole.

Beyond the central auditorium, the program of the building includes a rare book collection known as the Cervantina, which houses the world's largest collection of works by Cervantes as well as some of the earliest correspondence between Columbus and Queen Isabella of Spain regarding the discovery of the New World. In addition, the building houses the office of the president of the university, conference rooms, administrative offices, and informal working areas.

**REINVENTION
COMPLETED 2020
MONTERREY
MEXICO**

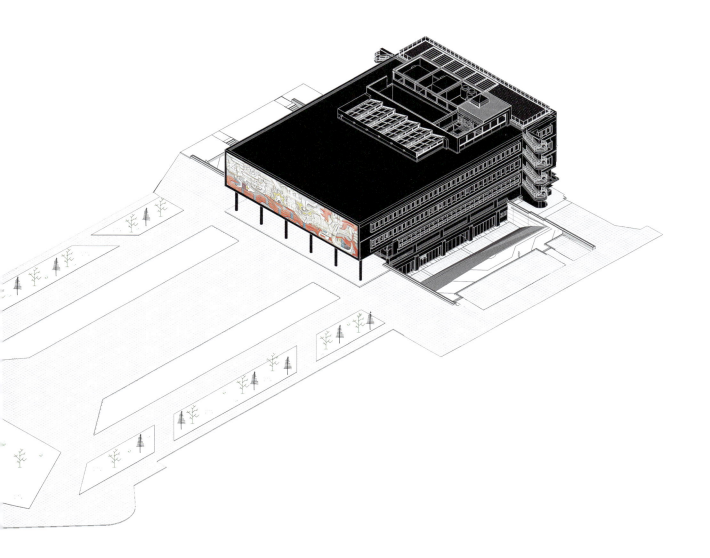

"I WAS SEVENTEEN YEARS OLD WHEN I ENTERED MONTERREY TEC UNIVERSITY FOR THE FIRST TIME AS AN ASPIRING ARCHITECT. THE RECTORÍA WAS THE MOST IMPORTANT BUILDING ON CAMPUS. IT WAS A BIT INTIMIDATING, SOLEMN, MODERN, SACRED, AND FORMAL. THREE DECADES LATER, I WAS APPOINTED AS THE ARCHITECT TO ADAPT IT TO A NEW FUTURE. I WAS CONFRONTED WITH A DIFFICULT DILEMMA. MY SOLUTION WAS TO ELIMINATE THE SUPERFLUOUS, SEEKING TO EXPOSE ITS NATURE, ITS ORIGIN. TRANSPARENCY UNCOVERED ITS ESSENCE, FULL OF LIFE, AND PROVIDED AN ESSENTIAL VALUE … DEMOCRACY."

At the same time, the building's use has evolved since it was constructed. It was initially used as the central library. Since this time, rooms have been subdivided, work habits altered, and the quantity of materials stored in the Cervantina and elsewhere increased. In the process, some renovations have been carried out. These have mostly consisted of adding new pieces of furniture and making minor surface alterations to give the building a more contemporary feel.

The result of all these modifications over the years is that the building retains its historical character in some areas, but not necessarily in others. A clear sense of cohesion is lacking. Most importantly, however, the spaces do not function optimally. Many on campus feel that the building appears closed and uninviting. It lacks transparency and a logical internal flow. The extraordinarily valuable collection housed in the Cervantina is not even known to many potential users, and the functioning of the central lecture hall is less than ideal. Finally, the basement level lacks natural light, and the vertical circulation does not meet current standards.

In this context, the leadership of the university decided that they needed to make a significant improvement. In developing a design solution that responded to this choice, it was imperative that the building retain its historical character. In particular, the design brief expressed the importance of respecting the murals in the lobby and on the facade. This approach would help ensure that the new design would appear to be a harmonious extension of the original intent.

In considering the renovation that we would come to call "Transparente," it is important to understand the client and role they play in education in Mexico. Instituto Tecnológico y de Estudios Superiores de Monterrey (ITESM), also known as Tecnológico de Monterrey or simply as Tec, was founded in 1943 by industrialists in Monterrey. Since its foundation, it has grown to thirty-two campuses in twenty-five cities around the country. Many consider it to be the preeminent university in Latin America. The business and medical schools are widely considered to be top ranked in the region.

The university was founded by Eugenio Garza Sada, an heir to one of the city's most influential industrialists. One of the primary goals of founding the university was to provide highly skilled personnel to the rapidly accelerating corporations located in Monterrey in the nineteen-forties. The university began operations in a rented building which it soon outgrew. In 1947, Enrique de la Mora was commissioned to design a master plan. Given the strong links

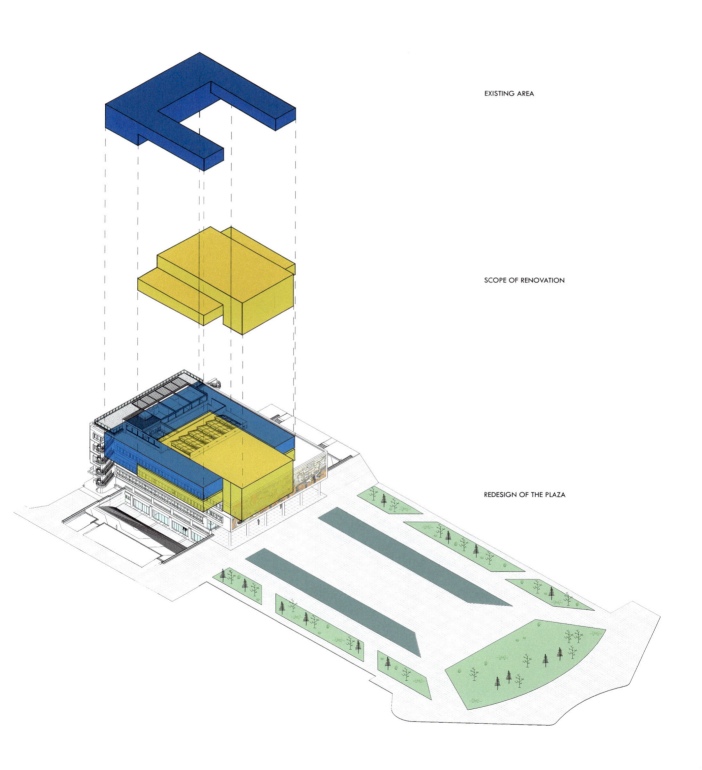

between the Mexican and US economies, the early leaders made international presence and recognition a priority. As a result, in 1950, the university became the first foreign university in history to be accredited by the Southern Association of Colleges and Schools (SACS), one of the six regional accreditation agencies recognized by the United States Department of Education.

The building site is located on the corner of Avenida Eugenio Garza Sada and Avenida Fernando García Roel on the campus of Tecnológico de Monterrey. The building serves as the symbolic entrance to the university and, as a result, is one of the most prominent sites on campus.

The site is defined in part by the angle of Avenida Eugenio Garza Sada that runs at a roughly forty-five-degree angle from northwest to southeast. This angle is in contrast to the orthogonal north-south, east-west planning of the campus. The building itself sits along the central axis of the campus with a plaza and fountains in front of the building and a quadrangle defined by two long linear buildings behind it. A smaller pavilion is located in the center of this quadrangle while additional linear buildings lie beyond the limits of the quadrangle to the east.

In approaching the renovation, there was a lot of concern about doing an intervention in an iconic building. Nevertheless, the facade in the lower level was preventing the mural from being given an urban context due to its lack of transparency and obstruction by mullions. At the same time, the glass was not performing to current energy standards. It was also crucial that the renovation not be undertaken as a series of fragmented parts. The building needed to be treated as a whole. The initial inspiration was driven by the theme of innovation in the mural in combination with the new entrance to the campus designed by Mario Schjetnan, which lowered the fence and created a berm. The project would follow this lead of openness and be about reimagining great spaces, creating clear circulation, fostering democratic space, and transforming a mysterious and hermetic building into something extroverted and open.

STRATEGY

The transformation of the building would be accomplished through the application of a few great ideas:
1) creation of grand spaces in synchronicity with the scale and importance of the building;
2) creation of a clear and legible circulation concept;
3) recovery of the original spatial relationship between the access plaza and the building, which speaks again about concepts of openness and democracy;
4) respecting the past through a thoughtful and minimal intervention paying special attention to materials and systems;
5) focusing on functionality to accommodate change and provoke seamless flows among all spaces;
6) striking a balance between preservation of the building's special character, quality, and historical significance and facilitating change in a way that sustains it into the future;
7) ensuring that the new layers represent the ideas, technology, material, and architectural language of future generation;
8) focusing on the quality of the relationship between old and new, and not in the architectural language per se;
9) designing quality in the new Rectoría defined by scale, form, material, color, and detail; and
10) ensuring that the Rectoría reflects the new spirit of Monterrey Tec.

A building that has one or two strongly executed ideas will always be better than one with many. In this sense, the strategy was not about being minimalist, but about removing what was superfluous and getting to the essence. At the same time, functionality was important. The building had to outlive many generations and live into the future.

With a building such as the Rectoría, it is important to treat it as an archeological project. The initial sketches were an attempt to 1) create a hierarchy of the myriad parts, 2) identify the client's goals, and 3) establish guiding principles for the design. This holistic approach was initially something of a surprise to the client, however, as they had imagined simply enhancing each floor. Such an approach would create a solution driven by interior design rather than an understanding of the building's architecture. It would lack cohesion. To address this possibility, the proposal created clear circulation by opening up the building—in some cases by demolishing slabs. This approach would use architecture to create a feeling of openness and democracy. The facade was outdated and needed to be revised. The building had to be more welcoming.

1. SEAMLESS FLOW + CONNECTIVITY
2. TRANSPARANCY + OPENESS TO PROMOTE INTERACTION
3. IMPROVE DAYLIGHT, NATURAL VENTILATION AND REDUCE ENERGY CONSUMPTION

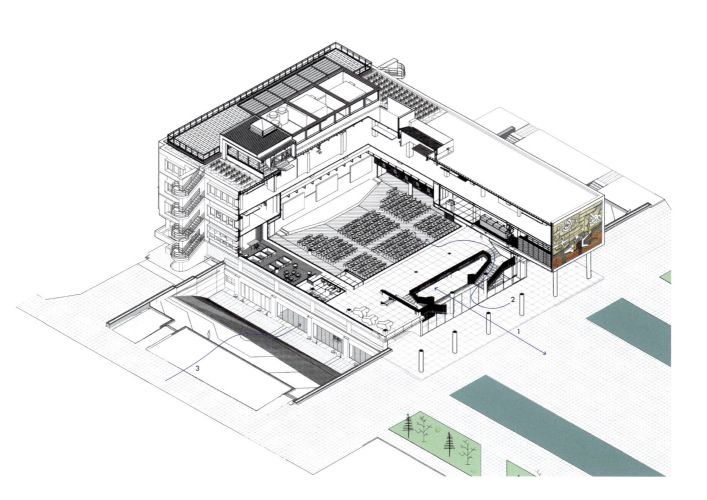

In moving forward with the design, the client was very cautious because the building was so important to the school. It was important to develop a narrative strategy for exploring alternatives that could help the client and other stakeholders understand the intent and arrive at a definitive agenda. This strategy would go beyond materials and finishes; instead, it would be about connectivity and transparency in an almost metaphysical sense. This notion can be seen in the new two-level hall connecting the ground level to the basement level. The hall itself is defined by a double-height space with a set of stairs and seats connecting the two levels. Coworking and gathering spaces form the perimeter of the two-level hall. Once on the lower level, visitors can see that a similar strategy has been introduced on the two parallel sides of the building, creating a stepped area that allows light to enter the once dark basement. Directly above this hall is the two-level Sala Major, which serves as a primary place for lectures and gatherings. While the form was not altered, the surfaces and furniture were updated to enhance comfort, improve acoustic performance, and provide up-to-date audiovisual equipment.

Adjacent to the upper level of the Sala Major and across a central atrium that runs from the entry level up two levels is the Cervantina, the rare book collection. In addressing the renovation of this very important space, it was necessary for it to be immediately visible upon entering. This would be accomplished by expanding the atrium, which required cutting into the slab and making the space three rather than two levels high. Visitors could glimpse the bibliographic treasures immediately. Unfortunately, this goal was not achieved. In not implementing this aspect of the design, a certain element of the holistic vision of connectedness was compromised. Nevertheless, many other design decisions regarding the Cervantina were implemented, including preservation of much of its existing character, expressed in elements such as the color of the floor and the vintage nineteen-fifties furniture.

The design process involved an ongoing series of presentations to a range of stakeholders that included the financial committee, board of the school, experience designers, technology providers, and building operations and maintenance. In the process, the client and design team found a number of areas where they were not in agreement, some areas where compromise was required, and some areas where they aligned completely. The process was also guided by the archeological aspect of renovating such a building where new elements were uncovered that pushed the design in one direction or another. This process could not have occurred without an extraordinary contractor and construction team, who approached the project with great sensitivity and embarked on some incredibly challenging endeavors.

THE RESULT

HIGH-PERFORMANCE FACADE WITH A FRAMELESS, STRUCTURAL GLAZING ENCLOSURE

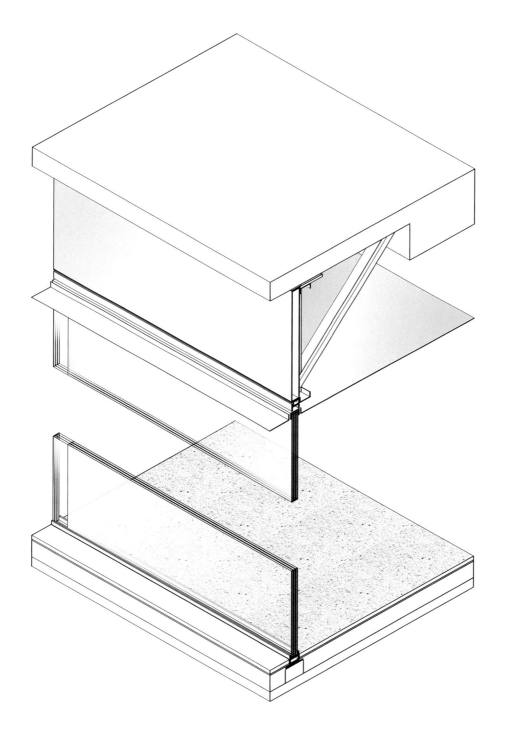

In the end, the essence of the design remained intact. The biggest contrast between the intent and execution can be seen in the approach to the interiors. In the beginning, the idea was to create a more neutral framework, almost like a canvas, that allows the building's occupants to do many things, as opposed to fixing the building in a style that would become outdated. The architectural strategies aimed for this and succeeded. The materials and finishes, however, reflect some disagreements.

One example is the design of a Corten steel stairway for the lower auditorium. This highly monolithic element was meant to feel as if it had been there since the beginning—since the building was built, as opposed to making it feel new by adhering to a particular trend, such as wood. This is similar to our approach with the Diablos Rojos baseball stadium in Mexico City, where the truncated pyramids look new from a distance, but when you get closer, they look as if they have been there for a long time. Most people supported our approach. For some board members, it was too bold.

Another example is the design of a soffit for the portico and some of the public spaces. It was organized via the grid of the building and created a series of linear lighting elements. The soffit would reflect movement and emphasize the grid of the building. It would serve as an important layer in the interior enclosure of the spaces. Instead, the client chose drywall and downlights. Perhaps this decision would be appropriate for a generic public space, but not for the most iconic building on the campus.

Finally, the main auditorium was designed using a strict palette of colors to create a canvas where anything can happen. Most of the ideas were followed, but the walls that required acoustic paneling were a missed opportunity to give the building character and to connect to the heritage of the building. While the client wanted to cover it with translucent panels, it was important to maintain the grid of the ceiling. Covering them would have been a shame, as the original ceiling was constructed of some very expensive and highly detailed elements that would be very difficult to build today.

Outside the building, the plaza will be restored in a later phase and connect to Mario Schjetnan's intervention. The idea is to return the space to its appearance in the nineteen-fifties. The planters were built in the nineteen-sixties as a response to student riots; they are meant to promote flow rather than create a space where people can linger. The idea is to go back to the origin and make it more about a plaza in front of an important building.

CONCLUSION

The prominent landscape architect and childhood friend of González Pulido, Claudia Harari, will guide the landscape design and the idea of extending democracy beyond the immediate surroundings of the building and into the campus.

In the end, we felt that if we had been more involved with the decision-making process, we would have suggested that emphasis should have been placed on a phase 0. This would have required a more thorough feasibility study to arrive at a realistic budget. We felt this would have been particularly important in the context of a renovation and would have served as a means of understanding the various risks that might be encountered once walls and floors were opened. Doing so would have helped to establish a realistic vision and budget for the project. We felt that having a clear picture of the scope and limits would have helped us to make more informed decisions and ensure that we did not lose control of some aspects of the project as the reality of the budget and limitations of the existing building emerged during the design and construction process. In our view, the architect should have a sense of the big picture so that he or she can advocate for one strategy versus another based on how it works as part of the whole, both at the time of design and in the future. This is something best addressed at the contractual level, which was not done with the Rectoría or with the bioengineering building, Tec Nano.

Another important lesson we learned was related to the approval process. While the board or financial committee was always very supportive, the process often lacked formality. Sometimes this was an advantage, while at other times it led to an ambiguous decision-making process. In these cases, the situation was complicated by a lack of transparent communication, which led to a dilution of some of the key design ideas. It is our belief that the architect must be present throughout the entire process and be allowed to present his or her ideas unfiltered by intermediaries if the client—in this case the board of the university—is to get a full understanding of the project that they can use to make decisions. Clear communication allows all of the parties to understand the reasons behind arguments so that subjective positions are avoided and, even if all parties do not end up supporting the idea, decisions are made from an informed, rational perspective.

The final product, however, is remarkable. Transparente would not have been possible without the tenacity of the local construction crew, who dealt with a fragile building. Great respect should be paid to all the brave people who made this success possible.

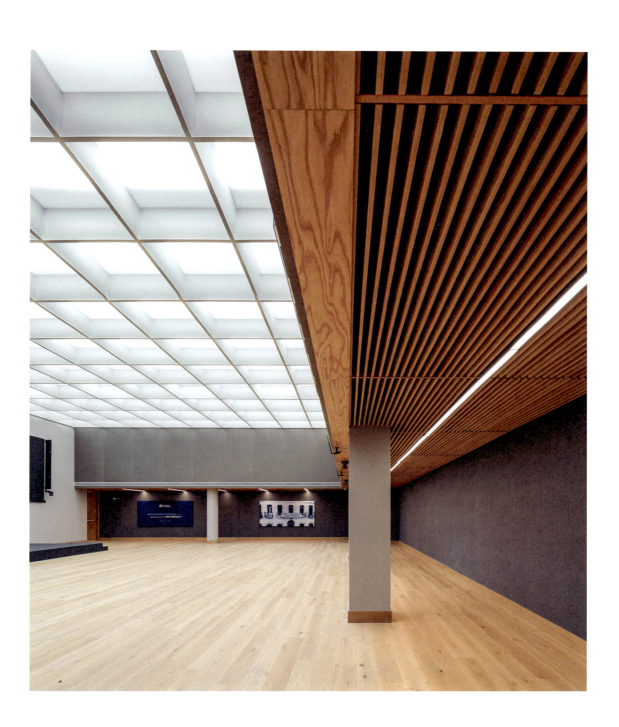

AS DESIGNED

AS BUILT

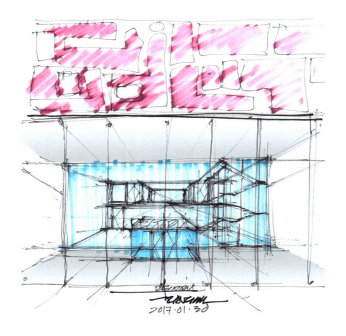

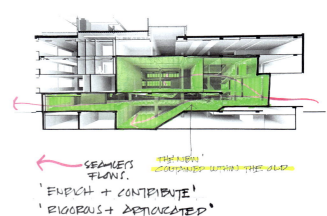

← SEAMLESS FLOWS.   THE NEW CONTAINED WITHIN THE OLD
'ENRICH + CONTRIBUTE'
'RIGOROUS + ARTICULATED'

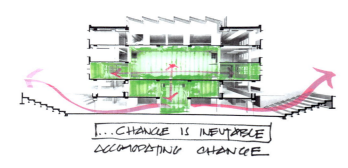

…CHANGE IS INEVITABLE
ACCOMODATING CHANGE

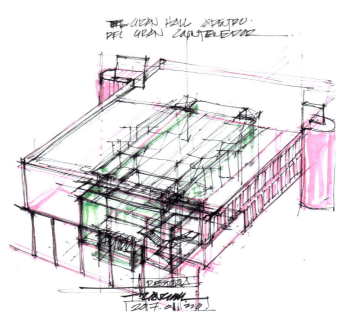

EL GRAN HALL DENTRO DEL GRAN CONTENEDOR

TWINNING

Attaining an accurate survey of the land on which one plans to build, or of the building that one plans to renovate, is an essential starting point for any design endeavor. It is imperative to know the spatial constraints, the quality of the surface on which one will build, and the relationship between the site and the surrounding area. In the case of renovations, one must understand the existing building systems, the structural capacity, and the material quality in addition to all the spatial and site-specific constraints. In the adaptive re-use projects that the firm has been involved with recently, it has been important to insist on accurate as-built models that can be attained via laser scanning technology to arrive at a point cloud that can be translated into a BIM model. Failure to take such steps will likely lead to an intervention that takes longer and costs more. Ultimately, the result may be an inability to serve a particular program over a period of time and the need to search for a true solution. This need has led to various methods of surveying a building and site in order to create the starting point for a project. These surveys have historically been representations of specific aspects of the site, and they select for a particular use of the survey. They have been drawn in two dimensions on paper. As such, they balance the amount of information with the legibility of the drawing. The result is a document type that has served generations of engineers and architects sufficiently to create a wide range of impressive buildings and pieces of infrastructure. These documents, however, do not capture the full reality and, as a result, often lead to surprises that occur during excavation and construction.

The problem of encountering unexpected elements below ground and during a renovation has become increasingly common when building structures on the same sites repeatedly, filling the ground with new generations of infrastructure, and finding new economic, environmental, and cultural pressure to reuse existing buildings. Crossrail in London, for example, which introduced a new subway line to the city, required extremely precise surveying and modeling in order to enable the new tunnels to fit between existing buildings and infrastructure. In some cases, the space was so constrained that there were only a few feet on either side of the new tunnel. To achieve this goal, engineers used the most advanced digital surveying technology available to develop a highly detailed model of the existing condition.

Achieving a level of accuracy that essentially creates an exact digital representation of the world is known as digital twinning. The desire to create a digital twin began outside the realm of architecture and cities, in the realm of industrial machinery. General Electric, among others, created a digital twin of their jet engines that connected to actual engines via sensors that monitored their operation in real time. This allowed them to better understand the

TWINNING

performance of that engine, optimize performance, predict when it would need to be serviced—a service called Predix—and schedule maintenance before a failure occurs in order to improve operational efficiency. The success of their work with jet engines led them to create an entire division of the company, GE Digital, that sold their Predix Platform to other manufacturers and endeavored to create a digital model of all the other things produced by GE.

While the idea of creating a digital twin of something a company manufactures and for which it already has a digital model presents one set of challenges, the idea of creating a digital twin of the built environment presents an entirely different set of challenges. While a manufactured product is likely to match the plans, a building often goes through a variety of iterations. Drawings evolve even after architects submit construction documents for bidding. Contractors sometimes make further alterations to past shop drawings based on conditions encountered in the field. The result is a building that might not completely reflect the digital model of the architect.

In this context, designers, contractors, and technologists have sought not only to build buildings that more accurately reflect the design intent, but also to map what has already been built. The former is facilitated by enhanced BIM standards, coordination of the BIM model across disciplines, new contracting methods such as integrated project delivery, and laser scanning technology coupled with clash detection and augmented reality. Some companies have sought to use radar technology to map what exists beneath the ground, while others have used laser scanning technology to give owners accurate as-built drawings to aid operations. Still others use photo technology to map streets and interiors to aid navigation and commerce. In the context of architecture and engineering, some firms are developing their own proprietary digital-twin software to more accurately model and track structural and building performance over time.

It is our goal to incorporate many of these approaches into our practice. More broadly, we would like to contribute to the broader effort to map the existing built environment in the hope of improving overall efficiency. In particular, we see tremendous opportunity to map the many historical works of architecture that were designed prior to the digital era. As an educational tool, they offer tremendous value to the next generation of architects as well as a to a much broader community interested in our shared cultural heritage. At the same time, as a potential network, they offer a tremendous capacity to navigate a global digital city while also using this digital city as an aid to engaging the physical world.

> "WHEN I ACTUALLY APPROACHED THE DESIGN OF AN INTERVENTION FOR THE RECTORÍA THAT WOULD ADDRESS SOME OF THESE DEFICIENCIES, NEGOTIATING THE LINE BETWEEN OLD AND NEW WAS CHALLENGING. THE QUESTION OF WHERE ONE DRAWS THE LINE ALWAYS ARISES."

TWINNING

Given that the adoption of digital twins is in its earliest stages, it is worth considering some of the broader implications and how they might impact our practice and what we design. Digital twins offer the potential to create a complete data set that represents and tracks the built environment in real time. A complete data set of the performance of our society and the things and places comprising it could be created as a total integrated "machine" that can be optimized and made to work efficiently. A data set of this kind and the algorithms that relate and make sense of it using different variables and graphic interfaces could be used to balance all the different hopes and desires of the global population within the context of limited resources. Doing so could, potentially, alleviate much of the stress placed on populations currently suffering, as well as help to alleviate conflict and violence via an equitable distribution of resources. An efficient digital representation and resource allocation strategy that is the direct output of the system of capital investment, construction, and manufacturing could, perhaps, help to address inequality as well as the degradation of the environment. This would imply using the system to foster equality rather than using the knowledge thus gained to further concentrate wealth, put up walls, and subjugate people. In this sense, it might allow us as architects greater opportunity to build projects for a wider range of people as a result of more resources being available. At the same time, it might allow us as designers to visualize a more complex way of embedding our projects in the world—from supply chain to energy consumption and broader ecology.

At the same time, it is important to consider the implications for privacy, control, and authority raised by the use of digital twins. The desire for an accurate representation of the world is by no means new. One can see desires to map the earth in many ancient civilizations. The desire and capacity to map the world has grown in conjunction with technologies and tools that have aided navigation. This process has concentrated a tremendous amount of power in the hands of the manufacturers of navigation and traveling technology, and of the machines and mining equipment needed to produce the energy to sustain these technologies. It has also concentrated power in the hands of governments and private corporations that control this equipment and make the benefits of this control available to their populations. The dominance of mechanization is often overlooked when discussing the aesthetics of the modernist movement and its role in shaping the appearance of architecture today. The flows and barriers, population concentrations and rights, wealth and disparity, and the urban form and architecture that result are perhaps a more significant outcome of the machine age than streamlined windows inspired by steamships.

TWINNING

With this framework in mind, the desire for a digital twin can be reframed, not just as a question of making it possible to build more efficiently, but also as a way of falling in line with the legacy of the colonization of space and the quest for efficiency. It can also be seen as a process that cuts off the possibility of the unexpected, serendipitous, and experimental. As a practice engaged in master planning, this capacity may seem quite appealing. It could allow us to better predict how people will use space and embed flexible strategies that allow that space to evolve over time. At the same time, it may create opportunities to include unplanned spaces where the unexpected can occur. In other words, it means to argue for improving the efficiency and predictability of the vast majority of spaces while still allowing for some spaces that are slow, inefficient, relaxed, off-the-grid, and disconnected from the twin.

It is also important to consider the risks associated with concentrating even more power in the hands of those who control the digital twin. Moreover, as digital twins become increasingly capable of analyzing, optimizing, and even managing the physical world, they become proxies that are as important—if not more important—than the physical world. In many ways, this is a similar moment that faced the Internet two decades ago, when its architects were confronted with the question of whether it would remain open or be commercialized. While at some fundamental level the Internet remains free and open, commercialization has been accelerated, such that the majority of the time spent, not to mention the bandwidth used, is not in the wild, unfettered corners of the Internet. In the present context, it might be possible to take an alternative path whereby digital twins remain a fundamentally common asset. This would not only ensure that the model of different properties would be able to communicate with each other, but that the models would be maintained over time. It would also return the privatization of property that so often occurred via acts of appropriation and violence to the general population. It would also make the argument that although one owns a specific place, where one is entitled to build and dwell, one does not own the digital representation of that place. This also raises the question of degrees of access and security. The result, however, would likely create an opening that might begin to restore balance and support broader social equity. It also might create a platform that supports considerable creativity. For designers, this would open the possibility of designing both the physical and the virtual realm of a new project. It would be possible to add elements that may be financially or even physically unfeasible. At the same time, it could create room for including a greater narrative dimension to a building.

TWINNING

While the capacities and opportunities presented by creating a digital twin are vast, and while a comprehensive twinning of the world presents untold opportunities, the route to achieving this vision is opaque. Moreover, it is already becoming clouded by private companies hoping to reap considerable reward for the investment they make in creating the twin to begin with. The next step would be to consider funding models that could support the creation of digital twins without resorting to privatization. One idea would be to use tax revenue to fund the creation of such a platform. Another would be to charge building owners rent for use of the platform, which in turn would pay for itself via enhanced operational capacity and energy efficiency. Whatever the case may be, it is vital that such a digital realm be developed to enhance the efficiency of the built environment, ideally while remaining a public asset that architects, among many other stakeholders, can collectively help shape.

"IN MY OPINION, BOLDNESS IS ALWAYS WHAT MAKES ONE STRONGER BUT ALSO WHAT CAN BRING ABOUT DEFEAT. BOLDNESS WILL ALWAYS BE CONTROVERSIAL."

CHAPTER NINE

Media and mediation have long played a role in how cities and buildings are designed. While the use of the term "media" is evocative of the late twentieth and early twenty-first century and has been chosen as a means of investigating how current trends are affecting architecture, past terms such as frescoes, sculptures, friezes, stained glass, carvings, insignias, family seals, and public sculptures can be understood to have accomplished similar goals. Even bells, clock towers, chanting, and pageants can be seen as extending media of some sort into the built environment and affecting its form as a result. Much later, public address systems, timetables, advertisements, and company logos continued this tradition.

The use of various media has also become a design tool. This occurs both through the generation of renderings, animations, and immersive virtual environments as well as through the use of screens and projects to help clients visualize future space. These visualizations play an instrumental role in reconciling different interests, opinions, and forces during the design process. Once a building is complete, the specific design can play a role in reconciling forces within a community or neighborhood. Finally, media can be used as a vehicle for disseminating ideas on works of architecture via text and images in some form of publication.

All of the projects presented in this volume have used these different forms of media and mediation to varying degrees. The two projects included in this chapter make "media" and "mediation" their central theme. Radart uses the form and appearance of the building to communicate what is taking place within. The goal of this strategy is, on one hand, to attract attention and investment in the work taking place within the building and, on the other hand, to visually reflect the building's energy consumption and overall sustainability in the hopes of improving efficiency.

CHAPTER NINE

At the same time, it reflects a philosophy of transparency and spatial structure that supports communicating internally in order to foster discourse and reconcile diverse viewpoints.

The Smart Salon prototype developed for Ted Gibson creates an immersive, mediated environment driven by communicating and delivering clients' desires to transform their appearance. The vast majority of the clients engaged in this experience work in media professionally. In this capacity, they often are called upon to reconcile various forces through their presence. This may involve mediating between two viewpoints as a host of a show or newscaster or playing a role in a film or serial that puts them between two points of view or locations, or confronts them with challenges to overcome. The salon itself was designed in partnership with Amazon and intended to be the world's first smart salon. The salon merges cutting-edge smart home technology with a signature luxe, premium salon experience. In many ways, it was an opportunity to create a space where the architecture would not stop at the walls but would extend into the surrounding space through the radiation of sound and light. Moreover, the space would be controlled by the guest's voice and transformed to suit his or her specific needs.

In both of these projects, media and mediation are not just concerned with technology, but with the use of technology to communicate and ideally to resolve potential conflict. The essay "Pervasive Media" explores these themes in a broader context—specifically, the scale of urbanism and the city. Ultimately, the argument is made that while media are common, they rarely support knowledge, progress, and the reconciliation of forces. Instead, they are mostly used to sell goods and keep power structures in place. The essay concludes by exploring why it might be worth considering an alternative and how this might be achieved.

SMART SALON

INTRO

Over the past several decades, the retail landscape has changed dramatically. The cost of space has increased and this, in turn, has made it more costly to house inventory such as beauty products. At the same time, shoppers have increasingly elected to purchase products online. This has been due in part to lower costs, as well as to the convenience of having the products delivered directly to one's place of residence.

As shopping habits have changed, so too has the nature of the stylist. Stylists have become increasingly entrepreneurial. They have found greater independence from the salon via social media. This has led to a capacity to move from one locale to another with greater ease. Salons have responded by offering greater flexibility and allowing stylists to work on a more temporary basis rather than having a permanent station.

It was in this context that Ted Gibson and his partner Jason Backe found themselves in when they decided to close their forty-seat salon in New York. During this period, they found themselves working between the East and West Coasts. Ultimately, they decided to relocate to Los Angeles and develop a salon tailored to the entertainment industry. At the same time, they were interested in creating a space to serve a younger crowd of entertainers and influencers rather than the more established socialite and fashion clientele that patronized their New York salon.

The type of space that would draw the necessary interest would have to be quite different than what had served them in the past. Whereas the grand and the great were once considered attractive, the intimate, unique, and relatable had increasingly become a focal point. People were more interested in spaces addressed to the scale of the body and experiences fostering exclusivity and quality. This shift, in turn, presents the opportunity to consider what one can accomplish at a small scale that cannot be done at a larger scale. It creates an opportunity to work within budgetary and time-frame limitations to achieve something remarkable.

In order to address these limitations, a modular solution was offered. This included the repetition of five semi-enclosed pods. Each varies slightly and can be manufactured with the aid of digital fabrication technology. Each pod ("cloud") allows for a unique atmosphere that can adapt to a particular client's preferences for lighting and music while also providing visual isolation from the other guests in the salon. These pods sit within a neutral white environment that provides a bright backdrop to serve as a stage for guests.

HAIR AND BEAUTY SALON
COMPLETED 2019
150 M2
BEVERLY HILLS
USA

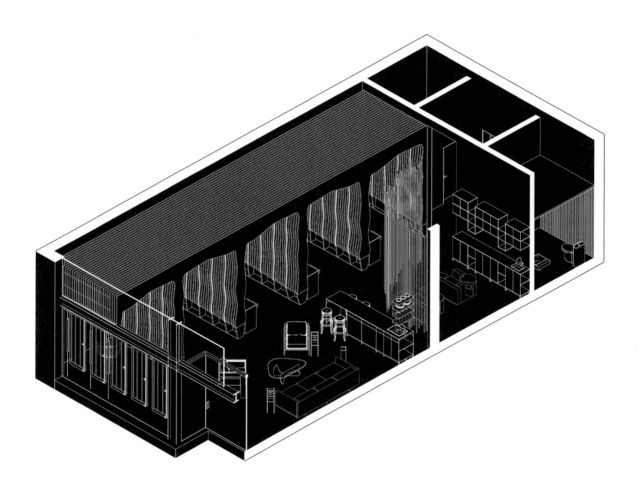

"THE ARTIFICE OF PRODUCT AND BRAND DESIGN, FOCUSED ON CONSUMPTION AND EMOTION, WHILE UTILIZING INTEGRATED TECHNOLOGY AS THE INTERFACE. THE 'SMART SALON' EXPLORES PRIVATE AND PUBLIC BOUNDARIES IN A SMALL FOOTPRINT, SEEKING TO PRESENT THE ESSENCE OF THE BRAND AND TO CONNECT IT WITH THE FUTURE OF RETAIL AS A TYPOLOGY. IN MY EXPERIENCE, THE SMALLEST PROJECTS ARE OFTEN THE GREATEST DISRUPTORS, FERTILE GROUND FOR EXPERIMENTATION; THE RESTRICTIONS ON BUDGETS AND SPACE ARE DRIVERS OF INNOVATION."

Beyond the series of pods lies a waiting area in lieu of a reception desk, a washing area screened by a curtain of thin Plexiglas rods, and a powder room with custom wallpaper.

The guest experience, as well as the broader salon, is powered by Alexa through a partnership with Amazon. In addition to controlling lighting and audio, the partnership with Amazon also makes it possible to scan styling products on shelves in the salon, add those products directly to the client's shopping cart, and then have them delivered later that day. This will be the first cashier-less retail establishment that Amazon has created through partnership with a brand that is not their own. As the first "smart/intelligent salon," it will set a new standard for the industry and become a prototype for future salons by Ted Gibson and Jason Backe. Each cloud will offer different ambient lighting options like "Everyday Sunshine," "Moonlight," and "Indoors" to view hair color and styles in various light and ambient settings. Additionally, each individual cloud will feature an Amazon Fire Tablet, Amazon Prime Video application, and Sonos speakers for truly personalized entertainment programming and music options. The salon itself will be entirely voice activated through Amazon Alexa, and a state-of-the-art entertainment lounge will welcome guests instead of a traditional salon waiting area.

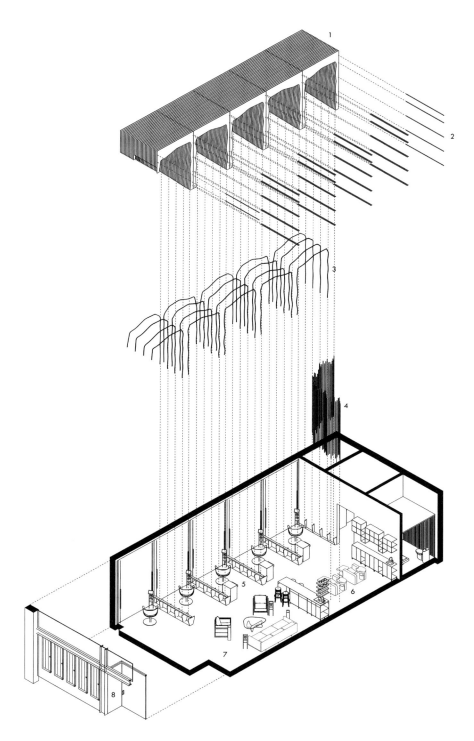

1. MDF CLOUDS
2. STRUCTURAL BRACING TUBES
3. LINEAR LED LIGHTING, VOICE ACTIVATED THROUGH ALEXA
4. ACRYLIC RODS
5. INDIVIDUAL BOOTH
6. WASHING + COLORING STATION
7. ENTRANCE / LOUNGE
8. BARCODED INTERACTIVE FACADE

CLOUD STRUCTURE

CLOUD DETAIL

RIB ELEVATION DETAIL

RIB PLAN DETAIL

CLOUD PLACEMENT DETAIL

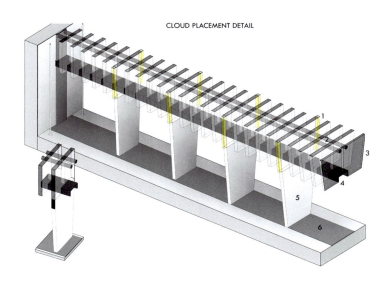

1. LED STRIP LIGHTING
2. THREADED STEEL ROD
3. MDF RIB
4. STEEL CHANNEL
5. STEEL LEGS
6. STEEL PLATE

"EACH POD ALLOWS FOR A UNIQUE ATMOSPHERE THAT CAN ADAPT TO A PARTICULAR CLIENT'S PREFERENCES FOR LIGHTING AND SOUND WHILE ALSO PROVIDING AN ATMOSPHERE OF INTIMACY AND ISOLATION."

ASSEMBLY CONCEPT
MDF RIBS - CNC CUT

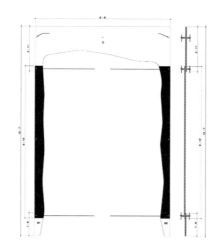

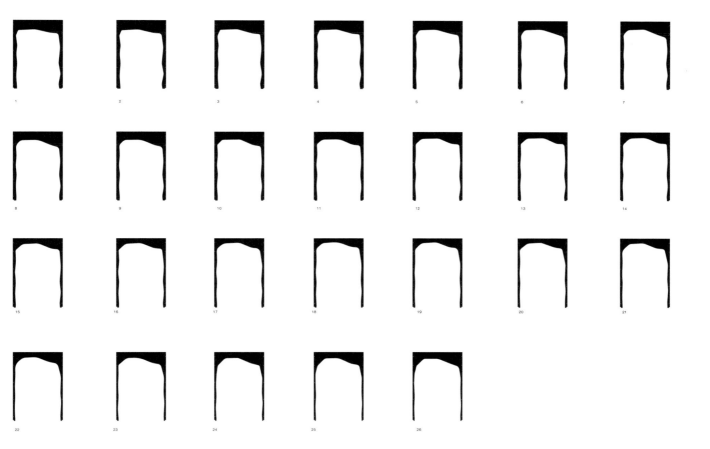

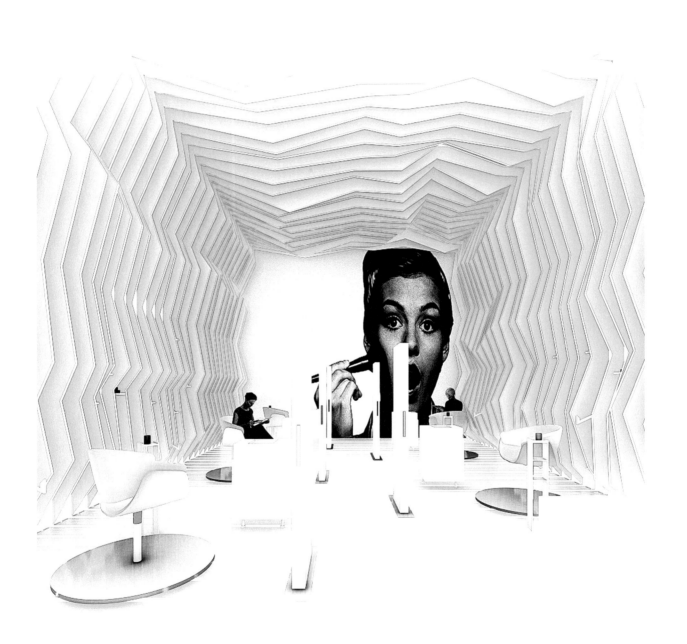

INITIAL CLOUD CONCEPT

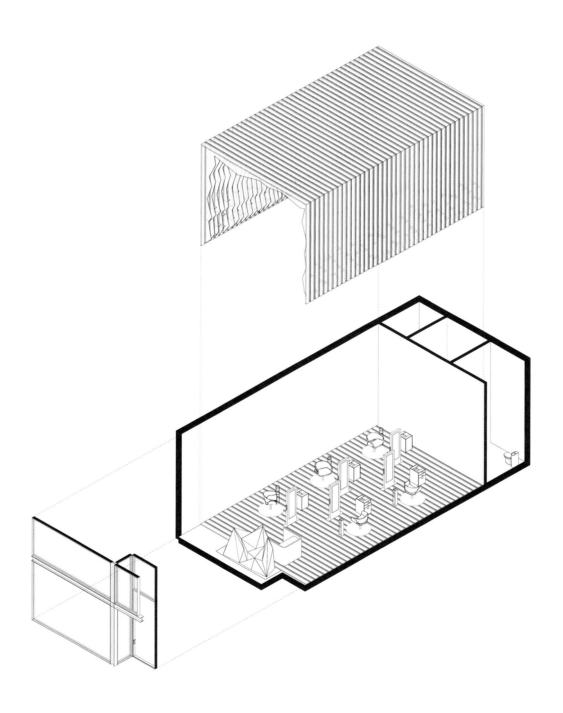

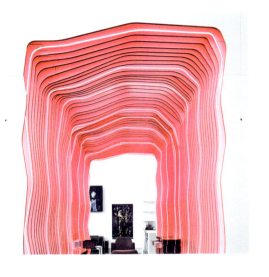
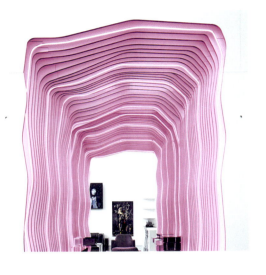
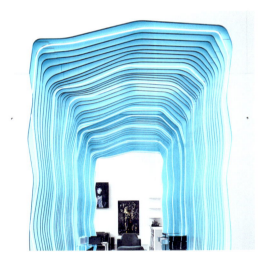

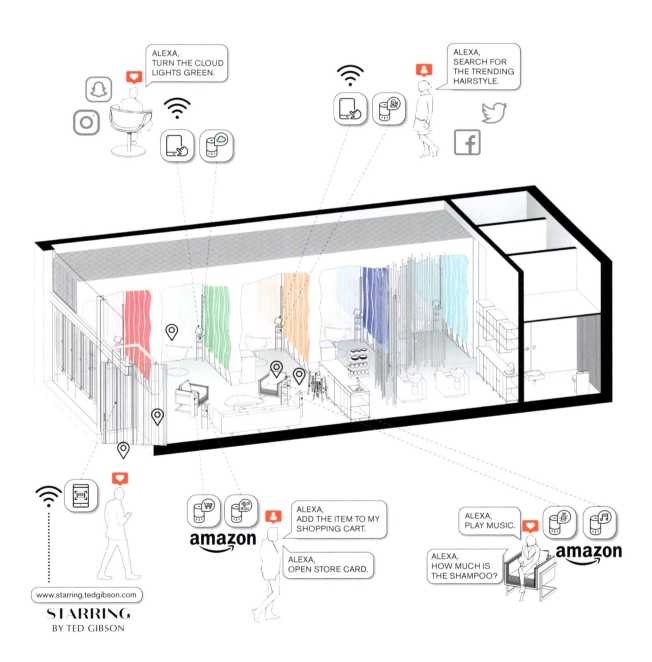

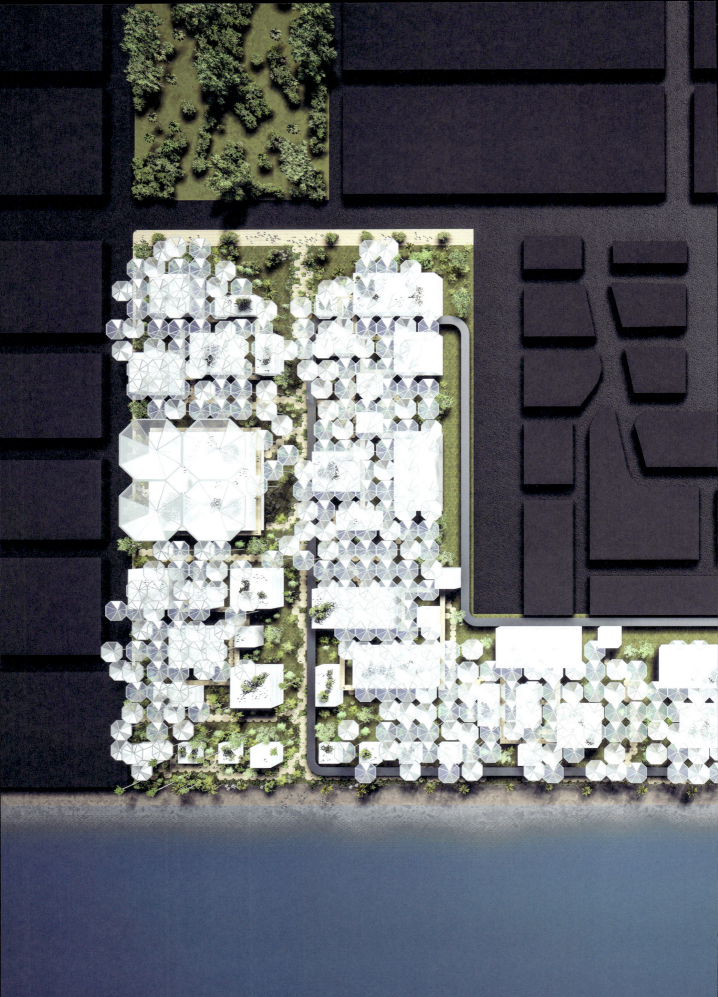

RADART

INTRO

Radart is an incubator that brings together established corporations, entrepreneurs, and sources of funding. It is a collection of research areas, labs, shared tools, classrooms, auditoriums, and cultural spaces balanced equally by open spaces where ideas are cultivated and exchanged. Moreover, it is a place defined by unique architecture and urbanism, in which the modular components serving these programs are connected by ground and aerial paths, electric vehicles, and elevated trains, and covered by dynamic fabric umbrellas reflecting the activities within. It is also a car-free oasis that is open to the city and defined by smart and sustainable urban systems showcasing the latest in waste, water, mobility, and energy management. This collaboration will capitalize on the legacy of manufacturing while also redefining Tijuana as a center of the globally connected knowledge economy.

Any visionary project must address a pressing problem that faces the community or the broader world. It is not enough merely to conceive of an innovative building, campus, or city and assume that people and companies will want to live and work there. It must be conceived by adopting a holistic approach that looks at the elements and systems necessary for a successful ecosystem. Pressing problems related to workforce, data, security, customer service, supply chains, new markets, and quality face all corporations. The way we live, and the consequences of our lifestyle, present new challenges for our economy and environment. These problems offer a chance for innovative solutions. Radart is a place to attract companies interested in solving these problems. Doing so will attract a broader range of interest from a wider range of corporations. It will also create a space that aims to solve more fundamental problems whose solutions will represent valuable innovations that provide a very strong return on investment.

What, then, are the most pressing problems facing life in our cities and the world? While a wide range of concerns from economic inequality to lack of access to adequate healthcare, clean water, and sanitation all exist, six basic areas are applicable to major sectors of the economy and will attract corporate interest. They include the following: 1) mobility and congestion; 2) housing and affordability; 3) inefficiency of buildings and construction; 4) aging and new infrastructure; 5) retail and how we consume; and 6) education and research. These are all connected to the sustainability and resilience of our cities and world.

CONCEPT

An open system of spaces, programs, and innovations that will contribute to economic prosperity and catalyze broader regional development will begin to address these problems. This project will be more than a building. It will

URBAN DEVELOPMENT PROPOSAL 2019
125,375 M2
TIJUANA
MEXICO

"AS ECOLOGY SEEKS TO UNDERSTAND THE VITAL RELATIONSHIPS BETWEEN LIVING ORGANISMS AND THEIR ENVIRONMENT, RADART SEEKS TO CONNECT BUILDINGS AS NON-LIVING ORGANISMS IN A MORE DYNAMIC WAY WITH BOTH. THE CORE OF THE EXPERIENCE IS TO MAKE THE BUILDINGS MORE HUMANE AND NATURAL, NOT BY WAY OF BIO-MIMICRY, BUT BY RESPONDING TO EXTERNAL AND INTERNAL FORCES AS 'LIVING ORGANISMS' THROUGH A SERIES OF ADAPTIVE SYSTEMS. THE GOAL IS TO CREATE AN ENVIRONMENT IN WHICH OUR METRICS OF ENERGY CONSUMPTION, POLLUTION, WATER AND WASTE MANAGEMENT, EMBODIED ENERGY, MOBILITY, AND RECYCLABILITY ESTABLISH A FRAMEWORK FOR FUTURE URBAN INSERTIONS."

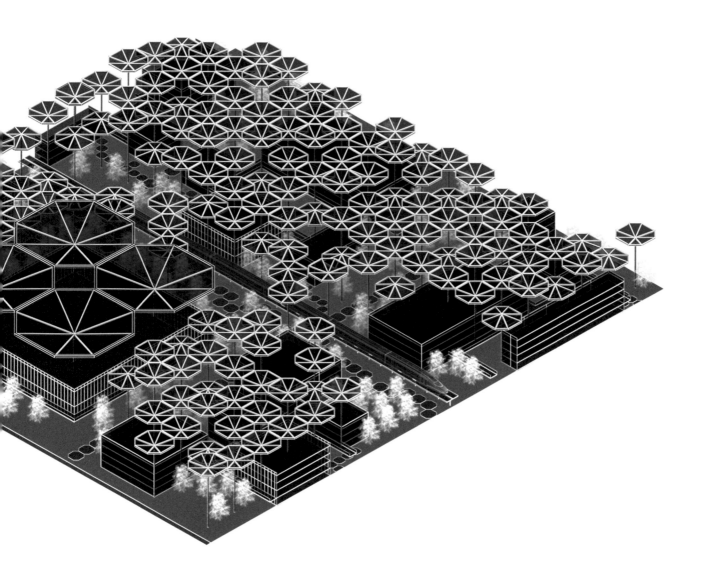

be a framework for development that can expand as demand increases. Contrary to past visions of grandiose smart cities requiring massive infrastructure investment, Radart will be a set of innovative urban elements. These will address mobility, building enclosure, structural systems, energy, waste, freight, and overall sustainability and resilience. They will be deployed gradually in order to serve research spaces and labs as well as cultural, social, retail, hospitality, and wellness zones.

This framework is the platform on which innovation will occur. At the heart of this platform lies the relationship between research and lab spaces as the location where ideas are generated and developed, respectively. They will be highly flexible spaces that can be configured in a variety of ways in order to meet evolving needs and create ideal adjacencies between different groups working within the space. These groups will essentially be divided into four categories: large corporate partners, small start-ups, visiting innovators, and venture funds. These groups will be supported by tools and equipment sponsored by the corporate partners that can easily be moved to different locations to support specific endeavors.

The specific spaces in which these groups work will be organized as a campus with related endeavors clustered around open spaces that support collaboration on the ground level and are connected via bridges on the upper levels. The spaces between the interior of the lab or research spaces will be flexible and easily opened to the surrounding covered courtyards. These central gathering spaces will be protected from the elements by a network of umbrellas that can be extended as the open system grows over time to meet specific project demands. They will also be filled by zones dedicated to culture, social activities, retail, hospitality, and wellness that will serve those working in the research spaces and labs as well as exist as potential test sites for products developed on-site before they enter the broader market.

This open system will support innovation in both manufacturing and digital technology. With this goal in mind, the companies that are attracted should not be limited by the sector they serve. Instead, the focus areas should be defined by more fundamental technologies that can be applied to four initial areas of focus:
1) big data, data science, and Internet of Things;
2) artificial intelligence and machine learning;
3) new materials and material science; and
4) robotics, advanced manufacturing, and automated construction.

ENERGY FOREST

INVERTED OCTAGONAL UMBRELLAS COLLECT WATER THROUGH CONDENSATION AND RAINFALL

THE UMBRELLAS ARE MADE OF ETFE MEMBRANES AND TUBULAR STEEL STRUCTURES

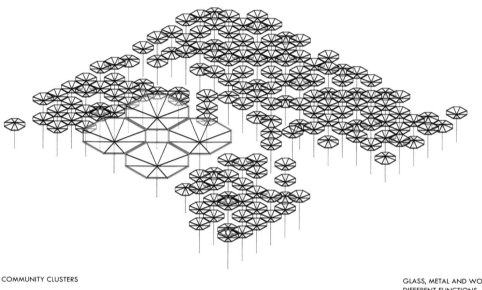

CREATIVE COMMUNITY CLUSTERS

GLASS, METAL AND WOOD PAVILIONS REPRESENT DIFFERENT FUNCTIONS

THE SITE IS ACCESSED BY A PEDESTRIAN SYSTEM OF PATHS OR A LIGHTWEIGHT RAIL SYSTEM

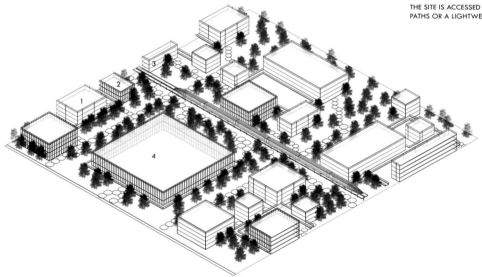

1. OFFICES
2. RESIDENTIAL
3. RETAIL
4. AUDITORIUM

CONTEXT

Ideally, porous boundaries between these different areas facilitated by the physical architecture would be created in order to enhance collaboration and sharing of expertise. Projects might then emerge that actively integrate innovations in these respective areas.

In order to realize this vision, leading companies in these respective fields should serve as anchor tenants to begin to set an agenda of challenges and problems they would like to overcome. Venture funds interested in supporting early-stage companies could then be introduced as partners. With this framework in place, an open call would be held for companies to apply to be residents of the space for a particular term to help develop an idea or take an existing company to the next level through corporate partnership. Talent could be cultivated locally as well as from the West Coast of the United States and via strategic partnerships with cities in Asia.

As the largest transnational metropolitan area in Mexico, Tijuana has a population of more than 2.23 million inhabitants. It is the most visited border in the world. Its rich gastronomic culture makes it the capital city of craft beer in the country and the most important in terms of Mexican-Mediterranean cuisine. Tijuana has been characterized by the interest of foreign investment thanks to its tariff-free factories, technology services, and assembly and manufacturing plants. Tijuana could be seen from another perspective—one in which it is not only a means for investment, but a starting point for the creation of an ecosystem that will open doors not only with its near border, but exponentially through connecting to the center of the country, Silicon Valley, and Asia. Its geographical location is a key point for these connections. At the same time, the concept is strategically located with views of the sea.

Tijuana is also a locale with a diverse population with respect to education and skills that will help supply the talent necessary for Radart to succeed. The proximity to universities is important for creating links between them and making a virtuous circle between education, entrepreneurship, and technology. The city must cease to be seen as a place where only labor is obtained. While the workforce is very valuable, there are many people who are prepared to become a higher-level workforce for companies making an investment in the region and new, innovative technology.

DESIGN

A logic of adjacencies will fuel creativity and growth. The system will include adjacent research and lab spaces, supported by a network of tools and dotted with cultural, social, retail, hospitality, and wellness zones serving the community and acting as sites where potential new technologies can be tested. These spaces and programs will be supported by corporate partners and

PROCUREMENT OF WILD NATURAL ENVIRONMENT

PRESERVATION OF MAXIMUM WATER ABSORPTION

PROMOTION OF A NATURAL ENVIRONMENT FOR
PEDESTRIANS BY USING INDEGENOUS SPECIES

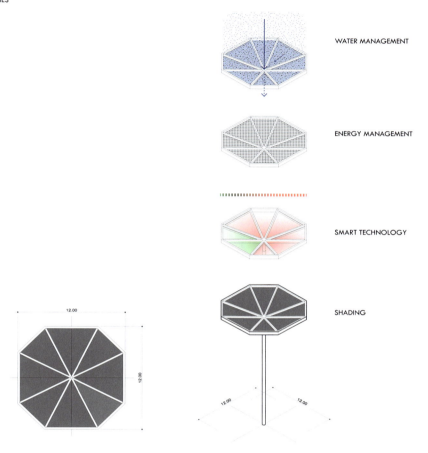

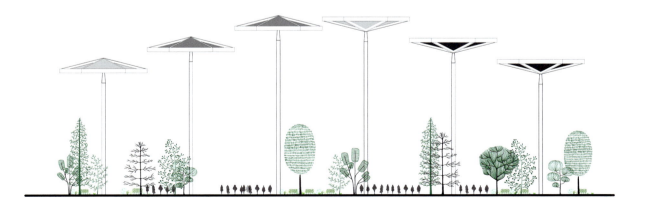

venture funds as anchor tenants and populated by start-ups and new companies. They will offer both permanent homes and residencies for innovators as well mentorship and a general sense of community.

These programs will be distributed across an initial set of fifteen buildings. Each building will be 5,000 square meters. We imagine that there will be a 1:1 ratio between built and open space, resulting in a total project footprint of 125,000 square meters. The perimeter of the site will be permeable to the surrounding city and will appear almost like an oasis from the broader urban fabric. Within the complex, clusters of buildings will form around specific research initiatives. These clusters will be served by two larger clusters of four umbrellas that serve as event spaces—one for internal events and one for city events. The latter will include an auditorium and enjoy ocean views.

The project will be constructed with a modular system that will accelerate building. This system will work at both the macro and micro level. At the macro, it will include a collection of elements such as ground paths, elevated paths, pavilions, courts, and dynamic roofs expressing the energy performance of the building through color. These dynamic roofs could also be used to express other aspects, such as air quality and special events taking place within.

At the micro level, the modular system will be deployed as structural and facade units within each pavilion. We imagine developing modular interior systems as well that will make it easier to reconfigure space without having to demolish walls. This can be achieved through running systems in the baseboard or at the ceiling level rather than embedding it within walls. We also imagine that this modular system could be produced locally and take advantage of locally available materials. This will support flexibility and allow companies to expand as they grow while also creating flexibility in adjacencies between companies.

The facades of these structures will be retractable in order to enhance the connectivity between inside and outside while also supporting connection between shared meeting, collaboration, and common spaces. These common spaces will in turn be covered by modular umbrellas to enhance their thermal comfort and offer protection from rain.

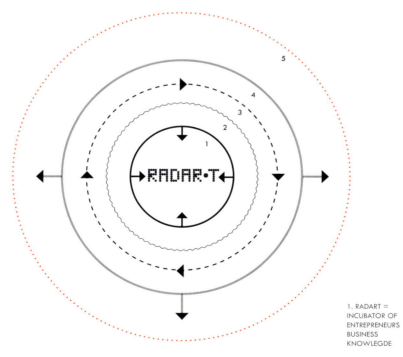

1. RADART =
INCUBATOR OF
ENTREPRENEURS
BUSINESS
KNOWLEGDE

2. INFRASTRUCTURE / ARCHITECTURE

3. CROSS-POLLINATION

4. INNOVATION IN TERMS OF
MOBILITY
BUILDING EFFICIENCY
HIGH-TECH INFRASTRUCTURE
E-COMMERCE
DATA SCIENCE
ROBOTICA
ARTIFICIAL INTELLIGENCE

5. TIJUANA AND THE WORLD

"I BELIEVE THAT THE ERA OF THE GARDEN HAS BEGUN WITH THE 2020 PANDEMIC. INSTEAD OF BEING DEFINED BY LOTS OF PEOPLE CONGREGATING IN TRADITIONAL PUBLIC SPACE, THIS NEW ERA WILL BE DEFINED BY PEOPLE FINDING THEIR OWN PRIVATE SPACES OUT OF DOORS WHERE THEY CAN BE PRODUCTIVE."

REALIZATION

The entire open system will be supported by a mobility strategy that reduces private car trips. Supporting programs within the development will be created to limit the need to travel off-site. Parking will be eliminated, rapid transit will be cultivated, and ride hailing lanes at the perimeter will be integrated in order to anticipate the arrival of autonomous vehicles. Throughout the complex, bike lanes, scooter lanes, an electric train, and walking paths that connect the buildings will be provided. Finally, an autonomous electric vehicle system to support trips from one end of the site to the other will be introduced.

The project will be powered by a core set of digital services that others can build on, an advanced energy management system, a flexible building and tenant management platform, a mobility management system, and an active stormwater management system. The project will be supported by an advanced power microgrid, smart water system, and underground freight delivery system. Finally, we will use waste as a resource by actively cultivating a circular economy.

Looking forward at the challenges of realizing this vision, we feel that it would be essential to develop a viable business plan and set of partners from the beginning. Beyond the precedents for a smart city or campus, there are a number of precedents for creating an incubator to support partnership between major corporate partners and entrepreneurs. Further, precedents exist for turning cities and regions into innovation hubs. These include the organic evolution of Silicon Valley and Palo Alto into the global center of digital technology. At the same time, they include the push to turn Cambridge, MA, and Boston into a center of biotech innovation and the current push to turn Atlanta into a tech hub of the East Coast of the United States. In each case, strong partnerships have existed between universities and private companies.

If we are to collectively address these problems, we feel that it would also be important to support policy analysis. A policy group would be capable of advocating for new local, national, and global strategies that are aligned with and make possible innovations coming from the hub. This would create an internal capacity to market new products and services in order to ensure that they receive the best chance of success and that Radart flourishes as a vibrant entrepreneurial ecosystem.

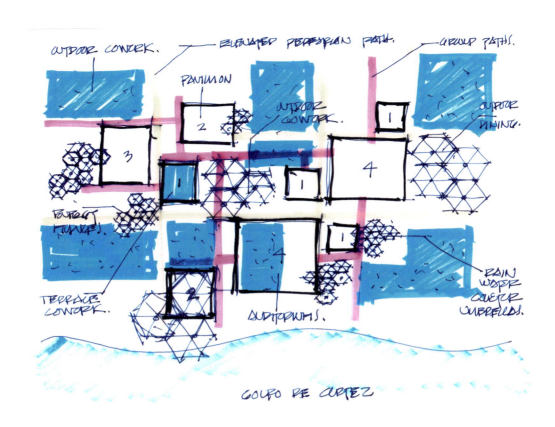

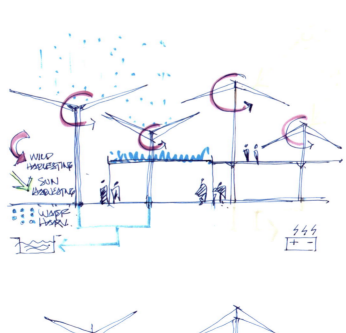

PERVASIVE AND PERVASIVE OF MEDIA RESTORATION MEDIATION

Digital screens have become a pervasive presence. They are carried in pockets, provide guidance through cities by aiding navigation and transportation services, and often make it possible to begin and end the day by receiving news and entertainment. During the workday, they have become one of the primary points of engagement. This is true not only in professional and service-oriented occupations, but also in manufacturing, logistics, construction, and maintenance. For those engaged in the design, construction, and maintenance of the built environment, the screen has become the primary surface through which design occurs. Contractors increasingly construct buildings while using a paperless jobsite. Augmented reality on mobile tablets is being used to validate the accuracy of construction, and tablets have become pervasive in operating and maintaining buildings once they are completed. At the same time, screens are integrated into the finished product to support the end users. While this presence and functionality is often taken for granted, it would be worth pausing to consider whether the ubiquity of screens is a "good" thing, how they are functioning, and how they could function. From a design perspective, this is important because it helps to guide how screens and other media devices of various scales might be situated within a given project. In principle, it would be possible to add media devices to architectural elements such as walls, windows, roof, doors, etc. This could help us to better understand how individual parts might relate to the overall hierarchy of the whole within a design, as well as the role that such devices might play in the overall image of an architectural work.

A few of our buildings have incorporated media devices as a prominent design feature. The Diablos Rojos baseball stadium in Mexico City makes use of a custom-designed central media screen that greets the visitor as they approach the main entrance beneath the PTFE-clad roof. This screen essentially mediates between the interior of the stadium and the public plaza. It offers a glimpse of the action to come while also serving as a powerful communication tool to convey the Diablos brand to visitors. In the case of Radart in Tijuana (Baja California, Mexico), the canopies of the modules covering the outdoor spaces were made communicative through projections that conveyed the building's energy performance and overall sustainability. This strategy again allowed us to communicate an interior quality to broader public in order to draw interest and contribute to the overall identity of the project. We have also introduced media devices in the lobby of the building we designed in Guangzhou, PRC, the GICC, which uses illuminated characters to tell a story. In the Smart Salon in Beverly Hills, we deployed integrated screens as well as a mediated light and sound environment, and the way that murals are preserved and reframed in our project Transparente for the Rectoría of Monterrey Tec in Monterrey, Mexico, likewise relies on embedded media. Other uses for media can also be seen in projects such as Harmony Bridge in Guangzhou, China, and Monarca in Santander, Spain.

PERVASIVE AND MEDIA OF RESTORATION MEDIATION

In this sense, media has the capacity to create a buffer or reconcile a building's relationship to inhabited spaces—often between interior and exterior, public and private. Mediation of this type occurs whenever we use a map to navigate the world or understand a message displayed on a mural adorning the side of a building or interior of a room. Historically, these instances of mediation have helped people to read and engage with their environment. Since the introduction of digital media, instances in which digital screens help us to navigate and engage physical reality are increasingly common. In some cases, digital surfaces have created something that stands in-between the body and the world. In doing so, they have also created the potential for us to have avatars or proxies that exist within that surface to fulfill needs not fulfilled in the physical world. Creating distance or adding something in-between the subject and the world they inhabit affects the physical constitution, design, and construction of that world. This mediation sets the parameters for what is needed from a habitat—both to compensate for the deficiencies of mediation and to complement them. Each subsequent new media supported by new technology requires a unique habitat that the architect must design. Creation of such a new approach to space based on media can be seen in the design of Radart and FGP ATELIER's more recent work in master planning, which incorporates artificial intelligence in the planning process itself.

In approaching such projects, it is worth considering how one ensures that media supports mediation rather than just becoming a decoration or distraction. In many cases, the way that media is involved in people's lives and sited the city has been instigated in such a way that mediation between occupant and space does not occur. Instead, an illusion of mediation exists. Desires are displaced rather than fulfilled. They are consolidated within the digital surface of the media experience. In their absence, there is a void of investment in the physical world. All profits are increasingly being made and spent within the digital realm as a tight, integrated, and homogenous zone where all real difference and conflict is suppressed.

In considering how future projects designed by the Atelier might counter this trend, we can draw on some of the past experiences of introducing media devices noted here, while also drawing on a much longer legacy of siting media in the built environment. In many ways, it would be possible to retell the entire history of architecture by tracing the different ways media is sited. This would begin with the earliest cave paintings and extend through stained-glass windows in churches, paintings in chapel alcoves and the great halls of private villas, sculptures in piazzas to commemorate victories, and murals on the sides of buildings to celebrate narratives. At the same time, this history would also include the radio sitting by the fireplace as well as the newspaper on the front step, in the newsstand, or at the breakfast table. It would come to include bookshelves, libraries, television, movie theaters, and now laptops and tablets moving through myriad spaces.

> "BAD DESIGN DOES NOT COMMUNICATE ESSENTIAL VALUES. IT IS LIKE A BEAUTIFUL COSTUME MADE OF DAZZLING FORMS THAT FAILS TO SUPPORT HUMAN INTERACTION AND COMFORT."

PERVASIVE AND PERSUASIVE MEDIA RESTORATION OF MEDIATION

 PERVASIVE AND OF | **MEDIA RESTORATION MEDIATION**

The current relationship between media and architecture has been determined by infrastructure and distribution networks. This relationship is defined by a hierarchy of media and the spaces in which they are encountered. Each is sited within the city at a particular location that has come to be associated with its qualities and served by infrastructure scaled and tailored to its needs. While the media of the past are still encountered, some examples of how new media is sited in relation to architecture include large screens such as digital billboards along roads, on buildings, and in public plazas, televisions in restaurants, screens in elevators, large projection walls, colored facades and rooftops spelling out messages, radio and dashboard screens in cars on roads, earbuds connected to smart-phone screens or tablets moving through buildings, tablets used as augmented reality devices to maintain buildings and equipment, screens embedded in walls that control building systems, computer screens mounted on desks, screens used to order food at restaurants, smart watches moving through buildings, screens at the gym, and digital public sculpture.

This recent history, when viewed within the broader history of the relationship between media and architecture, suggests that media devices are unable to support mediation with the physical environment in part because they are disconnected from the physical world. They are also ubiquitous, marking a disjunction between the temporality of media and that of the human body and revealing the competing temporalities of different media delivered digitally. The fleeting nature of digital media infrastructure and its capacity for replacing one piece of content with another open it up to control by corporate forces. Disconnection and ubiquity make it difficult to form communities that use media as tools of reconciliation directed at specific material conditions. The disjunction between media time and corporeal time contributes to further alienation from the self, while competing media make it difficult to focus processes of reconciliation. Instead, these processes are dispersed across a range of platforms. Their fleeting nature makes it difficult to inscribe the consequences of mediation in the world in such a way that benchmarks are registered and surpassed with time.

The lack of mediation is important because of the role that circulating and siting media have played in the reconciliation of societal forces. While media can be used to convey a simple message that may have little consequence, they can also perform a much more significant role in society—often through the cumulative activities within media, collective activities across media, and through understanding the hierarchy of media and its relationship to underlying forces. This process makes it possible for media to serve as the site where different physical realities are represented, how that representation is debated, and how physical reality is changed as a result. It is here that opposing societal forces, such as between the cultural and material realms or the superstructure and the base, can be worked out.

PERVASIVE MEDIA AND RESTORATION OF MEDIATION

In the context of architecture, a building is determined by and through language, labor, material, the client's desires, the architect's ambition, site, cultural context, time, and money. There have been many instances in the practice of FGP ATELIER in which we have found ourselves confronting these forces and taking on the role of mediator.

It is also important to understand how media siting is changing and what it means for media to become increasingly ethereal and ubiquitous in buildings. This is especially important given the control of this ubiquity by large digital corporations—as suggested above—but also by venture funds and investment trusts that have the capacity to foreclose independent platforms, open media, free exchange, and dissent—all means that are potential tools for those seeking to reconcile negative living conditions, wages, or personal freedoms. In this sense, it is important to ask how architectural design can work with media in reconciling opposing forces and helping to create a better society.

As designers, we have the opportunity to introduce moments within broader architectural projects that address some of these concerns. Architecture in collaboration with media can create site-specific encounters that challenge the ubiquitous media network and provide an alternative experience. Doing so might support the reconciliation of people with the places they occupy. In order to restore the promise of genuine collaboration between architecture and media and the possibility of genuine mediation, the specific media with which architecture might collaborate should be further examined. In this context, collaborations between architects and artists offer a unique opportunity to work together to surpass disciplinary limitations and confront some of the challenges described here. At the same time, by building on the reflections in "Twinning," it would be possible to explore how a digital twin could be used to improve architecture and infrastructure through digital tools and media supporting investment in physical space.

In this context, we have begun thinking about ways that we can integrate a building's digital life earlier in the design process while also considering what should be inhabited virtually and what should be inhabited physically. This approach might create new potential for architecture, space, and design to cultivate alignment with specific narratives, content, values, and meanings. Some of these ideas are beginning to be explored by FGP ATELIER's new research arm, the Building Research Institute, and its One City initiative. Whatever the specific context for exploring these ideas might be, this sort of allegiance would ideally create room for architecture to participate in the broader reconciliation of societal forces and, in doing so, support progress and opportunity.

"DIABLOS IS A GOOD EXAMPLE OF A BUILDING THAT DRAWS ON CONTEMPORARY DIGITAL TECHNOLOGY WHILE ALSO RELYING ON THE CLASSICAL TOOLS OF ARCHITECTURE—FORM, LIGHT, COLOR, TEXTURE, RHYTHM, AND FLOW—THAT TOGETHER FORM AN ATMOSPHERE AND EXPERIENCE."

CHAPTER TEN

Modularity—and its close cousin, scalability—characterizes several projects presented in this book and lies at the heart of our practice. We begin by exploring how modularity can be employed in different contexts and at different scales with an overview of recent work. Some of these projects—Spacecraft, the Alfredo Harp Helú Stadium, and Educational Pavilion—have been described in more detail elsewhere in this book. Others—New International Airport Mexico City at Texcoco (NAICM), Knowledge Training Center (KTC)—are introduced here to deepen the discussion.

The modular approach of NAICM was driven by soil conditions that made it desirable to distribute the weight of the structure to a number of columns rather than rely on long-span structures and single points of support. This led to a column sitting on a concrete pad above a three-meter-deep, pontoon-like structure. This approach made it possible to displace significantly less soil than would have been required for other approaches.

In developing this modular unit, a number of services, such as drainage and electricity, were bundled into the column. This unit was then repeated throughout the building and used to break down the overall scale, while the overall height of the section was also adapted to the scale of the landside and airside spaces. With Spacecraft, by contrast, a unit was repeated to create various living configurations within a flexible building supported by a space frame. Somewhat similarly, the modular unit designed for KTC was used to provide a range of educational services while also serving as the source of energy for the complex.

CHAPTER TEN

For the Alfredo Harp Helú Stadium, a series of eight roof modules were developed as the primary architectural gesture of the stadium. Modularity made it possible to fabricate the trusses within the controlled setting of a factory and then use a crane to hoist them into place. Once secured, they were then clad with a PTFE membrane. Finally, the entire Educational Pavilion was conceived as a kit of parts that could be disassembled, moved, and expanded.

Following the overview of modularity in our practice, we focus in detail on two transportation projects that utilize modularity extensively. The first is the competition entry for Guadalajara Airport Terminal 2 (GDL T2), which explores how complexity can be created from a simple unit. This premise allows for different lighting conditions to be created while also making it possible to design different textures and experiences for the specific programs throughout the building. The modular system would also enhance the overall constructability of the project.

The use of modular systems in the design of the new Felipe Ángeles International Airport At Santa Lucía, currently under construction, is primarily driven by the time and budget constraints of the project. It was very important to develop a system that could be built quickly in order to meet a rapid construction time frame. It was also important that it be designed in such a way as to support ease of constructability. At the same time, the prominent nature of the project for Mexico meant that the building had meet high design expectations and create an exceptional traveler experience.

III_AMBITION

CHAPTER TEN

III_AMBITION

This is achieved through the detailing of the modular system, the scale of the spaces, the introduction of natural light throughout, and the integration of greenspace and a monumental public plaza as part of the journey through Santa Lucía.

While these projects are related through their use of modular architecture, they are also related through their typology. Experience with this typology is part of the genealogy underlying the work presented in this book. It is anchored in Francisco González Pulido's experience working on the O'Hare International Airport Facade Enhancement. This project created an opportunity to become deeply familiar with the aviation architecture of one of the world's busiest and most complex airports. The enhancement involved renovating the entire arrival experience for Terminals 1–3 in order to accommodate greater check-in volume and a more efficient circulation system. Shortly after this project was completed, work began on the Cologne/Bonn Airport. This airport offered a chance to develop a highly efficient structure and energy-efficient building in close collaboration with Werner Sobek and Matthias Schuler. Their collaboration grew out of other high-performance buildings they had worked on together and formed the basis of what became known as "archi-neering." This approach would later be applied on a much larger scale with Bangkok's Suvarnabhumi Airport.

The collaborative architectural work on O'Hare, Cologne/Bonn, and Bangkok formed the backdrop for the independent design work on the competition entry for Terminal 2 in Mexico City, a number of competitions in Asia, and the projects presented in this chapter.

CHAPTER TEN

Although each of these projects makes use of a modular system, the specific context, scale, and program led us to temper the concept of modularity according to the context. In this sense, while "the modular" is a universal concept, it is only as successful as its dialogue with the specifics of a given project. Too many projects seek to blindly deploy a unit across geographic, climatic, and cultural conditions. The result is a homogeneity that ultimately renders the building less successful and interesting than others. The effect is to give the concept of modularity a negative connotation. The work presented here is intended to illustrate how the constraint of modularity can be an opportunity for creativity that supports work which is highly sustainable and contextual.

Modularity has interested González Pulido since he began studying architecture and lies at the heart of our practice. We expand on this topic in the essay "Dry Architecture," a name chosen to mark a contrast with a more plastic architecture often associated with cast-in-place concrete. It also has been chosen to contrast more fluid and amorphous architecture. In this sense, it is slightly more sober and exhibits a drier sense of humor, as it were, one that might be more appropriate for the current period in history.

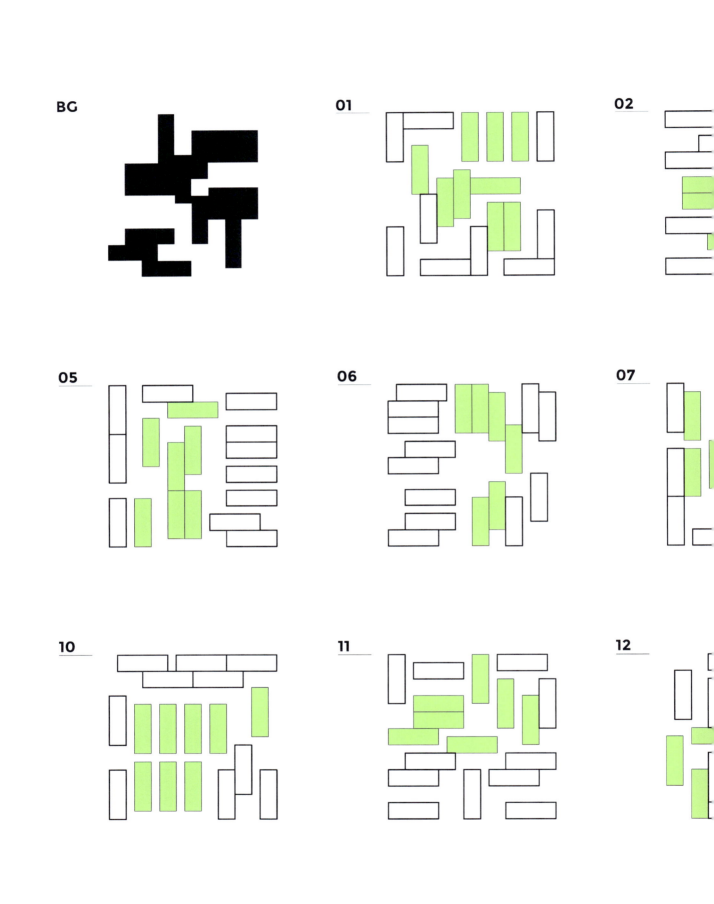

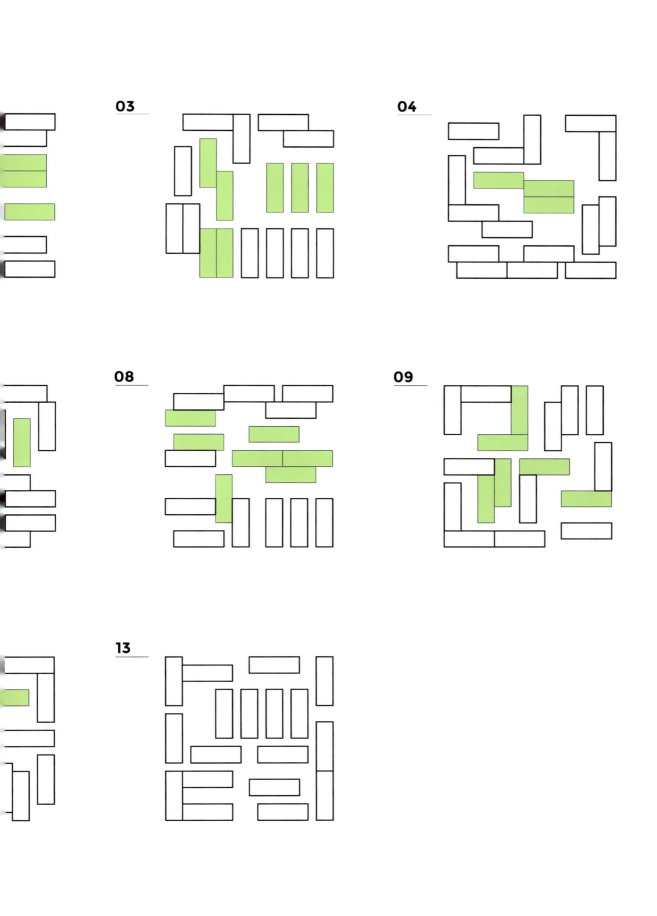

MODULAR

The concept of "the modular" in architecture is, in many ways, a modernization of "the module" in architecture. The module is a rather ancient concept found in such materials as stone, brick, and tatami mats, among others. These building blocks formed the units that defined the broader structure. In the case of stone and brick, the unit primarily defined the facade, while in the case of the tatami mat, it defined the overall dimensions of the plan.

During the early phase of modernity, bricks were standardized in order to make building more unified and efficient. As this occurred, steel components and balloon-frame construction were undergoing a similar process of standardization. However, these elements could still be combined in an almost infinite number of ways to yield spaces of wide-ranging dimensions. This made the building process a largely one-off endeavor that fell short of the new production capacities achieved by factories producing ships, cars, and airplanes.

With the rise of modernism in the early twentieth century, architects began developing modular systems that went beyond the unit to encompass the broader container of the user's space. This can be seen in Le Corbusier's development of his modular system, which uses the golden ratio as a means of determining the proportion of everything from furniture to expansive building complexes. It can also be seen in the modular systems developed by architects such as Buckminster Fuller and Ludwig Mies van der Rohe. Fuller considered how the geometry of the carbon atom could be scaled to create domes ranging in size from those appropriate for a single-family home to those that could cover an entire city. Mies van der Rohe, on the other hand, was more concerned with developing an ideal grid that could regulate the deployment of a standardized kit of parts, which could be used to serve different programs.

Several projects presented in this book make use of modular systems that draw upon this legacy. They roughly fall into three categories: the unit (defined as a container housing a specific function that can be repeated any number of times within an overall structure), the component (defined as an element playing a significant role—often structural—in the construction of the overall project), and the kit (defined as a collection of parts). Spacecraft and the Knowledge Training Center fall in to the first category; the New International Airport Mexico City at Texcoco and the Alfredo Harp Helú Stadium in Mexico City fall in to the second category; the Educational Pavilion falls into the final category. In what follows, the specific way in which each modular system was developed will be explored in turn.

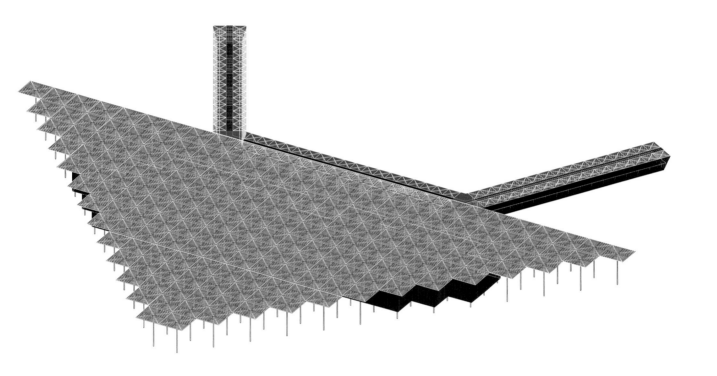

MEXICO CITY INTERNATIONAL AIRPORT

"ONE OF THE MOST EVERLASTING IMPRESSIONS IN MY LIBRARY OF IMAGES IS THE IMAGE OF A VOLKSWAGEN BEETLE COMPLETELY DISASSEMBLED AND REORGANIZED IN A KIT OF PARTS. I HAVE ALWAYS BEEN ATTRACTED TO THE CONCEPT OF THE CELL AS THE ORIGIN OF LIFE, AND THE PART AS THE ORIGIN OF A PRODUCT. WHEN I WORK ON PROJECTS ON A MASSIVE SCALE, I ALWAYS START WITH THE SMALLEST UNIT. RATIONAL COMPLEXITY AS THE BY-PRODUCT OF LOGICAL AND SIMPLE STEPS FUELS MY DESIGN PROCESS; IT ALLOWS ME TO GO BACK TO THE ORIGIN AND REDISCOVER WHAT GENERATED MY DECISIONS AND REPROGRAM IF REQUIRED."

Perhaps more than any other project considered here, Spacecraft builds on the modernist tradition of a spatial unit that is defined by what a person needs to dwell. The unit is geared towards meeting an individual's (or individuals') needs at all times of day or night as they go about a diverse range of activities. The space can be configured for living, sleeping, cooking, bathing, and entertaining. It has sufficient space for storing the various items needed for these activities, so that they do not interfere with the current task at hand.

The modular system is also driven by the modernist fascination with efficiency and using as little space as possible to serve a particular set of functions. As a result, unlike Le Corbusier's deployment of modules in a housing complex, such as the Unité d'habitation, where different functions are each given a discrete space, Spacecraft combines all functions within a single volume that can be reconfigured to meet different needs over the course of the day. This is achieved primarily through the wall system and a moveable "wet box." The wall system can be unfolded to reveal tables, benches, and a storage space. At the same time, the system serves as a shade or screen, giving privacy to walls that would otherwise be open to view from the exterior of the building in which the modular unit is contained. The "wet box" is a quartz-clad volume that can be moved throughout the space and used as a divider if desired. It can also be moved into a corner for maximal openness of plan.

The basic modular unit is, generally speaking, designed for an individual. If desired, however, the unit can easily be combined with others to form a suite. In this case, it is possible that a single "wet box" might suffice. Nonetheless, the functioning of the wall system as well as the ability to constantly reconfigure the space to meet different needs remain essential.

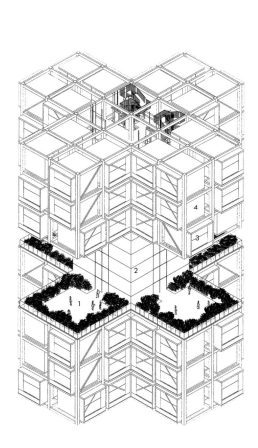
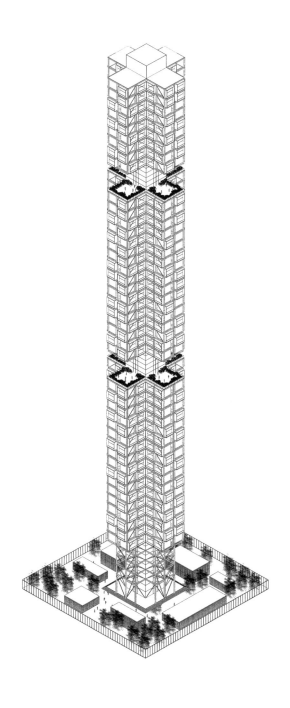

1. ELEVATED GARDEN
2. MECHANICAL AND VERTICAL CIRCULATION CORE
3. PREFAB LIVING UNIT
4. COMPOSITE SKELETON

The Knowledge Training Center (KTC)—designed for the first Chicago Architecture Biennial—uses a modular unit to address the demand for education rather than housing. The goal of the Knowledge Training Center was to create a place where people can trade knowledge without using currency by contributing their own knowledge. The project consisted of 234 modular cells, lightweight, prefabricated classrooms equipped with a screen and outfitted with a floor on which students can sit. Of these, 117 were mother cells generating their own energy, while the other 117 were surrogate cells that charged from the others. Lectures would last forty-five minutes and could be scheduled via an app. The site called for a 50% density ratio across each layer of the thirteen floors. A paranoiac-critical method was used to stack the cells as fast as possible without a pre-designed plan. By intuitively building the space, a pattern was uncovered. Rules emerged, and every floor was different. The open spaces thus created became quite interesting, with vertical and horizontal relationships creating a sense of urban connectivity. The space inside was almost like a cave. In order to expose that space to the exterior, a system was developed that would allow the building to open in the summer and close in the winter.

The modular approach to this design made it possible to extend the building program to meet growing demand. Moreover, it allowed for the solution to be tailored to different sites and potentially fill gaps in the urban fabric. The symbiotic relationship between cells that provide power and those that consume power can be used as a model for deploying the strategy in a range of situations. The system can be easily and economically distributed across vacant sites in communities that are in need of enhanced educational options and could benefit from a solution that is not simply a one-off development, but rather connected to a broader network that can help power and sustain programming and infrastructure.

At the same time, the solution is tied to a broader trend towards distributed knowledge and learning. By using screens and other digital technology, the project creates room where mediation can take place. More specifically, a space is created in which a base level of knowledge, perhaps the result of a specific socio-economic situation, can be elevated so that the student has greater opportunities. This will in turn support the broader reconciliation of societal forces and help to alleviate entrenched societal situations that give some people opportunities while keeping others in a state of perpetual poverty.

In this sense, the specific form that was proposed was merely a provocation. The modular units can be stacked in any number of manners. They can be added over time and configured to suit the local culture. At the same time, the notion that the building could open and close at different times of the year was proposed to suggest that the complex could evolve over time and that it would be possible for some of the units to be moveable and perhaps even be combined with other units to accommodate larger classes. In this sense, the project is more of a framework for thinking about education and the right—one we all should have—to contribute to and access knowledge.

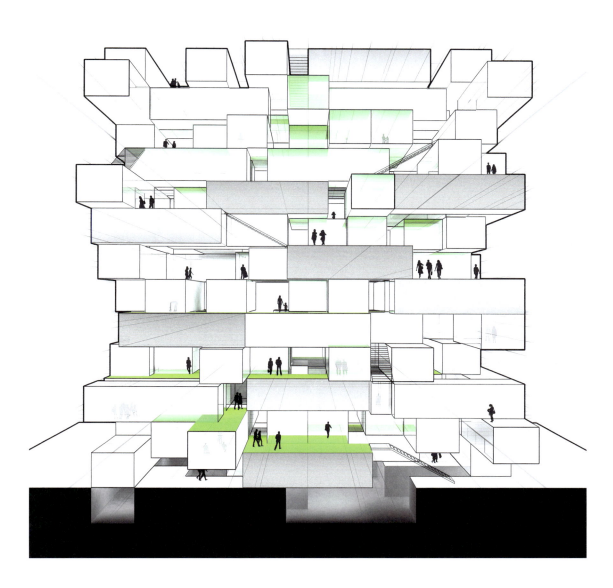
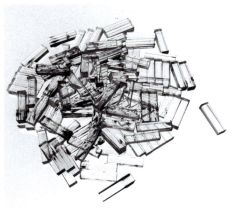
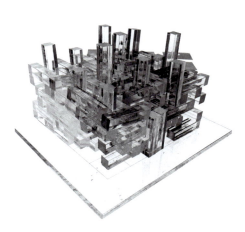

The modular approach proposed for the New International Airport Mexico City at Texcoco (NAICM) was driven in part by the challenge of building on poor, unstable soil. The interior spaces are monumental. They are modularly designed and true to the scale of Mexico City. The logic of the space follows a free configuration. It is independent and super-adaptable. The scale of the building and the soil conditions made a modular solution ideal. This was due in part to the way in which a modular structure can be repeated throughout, tailored to different programs, adjusted in height, and used to break down the immense scale of the project. At the same time, by defining the module as a column supporting a roof structure that radiates from a central point of support, the module would contribute to an even distribution of the structural load. This was important because it would reduce the need to drive significantly deep piles and displace a significant amount of dirt.

The buildings float on the site thanks to a post-tensioned slab that eliminates the need for excavation and deep piles. This would in turn result in a reduction of thirty-six months in the execution of the work. The foundation of the modular system is a box defined by a grid of three-meter-high beams. The foundation concept is based on an aircraft carrier. Three meters of soil are removed, and its weight replaced by the foundation. One column supports the structure. It provides energy and collects water that is transferred to a cistern. It was also intended to bring air into the space from a geothermal system. The lighting and all the wiring are also integrated into the columns. Their design reflects the idea that a component can do more than one thing. Each column then connects to a cruciform structure that is thirty-six by thirty-six meters. The strategy was to create a very rigid frame via a flat structural plate. The question then became how to embed cables in the fabric to create a stable roof plane. It was an exercise in pushing the limits of how textile technology could be applied within large-scale architectural projects.

182 CANOPY MODULES

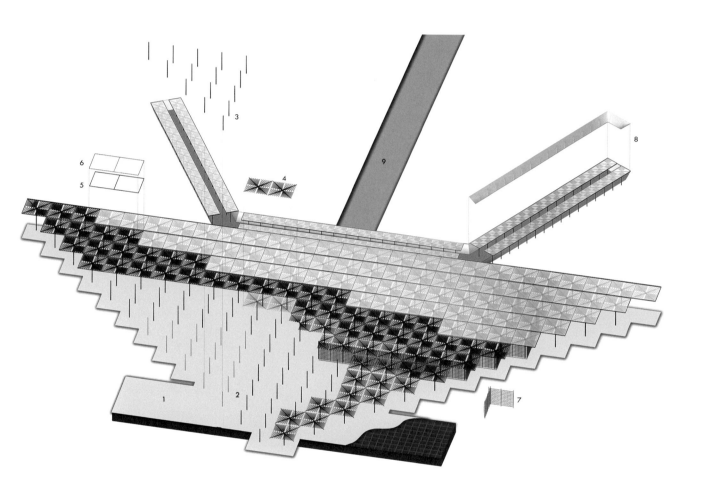

1. FOUNDATION AND BASEMENT
2. SLAB ON GRADE
3. COLUMNS
4. PRIMARY AND SECONDARY CANTILEVERS
5. EDGE BEAM
6. PTFE COATED GLASS FIBER FABRIC
7. FACADE STRUCTURE
8. GLASS ENCLOSURE
9. CONNECTION TO SATELLITE

The design is based on a light steel frame covered by a textile structure. The structure of all umbrellas is identical, which will allow industrial prefabrication. Loads are spread evenly over a wide area, which is more economical. Each umbrella is divided into four identical parts. The assembly of each will be carried out on land and then lifted into position by means of cranes. In order to reduce the weight of these elements, two measures are applied: 1) the secondary overhangs are divided in two, thus saving material and allowing the central insulating layer of the roof to be placed without interruption; and 2) the hollow section of the overhangs is optimized by introducing openings in structurally less-active areas.

This umbrella is a prefabricated element that is not only instrumental in reducing the time of construction, but also has two key sustainable features. It filters light and collects rainwater to supply the airport and mechanical demand. The canopy itself has three layers. The underlayer is perforated ETFE and is more transparent. The middle layer is polycarbonate for thermal and acoustic performance. The outer layer is PTFE. Acoustically it is very efficient, while also allowing for 5% daylight transmission, which is further supported by the south-facing orientation of the site. This is enough to keep the lights of the public space off throughout the day. It will ultimately be illuminated naturally 80% of the time. This will have a huge impact on energy consumption.

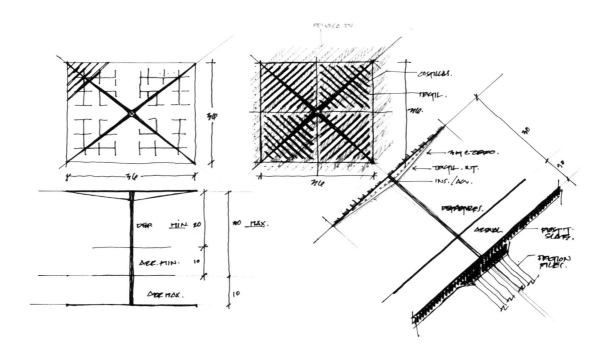

36M X 36M CANOPY MODULE

ETFE MEMBRANE

SECONDARY STEEL STRUCTURE

POLYCARBONATE LAYER

PRIMARY STEEL STRUCTURE

LED LIGHTING

PTFE MEMBRANE

STEEL COLUMN

POST-TENSIONED SLAB

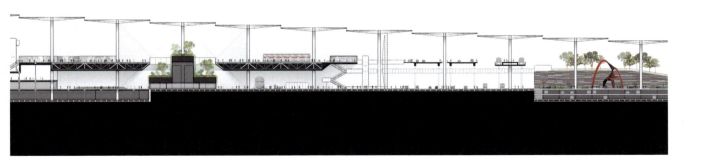

While the modular unit of NAICM was present throughout both the plan and section of the building and effectively created the overall structure that defined the project, the use of modular systems in the Diablos Rojos baseball stadium in Mexico City was somewhat different. A distinct approach was taken to the system that would be used to create the roof covering for the bowl seating and public circulation, while the systems used to create the spaces to house public functions and vertical circulation were differently conceived. A steel truss system was used to create the roof. The design called for six identical modular units to form the wings of the roof and two identical mirrored units to form the canopy covering the entrance to the stadium. These units were analyzed and coordinated in BIM and the field of the stadium became, in essence, a makeshift factory in which the 20-by-120-meter units were fabricated. They were then hoisted into place and connected to the support structure via a series of unique connection points. Once in place, the units were bolted and welded together to form the diaphragm structure. Finally, a layer of PTFE was attached to the outer layer of the truss system. Eventually, the client plans to add a second layer to the underside in order to complete the structure and enhance the overall monolithic appearance of the roof as it was originally designed.

At the same time, the support functions below the canopy were housed within a cast-in-place concrete frame structure that formed the truncated pyramids. This structure was in turn clad with a series of precast modular panels that were made in a local factory. The concrete integrates aggregate from local volcanic rock to give it a dark appearance. Manufacturing the panels in a factory made it possible to achieve much higher tolerances and a higher level of precision. In many ways, this approach updates the module of something like brick or stone for the twenty-first century.

The contrasting approaches to modularity and prefabrication give the roof the appearance of being a lightweight, floating structure above a heavier structure anchored to the ground. The specific use of PTFE and concrete allowed for contrast between rough and smooth textures, which further helped to define the identity of each element. Ultimately, the trapezoidal pyramids feel connected to the earthy, utilitarian functions of the ballpark, while the roof feels connected to the heavens and serves as the visual link between the stadium seating and the playing field.

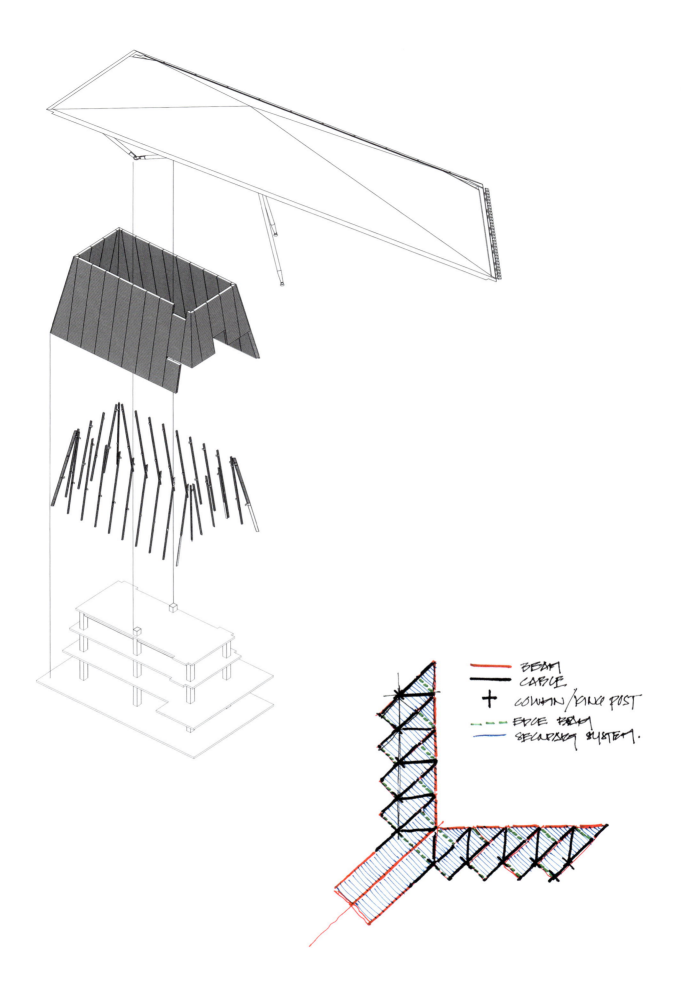

The Educational Pavilion in Oaxaca is, in many ways, the most Miesian with respect to the role of modularity in the design of the project. While the other projects utilize a spatial unit and custom-designed structural systems and cladding modules, the Pavilion is defined by a nine-by-nine-meter grid in which each unit is 1.2 meters, with the overall height measuring 6.4 meters. A kit of parts was then designed to work within the 1.2-meter modular unit. This kit includes columns, beams, tempered glass, braces, brackets, metal grating for the floors, clips, and bolts. All of these parts are intended to be connected in such a way that they can easily be taken apart, packed, and moved to a new location. At the same time, the system is designed in such a way that the overall dimensions can be expanded beyond the dimensions of the current pavilion.

The modular system was developed specifically for this purpose. With the exception of the glass from Saint Gobain, all of the components were custom fabricated by local craftsmen. Many of these craftsmen had limited experience of working with such a contemporary approach to design and construction. Nevertheless, their experience with the traditional crafts that define architecture in Oaxaca led them to deliver a very refined product. Overall, using local talent and a custom-tailored system made it possible to develop the lightest and most efficient solution.

Repetition of the modular unit plays a significant role in the overall experience of the Pavilion. Given that the enclosure is entirely glass, the visitor becomes quite aware of the various solid elements that support the structure and hold it together. These elements are encountered in a regular repetition that highlights their presence and consistent structure. They are shown a certain reverence in the way they stand out from the glass. This allows for further attention to be called to the contrast between the historical structures of the former monastery in which the Pavilion is located, which are all built according to a traditional "wet" approach to architecture, in which the various components are fused together. They would be rather difficult to separate if moving or recycling the building were considered desirable.

These projects all adopt a modular approach to the design and construction to enhance a building's overall efficiency from the perspective of planning, energy, and construction. This approach is applied in each project at a very different scale. In the case of KTC and Spacecraft, the modular system creates a compact structure that is focused on a central space and the introspection required to learn or dwell. The ultimate configuration is indeterminate and capable of meeting evolving demand. The design offers a highly economical means of creating a system that can be deployed on a wide range of sites and adapted to a range of contexts. The specific materials selected to build each unit could easily be chosen on the basis of climate conditions, while the overall height and density could be tailored to the availability of land.

By contrast, NAICM and Alfredo Harp Helú Stadium are expansive structures that create a very large covering for a wide range of programs underneath. The building form and size is fixed rather than indeterminate. In the case of NAICM, the broader masterplan was conceived in such a way that the airport could expand during later phases. Such expansion could naturally be accommodated by the continued use of the modular system as the fundamental unit of future concourses and ultimately the second planned terminal on the opposite side of the airport. The modular system could also be adjusted to address different soil conditions and climates and scaled to accommodate airports with different capacities. At the same time, a similar structure could be used to house a wide range of programs that require an expansive roof covering.

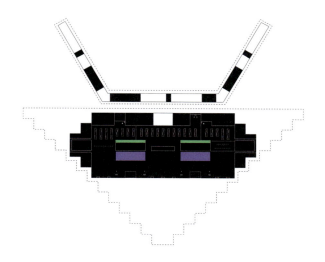
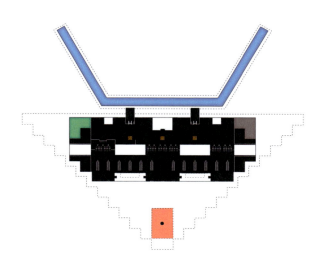
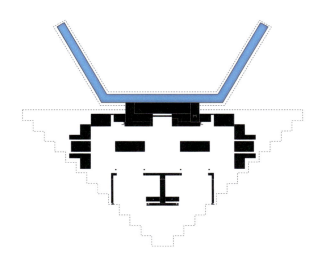

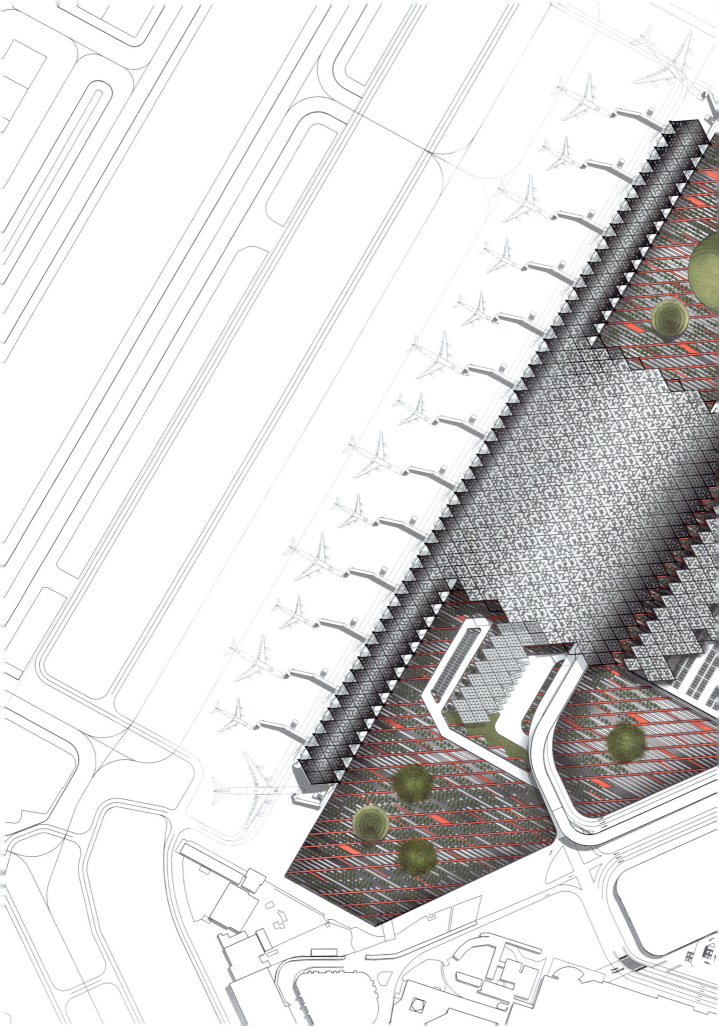

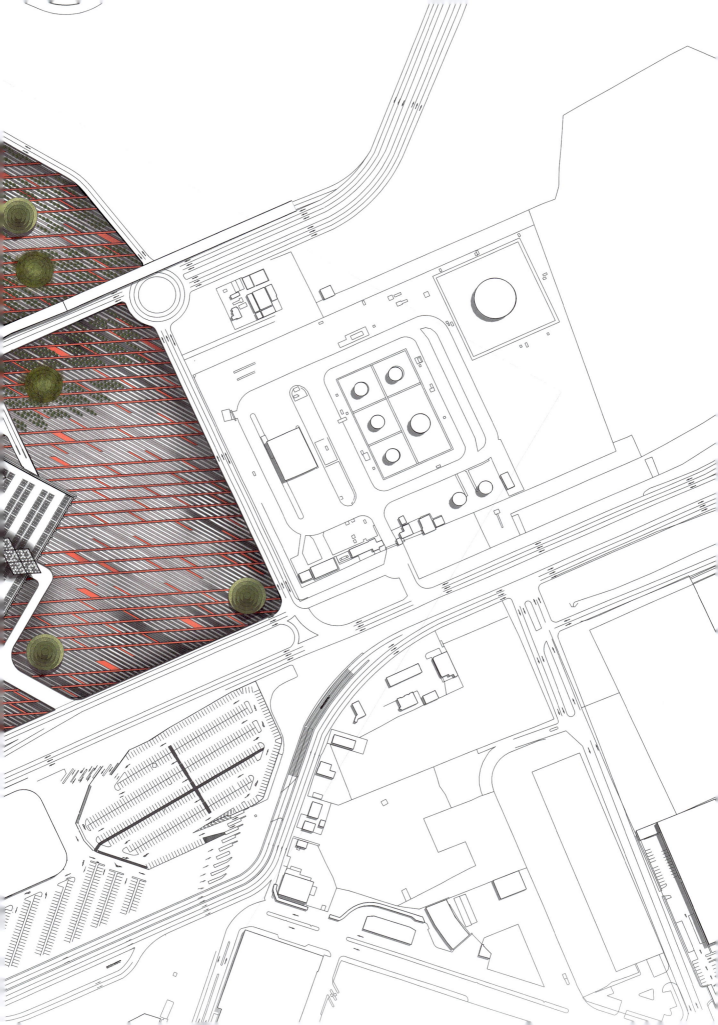

GUADALAJARA
T2

AIRPORT COMPETITION 2019
130,000 M2
GUADALAJARA
MEXICO

INTRO

The new terminal for the Aeropuerto Internacional de Guadalajara grows organically from the architectural, cultural, and ecological context of Guadalajara, which is reflected in its specific form, materiality, and inclusion of local artwork. The building is defined by a number of characteristics, which include an expansive diagrid roof covering the terminal, roadway, and jet bridges while also transitioning to form the enclosure of the concourse. A columned facade is connected by arches that flow from the arc of the roof before bending toward the ground. The column and roof structure form inhabitable interstitial spaces that accommodate the arrival and departure roadway on the landside and jet bridges on the airside—imparting a sense of symmetry and cohesion to the building in the process. The monumental facade is also used for the display of a rotating series of artworks that reflect local culture on the facades perpendicular to the arched facades. The design creates a contrast between the more ancient feel of the parking garage and the contemporary feel of the terminal. This contrast in turn creates a strong sense of transition that is expressed throughout the building via material, light, and form. Finally, greenery is brought into the building and integrated with the surrounding landscape, which includes ample greenspace and places where people can relax. Together, these elements give the design a unique contemporary identity that will distinguish the new terminals from their counterparts elsewhere in the world while also evoking a sense of nostalgia for the early days of jet travel and the great aviation architecture of that era.

A project is always to some extent the offspring of its predecessor, shaped by the addition of new knowledge. In this case, lessons learned in designing NAICM have been brought to GDL T2. First, it has a similar cultural context in terms of the people, the contractors, and budgets.

The form of an airport is heavily constrained by the relationship between the way travelers embark and disembark the aircraft, on one hand, and on the other, all the activities that must occur before and after to make the process safe and successful. Apart from the need to meet the stringent requirements of passengers and support staff, an airport's form is limited by runway configurations, existing aviation infrastructure, and the need for an efficient layout that can serve a maximum number of planes and passengers to support the operational costs of an extremely expensive piece of transportation infrastructure.

DESIGN

While innovative master plans have been proposed for new airports that enhance the connection between gates and retail while reducing passenger travel time from the point of entry to the most remote gates, many of these

"ONE CAN LIVE IN AN AIRPORT THESE DAYS. I HAVE ARRIVED IN CHICAGO ON DELAYED FLIGHTS IN THE MIDDLE OF THE NIGHT AND ENCOUNTERED CAMPERS INSIDE THE CHECK-IN HALLS OF THE TERMINALS COEXISTING WITH NOISY MAINTENANCE CREWS AND SLEEPY SECURITY GUARDS WHILE PRETENDING TO BE PASSENGERS ON A DELAYED FLIGHT OR WAITING FOR AN EARLY FLIGHT. DURING THE DAY, CAMPERS ROAM, SOCIALIZE, EAT, NAP, AND SHOP, ALMOST UNDERCOVER. THE COMPLEXITY AND SCALE OF SOME AIRPORTS ALLOWS FOR MANY FORMS OF EXTREME HUMAN BEHAVIOR THAT CAN ONLY COMPARE TO WHAT OCCURS IN THE CITY. WE HAVE A RESPONSIBILITY TO FOCUS ON OUR PATTERNS OF BEHAVIOR AS MUCH AS ON OUR PATTERNS OF CONSUMPTION."

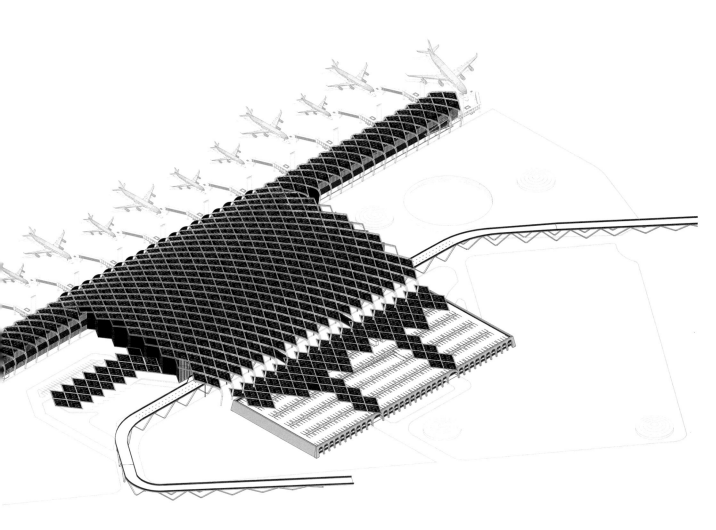

innovations have been realized on greenfield sites that offer a tremendous degree of flexibility. In the context of the site of the Aeropuerto Internacional de Guadalajara, the constraints are quite extreme and thus require a very straightforward master plan and work of aviation architecture.

In spite of—or perhaps by capitalizing on—the limitations of the plan and form, tremendous opportunity exists to create a significant work of aviation architecture that is not only innovative but also grounded in building within a broader cultural context, such that it is infused with local architectural tradition. In this way it is possible to create an affinity between the scale of the airport and the scale of historic buildings, such as cathedrals and large public markets. These disparate typologies bring people together from diverse backgrounds to share in a common activity. The result is a place with which people can identify and in which they can feel pride of ownership.

A key aspect of this pride is the way in which the architecture of the place synthesizes a much deeper tradition. This tradition is traced in the particular material, color, light, texture, and atmosphere as a culmination of the activities, efforts, and desires of generations of families—some of whom may still contribute to the culture of the present. If designed successfully, the quality of the space can resonate beyond the limits of a particular locale as something significant and attractive. In the process, the new work of architecture contributes to the city's identity and standing around the world. It surpasses its necessary functionality as a work of exceptional transportation infrastructure and becomes a true generator of sustained, long-term value at both the economic and the cultural level.

While this connection could be expressed formally, an opportunity exists to express it programmatically by hybridizing the airport with the museum. While the museum may bring together objects from different eras gathered from different locations, the airport and air travel in general do the reverse, making it possible to quickly travel to different sites around the region, country, or world in the present moment. In making this connection, we do not see a museum in the passive sense, as an institution that seeks only to preserve the past, but rather as one that preserves cultural memory in the present while also actively cultivating current cultural producers. Moreover, we do not see the character of these great cultural spaces as confined to the objects and programs within, but as embodied in the design of the spaces, the structure of the building, the materials chosen, and the overall atmosphere. This holistic union helps to create a unique, almost reverential experience that maybe, just maybe, will cause us to slow down for a moment, look around, pause to eat

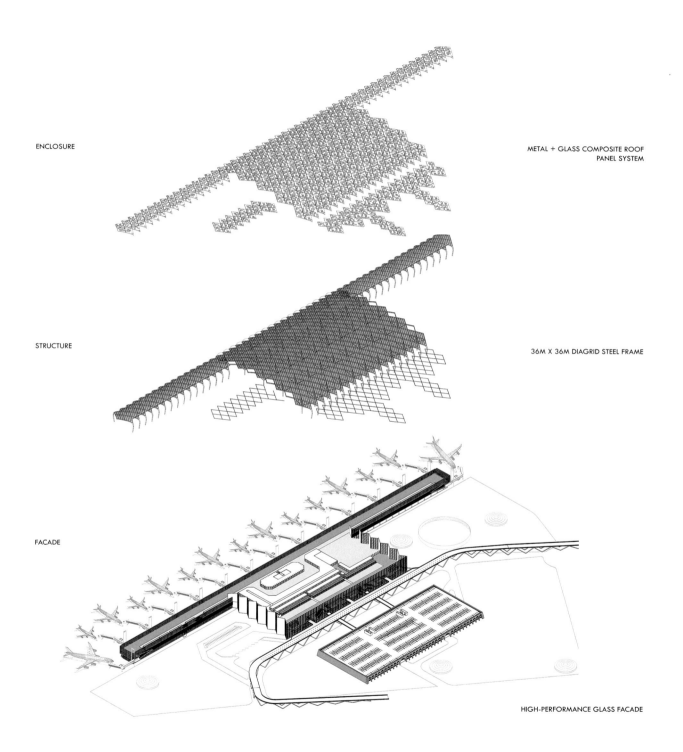

something together or buy something to remember the moment, and feel a genuine connection to the place that lingers profoundly in one's memory and perhaps even urges us to return.

Transitions between different portions of the airport play a significant role in the design. Distinct formal languages characterize the parking garage and terminal building in order to give them each their own identity. The terminal exhibits a highly technological approach that uses contemporary materials, while the parking garage appears rooted in an ancient tradition through the use of patinaed black stones. The contrast helps to break down the vast scale of the airport by avoiding a completely homogenous experience, as well as to create a memorable transition between the garage and the terminal. Crossing the road that separates the two buildings gives one a true sense of arrival. A similar experience greets those who arrive by car as they travel the covered roadway before seamlessly transitioning into the interior of the departures hall.

Throughout the building, similar moments of transition are marked by changes in the formal or material language of the building. In some cases, this might be a shift in the pattern density of the terrazzo paving, or a change in surface textures. In other cases, it might be walking in an interstitial space between the glass curtain wall and series of columns as one descends the jet bridge before boarding a flight. Some of these transitions are quite distinct, while other are far subtler. Together, they help to give each part of the building and journey a sense of identity that supports ease of navigation and forms the foundation of a memorable experience for the traveler.

In tracing Guadalajara's cultural context in the design, we have looked to local buildings from the classic and modern periods, drawing inspiration from iconic structural elements—particularly the vaults of the arcade of the Templo Expiatorio del Santísimo Sacramento—and collecting patterns, colors, and textures of materials that we find throughout Guadalajara. Through a careful combination of these elements within the context of a design practice driven by the intersection of architecture and science—as reflected in advanced building materials, structures, and systems—we have created a work of architecture with a sense of place, a terminal with a unique identity that will contribute to the overall quality of the Aeropuerto Internacional de Guadalajara. This quality helps orient travelers within the building and lets them know that they have arrived in Guadalajara. Moreover, the architecture conveys a sense of Guadalajara as a place of cultural distinction within Mexico and the world.

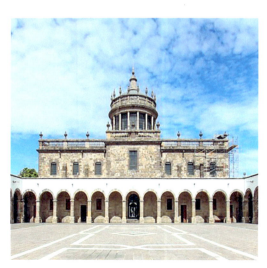
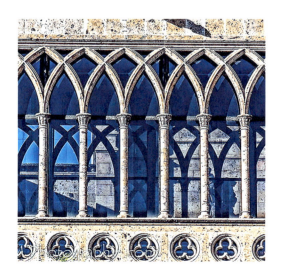

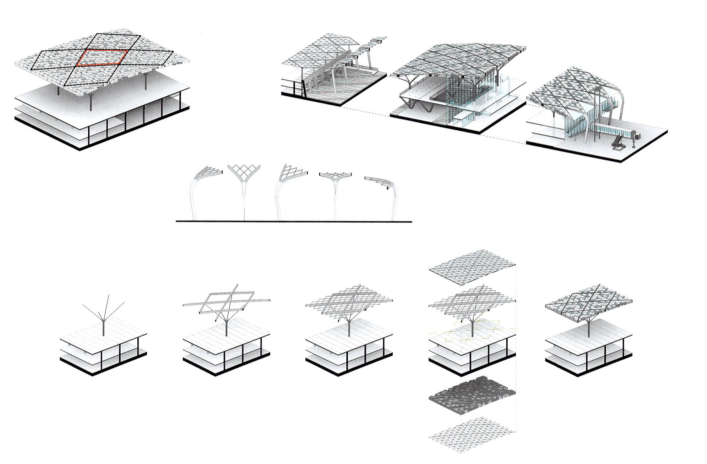

"GARDENS THAT LIVE WITH THE NATURAL LIGHT AND ART OF MEXICO WILL EXIST THROUGHOUT THE INTERIOR OF THE AIRPORT. THE GREAT HORIZONTALITY AND HEIGHT OF THIS AIRPORT WILL BE ENRICHED BY THE PRESENCE OF NATIVE VEGETATION THROUGH STRATEGICALLY LOCATED GARDENS.

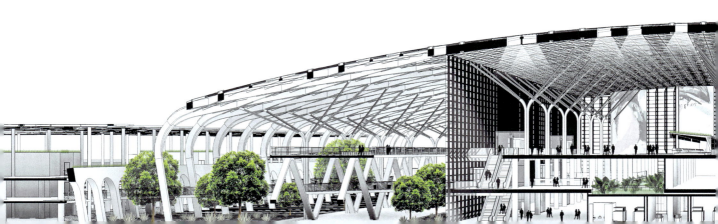

IN ADDITION TO ENHANCING THE BEAUTY OF THE INTERIOR SPACES, THEIR FUNCTION WILL BE MULTIPLE: PURIFY THE AIR, PROVIDE NATURAL HUMIDIFICATION, AND SERVE AS BACKWATERS, HELPING TO CALM THE ANXIETY OF PASSENGERS AND BRING THEM CLOSER TO THE DIVERSITY OF MEXICAN FLORA."

At the most fundamental level, our design is guided by transforming local techniques into sophisticated art, spaces defined by light and shadows, and lightweight structural systems. The famous arches of Guadalajara's historical architecture are a primary source of inspiration. The arches become members carrying the structure that covers the facade of the terminal building. These arches are rounded to evoke memories of the architectural roots of the state of Jalisco. The same source of inspiration informs the cover, resulting in skylights addressed to the airport passenger transit areas. These skylights enact a play of light and shadow, simultaneously opening and closing the spaces. The interlocking of the arches and points at which they join distributes the structural effort throughout the entire cover, making a modular system that is both light and simple. It is replicated throughout the volume.

These sources of inspiration all come together in the roof structure, which arches from one side of the terminal to the other. On the airside, this structure covers the central section of the concourse. On either side of the point at which the terminal and concourse intersect, it seamlessly transitions to cover the concourse with a shallower arch. As the arch descends to meet the facade of the building, the points of the diamond-shaped roof elements transition to become a column. The triangular area in-between each of the horizontal structural members is webbed with PTFE to protect passengers as they board and disembark from the airplanes. This formal language allows the facade and roof to become a unified whole. The two elements work together to create a very impactful image of the airport as the traveler arrives and departs. As one approaches the concourse, it becomes clear that the extremely long facade of the concourse has been broken down into segments that humanize the building. This approach contrasts the many airports around the world with extremely long glass curtain walls that lose all sense of human scale as a result of their sheer immensity. Such an approach to the design of the facade further enhances the uniqueness of the airport and its connection to local design traditions while also offering a novel and forward-looking approach that pushes the boundaries of what airport architecture can be.

The functionality of the roof shell/vault/column system is extended on both the land- and the airside by allowing arrival and departure circulation to exist within. On the landside, this occurs by allowing the roadway to slip under the cover of the roof. The traveler is now enveloped within the shelter of the roof structure and able to move freely, protected from the weather by the elegant formality of the columned arcade. Travelers will enjoy a similar experience upon leaving the airport. Instead of immediately entering a boarding ramp that protrudes from the building, travelers descend a portion of the

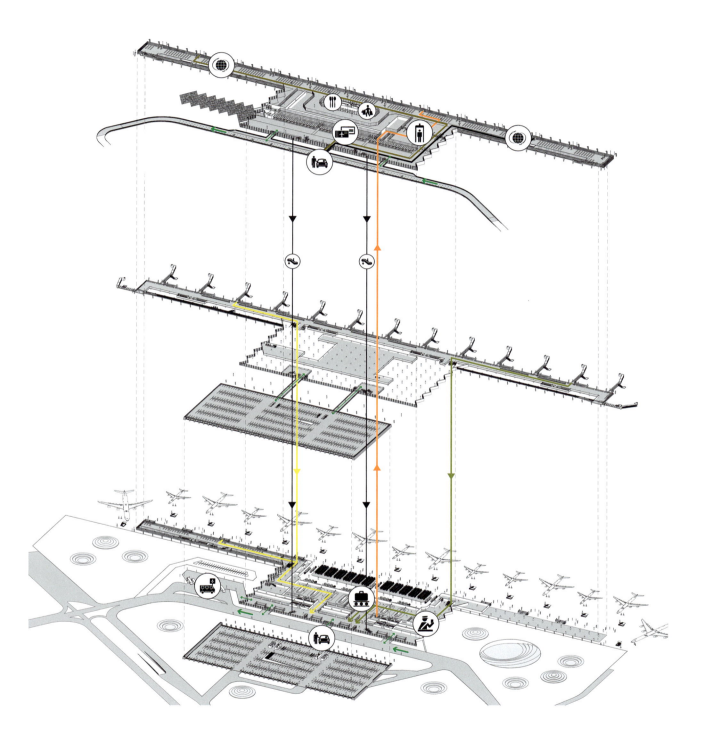

ramp between the glass wall of the concourse and the columns supporting the roof. This experience allows them to move within the colonnade—mirroring their experience of entering the airport and enhancing the overall identity of the airport and its association with Guadalajara. In both cases, the line between interior and exterior is blurred to enhance the continuity of airport operations with its environment while also providing room for travelers to reflect on the significant transitions between places and environments that occur while traveling. While the roof/column/vault system defines the land- and the airside, alternating glass and solid walls define the sides of the vaulted terminal perpendicular to the concourse. The solid portions are devoted to local artwork, while the glass walls bring daylight into the interior of the terminal.

Inside the terminal, the space is divided between areas for check-in, security processing, and retail. The roof is supported internally by a series of columns that branch to intersect with the cross-points of the diagonal frame. The solidity of the roof is broken by a series of triangular skylights, each occupying half a diamond roof module, that further enhance the daylight within the terminal. The structural system and uniformity of the roof shell make the planning of the space highly flexible, so that the layout and size of the respective programs can evolve as aviation demands change.

Ultimately, the most unique aspect of the building is the experience of deplaning in an indoor-outdoor space. The building is defined by a modular system that allows it to expand into a large diaphragm. The distribution of the program also proves to be somewhat innovative. Traditionally, the check-in counter zone is quite deep. By contrast, this design creates more depth in the retail space. This reflects a belief that the check-in area will become increasingly small as this process becomes digital. This idea came from NAICM, where the least space is allocated to areas where it is undesirable for people to congregate. It is also reflected in a competition design for an airport in Ho Chi Minh City. The focus in these projects is on the space just beyond security, where people spend the most time. Finally, the roof in this and other projects mediates light through a balance between opaque and transparent surfaces. This enhances both the departure and arrival sequence and reflects an overall commitment to sustainable elements.

ARRIVING IN VEHICLES

Signage to limit speed of vehicles, saving fuel and encouraging travelers to look around.

SURROUNDING VIEWS

Landscape comprising a limited variety of local vegetation, requiring less water for maintenance.

VISIBLE GREEN ENERGY

Photovoltaic solar panels ceiling mounted on the roof of the parking lot generate electricity for extreme lighting.

DRIVING UNDER THE CANOPY

A series of black steel colums and light umbrellas form a canopy along the driveway. You can learn more about their considerable quantity of recycled content by reading the signs.

INTERIOR-EXTERIOR

The design of the terminal building is light, transparent, and utilizes low-emissivity glass to allow maximum natural lighting of interior spaces and promote orientation.

CULTURAL LINK

Twelve elements of 10 x 30 m help integrate interior and exterior space by incorporating urban art in the building's facade.

RESTAURANTS, SNACKS, OR RETAIL

This airport encourages customers to reduce single-use plastic. Goods are delivered in cloth bags and containers that are composted on location. The restaurants could use products from on-site farms, fed with recycled water.

TERMINAL

The terminal is built on a large scale but is not extravagant. It is profitable because it is modular. The glass facades and skylights allow daylight to pass through, providing a view of the sky from any point in the building and reinforcing the principles of biophilic design.

RELAXATION AREA

Opportunities exist inside the airport to create wellness spaces like massage centers and rooms for yoga and meditation as well as rest areas with a view of the terraced gardens on land- and airside.

AIRCRAFT VENTILATION

Fixed GPU/PCA generate considerable fuel savings. Service vehicles that cater to the aircraft use an electrical charging method.

PRE-BOARDING BRIDGE

The design of the terminal building is light, transparent, utilizes low emissivity glass to allow maximum lighting of natural spaces interiors and promotes orientation.

FIRST LOOK AT THE FACADE

The glass of the facade incorporates a space of 16 mm following international standards for noise reduction.

INTRODUCING MEXICO

Low-energy screens show information about the geography and culture of Guadalajara as a first introduction of the country to arriving passengers.

DEPARTURES AT APRON LEVEL

Egress in the arrivals area is surrounded by greenery. Together with the green wall along the perimeter of the parking area, they create a "green canyon" that blocks noise from surrounding areas.

WAITING AREAS IN ARRIVALS HALL

While waiting for family, friends, or a taxi, travelers can read relevant information about the building and its impact on the carbon footprint. Our goal is to achieve at least a 30% reduction in energy, water consumption, and waste disposal.

BAGGAGE CLAIM

While waiting for your bags on the conveyor belt, the focus is on sound. Light Mexican music and classical music produce a calming effect, preparing passengers to go out into a new country and leave the tensions of the trip behind.

IMMIGRATION

As you queue to go through immigration, you are greeted by walls incorporating the work of local artists and promoting the culture of the region.

WALKING THROUGH THE BUILDING

The roof, lighting patterns, and materiality assist orientation as you wall down the hall towards immigration. The clean, orthogonal design of the pathway helps achieve efficiency of flow.

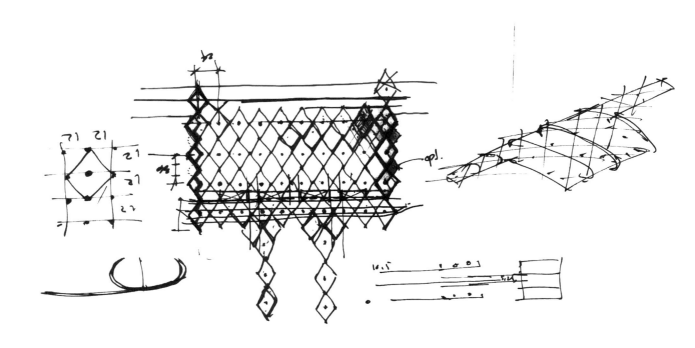

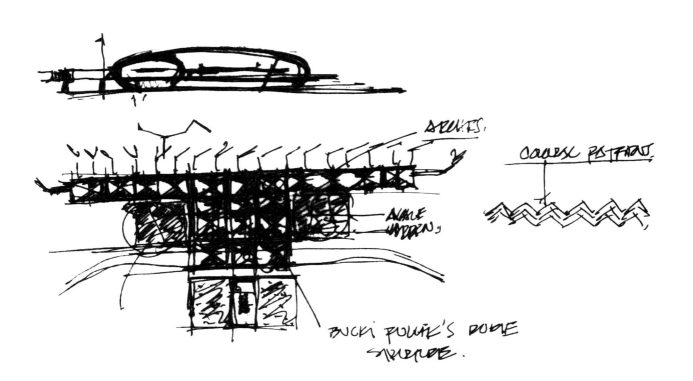

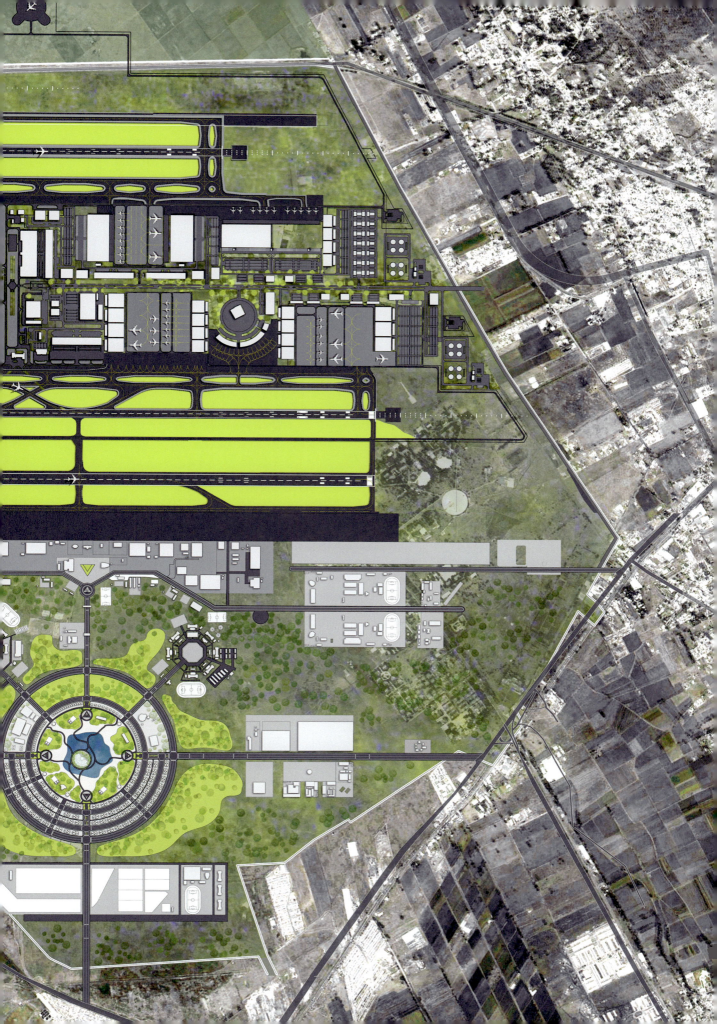

AIFA

INTRO

The new Felipe Ángeles International Airport at Santa Lucía (AIFA) was designed to be an iconic landmark for Mexico. The context in which the project arose made it essential that the design adhere to a strict budget and tight deadline for completion. In order to achieve these goals, an integrated design approach as well as an integrative process and team were proposed. At the same time, it was important that the airport be both expandable and sustainable. These characteristics would ultimately combine to form a work of exceptional architecture and urban planning befitting Mexico's growing presence on the global stage.

Currently under construction at the time of publication, AIFA is designed to be more than just a building: it is conceived as an urban complex defined by a grand roadway running along a strong axis that provides a processional approach to the terminal building and concourses. It will include an airport city, intermodal station, cargo terminals, general aviation facilities, and military city that itself will have a military aviation museum, school, and residences, among other amenities. These various components will be planned to work in harmony and are to be achieved over a series of phases on a site that can accommodate tremendous expansion, so that the airport can ultimately become a major player within the burgeoning aviation network of Mexico.
While travelers will see the iconic shape of an airport that will one day become synonymous with arriving in Mexico as they approach from the air, they will ultimately encounter this building in many diverse manners. Approaching, travelers pass by the grand rotunda that will signal the beginning of the departure sequence. As their vehicles near the drop-off, they will be surrounded by lush trees and catch their first glimpse of the honest, straightforward, and efficient terminal. Those arriving by train will be brought directly into the heart of the complex and join those arriving by car, bus, and taxi in the "Plaza Mexicana." After arriving under a series of ETFE canopies, passengers will then pass over a series of bridges that further signal that they are embarking on a journey.

The Plaza Mexicana will be a unique space, the likes of which will not be found in any other airport in the world. It will help make Santa Lucía into an urban place that reflects Mexican culture, aided by outdoor events, art, and exhibitions where all flows of the airport come together. The Plaza Mexicana is situated along the primary axis of the master plan and in relation to the central landscape element at the entrance to the airport city. This feature is the first grand landscape element visitors encounter that announces the presence of Santa Lucía Airport.

**AIRPORT
UNDER CONSTRUCTION
215,000 M2
SANTA LUCÍA
MEXICO**

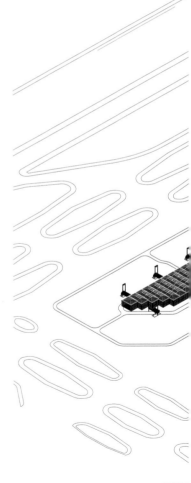

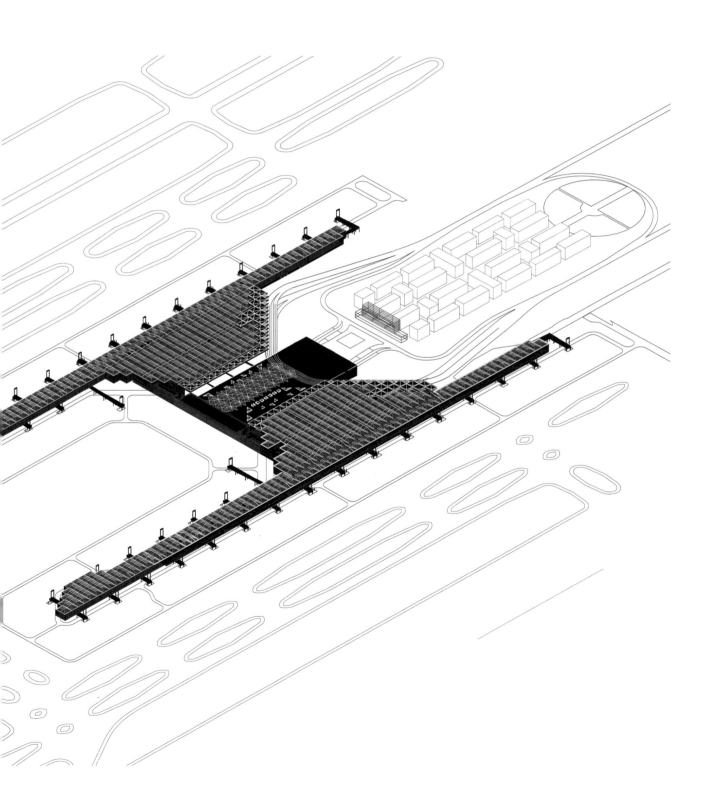

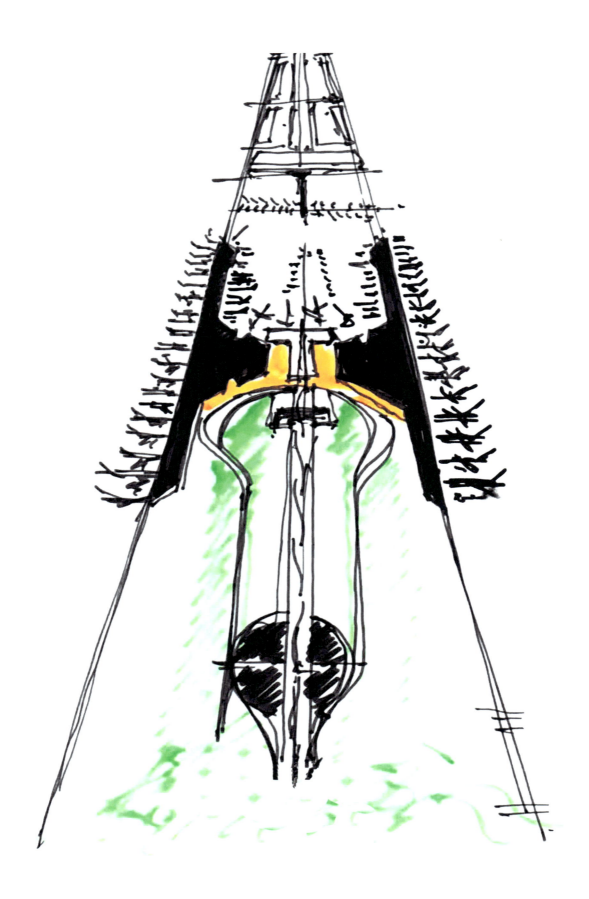

"SO MANY PEOPLE HAVE ASKED ME: WHY? WHY DID I DECIDE TO RETURN TO MEXICO AFTER TWENTY YEARS AND DESIGN THE FELIPE ÁNGELES PASSENGER TERMINAL AND MASTER PLAN FOR THE NEW AIRPORT COMPLEX IN SANTA LUCÍA?

THERE IS ONLY ONE ANSWER TO THAT IN MY MIND … I WAS INTRIGUED BY THE OPPORTUNITY TO DESIGN MASSIVE INFRASTRUCTURE USING A KIT OF PARTS, AND IN DOING SO, DEMONSTRATE THAT MEETING THE BUDGET AND THE SCHEDULE WITHOUT COMPROMISING DESIGN EXCELLENCE AND CONSTRUCTION QUALITY WAS POSSIBLE. WHICH, IN MY EXPERIENCE, IS ATYPICAL IN PROJECTS OF THIS SCALE AND COMPLEXITY.

MY GOAL WAS NEVER TO BUILD A MONUMENT, BUT RATHER TO CONSTRUCT A MACHINE, A FORMULA 1 BUILDING IN WHICH NOTHING IS SUPERFLUOUS. MY FOCUS WAS ON OPERATIONAL COSTS, EFFICIENCY OF FLOWS, LEGIBILITY, LOWER ENERGY CONSUMPTION, FUNCTIONALITY, EASE AND SPEED OF CONSTRUCTION, PASSENGER WELLNESS, BUDGET CONSCIOUSNESS, AND A STRONG CONNECTION TO THE ENVIRONMENT.

WHY A MACHINE?

WHEN A BUILDING IS BUILT WITH PUBLIC FUNDS, ALL PARTIES INVOLVED HAVE A FIDUCIARY RESPONSIBILITY. IN THAT SENSE, A SCIENTIFIC APPROACH GUIDES A RATIONAL PROCESS. BEAUTY CAN CERTAINLY BE DESIGNED, BUT FOR ME, BEAUTY EMERGES FROM UNEXPECTED PLACES; THE SCIENCE OF PERFORMANCE IS ONE OF THEM, FOR ITS LONG-LASTING VALUE."

The experience of crossing spatial boundaries is a theme repeated throughout the airport in order to help orient travelers. It takes place at key junctions: when one leaves the parking garage by passing through a series of planted terraces, as one enters the colonnade at the arrivals level, as one passes through the glass wall separating the interior from exterior, as one notices the continuity of exterior columns inside the building, when one passes through security surrounded by lush interior gardens on either side, when one enters the dense retail sequence dotted with gardens, and when one is set free in the light and airy concourse before a final transition through boarding bridges and taking flight and having a chance to see where this entire sequence has occurred before disappearing into the clouds. The consequence of this strategy is to give each part of the sequence its own identity, so that traveling becomes a real event that one can cherish rather than an ordeal through which one must pass.

At the same time, the building and master plan are harmonious. The variety of experiences and needs that the building supports is achieved through a common architectural language and modular building system. This system is designed to be efficient, economic, and sustainable. As a kit of parts, it can be combined and varied to achieve diversity out of commonality. The result is a set of spatial experiences that are achieved in a strategic, cost-effective manner. Overall, the building is both a humble machine whose specific design is derived from the most precise analysis of aviation requirements to attain optimal functionality and a great place to spend time before and after taking a flight. As such, it will effectively serve Mexico and the world from the day the doors open, as it expands, and for decades to come.

Cities and regions face increasing pressure from growing populations, expanding economies, evolving transportation modes, and an environment defined by greater extremes and severe events. In this context, the centralized infrastructure bearing the primary burden of a city's air transportation needs can present new challenges. The facility can end up being strangled by proximate growth that makes expansion difficult and congestion severe. Keeping existing facilities open during expansion can be difficult. At the same time, the facility may not be entirely resilient in the face of an earthquake or extreme weather event.

In order to address these challenges and the evolving nature of cities, planners have begun to think about networks of cities that form a region. This is the case with clusters of cities such as Amsterdam, The Hague, Utrecht, and Rotterdam in the Netherlands; Bonn, Cologne, and Düsseldorf in Germany; and New York, Jersey City, and Newark in the United States. In each case,

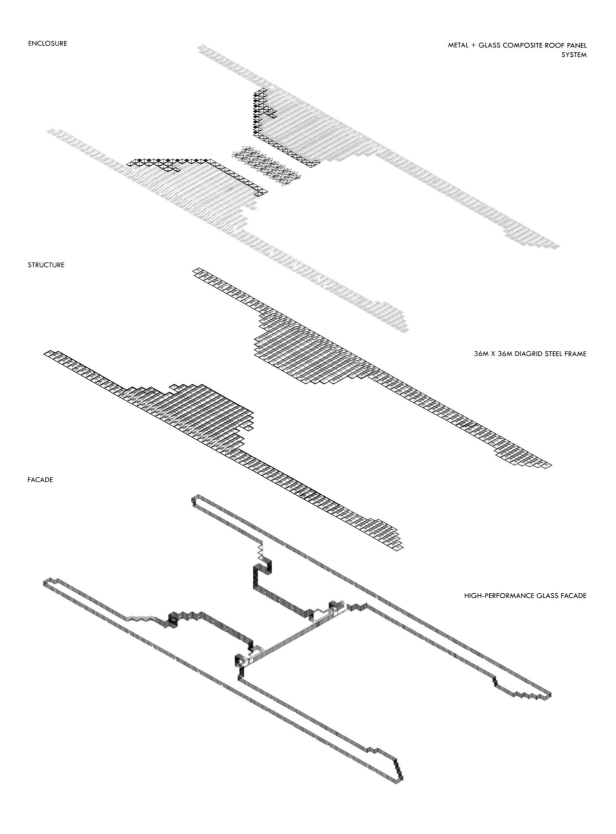

AUSTERE

It is a design that eliminates what is not essential to make way for an authentic beauty: a pure beauty based on design principles that are logical and rational.

EFFICIENT AND FUNCTIONAL

A building and an airport complex that are clearly organized and therefore legible, with optimal circulation routes for all flows: passengers, baggage, vehicles, and services.

SUSTAINABLE AND POSITIVE

A building that, in a simple way, reduces energy consumption, emissions, waste generation, water consumption, and the irrational use of resources in its construction, and that has a positive impact on the community in which it will be developed.

EASY TO BUILD

An architectural proposal based on a selection of "Mexican" materials, a building that represents Mexico for its constructive ingenuity and its simplicity in the use of materials and systems.

URBAN AND CONTEXTUAL

AIFA will be more than an airport, it will be a city with a positive impact within an ecosystem. Respectful of pre-existing architectural elements such as the Hacienda de Santa Lucía, it will generate urban activity that will have a positive impact on the local and national economy. It will have an adequately sized hotel, parking, retail, and back-of-house areas. It will seek the integration of native species and, as much as possible, it will not disrupt the existing ecosystem.

FLEXIBLE AND MODULAR

The established budget and schedule call for design and constructive intelligence to generate a simple but innovative concept based on prefabricated and modular systems that will guarantee quality, execution, and adaptability to future growth. With an initial phase of 20 million daily passengers (MDP), it can be expanded in future stages that allow it to reach a capacity of 85 MDP if necessary. AIFA is in this sense an ideal and strategic option for maximizing the potential of this initiative.

INCLUSIVE AND SAFE

AIFA will be a building for everyone. It will be transparent, democratic, open, connected, intuitive, and simple. It will be a place where the cultural and social diversity of Mexico converge, while also being a place where the safety of all users is guaranteed.

EMBLEMATIC

AIFA will be the creation of a multidisciplinary team of Mexicans committed to a single mission: to provide Mexico with a scalable airport system that will not only meet growing demand but will also be an example of the beauty of functionality and become the "Airport System that Will Move Mexico."

the region benefits from a network of international airports that serve the needs of the population. The network can handle micro-climatic weather variations, while each facility is able to grow without disrupting the operations of the others.

This trend, which privileges regional aviation infrastructure networks, serves as the inspiration for the future of Mexico City's aviation infrastructure. The current administration envisions an airport system rather than an airport hub. A system of three airports will work conjointly to supply a projected demand of 160 million passengers by 2052. The Santa Lucía Air Force Base will serve as the location of one of these three airports.

The Santa Lucía Air Force Base in Santa Lucía, Zumpango, is located approximately forty-five kilometers from Mexico City's International Airport. The base itself is named after the Hacienda of Santa Lucía, which has been recorded by the Landmarks Commission as the oldest in Mexico. In addition to an existing runway, hangars, and military city, the base also is home to a military aviation museum that will be expanded.

Beyond being able to support a regional system, the construction of a new airport at Santa Lucía has advantages over expanding and replacing Benito Juárez International Airport at Texcoco. While a new airport at Texcoco would have required the demolition of the existing airport once completed, the construction of Santa Lucía Airport will allow Benito Juárez International Airport to continue to operate in addition to Santa Lucía. Santa Lucía Airport will not only serve Mexico City, but other cities in the region as well. Once all phases of the airport's construction are complete, Santa Lucía will be able to handle 85 million passengers and will be the largest cargo terminal in the Americas.

An airport cannot be planned with a short-term or even mid-term goal in mind. It is important to think long-term. The site in Santa Lucía is large enough to accommodate such long-term goals through significant growth over a period of more than thirty years. At the same time, it will be possible to preserve and enhance the military base and the historic Hacienda of Santa Lucía. This will make it possible for the airport to become the largest cargo hub in the Americas and to play a vital role in regional and international passenger air travel.

The realization of this vision presents a range of challenges. Airports are among the most complex building typologies. They are subject to extreme and wide-ranging demands from their users. Passengers are comprised of groups of international and domestic travelers, business and leisure travelers, occasional and experienced travelers, young passengers and older passengers who might have mobility issues, families and those traveling alone, disabled and able-bodied travelers, and all combinations of these categories.

The vision for the airport is achieved through fusing architectural and engineering principles to form a new experience that is true to its functionality and easily adaptable to future interventions. The buildings will have a positive impact on the environment by using less of everything to create timeless beauty. Architecture, landscape, structure, and energy work in unison to create a building that is advanced, forward looking, functional, contextual, efficient, and highly performant. A minimal attitude in the selection of materials and conscious design of all building systems ensures an efficient use of resources and a positive attitude towards the environment. The idea is not to add but to subtract and yet achieve a higher standard.

The master plan of the airport has been achieved by carefully analyzing past airport typologies to design the best solution for the site and volume of air travelers, and by collaborating with the best aviation planning and programming consultants. The design values functionality over grand aesthetic statements while still delivering an iconic, uniquely Mexican airport that can serve as gateway to the world. The design has been arrived at with a local building and architectural tradition in mind. The design is also ideally suited to the local ecology. It is conceived as a series of modular units and kit of parts that will allow us to build a large building quickly with very simple, economical means.

The building has been designed with advanced data and analytic tools that can optimize baggage and passenger flow and help determine gate location based on passenger types. At the same time, the building has been designed for change. Processes are not hardwired into the building, so that it can evolve and have a long life. The building has been designed for ease of wayfinding, which supports comfort based on a narrative that has a broad range of stakeholders. An architectural solution was thus arrived at by relentlessly focusing on passenger experience, using custom simulations of passenger behavior to create a layout that brings together an optimal balance of commercial, planning, and spatial considerations that will maximize commercial activities and passenger satisfaction levels. In the process, intelligent building systems have been integrated to support ease of operations and maintenance.

Over the course of the design process, the span of the roof structure raised a number of questions. In the end, a long-span structure was rejected in favor of a short-span structure that was more appropriate to the time and budgetary constraints. In making this decision, modules of 18 by 18 meters and 12 by 18 meters were adopted. This choice was based on the widespread use of this module in aviation architecture, as well as the fact that the module would still allow for a relatively large span. The roof structure for this module was initially a pyramid, as opposed to the vault structure that was ultimately adopted. The pyramid structure would have been structurally more efficient, easier to fabricate offsite, and, as a result, would have resulted in savings of 30%. However, it was rejected in favor of the vault structure for unknown reasons.

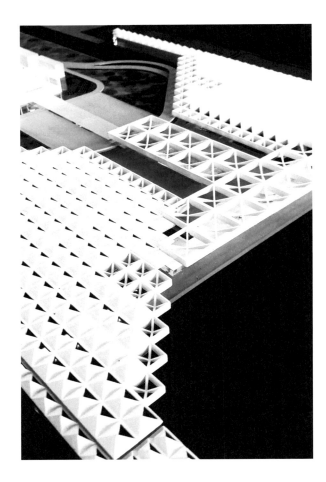

The seismic requirements of the structure also played a significant role in how the design of the building evolved. At one point during the design process, the structure was braced with a series of diagonals that made a significant impact on the overall feeling of openness within the building. They also potentially posed an impediment to motion. In this context, it became clear that outside engineers should be consulted to explore alternatives. This resulted in the development of a system of seismic isolators that made it possible for the building to move independently of the ground. This would allow for the building to perform throughout the year, even in the event of an earthquake.

Santa Lucía is conceived in three manageable phases that limit the need for an extreme upfront investment while also making it possible to grow over the course of several decades as demand increases. The first phase will support 20 million passengers, and the final phase will support 85 million passengers. The airport will be served by three commercial runways and one military runway that can be used for commercial purposes when needed. The length of the runways

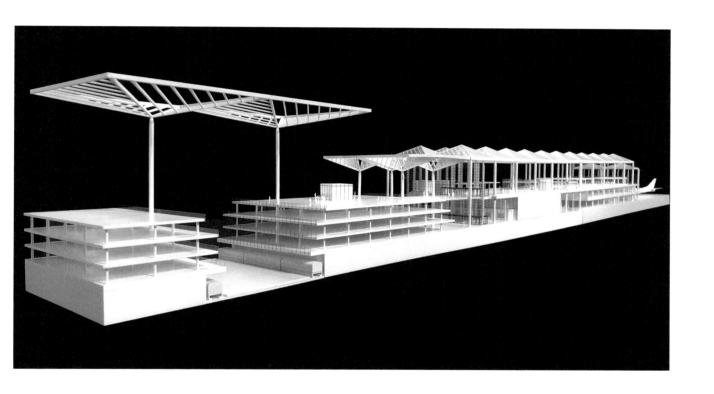

"OUR RESPONSE WAS RATIONAL, DRIVEN BY MODULARITY AND CONSTRUCTABILITY. IT WAS DRIVEN MORE BY HOW IT WOULD BE BUILT THAN JUST BY DESIGN. MORE THAN ANY OTHER AIRPORT THAT WE HAVE IMAGINED AND DESIGNED, AIFA IS THE ULTIMATE MACHINE."

extends up to 4.5 kilometers to allow for the largest planes and long-distance travel. The control tower will reach a height of ninety meters and is planned along the axis of the terminal building on the airfield side. It will be accessible from the service area on the east side.

There are six points of entry into the check-in hall—three from the Plaza Mexicana and three from the curbside roadway. The area immediately adjacent to the roadway is filled check-in kiosks. Kiosks will become increasing common in the future as airlines strive for greater economy by encouraging passengers to do as much as possible online, and as low-cost airlines and smaller, more efficient airplanes that can travel longer distances become more common. As a result, kiosks will likely replace many of the check-in counters, freeing up considerable space in the process. For this reason, a slightly smaller check-in pavilion was designed than might have been designed in the past. In addition, the pavilion has been designed in such a way that security can eventually be moved to where the check-in counters are currently, and additional retail can be added where security is currently located.

Typologically, the design follows a linear terminal concept comprising a pavilion and a pier. The diagram of the building is highly legible and makes it easy to navigate, with travelers essentially being given the option of turning right or left upon clearing security. The aircraft configuration begins with 33 contact stands in phase I, 68 during phase II, and 112 contact stands in the final phase. The building's design as a linear pier with a central terminal is based on a classic diagram and will be very efficient given the right mix of aircraft types.

The terminal pavilion is roughly 200 by 200 meters. It has five ticketing islands and is divided into three sections that contain the major spaces for processing passengers and baggage. The first section is the check-in hall. The retail is envisioned on the grand scale of a European arcade. This section is the largest portion under the terminal pavilion and includes interspersed pavilions that evoke the feeling of being in a village and moving through different neighborhoods. The idea behind this innovative concept is rooted in future development trends between landside and airside concepts, in which the latter has become highly profitable and is becoming "a destination" in its own right, a place where passengers want to be.

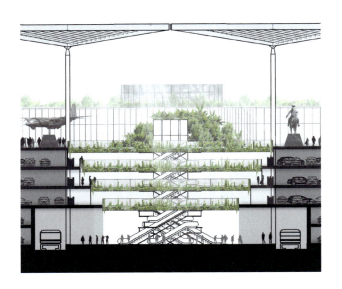
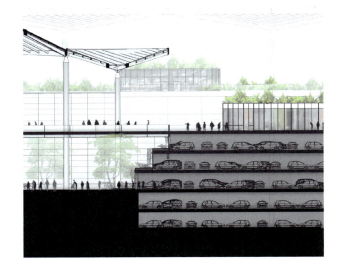
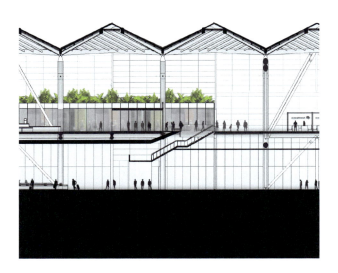
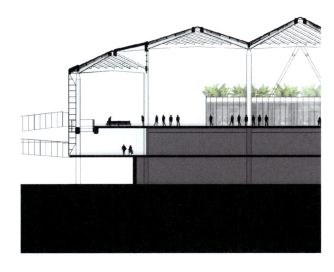

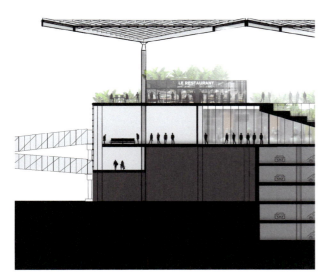
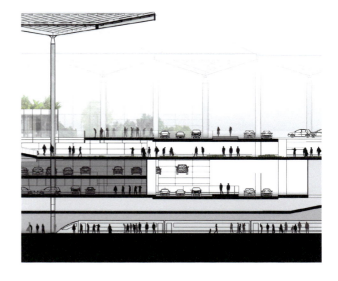
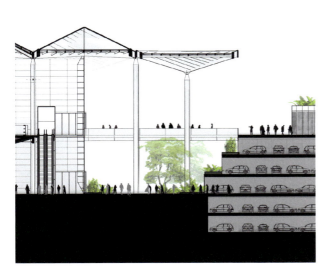
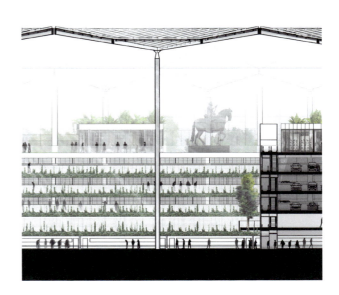

SUSTAINABILITY

The overall master plan of the airport is based on an axial organization of functions between the two main runways at 1.6 kilometers from each other. The axis forms the line of symmetry between the phase I terminal and the phase II terminal, with the Plaza Mexicana serving as the primary unifying planning element. This allows the width of the final phase terminal complex to be around 700 meters. This ultimately determines the overall scale of the airport and potential for future development. The area on either side of the axis is reserved for the airport city, which will include mixed-use buildings as well as a hotel on the landside.

Santa Lucía Airport make the passenger journey less stressful and more sustainable. Sustainability is about using less to do more. It is about enjoying the offerings of nature, which cost nothing and are priceless, while ensuring that they are sustainable for the future. AIFA encourages users to follow this ideology and embodies a new way of life and travel in Mexico. Our belief is that sustainability in architecture is not only about the quantitative benefits of construction, but even more about the qualitative benefits of design. This aspect is addressed at three levels: the regional scale, the site scale, and building scale. At the regional scale, AIFA proposes a new urban development that will transform Santa Lucía in many ways. Its infrastructural and economic impetus will help Mexico achieve the United Nations 2030 Sustainable Development Goals; specifically, the ones targeted at human well-being, clean energy, job creation, innovation, and sustainable communities. The intermodal transport hub at the heart of the development provides convenient access to the site and encourages users to avoid using private vehicles that will take longer and cost more. This, in turn, reduces the parking footprint and ensures air quality levels within World Health Organization recommendations.

At the level of the site or master plan, several design and planning features have been adopted that are consistent with the WELL Community Standard, LEED Neighborhood Development, and Sustainable SITES Initiative for land development. The project is being developed on an existing military base and will make use of steel and passenger elevators previously procured, thus reducing and reusing materials to make this endeavor sustainable from the start. The integrated project design and delivery approach further ensures thoughtfulness in planning and efficiency in construction and operations. The site presents an incredible opportunity to make a lasting impact on neighborhood and community development, upholding civic character and a sense of place to an extent unprecedented for an airport.

"THE DESIGN OF THE AIRPORT IS CONCEIVED AS AN URBAN EXPERIENCE ORGANIZED AROUND A GRAND OPEN SPACE. LA PLAZA MEXICANA SITS ALONG THE PRIMARY AXIS OF THE MASTER PLAN AND IN RELATION TO THE CENTRAL LANDSCAPE ELEMENT AT THE ENTRANCE TO THE AIRPORT CITY."

As the threshold to the aviation experience, the primary landscape feature marking the entrance to the site and the Plaza Mexicana will be a landmark of great cultural importance in Mexico. "Mind" and "Community" are vital concepts around which the site is planned. Every path is designed for the pedestrian scale, with tree canopies for thermal comfort and biophilic design incorporating blue spaces, plazas, indoor gardens, and green roofs. Restorative built spaces, all along the journey to and from the gates, not only rejuvenate the traveler but also celebrate the culture of Mexico through spatial organization and artistic installations. Cyclist and pedestrian infrastructure and physical activity spaces reinforce the concept of active design for movement. In addition, the site development aims at restoring native vegetation and using landscape for natural sound mitigation and water management.

At the building level, the prescriptions of SAGA (Sustainable Aviation Guidance Alliance) are considered, and design features of the building satisfy several of the WELL Building as well as LEED Transit goals. Sustainability is a technical as well as a social and behavioral issue. Hence, our sustainability focus is split into operations and design. Operations focuses on efficiency of energy and water use as well as waste management. Design entails orchestration of passenger flow as well as material and systems selection. Convenient access to resources, easy wayfinding, and elevated sensory experiences as part of passenger flow will contribute to user well-being.

The goal is to design systems that reduce operational costs, improve ease of operations, and enhance the longevity of the building. Light materials and systems will be utilized to reduce transportation cost, the need for excessive structure, and construction costs. Among other things, energy efficiency, renewable energy, and zero carbon emission will all be essential goals, and will be achieved through the use of advanced modeling technology, design solutions, materials, and systems. Passive systems and natural light will be used when possible. Intelligent building systems will be integrated to help reduce energy costs, ease operational burden, and enhance guest experience. Finally, materials that minimize the impact on the environment will be used.
Responding to the solar orientation, the building enclosure combines advanced high-performance glazing materials and high-performance roof cladding to achieve a high level of occupant comfort and enjoyment, while simultaneously reducing energy consumption.

The design of the building enclosure and the MEP systems will be designed in close collaboration between the architect and key engineers; conceptually, it is already based on concepts tailored to fit the Mexican climate. The

"PASSIVE SYSTEMS AND NATURAL LIGHT WILL BE USED WHEN POSSIBLE. INTELLIGENT BUILDING SYSTEMS WILL BE INTEGRATED TO HELP REDUCE ENERGY COSTS, EASE OPERATIONAL BURDEN, AND ENHANCE PASSENGER EXPERIENCE."

design strategies will be thoughtfully analyzed using advanced engineering and computer modeling to yield highly efficient yet highly comfortable and natural interior environments.

The resulting facade expression is integral to the building's form and structure and displays a visual logic that has a clear foundation in high-performance engineering. The goal is to dramatically improve the quality and enjoyment of the terminal environment by maximizing views and daylight while reducing energy consumption by minimizing direct solar gain. High glass walls will reduce both the demand for electricity and the electricity requirement generated by artificial lighting. This effort is guided by employing the following material and design concepts: high natural light transmission, very low solar heat gain coefficient, low reflectivity, color-neutral glazing for good interior light quality, maximize natural lighting/shading, use of natural light to eliminate artificial lighting during daylight hours, control of all terminal artificial lighting by daylight sensors, overhead glazing with 80% frit to limit solar gain while still providing very good daylighting, maximum glazing at eye level to promote ease of orientation and views, water efficiency with a goal of zero neutral, and waste control with a goal of zero neutral.

The forms of the vaulted roof structure are designed in such a way that they can collect water and create a reserve that can be treated for use in landscape and restrooms. This will help the building to be water neutral. Because of the large volume, a displacement system will be ideal for ventilation and conditioning. This will allow us to only cool the occupied zones of the building by using stratification that allows for air movement and exhausting of heat in an active and a passive manner. Preliminary analysis suggests that this strategy will reduce energy consumption by roughly 30%. The building will not require any heating, so there will be no boilers. With regards to direct energy production, photovoltaic panels will be introduced where possible. The use of a biodigester that will operate on gas generated by cactus is also being explored.

LANDSCAPE

The overall spatial concept is defined by a series of bands running north-south that divide the landscape into a series of zones and break down the massive scale of the project. As passengers arrive at the airport, they pass from one zone to another as they approach the terminal building. Each zone is defined by a different type of plant that is native to Mexico.

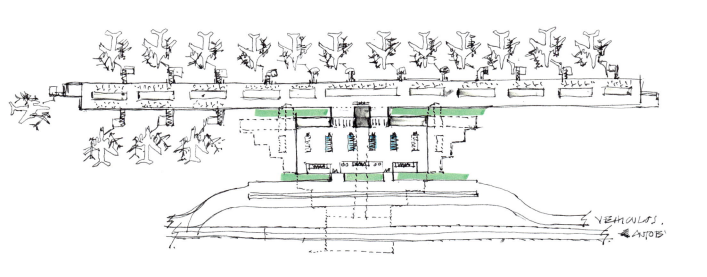
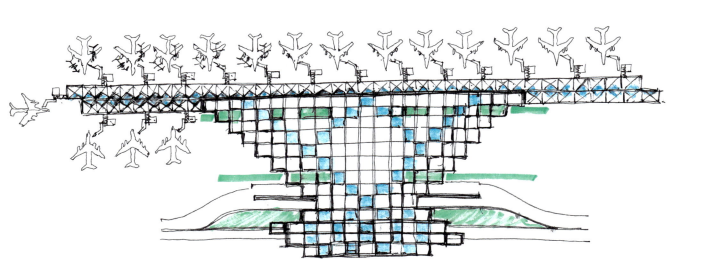

The first primary landscape element that the visitor encounters is the circular water feature, which also functions as a connection point between the northern and southern roadways. Half of the water feature is defined by a series of steps that gradually blend the elevated landscape to the east with the level of the water. A pier juts out over the water and allows visitors to walk out into the landscape feature and become completely immersed in the landscape.

As visitors approach the terminal, they pass through a series of zones defined by pine, agave, nopal, coral tree, and Montezuma cypress. They ultimately arrive at the Plaza Mexicana. This grand space is a mix of commercial elements and triangular botanical elements. Each of the commercial pavilions is designed with a green roof. In between, people circulate and find a series of benches and places to rest and gather.

Those passengers who park in the garage or arrive via bus or train progress to the upper departures level after encountering the gallery forest. This dense, shaded landscape zone will provide a sense of intimacy amid the grand overall scale of the airport. For those arriving, this inviting space, akin to an arcade, will be one of the first experiences encountered. Indigenous plants that require minimal maintenance are used throughout. Although some trees will have to be relocated, SEDENA, the largest reforestation organization in the country, will ensure a positive outcome with regard to vegetation.

Airports are typically dominated by both the enormous, paved areas of aprons and runways and the wide concrete ribbons of the landside road network. With this landscaping concept, the goal is to ecologically counterbalance these paved areas with a graceful natural landscape that brings a sense of beauty and pleasure to the visitor. The flowing line of green areas and delicate network of pathways create a beautiful, rhythmic pattern that ties the airport city and surrounding landscape to the terminals, thus creating a consistent landscape identity for Santa Lucía Airport.

WALL GRAPHIC INSPIRED BY AZTEC MYTHOLOGY

CHECK-IN CASEWORK

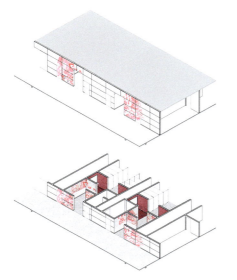

TERRAZZO FLOORING AT BOARDING GATE AREA

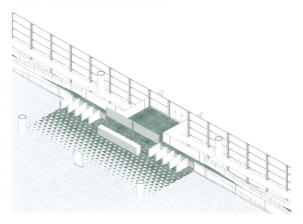

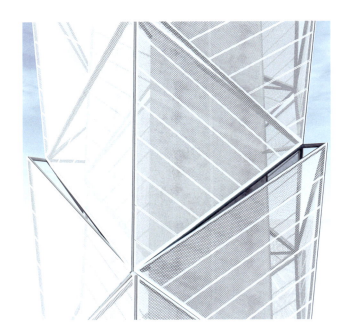

CONTROL TOWER

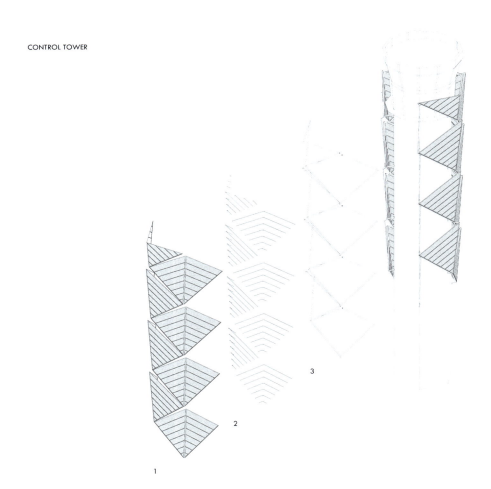

1. PERFORATED STAINLESS STEEL CLADDING
2. SECONDARY STRUCTURAL FRAMING
3. PRIMARY STRUCTURAL FRAMING

FACADE DETAIL

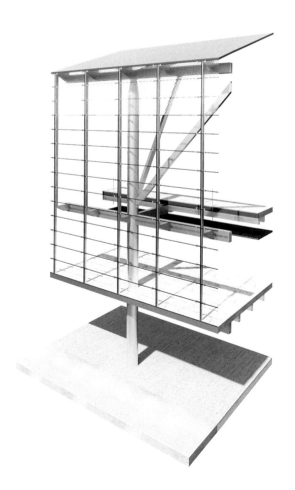

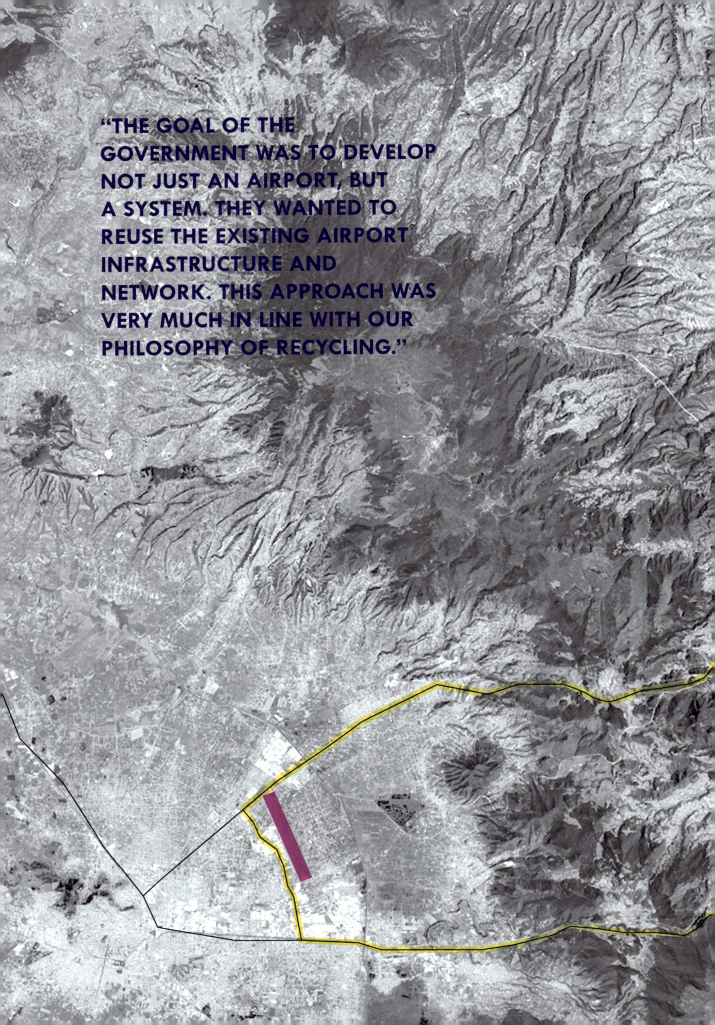

"THE GOAL OF THE GOVERNMENT WAS TO DEVELOP NOT JUST AN AIRPORT, BUT A SYSTEM. THEY WANTED TO REUSE THE EXISTING AIRPORT INFRASTRUCTURE AND NETWORK. THIS APPROACH WAS VERY MUCH IN LINE WITH OUR PHILOSOPHY OF RECYCLING."

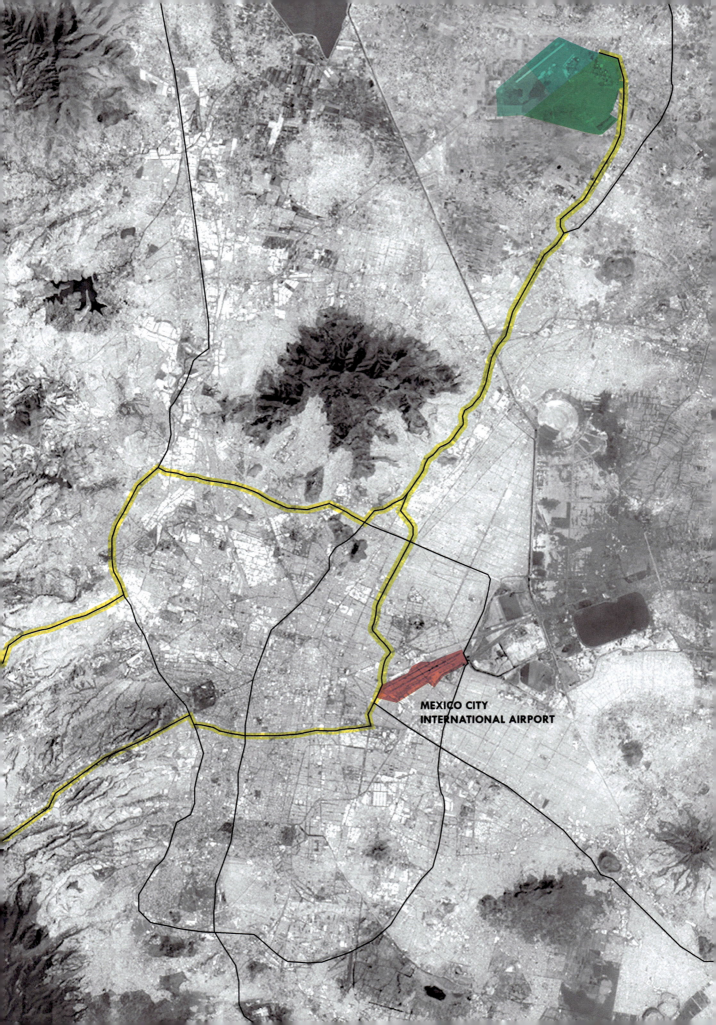

AEROSPACE
REVISION OF THE NATIONAL AEROSPACE STRATEGY
UPGRADE OF THE AEROSPACE SOFTWARE
=
SIMULTANEOUS USE OF NEARBY CITY AIRPORTS
=
SUSTAINABLE USE OF EXISTING INFRASTRUCTURE

RUNWAYS
TEST WIDTH AND LENGTH OF THE RUNWAYS IN CONNECTION
WITH THE
SURROUNDING PEAKS + EFFICIENT EXPANSION MODELS
=
1600 M : IDEAL FOR FUTURE EXPANSION
+ ECONOMIC ADVANTAGE BECAUSE OF EFFICIENT USE
COMBUSTIBLES IN THE CONTEXT OF PASSENGER AND CARGO
LOADS.

CONNECTIVITY
WITH CITY AND DISTRIBUTION OF CARGO

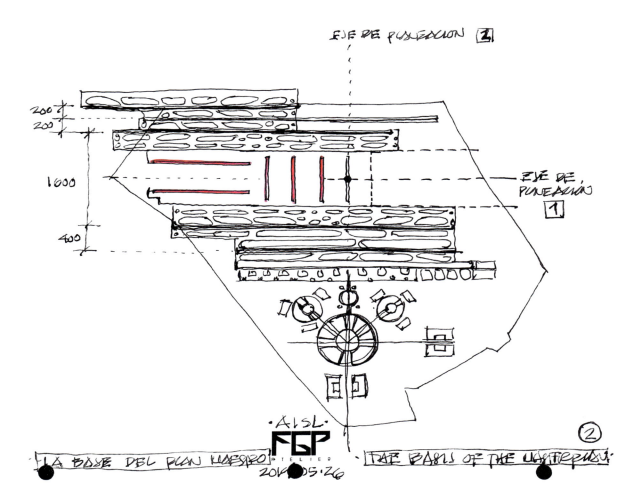

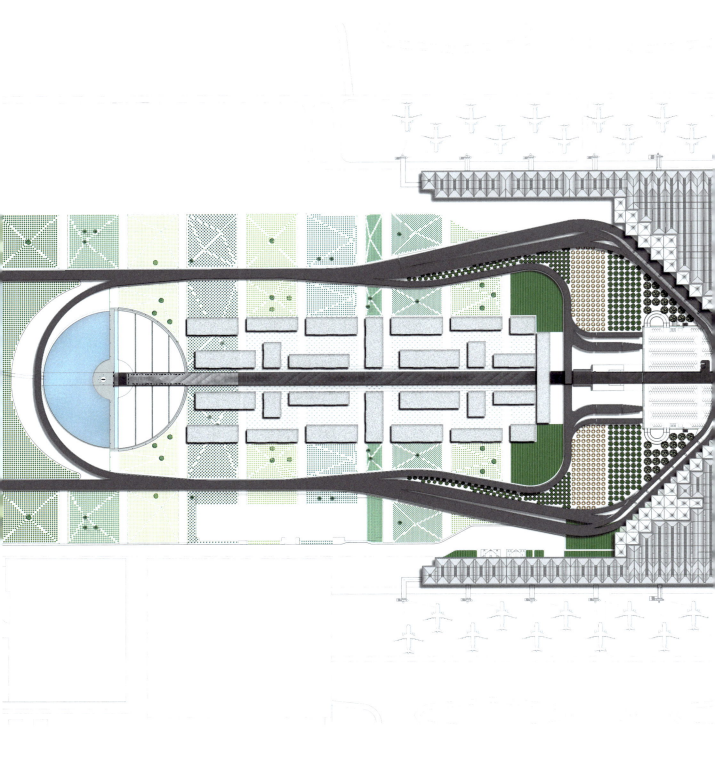

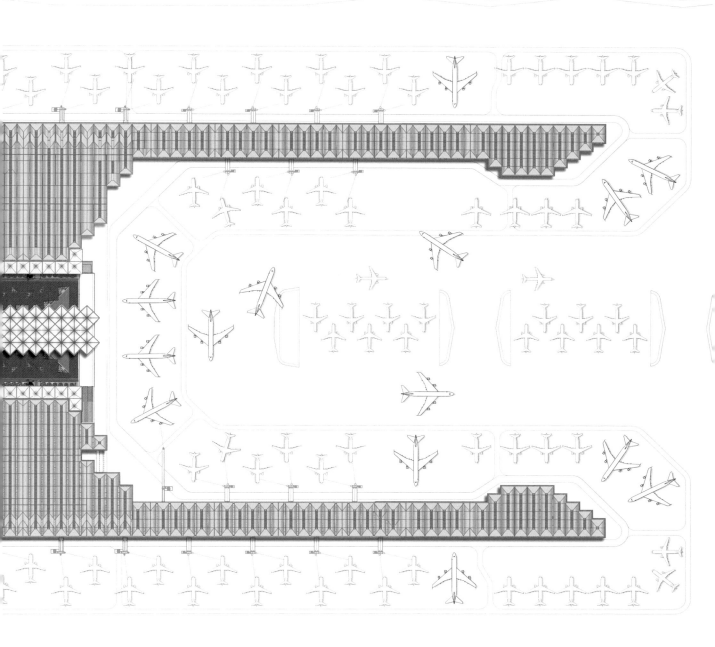

"THE DESIGN OF THE MASTER PLAN, TERMINAL, AND CONCOURSE SHOULD BE GUIDED BY THE PRINCIPLES OF MODULARITY, LIGHTNESS OF MATERIALS, EFFICIENT HIGH-PERFORMANCE MATERIALS, INTELLIGENT LAYOUT AND CIRCULATION PATTERNS DERIVED FROM A DATA-DRIVEN SCIENTIFIC APPROACH, RESILIENCY, EXCEPTIONAL ENERGY PERFORMANCE, AND EASE OF OPERATIONS AND MAINTENANCE."

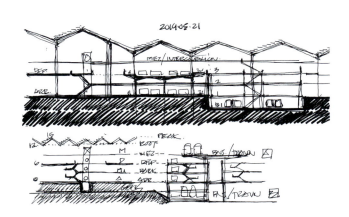

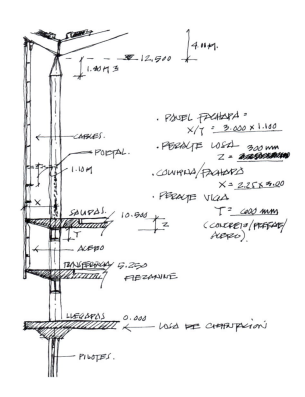

DRY ARCHITECTURE

The use of modular building systems has, over the past couple of years, become a topic eliciting wide interest from those involved in the industry as well as the general public. These building systems are of interest, in part because they offer an alternative to "wet" systems such as poured concrete or stick construction. Companies and institutions are looking for ways of standardizing the units used in the construction of their projects in order to reduce time, improve quality, and, as a result, reduce cost. At the same time, construction companies are working in rather different markets and, at different scales, have invested in factories and building systems to deliver modular solutions to their clients.

In the context of our own practice, what is often characterized as "modular construction" has come to be referred to as "dry architecture." For us, "dry architecture" describes a building or other structure that has the following characteristics. It (is):
1) based on a module or modular unit;
2) achieved as a repeated unit, component, or kit;
3) built in such a way that its parts remain autonomous and can be easily deconstructed;
4) utilizes only the elements and energy necessary to solve the problem;
5) supports faster and more cost-effective project delivery;
6) produces buildings that last longer and are more sustainable; and
7) results in an experience that is essential rather than superficial.

While these characteristics are reflected in many of the projects in this book, striving for a genuine intersection and balance of each characteristic continues to be a challenge to which each new project must rise. Each presents the possibility of creating a precedent that can enhance the efficiency of the building industry, increase quality, reduce cost, extend affordability, promote safety, create the potential for mass customization, and make cities better and more sustainable.

These trends are not entirely new. The use of prefabricated elements and even of largely prefabricated balloon-frame homes has become a standard feature of many suburbs throughout the United States. This trend extends back to the mass manufacture of homes by Sears, Roebuck and Co. at the turn of the twentieth century—a trend that quickly led competitors such as Montgomery Ward to offer similar products. It has continued with the development of concrete modular units that can be quickly assembled to create large swaths of social housing throughout Europe, as well with as the manufacture of mobile homes—the majority of which spend the entirety of their existence in the same location on what is likely rented land.

DRY ARCHITECTURE

Interest in modular construction goes even further back in history. If one looks at indigenous building systems, ranging from Japan and the South Pacific to the Middle East and North America, it is possible to discern standardized dwelling spaces that could be multiplied and combined to suit specific sites and programmatic needs. At the same time, architectural systems sought to standardize measurements and proportions based on the module or modular of the human body. This was the case in the classical architecture of Greece as well as during the Renaissance in Italy. The quest to define buildings based on the human body was reintroduced through the research of groups such as the Bauhaus and architects like Le Corbusier, who sought to base the proportions of his buildings on the Modulor, an anthropomorphic scale of proportions whose measurements in turn conformed to the golden ratio.

More recent interest in standardized units and spatial measurements has coincided with the continued proliferation of mechanization, which extended beyond the first wave of infrastructure—such as railroads, telegraphs, and factories—to the broad electrification of the world and all the new capacities it made possible. These new capacities supported the development of a wide range of new building materials and the broader revolution in building structure and cladding systems. With this revolution came the possibility of producing larger, stronger, lighter, and more connected elements. At the same time, the utopian notion of a harmony between the modular elements of machine, space, and the human body was propagated by thinkers such as Buckminster Fuller. They felt that humankind could find greater leisure through automation and the mass production of objects, use those objects during their leisure time, and dwell in highly performant enclosures uniquely tailored to the environment and the needs of human beings.

This utopian vision, in which people lived in pods as envisioned by architects from Archigram to Paolo Solari, collided with the reality of a specific demographic in need of housing. This demographic had, for the most part, grown up in crowded urban conditions or on family farms. Following World War II, most returned to increasingly crowded cities. When given the opportunity to own their own home with a yard, garage, and good school in the neighborhood, many embraced what was being sold as The American Dream. These families wanted a house that looked like a house and, increasingly over the years, a house that drew upon historic architectural styles. They did not want a futuristic, modular, small dwelling produced from high-tech materials. They wanted something warm, familiar, and sprawling—capable of housing a growing family and supporting a return to normalcy.

"MANY PEOPLE LOOK AT THE KIT-OF-PARTS CONCEPT AND THINK THAT THE KIT IS LIMITED. THIS IS NOT ENTIRELY TRUE. EVEN BEYOND THE RECENT TREND OF MASS CUSTOMIZATION FACILITATED BY DIGITAL FABRICATION TECHNIQUES, A KIT OF PARTS SUPPORTS ELASTIC SPACE THROUGH THE ADAPTABILITY IT MAKES POSSIBLE."

DRY ARCHITECTURE

Demographics have shifted, however, and with this shift has come a new set of preferences. These changes in demography coincide with an evolving climate, increased global population, diminishing natural resources, rising sea levels, and greater stress on existing urban fabrics. In particular, the growing global population will require the construction of an extraordinary amount of housing over the coming decades to meet demand. The logical conclusion is to build more housing in dense urban centers close to jobs, where it is supported by infrastructure that reduces reliance on the automobile. Unfortunately, this demand has led to rapidly rising land and rental costs in urban centers. A broad crisis of affordable housing has resulted. At the same time, the cost of labor in urban centers has continued to rise rapidly. The result is an economy that does not necessarily keep uniform pace with growth. One consequence is a striation of purchasing power across classes and geographic locales.

In this context, modular construction techniques can begin to address these concerns through the increased building efficiency made possible by constructing units in factories. Doing so requires a new approach to the module and the modular. What distinguishes past trends from present is the current emphasis on a total product: that is, a complete unit deployed in traditional and often urban contexts rather than a smaller modular unit or even a structure meant to be finished on site. As one might expect, this also marks a shift towards emphasizing consumable architectural products that can be marketed and purchased, much as one might buy other consumer products. This is a monumental shift for a building industry that often conceives of a building as a collection of sticks, sheets, systems, and products whose design is orchestrated by an architect in collaboration with sub-consultants, and whose construction is executed by a general contractor coordinating a similar set of sub-contractors responsible for the different systems.

While a modular building product such as room, suite, apartment, or house will naturally need to be made of smaller units, the idea of putting all these parts together in a factory and delivering them to the site as a ready-to-inhabit package is revolutionary in our field. There is little need to repeat all that has been said about the possibilities of such a revolution, or the broader shift toward manufactured rather than constructed buildings. What has been discussed less frequently, however, is the effects on design that result from different parties such as the manufacturer, contractor, investor, industrial designer, or architect driving this innovation. The specific party that guides the process and integrates the team deeply affects the spaces in which people live and the city more broadly.

DRY ARCHITECTURE

Today, it would be possible to infuse modular trends with the same high standards that have come to define industrial design in the era of the iPod. Keeping this desire in mind, we might consider a few possibilities presented by modular construction techniques through the lens of our design practice and try to imagine how we might push them further: 1) enhancing mass customization through difference and repetition; 2) combining modular units with highly customized spaces; 3) creating modular units with recycled materials; and 4) infusing the modular unit with a cultural dimension connected to the local site.

To visualize the concept of mass customization, let us begin by considering a box as our specific base unit. This box can be repeated without any variation at all, resulting in a uniform pattern—or one can change the orientation, configuration, order, scale, color, material, and combination in order to establish a particular pattern and purpose. Doing so can help tailor a general unit to a specific context and desired meaning. This meaning can be both explicit and latent, and the specific nature of the difference and repetition can be used to define a particular expression. The ultimate meaning can be both architectural and non-architectural. Capitalizing on this capacity would involve fully integrating a range of programmatic and technological developments. In many ways, it would follow on the exploration of mass-customization without a cost premium and with the enhanced desire that might come from having something custom tailored. Perhaps the first step would be to take seriously the presence of difference before repetition and consider the way in which a unit, even one mass produced in a factory, differs from others before it is repeated—likely through increased input from the end-user.

The second concept involves combining uniform, entirely homogenous modular units and custom-built, bespoke elements. The key is to create contrast between the two. Such an approach would support continuity with a more traditional approach to architecture and design while also allowing for economies of scale and construction technique. The overall building could support truly exceptional spaces intended to foster a unique experience within the broader homogeneity of the building. These spaces would serve as a break from what might otherwise be considered banal architecture. The result would be a contrast that would enhance both while creating unique spaces that would be highly attractive to potential residents. This has often been undertaken in the development of building podiums and special floors, or sky clubs that serve unique services shared by a select group of building tenants. These spaces can often be defined by special materials and forms that highlight unique views coveted by all members of the community.

"AVIATION HAS PLAYED A SIGNIFICANT ROLE IN MY LIFE AND CAREER AS AN ARCHITECT. WHEN I WAS GROWING UP, MY FATHER HAD A SMALL PLANE AND I ENJOYED LOOKING AT THE WORLD FROM A DIFFERENT PERSPECTIVE."

DRY ARCHITECTURE

In the current context, we might ask whether these spaces can be pushed to become even more phenomenal and generally exceptional. They could even be connected to a broader virtual or other narrative experience that might even connect to some master plan for a particular neighborhood or region. This would ultimately enhance the spatial experience of a building and its environs and help to create both lived personal experience and a macro narrative.

The concept of reuse in the context of modular building, our third possibility, has largely expressed itself in the form of shipping containers. These units are stripped, cleaned, and repurposed for a variety of uses, ranging from single-family homes to large commercial centers and civic buildings. In this context, we might ask whether it is possible to reuse a wider range of existing units for a larger number of new destinations. This might include repurposing mobile homes or abandoned houses that might be repackaged and moved to a new site—perhaps alongside hundreds of other such units. In the process, recycled and reused materials could be reinstalled within a modular framework. At the same time, we might consider modular frameworks—such as column grids of buildings that have fallen out of use or newly developed grids that can form the support structure for future construction. In this sense, we might think of modular construction not solely as the deployment of complete products, but also as the development of modular infrastructure that can support the gradual installation of varying modular units over time as demand changes.

Beyond these more formal and material approaches to modular structures, it might also be worth considering how new rigor can be brought to the process by considering the specific cultural and climatological dimensions of the site. This is to suggest that, on one hand, we might introduce something like a geometric logic that limits deployment and configuration of modular units, much like the systemic limitations deployed by conceptual and minimalist artists. On the other hand, we might introduce systems connected to meaning, program, urban form, and ecology that provide further clarity and guidance as to how and where modular units are deployed. Doing so will give the resulting structure a greater specificity that ties it to its environs—unlike the many structures that look as if they could exist anywhere, in any context or climate. This might allow the structure to transcend its initial purpose and take on a new role—though perhaps not in all instances; it may be an exception that occurs at some carefully chosen moment. This would essentially be to ask how a formal set of rules can liberate a modular system intended to solve a problem efficiently, releasing it from that largely quantitative demand so that it may ultimately instill a sense of quality beyond anything directly associated with the properties of the modular system.

DRY ARCHITECTURE

To a certain extent, modular architecture has been confined to the single- and multi-family residential market—in particular the prefabricate balloon-frame system and, more recently, steel-frame systems. Whenever these systems are used in commercial, industrial, or public buildings, it is usually in cases where a high degree of performance is required, and little formal expression is possible. These instances include warehouses, data centers, and hospitals. Rarely do modular buildings of this kind become architecturally significant.

As a point of contrast, major civic buildings are often defined by a highly specific, customized design solution. In recent years, they have become increasingly fluid and dynamic. They express a sense of movement and tension through unique spaces that become entwined with the identity of a place. In many ways, the form of these spaces is tied to the broader dynamism of society—expressing different perspectives, forces, and ways of using space. While these spaces are certainly novel, extraordinary, and compelling places to spend time, achieving such formal and structural acrobatics often comes at a high cost, which can place a large burden on taxpayers if the building is publicly financed. In cases where the building is not publicly financed, the formal extravagance may be tied to the ego of the building donor.

Dry architecture, on the other hand, is sobering. It offers a more straightforward approach that still has just as much capacity to generate unique, highly attractive, and symbolic spaces. At a more conceptual level, the notion of a "dry" architecture can be understood to extend beyond form to encompass the entire atmosphere that a building creates. The air of such architecture is more tightly regulated because it is circulated and cleaned in modular units rather than through a much larger air handling system. Such an approach might be particularly timely and pertinent to the global population in an era increasingly characterized by the prevalence of airborne infections.

Ultimately, the argument in favor of dry architecture can be linked to the many economic, social, and environmental challenges that the world will face over the coming century. On one hand, a modular approach allows for tighter control and efficiency during the manufacturing process and, on the other hand, frees up resources to invest in the sustainability and viability of communities. In this sense, dry architecture as a philosophy extends beyond the limits of building by advocating an approach to development that looks at a wide range of investments that need to be made—in infrastructure, people, and institutions—all of which must work together to produce a successful project.

"DRY ARCHITECTURE PRESENTS A GREAT OPPORTUNITY AND IS AN AREA THAT HAS NOT BEEN FULLY EXPLORED. IT INVOLVES THINKING ABOUT THE OTHER LIVES OF THESE MATERIALS BEFORE THEY ARE INSTALLED AND PERHAPS AFTER THEIR INITIAL USE."

COLLABORATION

With every project, there is always a moment—or sometimes a series of moments—that defines its result. In my experience, the nature of the collaboration that occurs during these moments is integral to the ultimate positive or negative outcome. How the collaboration is structured and who is called upon to collaborate is not, of course, a given and varies from one project to the next. It is often incumbent upon the architect to draw on their experience to help shape a successful collaboration that will serve the goals of the project and deliver an exceptional building.

Over the course of my career, I have had the opportunity to work in a wide range of collaborative environments that include everything from working in a design-build context as architect and general contractor to being an equal on a team of engineers and sub-consultants working to solve complex technical challenges on some of the largest projects ever built. Each has made a great impression on me, and this in turn has informed how I approach the next project in hopes of making the collaborative process more successful. They have also given me the opportunity to work with some of the most extraordinarily talented designers, engineers, consultants, and clients—some of whom I am fortunate enough to call longtime friends.

With my first project—Casa Veranda—the client, Wilfrido González Balboa (my uncle), knew what he wanted. He was a very successful man with a powerful intellect and driven mind. I, with my twenty-two years, of course, had never done anything professionally and so, in a way, the collaboration was more about arming myself with the tools to realize his vision. I had to build a team in a context void of any real technological base or foundation. This aspect of the collaboration was remarkable. For me, it was not about taking the role of chief architect. Instead, my role extended from designer and engineer to construction worker, manager, and contractor.

The physical context was extraordinary: the most spectacular site on a hilltop, surrounded by mountains and nothing else. Which, of course, was void of utilities and access. There is not a single moment when facing the everyday challenges of building the extraordinary that I do not think back to those wonderful days and the invaluable lessons learned.

In the process, I met key figures who left marks on my career. One of those figures was the engineer Villalobos. He became involved because I needed to build a road and a small bridge. In my approximation to the problem, Villalobos did not just tell me that I was wrong or solve the problem for me. Every time he corrected me, he would state the theory behind the reason for doing something in a certain way. In many ways, he was my first professional mentor in the business of building. His humility in spite of being such a great engineer taught me value of situational leadership.

The second residential project that I worked on was very different. I had a client—Addy Pulido (my aunt)—who knew what she wanted but was open to my guidance. Her husband, however, was convinced that he knew exactly how it should be planned. I felt that I knew how to solve all the problems and he felt otherwise. Arguments arose and, ultimately, I became more of a mediator by trying to establish how we could work together to realize a vision. This moment changed a lot of things for me. I started to question whether this was what I wanted to do—not in the sense of whether I wanted to be an architect, but whether I wanted to work at that scale. The smaller scale requires a different level of involvement, and emotions can run high because people are so invested in the space that they will live in.

I responded to this concern by turning my attention to competitions. It was my search for "freedom." It was my attempt to enter the world of architecture with greater purity and integrity, so that what I designed reflected my values and my ambition.

At this point, I achieved a certain level of success. My work started to resonate with the juries of these competitions. Of the four competitions that I entered during this period, I won three and came in second in the fourth. This gave me design confidence. But at that point, there was no real collaboration. I was dreaming of multidisciplinary collaboration, but there was no real culture of collaboration in Mexico at the time.

I ultimately decided to get a master's degree from Harvard and hoped that I would find a network for pursuing the collaboration framework I was seeking. Such a culture was virtually nonexistent. The practice of architecture at the time was very individualistic, which in my mind made it more about the image of things rather than their essence. There were, however, a few exceptional professors who channeled my interest in collaboration, which would become the platform of my professional life. They included Rafael Moneo and Spiro Pollalis at the Harvard Graduate School of Design, Marco Iansiti at the Business School, and the artist Krzysztof Wodiczko at MIT. I was struck by how Spiro saw my interest in learning more about the collaboration between architects and engineers and commissioned me and my classmate Pablo Vaggione to write three case studies on Frank Ghery's Guggenheim Museum in Bilbao. In doing so, we uncovered the truths behind what seemed to be the product of an exceptional collaboration. At the same time, I took a studio with Krzysztof and experienced a process that was focused on collaboration in the most radical way. He questioned everybody's role in the process of design and the reasons behind it.

It was there that I began to gradually see what I wanted to do collaboratively with other disciplines and emerging fields.

After graduating, I learned that Helmut Jahn was collaborating with two emerging yet leading German engineers, Werner Sobek and Mathias Schuler, and decided to come to Chicago. I began to work in his office in the fall of 1999, and I must say that it was not quite explicitly a culture of collaboration from an internal perspective. However, they were developing a culture of collaboration from an external perspective, and that was terrific. They were reaching out to all these great minds working in different fields. It was a very sincere engagement. It was not a disposable process, in which you get what you need from the collaborator and then walk away. There was strong involvement from the early stages that, in the end, was clearly reflected in the finished building.

Many of these experiments played out in projects we were building in Germany at the time. Where there was absolute respect for this process. They understood that these were buildings with purpose. The clients were willing to fight the necessary battles with us. In some cases, we had to challenge building codes. These collaborations were very symbiotic. All the buildings—Deutsche Post, Bayer, Sorono, Bangkok, Highlight Tower, Hegau Tower, Sign Düsseldorf, Mansueto Library, South and West Chiller Plants, Cologne Airport—all built between 2006 and 2007—were really the offspring of this symbiotic collaboration between engineers and architects. At the same time, there were situations in which the contribution of some was diluted in favor of promoting the role of the architect. This was a little hard for me to swallow. I thought that the sum of the parts was always stronger than the individual parts alone. This was becoming increasingly clear as the buildings became these fantastic machines that were the result of integrated doing and integrated thinking.

One byproduct of the relationship with Werner Sobek was the Triple Zero High-Rise Studio that we taught together at Illinois Institute of Technology. Our goal was to bring the collaborative process and methodology into an academic setting.

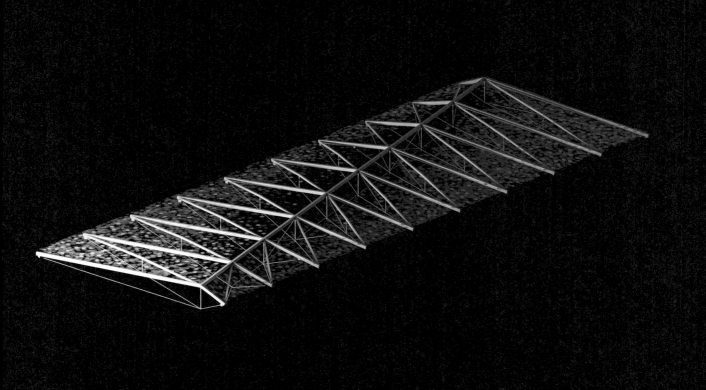

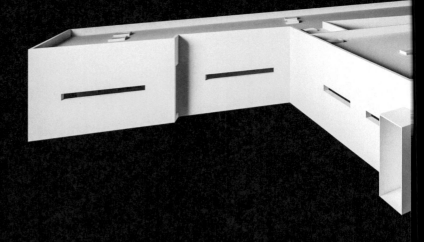

From each generation of those students, I had architects that I subsequently hired to work with me at Jahn.

During this period there were some extraordinary clients. MGM, the clients of Veer Towers, was one of them. They were realistic about their budget and expectations. They began talking with us because they respected our work, but they continued working with us because they admired our work ethic. I feel that the overall result was a real fifty-fifty collaboration between the client and the architect, and our ambitions were in sync. Of course, there were tough decisions related to the budget, as always. But MGM was willing to listen to us, because they wanted the best. When architects fail, it is usually because they fail to support their design or simply tell the client what they think they want to hear. By contrast, we fought and defended our position with arguments that were more scientific than aesthetic. I always reflect on how fortunate I was to have found a client that really supported our vision. They felt their vision was our vision.

Part of the success was directly attributable to Bobby Baldwin, who was an incredible project leader. He reported directly to the owner, Kirk Kerkorian.

He got involved in the smallest details without micromanaging. He was always there, until the end, when important decisions had to be made. Those presentations were so important: through them, we shared progress and got design approval.

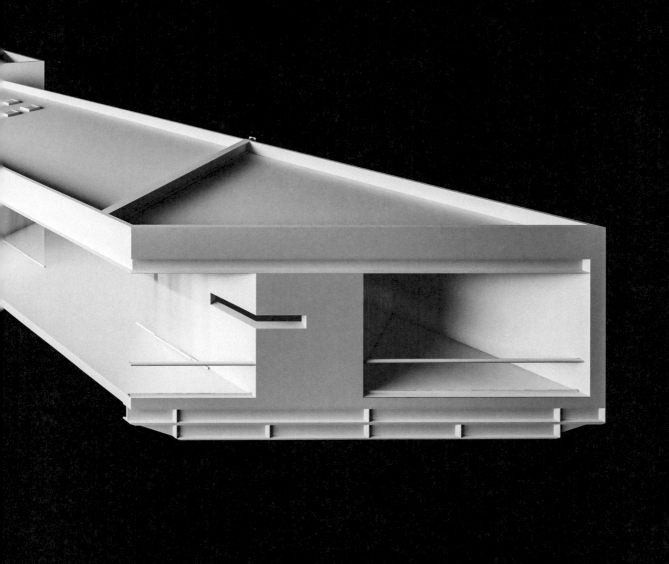

the facade, we were able to challenge the options available from US industry by investigating whether the facade could be produced more efficiently elsewhere. This led us to Hong Kong, where we looked at full-facade mock-ups. This was ultimately the option we selected. They even accepted our recommendations regarding contractors. They took all the right steps by hiring the best construction and project managers. They even built a massive office on site for all the architects working on the different buildings that were part of the project so that we could come together and work with our consultants every two weeks.

Not long after Veer, I had a very different experience with the master plan for Hudson Yards, in New York City. Helmut was deeply involved, because he had worked with the developer at Sony Center. My focus at that time, on the other hand, was opening new markets in Asia and the Middle East. As a result, he took the lead role in designing the proposal.

My favorite part of the proposal is a large, open space where I designed a concert hall and an amphitheater. It has an indoor use, but it is also an outdoor facility. In the winter, the outdoor space becomes the atrium of the complex and, in the summer, it is an arena. It is the only true public space on the large site. My belief was that the pressure to pack the site with commercial use from the development side brought the project to a place where there was no longer a good balance between the built and the unbuilt.

When the time came to present the project to the representatives of the city, who would decide who would get to develop the city-owned site, as well as to the general public, Helmut had a scheduling conflict with a sailing regatta, so he was unable to attend the presentation. I was very conflicted about going because it was not a design that I truly believed in. I think the *New York Times* critic at the time called it an "architecture of intimidation."

velopers and architects who were competing for the project. I traveled directly from Hong Kong and barely met the developer before the meeting. I was the third to present. Before my presentation, they were constantly texting me about new ideas for how to present the master plan. I was in a very difficult position, having to defend something that I did not believe in. I thought we could have done a much better proposal. Too much focus was placed on the buildings and not enough on the people. I think this really speaks of an unsuccessful client-architect collaboration.

Of course, I understand the client's perspective and their need to balance how much they are going to pay for a hugely expensive site with the technical challenge of building a slab to span the rails. Even though it was not an ideal collaboration, we did win the bid. As many people know, however, this was just before the 2008 financial crisis and another developer ultimately executed the project.

In 2007 and 2008, we were beginning to do a lot of work in Asia and the Middle East as the result of my business development efforts. It was still a very tough time. We saw great demand for scale and diversity of program. At the same time, we saw a new set of clients emerge. They were entirely new developers with little clue about what they were doing. They were good at putting together the numbers—the pro forma—but there was no real vision for the buildings. They had no mission to change anything. They were absolutely profit driven. And many felt the best way to achieve profit was to create spectacle. That was hard to watch. At the same time, we were given a lot of freedom and allowed to design what we wanted. And then the 2008 crisis happened, and China was the only market left. That changed a lot of things. It became very competitive because everyone was focused there.

We entered the market earlier, while it was still evolving. The Chinese government was trying to protect their architects. They set up a format in which there is the architect of record and the international firm. This was something relatively new to us. In Europe and the Middle East, we had always been in charge of the process from beginning to end. This new format was of concern to us because of the level of involvement required to achieve an exceptional result. We pushed them to embrace as much scope as we could. In some cases, we were breaking down our work into two categories: the visible and non-visible parts of the building.

We were willing to give the local firms the upper hand on the back-of-house so that we could control more of the front-of-house space. This approach was successful in the Shanghai Financial Center. In many ways, it was an atypical job in which we developed 70% of the design of the overall building complex to the level of construction documents, while our local partner completed the remaining 30% of the work.

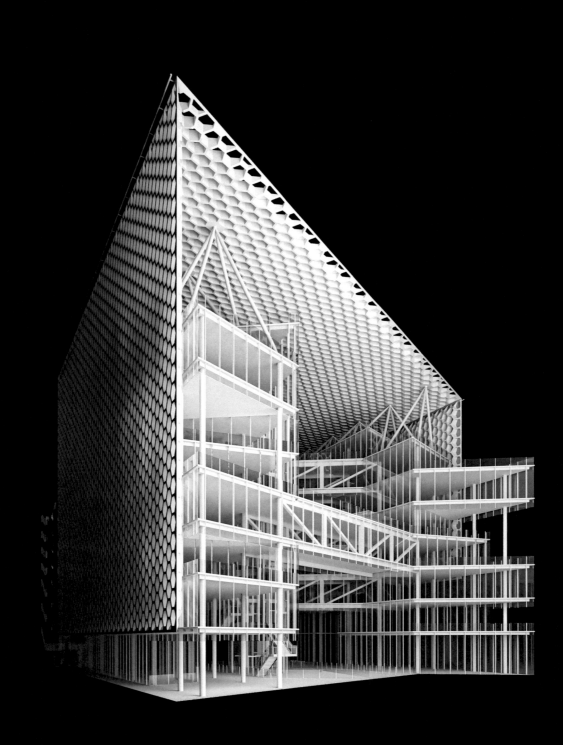

Shanghai Financial Center was quite significant. It began as a competition. I remember that Sir Norman Foster's team presented before us. Our design responded to the question of the competition brief with great specificity; hence, the city became a great partner. They understood what we were trying to do. They saw so much value in the creation of public space at a grand scale. They understood that we were creating vast public infrastructure through the gardens, theater, and museum. Each building had a club with a public component on the uppermost level. The city was ahead of its time. The embrace of public space was not what was happening in Shanghai at the time. A lot of buildings were post-modern. They were introverted. Our design was extroverted and grounded in public life. At the same time, the client was unwilling to challenge public rules. As a result, we had to re-plan the whole interior because of a new law that limited the amount of space a public official could have for an office. We also had to re-plan the whole facade based on a new code. The client, unfortunately, was not particularly supportive through these processes.

In every other job in China, we finished our design work at the end of the design development phase, in which all of the layout, materials, systems, and structure are fully specified and highly detailed. This phase immediately precedes construction documents that refine these drawings into a set on which a contractor can place a bid for erecting the building. My concerns back then were focused on production redundancy because of the cultural, language, and time-zone differences. In most cases, however, the results were remarkably positive.

We always felt that we achieved almost the same level of design quality that we achieved in other parts of the world.

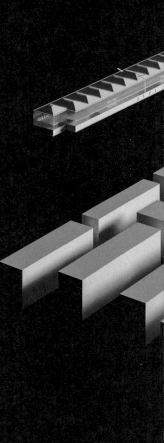

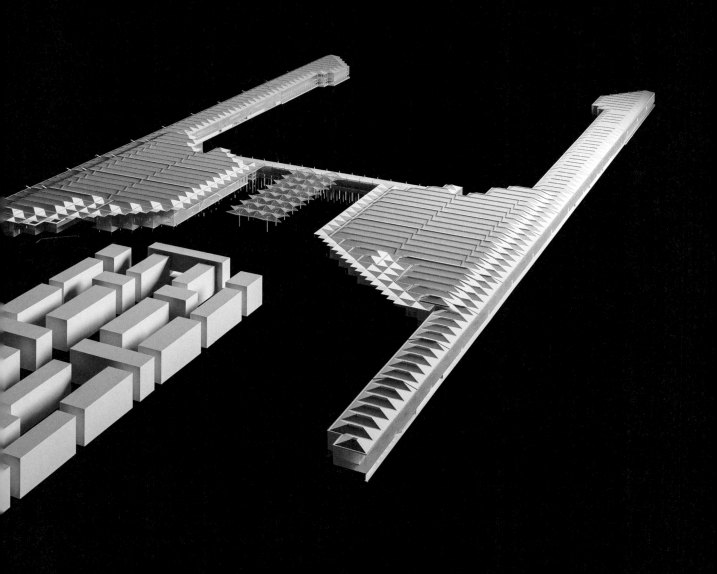

There were two atypical "children" from this time: Suvarnabhumi Airport in Bangkok and Japan Post. With Bangkok, we did everything. It was like a German building in Asia. With Japan Post, we did much less than we did in China. There was, however, great respect for our design ideas. The collaboration with the Japanese was excellent in the context of their technical understanding and respect for design ideas. Most of the boundaries that we negotiated with them were related to functionality in connection with cultural aspects of how they wanted to use space. With Japan Post, we had no engineers except for Werner Sobek on the facade. All other engineering was done locally with MJS as the architect of record. They were really remarkable.

A little later on, I had the opportunity to work with two incredible clients on Leatop—Mr. Fu and Mr. Lei. They were young entrepreneurs of the new China with a clear vision of what they wanted to achieve. The project began as a competition. I was the first one presenting. When I stepped down from the podium, they left the room and came to talk with me while there were still four other presentations to go. We spent three hours together discussing our design proposal. At that point, I knew that the job was ours. Every time I went to Guangzhou, they were waiting for me at the airport. We would always go to dinner and discuss every detail of the project. They were present and never felt they were too important to deal with even the smallest detail.

The building was built so well because of their involvement. At a certain point, I was extremely unhappy with the mechanical engineers and wanted to fire them, and they did just that.

At another point, I told them that it was possible to reduce the weight of the building by 30% and they immediately embraced the vision. However, it did require taming the bull that is the local municipality responsible for codes.

We had to challenge the codes in order to build an extraordinary building without compromises. I remember that one time I went to review the glass of the facade. There were different glass panels with ceramic frit reading blue, green, and red. It was terrible. We discovered that the frit was on the wrong interlayer. The building, however, was already one-third clad. I told them that they had to fight their contractor. They did just that and redid the glass.

Shortly after formally launching FGP ATELIER, we completed the Educational Pavilion. It was an incredible project that I had been working on independently for several years. Stakeholder engagement was essential. There were many groups interested in building a pavilion on such a significant historical site. These included groups like the Instituto Nacional de Antropología e Historia (INAH), the Instituto Nacional de las Bellas Artes (INBA), the local community, the historical preservation agency, environmental groups, the local artist community, and the local government. They all somehow felt they had a voice. It is remarkable that the building survived all of these voices and remained as it was intended to be. This was possible because people understood the mission of the building. I will always be thankful for the partnership that Luis Zarate, Alejandro de Avila, and I created. Each one of us was speaking from a different perspective while always putting the interests of the project first. In this sense, the project also survived its creators because nothing was driven by anybody's ego.

One of the first new projects that we landed after founding the Atelier was a 320-meter tower in Guangzhou, China. While we were also working on a competition for a tower in Shenzhen. In Shenzhen, we came in second place, and in Guangzhou we won.

The format of collaboration was the same as the other projects in China—a local design institute and local engineers. We recently broke ground on this project.

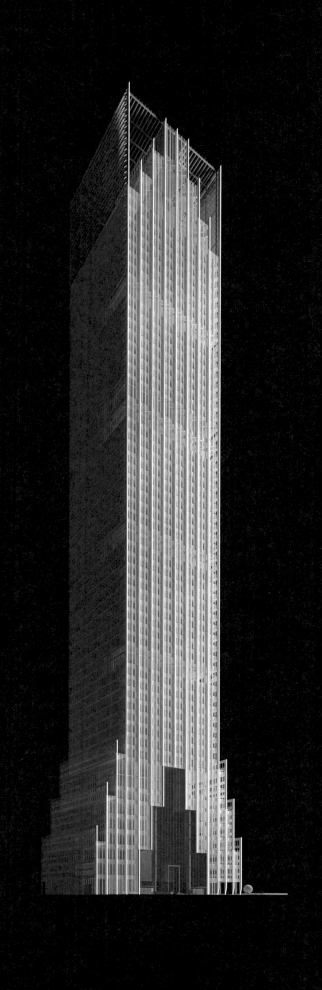

the only aspect of the project that we are revising right now is the lobby of the building, in order to enhance its cultural symbolism. The client was very similar to Leatop. They were young, visionary, and respectful of our ideas. I remember that the project began with them telling me they wanted a timeless classic building—like James Bond's Aston Martin in the form of a building.

By contrast, the design brief in Shenzhen called for something very different. We would later find out that what the design brief called for was not what they selected. We responded to what they requested, but they selected something that was quiet and introverted. When I talked to them about how the decision was made, they said that a very tall, extroverted building designed by KPF that moves a lot was going to be built nearby. The city felt that our building would compete with the KPF building, which was supposed to be the centerpiece of the master plan. So the city voted for a building that was less noticeable. Given that this was a unique competition that allowed for back-and-forth between the client and the architect, I wondered why they never mentioned this other building and their desire for a more understated building. I do not think that we ever really received a satisfactory answer. Which is common in such processes.

While we were starting these new projects at the Atelier, we were also finishing our work on the Diablos Rojos baseball stadium in Mexico City. Diablos is really the product of a visionary client. Without that client commitment, the building would be completely different. Diablos, in my opinion, is an excellent example of a symbiotic relationship between the client and the architect.

However, the collaborations between international and local engineers proved to be very challenging, even though culturally we were not so different. I felt that our Mexican engineers were not willing to challenge codes with performance-based analysis. Doing so would have made the building leaner and less expensive. The international engineers were always working on the edge of design. They wanted to design things to the limit.

We all knew this was technically possible, but the vagueness of the local codes and the fact that they are subject to the interpretation of the local engineer and those responsible for approving it made it very difficult for the building to be designed on the cutting edge of technology.

Construction administration was also very challenging because of the communication protocols that were established for the project. In many cases, our reviews remained unaddressed—sometimes for one or two months. By the time they responded, our original design intent could not be implemented, and an alternative had to be found, which was constantly compromising the design. When I walk that building, I feel that 30% of the things I see could have been built in the technological context of Mexico but were not executed properly because of poor coordination.

One of the best contractors on the job was Fapressa. They oversaw cladding the truncated trapezoids. They had been the contractor of Toyo Ito's Museum in Puebla, and I think that prepared them for their work on Diablos.

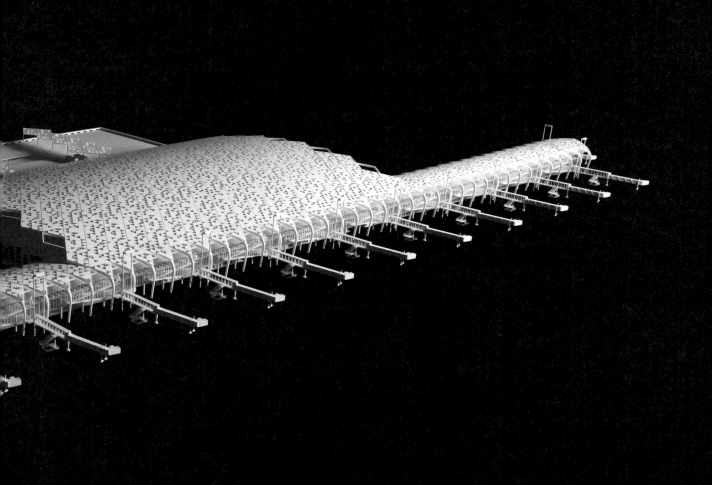

They were the only contractor that finished the job according to the drawings with no mistakes. They built mock-ups, did tests, and really thought through every detail. It was almost like working internationally. The result, nevertheless, is exceptional. I will always be thankful to my friend and exceptional Mexican architect, Alonso de Garay, for our partnership on this project. Each of us brought our own experience, vision, and strengths. I designed the roof, Alonso designed the interiors, and, in a fifty-fifty collaboration, we designed the rest jointly. We always strove to put the building first.

Another of the Atelier's early projects was the Ted Gibson Salon. Scale has never really driven my interest in deciding to pursue a project. Ted Gibson is a perfect example. Ted was a visionary. He was intrigued by our ideas and he chose to execute them with loyalty and great commitment. From our end, we supported a design-build process to achieve the project on budget. I think Ted Gibson Salon and La Hoja are excellent examples of fidelity to design intent in which the untouched design becomes remarkable. We have received good press on these projects—more so, I think, than on others in which the client has intervened in the design. I feel this is because good ideas have their own force and strength. When other forces influence and tame them, they start to dilute to the point that they lose their value. We value collaboration with our clients, but establishing boundaries is important for preserving the essence of things.

My work for Monterrey Tec represents a very important chapter in my life. This is not just because I went to school there, but also because I was selected to do three projects for them—La Hoja, the Rectoría, and Tec Nano. From a design perspective, La Hoja is the most remarkable of the three because it was built as the design intended. The Rectoría, however, was my biggest accomplishment for the institution so far because of what it represents. The symbolism and history of the building are so significant.

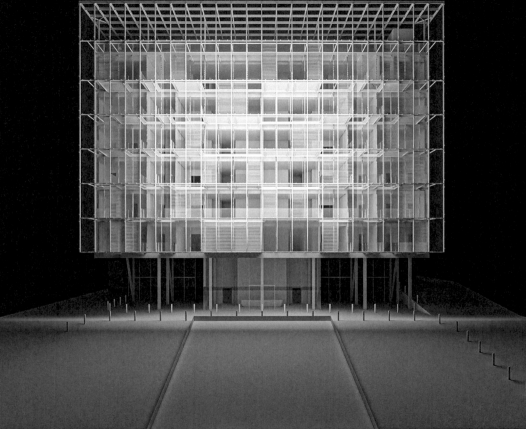

However, the leadership's lack of involvement at crucial moments, when important decisions had to be made, failed to support the original vision for this project. It changed the meaning and the result of the design. What is interesting is that not many of these decisions were connected to value engineering. They were connected to a misinterpretation of the architect's intent and a lack of communication among the collaborators. Instead of dealing with the leadership in making important decisions, the decisions were relegated to the management group. At some point, the project's core was lost. This was in part due to the fact that it was increasingly a design-build project, whereas aspects of the original building were being discovered and decisions had to be made on a daily basis. Given that we were based in Chicago and not always able to be on site, it was hard for our input to be fully integrated.

Having worked on many projects internationally and coordinated much more complex teams, I felt there were multiple ways of addressing that problem. In the end, perhaps, it just came down to the culture of construction in Monterrey and at the University.

The last project I undertook for Monterrey Tec was Tec Nano. The alignment of technical requirements and lack of feasibility studies led to difficulties. It made coordination in general quite challenging. We spent a great deal of time defining the technical boundaries of the building with the consultant and the client, and then fighting a budget that was established without feasibility studies. I felt that, culturally, it was very difficult for the University to fully embrace the recommendations of the international consultants. On the other hand, the international consultants were somehow too rigid with respect to their recommendations because of the culture of liability that prevails in the United States. This "inflexibility" in the eyes of the client was unacceptable within their concept of collaboration.

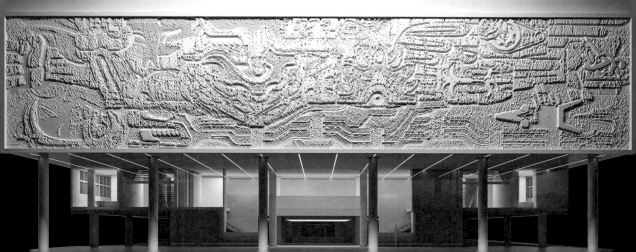

They felt that the consultants had to follow the client's wishes. Instead, they received international standards that conflicted with other, less expensive labs that they had seen. This led to direct opposition between what the client had established and what the international consultants recommended.

With this project, our role went beyond the traditional role of architect. We acted as mediators as well as project managers at some point. When we questioned construction costs, we even organized a bidding process that ultimately proved that our design could be built within the established budget. In the end, we designed an extraordinary building that required an extraordinary client, extraordinary consultants, and an extraordinary architect. For us, the building was in fact "the client," because the requirements were so specific that the building had to dictate its own future. I think this was never understood.

When we were approached to understand the potential of the Felipe Ángeles International Airport at Santa Lucía (AIFA) as a future node within the new aviation network of Mexico City and the country, I decided to divest myself of preconceptions and look at this challenge objectively and dispassionately. I took no political stance and withheld judgment on the decisions of former governments. Instead, I immersed myself in this challenge and sought a way to respond to it in consideration of the budget and the schedule.

It is my belief that public work must be executed with the notion that the funding is public. In that sense, my approach to Santa Lucía was not to design with excess, but to eliminate the superfluous and fulfill the vision of the current administration, that of austerity and efficiency.

In many ways, the project was quite atypical for a project of this scale because of the absence of a core group of engineers and specialty consultants. At the same time, I was committed to realizing the highest international standards under our leadership, in accordance with my previous experience on projects of the same scale and complexity. We were facing a different paradigm in which the minister of defense oversaw engineering, building, and coordinating for the entire project. We designed the master plan in collaboration with Aéroports de Paris Ingénierie (ADPi) and in coordination with the client—Mexico's Secretaría de la Defensa Nacional (SEDENA). We also designed the terminal building, the control tower, the intermodal station, the hotel, and significant public spaces. However, the client attempted to shift our role and that of the consultants from designers to design advisors. Therefore, the actual project now being built is not the one we designed.

I only hope, for the future of Mexico and its people, that the result of their decisions and endeavors will respond to the challenges and demands of the main international airport of the world's sixteenth largest economy.

I must, however, add a word of caution: in an airport, almost any change can have a significant impact on performance, functionality, operational efficiency, security, safety, and, ultimately, the profitability of this crucial piece of infrastructure. My work has been characterized as an integrated process in which technical expertise and collaborations are essential for success. When the architect is removed from those decisions, leaving those involved with little understanding of the reasons why the architect made the decisions in the first place, the results can be catastrophic. An airport is the ultimate machine. It is almost like the motherboard in a computer, where every aspect of the building contributes to making the passenger experience and the operations feel seamless. An airport is the first and the last thing that you see when you visit a place. It defines a country on so many levels. Architects understand this. Airports, however, are also political entities that are subject to many external forces.

Collaboration balances all such forces to produce an optimal product. It is critical for this building typology. As I think has become clear, I value collaboration tremendously. I put science in the center of our practice, in which architecture, urban planning, research, engineering, and technology all inform the process of creating remarkable buildings. This framework presupposes a highly synergetic way of collaborating among all parties involved. The culture of our practice has been defined by lightness, buildings with purpose, the search for simplicity, the size of the ideas, risk as a path for innovation, and imagination above ego. It is my belief that extraordinary projects need three ingredients: 1) an urban vision; 2) a client with vision; and 3) an architect who takes note. It is never scale that defines a good project. It is the scale of the ambition.

I have always been interested in the cultural aspects that influence our work through the site, climate, and technology.

The architect is responsible for providing each building with its own language, one that communicates with users. Together, the building and its users are responsible for communicating with their context and, over time, allowing the building to function as an integral part of broader urban, social, and ecological systems. Our most successful projects are the ones where all these factors translate into the destruction of archetypes in order to make room for the emergence of unique buildings grounded in collaboration, science, and imagination, which defines the design process and, ultimately, our lives.

Architecture has become spectacle; I prefer to think of my work as a stage. Life should be the spectacle.

Francisco González Pulido

Chicago

January 2021

PROGRESSION CAN ONLY BE THE RESULT OF GREAT COLLABORATION.
THEREFORE, I WANT TO EXPRESS MY DEEP GRATITUDE TO: WILFRIDO GONZÁLEZ BALBOA, ADDY PULIDO, DR. MANUEL RAMOS-ALVAREZ, VICTOR GARIBAY AND VICTOR GARIBAY JR., MANUEL GARCIA DIAZ, MARIBEL SANTAULARIA, FRANCISCO GARCIA DIAZ, WERNER SOBEK, MATHIAS SCHULER, YANN KERSALE, SAM SCACCIA, HELMUT JAHN, D. ALFREDO HARP HELÚ, ALONSO DE GARAY, EDUARDO NAVARRO, BRUNO ZEPEDA, ALEJANDRO P. CASTRO, DAVID GARZA, JOSE ANTONIO TORRE, BERNARDO HINOJOSA, MANUEL ALVAREZ, LUIS ZARATE, ALEJANDRO DE AVILA, MR. QUE, MR. QU, MR. FU, MR. LEI, MR. LOU, BOBBY BALDWIN, SVEN VAN ASCHE, AND RODOLFO MADERO, WHO AT THE TIME OF FINALIZING THE BOOK, AWARDED US WITH A NEW PROJECT IN MAZATLÁN, MEXICO.

FRANCISCO GONZÁLEZ PULIDO

Born in Mexico City in 1970, Francisco González Pulido graduated from Monterrey Tec with a bachelor's degree in architecture in 1991. He completed his first residential project in 1993 and won his first international competition in 1995, followed by his first high-rise building project in 1997. He was accepted to Harvard Graduate School of Design for a master's degree in 1998. His interest in science, technology, and business took him to MIT and the Harvard Business School. At the MIT Media Lab, he collaborated with media artist Krzysztof Wodiczko, who would be highly influential in the formation of his design philosophy. In 2000, González Pulido moved to Chicago to join JAHN, was made partner in 2008, and named president of the company in 2012. His designs from 2000 to 2017 encompass a wide range of buildings, from pavilions and boutique spaces to stadiums and airports, from speculative explorations to science facilities and skyscrapers across five continents. He founded FGP ATELIER in 2017.

Among his most important recent projects are the Land Rover Regional Offices in Shanghai, the 20,000-seat Alfredo Harp Helú Stadium in Mexico, the Shanghai International Financial Center, the Gate in Shenzhen, the proposal for Monterrey Tec's Bioengineering and Nanotechnology Laboratory, the 320-meter-high Guangzhou International Cultural Center, the 400-meter-high Nanjing Tower, the renovation of Monterrey Tec's historical Rectoría building, the first smart beauty salon for Ted Gibson in collaboration with Amazon in Beverly Hills, and finally the 20-million-passenger terminal building for Felipe Ángeles International Airport in Santa Lucía in Mexico.

**"BUILDING LIGHT IS NOT ONLY
A THEORETICAL BUT ALSO AN
ETHICAL POSITION …
LIGHTNESS IS PHYSICAL AND
METAPHYSICAL.
LIGHTNESS IS FOR ME ABOUT
LESS OF EVERYTHING,
TO MINIMIZE, TO SIMPLIFY;
IT IS THE ENDLESS SEARCH FOR
BOUNDARIES IN ARCHITECTURE.
GOING TO THE LIMIT OF THINGS.**

**HOW INVISIBLE WE CAN MAKE
SOMETHING THAT STILL PROTECTS
US …
HOW LIGHTWEIGHT WE CAN
MAKE SOMETHING THAT
BALANCES NATURAL FORCES …**

**I STRIVE FOR LIGHTNESS, AS I
BELIEVE IT IS A CONCEPT THAT
RESONATES DEEPLY WITH OUR
CIVILIZATION, CITIES, AND LIVES."**

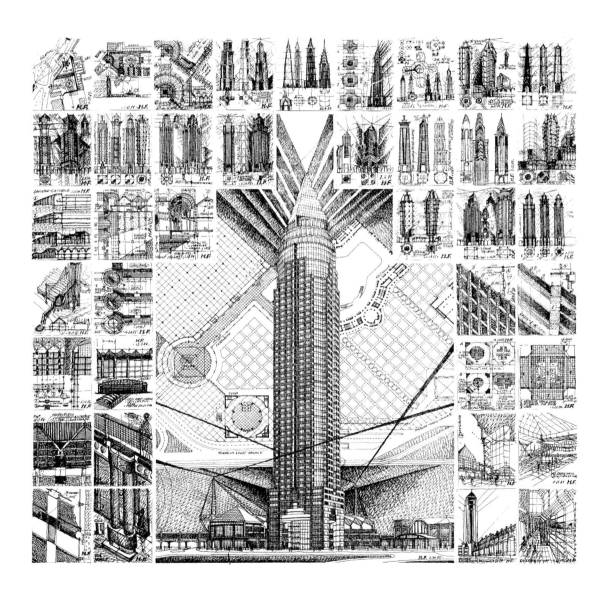

HELMUT

On May 8, 2021, my longtime mentor, partner, and friend, Helmut Jahn, passed away. Five days later, I am writing these lines about a relationship that will forever be like no other.

Our professional exchange began in the fall of 1999; however, the remarkable Thompson Center had been in the "architectural drawers" of my memory since the late nineteen-eighties, when I was finishing my architecture studies in Mexico. Our working relationship evolved rapidly and drastically in a short time, and it lasted up to Helmut's passing; we had a four-hour lunch in January of this year, and we planned to get together this summer for a recap. I will never forget the day of my departure from JAHN. It was a Thursday, August 31, 2017, after eighteen remarkable years together, to the day. I remember in particular what he said in his farewell speech: "Francisco, we have been partners and from now on, we might be competing for the same projects!"—I always loved that about him: he was fearless in expressing his mind and extremely competitive.

In the first six years, I was working for him; in the six years that followed, we were working together; and in the last six years, as we became design and business partners, our collaboration evolved and solidified. It was always poised with intensity; we could be completely aligned, even if we also had contrasting opinions about how to get there, but we always knew what the objective was because we believed in the same things. "If it works, it will be extraordinary"—that was our secret symmetry and ultimately what defined the nature of our collaboration.

It is difficult to define him in words, but I will try to give some images: Helmut had more energy, drive, determination, ideas, speed, order, hand-sketches, built projects, true friends, pens, intellect, impatience, rage, intolerance to small talk, confidence, freedom, obsession with solving problems, ability to simplify, flamboyance, ground, and wings than anybody I have ever met.

We traveled, designed, lunched, laughed, and worked together tirelessly. Our relationship was complex, one of contrast, affection, and opposition at times, but always one of admiration and respect. I became an architect by his side and learned, among many other things, what work ethic really means and why compromise ruins everything.

Helmut will always be a comet on a magnificent journey across the universe that will forever shine upon us, the ones who had the privilege of a moment in his unparalleled company.

Francisco

ACKNOW

AARON TABARES
ABBYGAIL JOSEPH
ABRAHAM CABABIE
ADAM SONABEND
ADDY PULIDO
ADRIANA ELIZONDO
ADRIANA PEQUEÑO
AGUSTIN PIZAR
ARMIN MOEHRLE
AISHA SETHI
ALBERTO ROSALES
ALEJANDRA HERNANDEZ
ALEJANDRO CASTRO
ALEJANDRO DE ÁVILA
ALEJANDRO MORALES
ALESSANDRO BANI
ALEX BRATTON
ALEXANDRA MRZIGOD
ALEXANDRA TONCAR
ALEXIS COVACEVICH
ALFONSO GONZÁLEZ MIGOYA
ALFREDO HARP HELÚ
ALFREDO HIDALGO
ALICE KRIEGER
ALICIA ANDONEGUI
ALLIE BILLINGSLEY
ALONSO DE GARAY
ALPHONSO PELUSO
ALVARO COVACEVICH
ANA FERNANDA GONZÁLEZ
ANA ISABEL LUNA GARCIA
ANA LORENA GONZÁLEZ
ANA LUCIA MACIAS
ANDREA HAASE
ANDREAS HOIER
ANDRES CONESA
ANDRES GONZÁLEZ-ARQUIETA
ANDRES SANCHEZ
ANDRES VILLASENOR
ANDREW CORNEY
ANDY RODRIGUEZ

ANGEL GONZÁLEZ LOYA
ANNA GUZMAN
ANNE GUTHRIE
ANTONIO MENDEZ VIGATA
ARTURO ARDITTI
ATUL TALWAR
AURORA DELGADO
BARBARA RANDOLPH
BELA MOTÉ
BENJAMIN MOLINA
BENJAMIN ORTIZ
BENJAMIN ROMANO
BERNARDO HINOJOSA
BETSY RODRIGUEZ
BETTY VILLARREAL
BILL BRADLEY
BILL HENDRICKS
BINKY SPOLARICH
BOBBY BALDWIN
BRIAN PAVLOVEC
BRUNO ZEPEDA
BURTON MANGAHRAM
CARL D'SILVA
CARLA PROKYWCA
CARLA SWITCKERATH
CARLOS CRUZ
CARLOS ESTRADA
CARLOS MOTIN
CARLOS MUNOZ
CARLOS NUNGARAY
CARLOS ROUSSEAU
CARMEN ESPINOSA
CAROLYN AGUILAR
CÉCILIA HURSTEL
CECILIA LOPEZ
CELIA ARREDONDO
CESAR DE ANDA
CHAD TISCHER
CHATA PULIDO
CHRIS DALMARES
CHRIS FITZGERALD

CHRISTIANE BAUSBACK
CHRISTINA LUCAS
CHRISTINE ABATTE
CHRISTINE WILLIAMS
CINDY WILD
CLAUDIA HARARI
CLAUDIA PULIDO
CLAUDIA ROJAS
CLAUDIA TAMAYO
COCO INES KENAR
COLIN SIPOS
CONSTANZA MARTÍNEZ
CONSUL. REYNA TORRES MENDIVIL
CRNL. CÁZERES
CRNL. PAVÓN
CRNL. VARGAS
DANIEL DE LA VEGA
DANIEL FESTAG
DANIEL LIEBESKIND
DANIEL LOFTUS
DANIEL PEROGORDO MADRID
DANIEL REYNOSO
DANILO MEDINA
DAVID BASULTO
DAVID BOWER
DAVID BROWN
DAVID GARZA SALAZAR
DAVID LIZARRAGA
DAVID SOLIS
DAVID WALKER
DAVID WEGTER
DEBORAH BLAINE
DENISE CAPLAN
DIEGO GONZÁLEZ ALANIS
DIEGO RODRIGUEZ
DIEGO RODRIGUEZ RENOVALES
DON PACO GARCIA
DONA CARMEN DIAZ DE GARCIA
DONNA ROBERTSON
DOROTA KENAR
DOTCHKA VELICHKOVA

EDGMENT

DR. SUN YI MIN
EDITH BISHOP
EDUARDO NAVARRO
EDUARDO SOSA
ELÍA GONZÁLEZ BALBOA
ELIAS FASJA
ELIAS PULIDO
EMILIANO GODOY
EMILIO GARCÍA
EMILY SANTOS
ENRIQUE G DE LA G
EUGENIO TAPIA
EUSEBIO SANTAULARIA
EVA FRANCH I GILABERT
EWHEN HOLOWKO
FABRICE QUEMENEUR
FABRICIO PEREZ
FANG LI
FARID REZA
FEDERICO ALBA GONZÁLEZ
FEDERICO BARBACHANO
FELIPE DIAZ DE LEON
FELIX WEBER
FERNANDO CALLEJON
FERNANDO GARCIA TORRES
FLORIAN ROUSSEL
FRANCISCO BARONA
FRANCISCO GARCIA DIAZ
FRANCISCO MADLA
FRANCISCO MARTINEZ
FRANCISCO ROJAS
FRANCISCO YEOMANS
FRANÇOIS BENIS
GABRIELA ESTEFANIA CANTU
GAZI NACIF
GEORGE BINDER
GERARDO FERRANDO
GERMAN ARVIZU LOYOLA
GERMAN CASTILLO
GERMAN CLARO
GERMAN CLARO JR
GILBERTO RODRIGUEZ
GLORIA ELENA DE LEÓN ORTÍ
GORAN STROKIRK
GOKAY CALIK
GRANT IRVING
GREG THOMPSON
GRETCHEN HELFRICH
GUILLERMINA PULIDO
GUILLERMO COETO
GUILLERMO PULIDO CABRERA
GUILLERMO PULIDO GORDILLO
GUNNAR HUBBARD
GUSTAVO MADRID
HAIDONG YE
HAOJIANG LIU
HARLEY JONES
HECTOR ARIAS
HECTOR CORREA
HECTOR MARMOLEJO
HECTOR TORREJON
HEIDI TISCHER
HELMUT JAHN
HELMUT SCHMIDT
HERNAN GARCIA
HERON RODRIGUEZ
HIMANGSHU KEDIA
HIROYUKI NIINO
HOMERO RIOS
HORACIO LOPEZ
HOWARD ECKER
HUI YU
HUNTER TURA
ILAN GEVA
ING. HECTOR CUELLAR
IRVING SHEN
ISABEL KLUNKER
ISMAEL GONZÁLEZ BALBOA
JAIME ALLAM GONZÁLEZ
JAMES STEINKAMP
JAIMIE HENRY
JAMIE ROSEN
JANETE ECKER
JAVIER JIMENEZ ESPRIÚ
JAVIER RATTIA
JAVIER SANCHEZ
JAY POPP
JEFF LUCAS
JESSICA HUENNEKENS
JESUS BARNEY
JESUS HERRERA
JESUS ORTIZ
JIM ANTELL
JOACHIM SCHUESSLER
JOAKIM WANDENHOLT
JOAQUIN BOEKER
JOAQUIN LORDA
JOE KHOURY
JOE WEIN
JOHN DURBROW
JOHN KEMPER
JOHN KOSAR
JOHN LUCAS
JOHN MANAVES
JOHN POTOCSNAK
JOHN SCHRADER
JOKIN LUISA
JORGE ALESSIO ROBLES
JORGE ARDITTI
JORGE ÁVILA
JORGE GUENDOLAIN
JORGE SAENZ
JORGE SAENZ JR
JORGE VALENCIA CUEVAS
JOSE ANTONIO FERNANDEZ
JOSE ANTONIO TORRE
JOSE CARLOS LOMBANA
JOSE DAVID GUTIERREZ LUNA
JOSE ESCALANTE
JOSE LUIS CORTES DELGADO
JOSE LUIS GRAUE
JOSE LUIS MALDONADO
JOSE RAMON GORDILLO

AGRADE

JOSÉ RODRIGUEZ	LUIS CONTRERAS	MARTY LEISCH
JOSEFINA POINSOT GARZA	LUIS GONZÁLEZ BALBOA	MASSIMILIANO FUKSAS
JOSEPH LARSON BILLEAUD	LUIS MENDOZA JUAREZ	MATHIAS SCHULER
JOSH GREENE	LUIS SAENZ	MATTHEW MESSNER
JUAN CARLOS AMARO	LUIS ZARATE	MATTHEW STYMIEST
JUAN CARLOS COLORADO	LUZ GARDELLA	MAURICIO ARDITTI
JUAN PABLO REYES	LUZ MARIA GARCIA	MAURICIO GONZÁLEZ ASSAD
JUANI GOMEZ DE FLORES	LYNN OSMOND	MAURICIO INGLADA
JUREK KENAR	MACIEJ KOURKA	MAYOR JAVIER MACIEL
KAREN IRVINE	MAGALI MORALES GONZÁLEZ	MAYRA GONZÁLEZ
KARLA SAENZ	MALCOM BARKSDALE	MAYRA MENDIETA
KAZUKIYO SATO	MANUEL ALVAREZ	MAYTE NEVAREZ
KENGO KUMA	MANUEL CUNG	MEGAN ANGUS
KEVIN SMITH	MANUEL FLORES GOMEZ	MELISSA MCCLAYTON
KIMBERLY CARUSO	MANUEL GARCIA DIAZ	MELODY ABLOLA
KO MAKABE	MANUEL IZQUIERDO	MICHAEL EDMONDS
KOKI MIYACHI	MANUEL VERTIZ	MICHAEL F. ROHDE
KRISTIN GARIBALDI	MANUEL ZERTUCHE	MICHAEL LEPISTO
KRISTIN WEEKS	MARA NUYENS	MICHAEL LI
KUN LIU	MARCOS ESCAMILLA	MIKE SABATINI
LANCE MCMASTERS	MARGARITA MORALES GONZÁLEZ	MILOS STEHLIK
LANCE ROSENMAYER	MARGARITA PULIDO	MIN ZHAO
LAURENCE BERTOUX	MARIA ANTONIETTA ESPOSITO	MIRIAM FLORES
LEONOR PINTADO	MARIA ISABEL PORRUA DE HARP	MIRIAM TORRES
LEOPOLD TEMPEZ	MARIA SAENZ	MOLLY O'DONELL
LESLIE HULSE	MARIA VILLARREAL	MONICA GRANJA VAZQUEZ
LETICIA BALBUENA	MARIANA CASTRO	MR. CHOW
LI XU	MARIANA GOMEZ PIMIENTA	MR. FU
LIANKA BEDESCHI	MARIANA MONTOYA	MR. LEI
LIDIA LEISCH	MARIANNE STROKIRK	MR. QU
LIE ZHANG	MARIBEL FISHER	MR. ZHANG LINHAN
LINCHAO MA	MARIBEL SANTAULARIA	MR. YU HUI
LIUFU JUN	MARIBEL TOMAS	MS. HE, MINLIN
LIZETTE DE LA GARZA	MARIE MARMOLEJO	NEETI MENON
LORENZO PEON	MARIELA GONZÁLEZ SIGOÑA	NINA LIEBESKIND
LOU XIAOJUN	MARIO CARRASCO	NORBERT WEICHELE
LOURDES PEREZ	MARIO PLIEGO	OLIMPIA PEREZ MORENO
LU SALINAS	MARIO SCHJETNAN	OMAR CHAVEZ
LUCA LANZETTA	MARK MANN	PACO ALVAREZ
LUCIO BLANDINI	MARTHA BOSQUE	PACO ZHOU
LUCIO MORINI	MARTIN DOLAN	PANAGIOTIS IREIOTIS

IMIENTO

PAOLA DE LA BARRERA	SANDRA KOMMENIC	ULISES MORELOS
PAOLO TIRAMANI	SANDRA LOPEZ-ACOSTA	VANESSA PULIDO
PATRICK BROWN	SANDY GORSHOW	VENE VELICHKOF
PAUL CREMOUX	SEAN SHELBY	VENISLAV VELICHKOF
PEDRO ALONSO RODRIGUEZ	SERENE KANNAAN	VICTOR GARIBAY
PEPE COMPEAN	SERGIO QUINTANILLA	VICTOR GARIBAY JR
PETER ZELLNER	SERGIO QUINTANILLA JR	VICTOR GUTIERREZ ALADRO
RAFAEL GAMO	SERGIO VALENTINI	VICTOR MARTINEZ RIVAS
RAFAEL HERNANDEZ	SETH GRESSER	VICTOR RAMIREZ
RAINER SCHMIDT	SHENGBO WANG	VICTOR SAENZ
RAINER VIERTLBOECK	SHIRA SIMON	VICTOR SÁNCHEZ BURES
RAQUEL LIEBERMAN	SHIRO NITANAI	VICTORIA GRIMES
RAQUIN LOIC	SHUYE JI	VOON FUI LAI
RAUL DE SANTIAGO	SHUYING XI	WAI MUN CHUI
RAÚL GONZÁLEZ ARREDONDO	SILVANO SOLIS	WALKER THISTED
RAUL GONZÁLEZ BALBOA	SILVERIO SIERRA	WAYNE GAW
RAUL PEREZ DUARTE	SOLEDAD LASCURAIN DEL RIO	WENJUN LUAN
REGINALD A. MONTEYNE	SPIRO POLLALIS	WENXIAO WANG
REN BIN WEN	STANLEY ZHAO	WERNER SOBEK
RENÉ BUSTAMANTE	STEPHAN RAU	WILFRIDO GONZÁLEZ BALBOA
RICARDO MONDRAGON	STEPHEN HAGENMAYER	XAVIER SORONDO
RICARDO RODRIGUEZ	STEPHEN KERN	XINGJIAN ZHANG
RICK MARSIGLIO	STEVE BABITCH	XINGNAN MENG
RITA BERGET	STEVE COOK	XOCHITL DEL CARMEN ARIAS
ROBERT BISHOP	SUZETTE BULLEY	GONZÁLEZ
ROBERT TAZELEAR	SVEN VAN ASCHE	YANN KERSALE
ROBERTO IÑIGUEZ	TAI ORHON	YESICA PAREDES
ROBERTO MUÑOZ	TAMINA WEICHELE	YOLANDA LEAL
ROBERTO RAMIREZ	TED GIBSON AND JASON BACKE	YORGO LYKOURIA
RODOLFO BARRAGÀN	TERRY BROWN	YUYING LIU
RODOLFO MADERO	TEODORO GONZÁLEZ DE LEON	ZHE ZHU
RODOLFO VILLARREAL GARZA	THADDEA MATHIESSEN	
RODRIGO MAISTERRENA	THOMAS WINTERSTETTER	
ROGELIO JIMENEZ PONS	TIM PERSING	
ROGELIO LOPEZ	TOBIAS DOLD	
ROGELIO SIMON	TOM DIORO	
ROLAND BECHMANN	TOM KOZLOSKI	
RON KLEMENCIC	TOM WIEBE	
RYAN BIZIOREK	TOM WILLOUGHBY	
SALVADOR ALVA	TOMAS CASTILLO	
SAM SCACCIA	TULAY ORHON	

editor
FGP ATELIER

sounding board
Gergana González Pulido

project management
Dorothee Hahn, on behalf of Hatje Cantz

copyediting
Irene Schaudies

graphic design
Francisco González Pulido
Mara Nuyens

production
Thomas Lemaître, Hatje Cantz

reproductions
DLG Graphic, Paris

printing and binding
Livonia Print, Riga

© 2021 Hatje Cantz Verlag, Berlin, and authors

published by
Hatje Cantz Verlag GmbH
Mommsenstraße 27
10629 Berlin
www.hatjecantz.com

A Ganske Publishing Group Company

ISBN: 978-3-7757-5057-8

cover illustration
Mara Nuyens

© 2021 for all plans, renderings, and sketches:

FGP ATELIER

© 2021 for photographs:

Paco Alvarez: pp. 346–51, 355, 358–59, 361–62, 365, 367–70, 373, 375

Andres Cedillo: p. 564

Rafael Gamo: pp. 6, 26–27, 30–34, 36, 39, 41–44, 46–49, 51, 62–63, 66–67, 70, 72, 75, 77–78, 80–81, 89, 92–93, 132–33, 134, 136–38, 140–44, 147, 149–51, 153, 155, 157, 160, 162–63, 165, 298–99, 304, 306–10, 312–13, 315, 342–43, 384–85, 388, 390, 392, 396, 398–99, 401, 444–45, 447–49, 564

Porcelanosa: p. 295

Dmitry Yagovkin: pp. 173–75, 176, 178, 181–83, 185–88, 190–91, 193–97, 199

YouTube: "Trabajando en la estructura del edificio terminal de pasajeros del AIFA," June 14, 2020: pp. 502–03